M W
& R

The Last Amigo

The Last Amigo

Karlheinz Schreiber
and the Anatomy of a Scandal

STEVIE CAMERON

HARVEY CASHORE

Macfarlane Walter & Ross
Toronto

Macfarlane Walter & Ross
An Affiliate of McClelland & Stewart Ltd.
37A Hazelton Avenue
Toronto, Canada M5R 2E3
www.mwandr.com

National Library of Canada Cataloguing in Publication Data

Cameron, Stevie
The last amigo: Karlheinz Schreiber and the anatomy of a scandal

Includes index.
ISBN 1-55199-051-2

1. Schreiber, Karlheinz. 2. Political corruption – Canada.
3. Corruption investigation – Canada. 4. Canada – Politics and
government – 1984-1993. 5. Canada – Politics and government – 1993- .
6. Airbus (Jet transport). 7. Air Canada. 8. Germany (West) –
Politics and government – 1982-1990. 9. Germany – Politics and
government – 1990- . I. Cashore, Harvey. II. Title.

FC630.C28 2001   971.064'7   C2001-930385-8
F1034.2.C28 2001

Macfarlane Walter & Ross gratefully acknowledges support for its
publishing program from the Canada Council for the Arts,
the Ontario Arts Council, and the Government of Canada through the
Book Publishing Industry Development Program.

Printed and bound in Canada

For David and Tassie and Amy
S.C.

For my mother, Sharon, and my wife, Alisa
H.C.

Contents

Acknowledgments

The idea of a book on Karlheinz Schreiber occurred to each of us more than three years ago. The story of this enigmatic middle-man was made all the more intriguing by the public relations and legal campaigns designed to obscure it. Canadians knew him as the figure at the centre of the Airbus scandal, a long-running saga that, for all the media's scrutiny, left a crucial question unanswered: Where did the money go? We had pursued the mystery independently – Stevie for *Maclean's* and Harvey for the CBC's *fifth estate* – but coop-eratively for many months. Eventually we saw the wisdom of tackling the subject together, sharing our experiences, information, contacts, and skills. The result is a far more comprehensive book than either of us could have accomplished alone. But it took more than the two of us; we needed help from many people, and none were more generous than our own tribe of journalists, both in Canada and overseas.

In Toronto, we want to thank Kit Melamed and the late Eric Malling who, when they were at *the fifth estate*, were among the first journalists to understand Schreiber's role in the Airbus sale. We are grateful too for the generosity of Jim Littleton and Sheila Mandel. The *Globe and Mail*'s Stan Oziewicz provided much helpful information, as did the *Toronto Star*'s Jonathan Ferguson, Bill Schiller, and Darcy

Henton, and a former *Star* reporter, Edison Stewart, all of whom assisted in fact-checking material. We would like to congratulate, in particular, the team at the *Star* who did extraordinary work on this story in December 1995; you will see their articles cited frequently in these pages. John Nicol, a senior writer at *Maclean's*, was always ready to lend a hand.

In Montreal, we relied on superb court research from Alex Roslin, who took time from his own assignments as an editor and investigative journalist to help us. In Newfoundland, we drew on the knowledge of the writer John Gushue, who has checked many details for us over the years. Gerardo Bolaños, a well-known political columnist in Costa Rica, also helped us with valuable research and interviews.

In Germany, we were touched by the hospitality and kindness of journalists who helped us beyond the call of duty, even to sharing their interview notes with us. Among these are John Goetz, Harvey's co-producer in Berlin; Mathias Blumencron of *Der Spiegel* in Hamburg; Conny Neumann in Augsburg, formerly of *Süddeutsche Zeitung* and now with *Der Spiegel*; ARD Television's Christian Nitsche, who is based in Munich; and two other *Süddeutsche Zeitung* reporters, Michael von Stiller in Munich and Hans Leyendecker in Cologne. Bruno Schirra of *Die Zeit* became a valued colleague.

Then there are the team of people who have worked on *The Last Amigo* as it took shape as manuscript and book. Our publisher and editor, Jan Walter, shared our faith in the project from the beginning. Barbara Czarnecki was our copy editor and more, improving and refining the manuscript in countless ways. Our lawyer Peter Jacobsen understands what we do almost better than we do ourselves and has been a rock for us. The editorial and publicity staff at Macfarlane Walter & Ross – especially Adrienne Guthrie and Kelly Hyatt – have been attentive and kind. Pat Cairns has enthusiastically organized the book's promotion campaign and all the events associated with its publication. We know many readers will turn to our index before they read anything else, and we thank Liba Berry for her fine work. For fact-checking in the final weeks we are indebted to Virginia Smart, and for research and acquisition of many of the photographs, we are grateful to Dolores Gubasta and Lenny Stoute at Klix. To Ingrid Paulson, the book's designer, and Marie Jircik, its typesetter, our thanks for care and attention to the smallest details. A special thank-you to Tara Cleveland, our talented Web designer, who developed the prototypes and ideas for www.thelastamigo.com (e-mail address: info@thelast amigo.com) so that readers may reach us easily.

A project like this, dealing with more than 10,000 pages of German documents, is a translator's nightmare, but several people turned material around for us quickly and efficiently. They include a brother-and-sister team, André and Danielle Mayer, and Sue Burkhardt, who did the bulk of our translations in Canada.

We are also fortunate to have wonderful agents by our side. Linda McKnight and Bruce Westwood have been both our sounding boards and our cheerleaders when we thought we'd never get this book done. Their patience is truly saint-like.

There is one other individual whose expertise and support have been invaluable. Hans Marschdorf, a distinguished forensic accountant from Germany, was the partner in charge of the Zurich office of Price Waterhouse before moving to Canada two years ago. Not only did he read our manuscript carefully, explaining the most arcane details of money transfers, numbered accounts, and shell companies, but he educated us in the everyday details of German business practice. No matter how trivial the question, how late the hour, or how far from home, he was always there for us, by phone or e-mail.

Each of us has travelled extensively across Canada and in Europe to gather primary material and conduct scores of interviews. Each of us has pulled hundreds of pages of material from requests under the Access to Information Act made to federal government departments in Ottawa between 1989 and the present. One access request alone took seven years to fulfill, and only after sustained court battles. We obtained material from the Department of National Defence, the Department of Public Works, the Department of Transport, the Privy Council Office, and the former Department of Regional Industrial Expansion, now called Industry Canada. We are indebted to the Canadian Broadcasting Corporation for access to its extensive resources, the product of more than five years of research. Those resources included countless in-depth interviews and several conversations with Karlheinz Schreiber;

banking records from Schreiber's Zurich accounts, complete with code names for Canadian and European friends; copies of Schreiber's 1991 and 1994 appointment diaries; and thousands of pages of German prosecutors' documents. All of this material represents an extraordinary archive of original research, amassed with the cooperation of valued contacts and colleagues.

Stevie Cameron writes: I first heard of Karlheinz Schreiber in 1988 when I was working at the *Globe and Mail.* Later I covered the story for *Maclean's* from the mid-1990s to 1997, and there I was grateful for the help of Andrew Phillips, then the national editor, and of the editor-in-chief, Bob Lewis. When my old boss from the *Globe and Mail*, Geoffrey Stevens, arrived as managing editor, he offered friendship and wise counsel, as always.

Some of the work for this book overlapped with my years as editor-in-chief of *Elm Street*; there, Greg Macneil, Lilia Lozinski, Bill Wolch, Heather McArdle, Liz Renzetti, Gwen Smith, and the rest of the gang were the best colleagues anyone could ever have. Cal Broeker, Lee Lamothe, Evan Jones, Bob Lindquist, Phyllis Bruce, John Pearce, and Marg and Cameron Brett have all helped in ways that I can never repay. So have an irrepressible sister team, Jen and Kate Robson. I have known this pair literally since they were born, and we have had many adventures together. When Jen worked as my assistant at *Elm Street*, she organized all my clippings and files for this book; later, Kate – on holiday in Toronto from her home in Italy – arrived at my house to catalogue masses of German documents.

Over the years, Bob Fife, now the Ottawa bureau chief of the *National Post*, has been a good friend and sounding board on this story; so has Rod Macdonell, a former Montreal *Gazette* investigative reporter and research associate on my last two books, *On the Take* and *Blue Trust*, who is now working for the World Bank in Washington, teaching investigative reporting in many countries. Rod covered the Airbus story for the *Gazette*, and his expertise and support were invaluable. I want to thank friends in Newfoundland: Russell Wangersky, the assignment editor for the St. John's *Telegram*, and Noreen Golfman, a CBC commentator and Memorial University professor, who offered help and good advice. There was another great pal in Regina, the author and lawyer Garrett Wilson, who never tired of answering my questions. I appreciate too the many kindnesses of the *Globe and Mail*'s Andrew Mitrovica, a dear colleague since our days together on *the fifth estate*. Marci MacDonald, a former *Maclean's* feature writer who now works for *U.S. News and World Report* in Washington, and who covered the Iran-Contra affair in Nicaragua, took me through the activities of foreign governments in Central America during the early 1990s.

I would also like to say how grateful I am to my colleagues at the *Globe and Mail*, especially editor-in-chief Richard Addis, deputy editor Chrystia Freeland, and managing editor Sylvia Stead, who have all understood the challenges of this book, offered excellent advice, and waited for me while I finished it.

Most of all, I am grateful to my family, who also understood. As David, Tassie, and Amy know, everything is possible when they are at my side.

Harvey Cashore writes: In the fall of 1994 *the fifth estate* assigned me to investigate a story about secret sales commissions, aggressive lobbyists, and connections to powerful politicians. None of us had any idea what lay ahead – it was probably better that we did not – but we knew this was the kind of assignment the CBC, as a public broadcaster, encouraged. I also believe it is thanks to the CBC and two of its managers that Canadians became aware of a story that would eventually make headlines around the world. Susan Teskey, then *the fifth estate*'s senior producer, committed us to the Airbus project in the first place; David Studer, the executive producer, has provided solid leadership to the team ever since. I will always be grateful for his private counsel and encouragement when it mattered most.

I am particularly indebted to those colleagues who endured my endless questions and offered me invaluable guidance: Sheila Pin, Jennifer Fowler, Howard Goldenthal, Theresa Burke, Jock Ferguson, Linden MacIntyre, Anita Mielewczyk, Oleh Rumak, and once again Kit Melamed. Other friends and colleagues at the *fifth* who, perhaps without knowing it, helped me prepare for this book are Gary

Akenhead, Colin Allison, Alistair Bell, Jim Bertin, Eleanor Besly, Deborah Carter, John Griffin, Mike Grippo, Nilesh Hathi, David Kaufman, Larry Kent, Marie-Françoise Raffougeau, Diana Redegeld, Ces Rosner, Hans Vanderzande, Brigitte Thompson, Michael Wasilewski, Jim Williamson, Trish Wood, and Larry Zolf. Annik Hilger and Betty Wall provided excellent translations.

In CBC management, I thank Sig Gerber, Don Knox, Bob Culbert, Tony Burman, and Jim Byrd. I must also acknowledge a group of first-class lawyers, some of whom I continue to work with. From Reynolds Mirth Richards and Farmer in Edmonton, Allan Lefever, Fred Kozak, and Don Lucky. From Torys, Bob Armstrong and John Koch. Robyn Bell, of Bennett Jones, and John Rosen, of Rosen Wasser, are a formidable and brilliant legal team. None ranks higher than Danny Henry, of the CBC's legal department, who is equally demanding and encouraging.

My friend and co-producer in Germany, John Goetz, deserves thanks for his commitment to the story, his ability to engage almost anyone in conversation, and his willingness to help at almost any time, day or night. I must thank him too for the title – the fruit of a discussion at a sidewalk café in Zurich in September 1999.

Thanks also to my informal support group: Wayne Chong, Doug Lefaive, Richard Leitner, my sisters Judy and Cecelia, my brother, Ben Cashore, who convinced me I should take the plunge into this project, and my parents, John and Sharon.

To the hundreds of people we interviewed, I simply say thank you for returning my phone calls. While many cannot be named, Gary Kincaid, Tom Ronell, and Fred von Veh deserve particular acknowledgment.

My boys, Massey and Jeremiah, did not see as much of their father as they should have in 2000. Evenings, weekends, and summer holidays were devoted to the book more than to them. I hope one day, when they are a little older, they will read this work and understand. To my wife, Alisa, who lived through it all with me: thank you, thank you.

1

The Arrest

The summer of 1999 has been oppressively hot and muggy in Toronto, and at the end of August, a dirty yellow smear of pollution still hangs over the exhausted city. The German businessman Karlheinz Schreiber is relieved to be sitting in the air-conditioned restaurant of the Westin Prince Hotel, a modern tower nestled in a green park in a northern suburb of the city. Schreiber, short and bulky at age sixty-five with grey hair combed over a bald pate, is inconspicuous among the early diners. There is little chance that any of these Japanese executives or visiting convention-goers will recognize him. The venue is equally convenient for Phil Mathias, a reporter with the *National Post*, whose offices are just a few blocks away. A few years younger than Schreiber, Mathias is white-haired and weathered. Together they sit hunched over their coffees, deep in conversation.

They look up, startled, when two strangers, men dressed in slacks and blazers, approach the table.

"Mr. Schreiber," begins one of the men quietly, "I'm Inspector Graham Muir with the Royal Canadian Mounted Police, and this is Inspector John Dickson." Instinctively, Schreiber shakes their outstretched hands. "Can we be seated?" asks Muir, as the RCMP officers drop their business cards on the table.

"We have a matter of some importance to discuss with you," announces Dickson. Muir asks Schreiber about his dinner companion. "Who is this gentleman?"

"This is Philip Mathias," Schreiber replies.

"Well, the matter which we have to discuss, you might want to consider a private matter, Mr. Schreiber," Muir continues.

"Whatever you have got to say, you can say it in front of Mr. Mathias."

Muir obliges. "I am placing you under arrest on a warrant outstanding from Germany, on matters presently under investigation by German authorities. It is a German arrest warrant. You are presently in our custody, however."

"I can't believe this," Schreiber says, looking down at the business cards. "I can't believe this. You are arresting me for the Germans?"

Muir tells him he is allowed to remain silent and that he has the right to call a lawyer. He explains that Germany has sent an application to the Canadian government for Schreiber's extradition. German authorities want him back in Bavaria to answer questions relating to an investigation of him for tax evasion and fraud. Inspector Peter Henschel, another plainclothes officer, is standing nearby.

Rattled, Schreiber asks if he can make some calls on his cellphone while he's at the table. "Yes," Muir replies. Schreiber calls his wife, Barbara; they talk anxiously for a few minutes. "Yes, Barbel," he says, "we were expecting something like this ... Don't cry." His next conversation is with Robert Hladun in Edmonton, a close friend and his lawyer for twenty years. Then he makes a quick call to another close friend, Elmer MacKay, a former federal cabinet minister from Nova Scotia.

As soon as he has finished, the police hustle Schreiber through the lobby and outside where two more officers are waiting beside two police cars. Mathias has followed them to the curb, but the officers pay him no attention as they briskly search Schreiber, handcuff him, and stuff him into one of the vehicles. The party then drives north of the city to the RCMP booking office in Newmarket; here Schreiber is formally charged, photographed, and fingerprinted. Inspector Henschel asks the new prisoner to empty his pockets, remove his belt, tie, jewellery, and shoelaces, and hand over the brown Louis Vuitton purse that hangs from his shoulder by a long strap. Henschel pulls everything out of the purse into a heap on a table, adds the contents of Schreiber's pockets, and sits down to make an inventory.

As the booking procedure continues, Schreiber is clearly in shock. "I can't believe this," he says repeatedly to the officers. "I can't believe you're arresting me on a tax matter. If I'd known this was going to happen, I would never have come to Canada." Henschel paws through the contents of the Vuitton bag while Schreiber shakes his head in disbelief. "I'm not naive. I have failed...I didn't think there was the smallest risk. I travel a lot, about 178 days a year...I'm a retired pensioner...I can't believe you'd extradite me on a tax matter."

Henschel doesn't respond to Schreiber's wails; instead, he's itemizing, in fascination, the pile on the table. First, there's the cash. A money clip from Schreiber's pocket holds several hundred Canadian dollars. Inside the purse there's an envelope with fifty $100 bills, also Canadian. In a leather billfold, along with a Swiss driver's licence, is another wad of fifty $100 bills, these in U.S. currency. A plastic envelope holds more bills; so does Schreiber's wallet. Henschel counts out $10,709.79 in Canadian dollars, $5,950 in U.S. dollars, and 10,000 Deutschmarks in ten DM1,000 bills. There's 7,370 Swiss francs, 435,000 Italian lire, 185 Dutch guilders, 231 British pounds, and 6,250 French francs – altogether, roughly $30,300 in Canadian money. And that's without counting the two fifty-peseta Mexican gold coins and the ten-dollar U.S. gold coin he finds.

"You shouldn't be walking around with all this money," Henschel says, glancing up at Schreiber. "You're like a walking bank."

Schreiber doesn't appear to find Henschel's little joke funny. Unperturbed, Henschel returns to his inventory. A Nokia phone with a spare battery.

"What's the number?"

Schreiber shrugs. "I don't know." The number, he concedes, might be in his Casio digital diary, one of the items in Henschel's pile.

"You never remember your own cellphone number," Schreiber mutters as he scrolls through the diary. Finally he finds it. "It's 416 578-4022," he says, and Henschel writes it down.

Henschel then makes a list of all Schreiber's identification papers. One Canadian passport, one German passport, both valid. A Canadian citizenship card. A German identification card. A German pensioner's card. A Canadian social insurance card. An Ontario health card, a German health card. A Swiss train pass. A Mercedes-Benz bank card, a Credit Suisse MasterCard and Visa, a Lufthansa Visa (expired), and two American Express cards (expired). There are two business cards, one giving his address in Pontresina, Switzerland, and another showing the address of his condominium in Ottawa. His German hunting licence is in the collection, along with a chequebook bearing the Ottawa address and a well-thumbed black notebook. There's more. A leather case with a tool kit and a Swiss Army knife. A leather bag with a gold bracelet and two sets of cufflinks. A flashlight with a built-in compass. A man's belt. Five key rings. A cigarette lighter, a cognac flask, three pairs of reading glasses, one pair of sunglasses, one case with two pens and a comb. A folding photo frame, hand cream, sun cream, a sewing kit, a small alarm clock, three plastic packs of medication and pill holders, four packages of lozenges, one bottle of eau de toilette, a nail file, two Wet-Naps, some Band-Aids, a handkerchief, and two emergency blankets. All of this has come out of the Louis Vuitton purse and Schreiber's pockets. Added to the list are Schreiber's Rolex watch and a gold necklace with two gold tags.

Henschel looks closely at the Canadian passport and finds a few slips of paper tucked inside. One bears the words to "O Canada," and another has the oath of allegiance to Canada that all new citizens have to swear. There are also the lyrics to "Wild Rose Country," a sentimental ballad with fond references to the province of Alberta.

As soon as Henschel completes the inventory, the Mounties lead their prisoner out to a police car and drive him back into Toronto to the Metro West Detention Centre, a holding tank for people who have been charged with criminal offences and are awaiting bail hearings. Later that evening, about 9 p.m., the RCMP issues a statement that goes out on the wire services, announcing Schreiber's arrest.

Schreiber's bail hearing begins two days later on Wednesday, September 1, 1999, when a white paddy wagon pulls into the provincial courthouse on University Avenue in Toronto. A crowd of some thirty reporters, photographers, and cameramen have been waiting for hours, gossiping among themselves, reading the papers, phoning their editors, or passing the time by watching Justice Frank Roberts process a steady stream of young men, all led in in handcuffs, most charged with rape, assault, or theft. The cops remove the cuffs when the accused joins the long row of fellow defendants in the prisoner's dock. Roberts dispenses with each case in a minute or two, putting most cases over to a later date. Handcuffed again, the men shuffle out, steered by the cops, while their lawyers bow and withdraw.

When there is no one left in the prisoner's dock, Justice Roberts's clerk tells him there's an "add-on" to the morning's schedule, a matter of an extradition treaty. Counsel for the accused has arrived from Alberta, but he hasn't been called to the Ontario bar so he can't be "gowned," in legal parlance. Ungowned, he can't speak for his client in this court.

The counsel is Bobby Hladun. Despite an overnight flight on the red-eye from Edmonton, he is relaxed, tanned, smiling; in fact, he looks like a hockey player who is aging gracefully, with his short-topped, silver-grey mane styled to fall just over his collar and his suit perfectly tailored to his slim figure. The judge asks him how the RCMP knew where to find Schreiber; Hladun says he knows none of the details, only that his client was sitting in a hotel having coffee when the officers approached him and told him he was under arrest. Roberts looks baffled and irritated. He reminds the room that he has an important murder trial starting any minute; he doesn't have time for this kind of nonsense. He adjourns the court for a couple of hours; confused, everyone stands while he stomps out, followed by the court officials.

At 2:30 Roberts returns, looking just as bad-tempered as he was in the morning. Tom Beveridge, the federal government lawyer representing the interests of the German government, informs him that a reporter intends to tape the proceedings. Roberts says he won't allow it. The *Globe and Mail*'s Stan Oziewicz – who had told both Beveridge and Hladun, as a courtesy, of his customary practice – moves quickly to the front of the courtroom to object. A ban isn't called for in this situation, he tries to say, but the judge frowns at the interruption and waves him away. Oziewicz is insistent. Roberts is annoyed. "You have no standing in this court," he snaps. "Sit down." Finally he agrees to look into lifting the ban for the day following, but for today nothing that is said in court can be taped.

A door to the left of the judge's bench opens and a police officer enters, followed by Schreiber and another officer. Schreiber's blue cotton shirt is rumpled, his grey plaid pants are baggy and riding low below his belly, and his hair is greasy and messed. His skin is sallow, dime-sized liver spots and pockmarks immediately noticeable. His mouth is small below a beaky nose, and his lower lip is thrust out in an unhappy pout. Like the homeboys who preceded him, he's handcuffed behind his back.

Bobby Hladun has been chatting to Phil Mathias, but as soon as his client arrives, he trots forward. Schreiber brightens a little when he sees Bobby. The officers lead Schreiber to the prisoner's dock and one of them removes his handcuffs. Immediately he reaches deep into the front of his pants and pulls down his shirt. He arranges his underwear, yanks at his pants at the waist, and tries to smooth his hair. It's unconscious on his part, a reflex action, a little embarrassing for the other people watching him, but they all understand. This man has slept in his clothes and has been handcuffed in the paddy wagon. His efforts to tidy himself before the judge arouse sympathy.

Because Bobby Hladun can't help here, the judge looks at Schreiber and asks if he has any submissions. Schreiber shrugs and spreads his hands out to show he has no idea what to say, then he looks to Hladun pleadingly. The judge allows Hladun to suggest that the hearing be put over until Friday. Roberts glances at Tom Beveridge, and he too suggests remanding the case until Schreiber finds a lawyer. The judge agrees and tells everyone to return two days later, on September 3. The police snap the handcuffs back on Schreiber and lead him away. Justice Roberts remarks to no one in particular that he has a really important murder case to hear, and he doesn't need any more of this.

The reporters milling around the courthouse are left with nothing, and most have little understanding of the case. If they recognize Schreiber's name at all, they connect it with the Airbus affair... and isn't that old history? Didn't the government apologize and pay him some money? Or was it just former prime minister Brian Mulroney they paid? There are no Canadian names in the warrant, so perhaps this is really just a German story. Even those who do understand what's going on – the senior correspondents from CBC Radio and Television, CTV, and Global – admit they've been told to keep their reports short and succinct. Their producers are nervous. Every journalist – especially the print reporters from Canadian Press and Southam News, both summer interns who are bright but unaware of the background – was told that any report has to include the boiler-plate paragraph stating that Brian Mulroney was cleared of any wrongdoing and the government apologized, and this case today has nothing to do with... well, anything here in Canada.

Reporters have copies of the German government's application for Schreiber's arrest, the document that outlines the case against him, but it's a thick file, nearly a hundred pages long. A minute-thirty on national television or radio means it's almost not worth the effort to flip through the pages. Print reporters have the space to make some sense of it, yet the only ones who try are the *Globe*'s Stan Oziewicz, in a piece published the next day, and John Nicol for *Maclean's* the following week.

For all their careful, bureaucratic language, the German documents reveal a wealth of information and a sense of urgency. There are two warrants in this file: the original arrest warrant, which arrived on August 27, and the amended warrant, which came in on September 2, both sent by Winfried Maier, a senior prosecutor in Augsburg, a town near Munich. Maier believes Schreiber is hiding in Canada; what he needs is help in arresting him, and he explains why: "Investigative proceedings are pending against the German-Canadian national, Karlheinz Schreiber, born in Petersdorf on 25 March, 1934, lastly residing at 86916 Kaufering, Raiffeisenstrasse, 27, for tax evasion and other offences," Maier writes. "The wanted person is strongly suspected of having intentionally concealed proceeds from commissions in the respective tax declarations of the years 1988 to 1993. He thus reduced income and trade tax by a total of [DM]25,724,844" – about C\$20.8 million.

Maier knows that tax evasion is not specifically listed as an extraditable offence in Canada's treaty with Germany, so he signals there's more to come: a new arrest warrant is imminent because Schreiber is also "strongly suspected of having committed bribery and aiding and abetting criminal breach of trust." The prosecutor's documents outline the course of the German investigation into Schreiber's affairs with cool precision, but the details are riveting: his bank records have been combed, his telephone calls traced, two of his former business associates were arrested and another is being hunted. There is a clear money trail and allegations that part of it runs through Canada. If convicted, the document states, Schreiber faces up to fifteen years in prison.

Should Schreiber be apprehended in Canada, Maier argues strenuously against granting him bail. Following searches of his home and business premises, Schreiber left Germany for Switzerland to evade prosecution by the tax authorities, says Maier. Fearing the Swiss might detain him on behalf of the Germans, "the wanted subject evidently decided to give up his domicile in Switzerland." And now he is in Canada. He has fled from two countries already and Maier is convinced that he will run again or, at the very least, will fight extradition so long that he will, in effect, be a free man in Canada. Back in Germany there is little chance of bail while awaiting trial; he has disappeared once too often for that to happen. Maier attaches the amended arrest warrant to his letter and crosses his fingers. All he can hope now is that the Canadians pay attention.

By the time the bail hearing resumes on Friday, September 3, the TV networks have pulled their stars from the story and sent juniors. The wire services continue to assign summer interns. Only the *Globe and Mail*, *Maclean's*, the *Toronto Star*, and the *National Post* have senior reporters in attendance: Oziewicz, Nicol, Tracey Tyler, and Mathias.

Few notice the new faces, the senior staff writers from *Der Spiegel*, Germany's largest and most influential newsmagazine, and from the magazine *Stern*. These reporters are quite familiar with the German arrest warrants and understand their significance to Canada. The Schreiber story is hot news in Germany, but the *Spiegel* and *Stern* correspondents sniff something much bigger about to break.

The mysterious woman sitting in the back of the courtroom on September 3 is Schreiber's wife, Barbara. She's an elegant, middle-aged woman with well-cut auburn hair, dressed in a good suit with a silk scarf tied around her shoulders. Every so often someone approaches to ask if she is Mrs. Schreiber, and she shakes her head. This is Canada and reporters are polite; they accept her fib as a request to be left alone. When Schreiber is brought in, he quickly scans the room and recognizes Eddie Greenspan, perhaps Canada's most famous criminal lawyer. Greenspan is known for his ability to juggle up to fifty high-profile clients at a time, for his addiction to junk food, and for the television series he hosted on sensational legal cases.

"Glad to meet you," Greenspan says firmly to Schreiber, who nods gratefully, unable to shake hands because his are still cuffed behind his back. He seems tidier than he was on Wednesday, but he wears the same pants and shirt. The handcuffs are removed and Schreiber sits down. Hladun comes over and they talk in a whisper while Greenspan snaps open his briefcase. Greenspan turns with a scowl to a handful of anxious young lawyers at the back of the court; one, Alison Wheeler, is holding a fistful of yellow markers bundled together with rubber bands. "Where's the pub ban section?" he demands. Wheeler frantically flips through a thick red book, finds the highlighted section, and brings it to Greenspan. As he breezes through the section, Greenspan looks up and carefully searches the faces in the courtroom.

Stan Oziewicz has been busy; he's brought Tim Trembley, a lawyer for the *Globe*, who gives Justice Roberts some of the case law on tape recorders in court. After discussion everyone agrees that reporters can tape the hearing, and that there will be no publication ban. Roberts notes testily that Phil Mathias got his first name wrong in a Schreiber story in that day's *National Post*, calling him Fred instead of Frank. Then he leaves to attend to his murder trial. His replacement on the bench is Justice David Humphrey, formerly a legendary Toronto criminal lawyer.

Tom Beveridge, the deputy section head of criminal prosecutions for the federal government's Toronto office, is acting for the Federal Republic of Germany. He begins by running through Maier's warrant and the Germans' case against Schreiber. He mentions that although Schreiber has a residence at 7 Bittern Court in Ottawa, the neighbours in the complex say they haven't seen him there since the Airbus story broke in 1995. In response, Greenspan paints his client as a Canadian citizen who bought a home in Ottawa in 1989, owns other property there, and has been living in Toronto for the past four months. "This sixty-five-year-old man who appears before you has never been charged and never been convicted." This statement, along with the lines that this is "just a tax dispute" and that the Germans are on a "fishing expedition," becomes the heart of his argument for bail.

Unruffled by Greenspan's hyperbole, Beveridge continues laying out his case by calling Peter Henschel to the witness stand. Inspector Henschel, tall, slim, and preppy in a blue shirt, silk tie, and blazer, looks young but tells the court he's an eighteen-year veteran of the RCMP and works in the Commercial Crime Division in Ottawa. He is, he concedes laconically, "somewhat familiar" with the case. An understatement; this man is one of the lead investigators in the RCMP's investigation of the Airbus affair. Schreiber's arrest, he explains, came after German phone taps showed calls to the house of someone named Greg Alford and to his cellphone. A couple of the calls, the ones to the cellphone, had come from Barbara Schreiber's mother's home in Germany.

Once they knew Schreiber was using Alford's cellphone, they began watching Alford's house in northeast Toronto. Two days later, on Monday, August 30, Henschel heard that Alford had picked up a man and a woman on Bloor Street in Toronto, a couple who resembled the photographs they had of the Schreibers. The surveillance team followed Alford's car back to 102 Bloor Street West, where the Schreibers got out. The officers discovered that in the middle of the most expensive shopping street in Canada is a private luxury apartment hotel called Bridge Street Accommodations. It offers furnished apartments, from small, studio-sized units to two-bedroom suites, and caters to wealthy guests who need a place for a few days or a few months.

The hotel security chief said Schreiber arrived at the beginning of June but wasn't using that name; instead he was known to him as Mr. Hermann, which is Schreiber's middle name. It was Alford who had made all the arrangements, ordering that the name Hermann not be posted in the hotel's electronic directory. Because no name was posted, there was no way to call the suite. If there was any kind of emergency, the hotel was to call Alford. The Mounties checked for any record of long-distance calls to Germany from Suite 511, but there were none. Any calls Schreiber made were from a cellphone.

After the break, Greenspan has his chance to question Henschel. He asks if Henschel and his colleagues were the ones in charge of the RCMP Airbus investigation. Henschel won't be drawn into this; all he'll say is that he can't comment. Greenspan demands to know if Henschel thinks any of the documents in Schreiber's purse are forged, or if he has any proof that Schreiber was fleeing Switzerland or that he refused to deal with his tax problems. Greenspan attempts to portray a man going about his business with nothing to hide, even making restaurant reservations in his own name in Toronto. He asks the officer if he's aware of active lawsuits Schreiber has filed, including one against the CBC stemming from the broadcaster's coverage of the Airbus story. In fact, this lawsuit, filed in 1995, has been dormant ever since because Schreiber said he was unable, for health reasons, to come to Canada for questioning by the CBC's lawyers. But Henschel can only respond that yes, he is aware.

"He has never backed down from a fight in a courtroom," declares Greenspan with passion. He is trying to show that his client feels wronged and will fight no matter how much it costs, and that he moves about Toronto openly; he uses a fake name and Alford's cellphone only to avoid the press. "He sees the people he wants to see, but not the press – whom he doesn't want to see."

Although Greenspan has just met his client, there is no uncertainty to his performance. He keeps up a running stream of inside jokes that Justice Humphrey rewards with frequent chuckles. The two are comfortable with each other; the judge's son, also named David, practises law with Greenspan's brother Brian, another criminal lawyer almost as famous as Eddie. Beveridge, on the other hand, wins no smiles from Humphrey; their relationship is all business.

Greenspan has represented Schreiber for only a day, but his central line of defence is already clear: he will argue that Canada's new extradition law, passed on June 17, 1999, offends the country's Charter of Rights and Freedoms. His client is being detained for an investigation, not a trial, and that is unacceptable. If the judge should let him out on bail, he won't flee; he'll stay put in Ontario, at either the Ottawa condo or the Toronto hotel. The Ottawa house is worth $330,000, and his wife is willing to put up $200,000 in cash. Surely, says Greenspan, this is more than adequate surety for bail, though the very idea is offensive, he says in his summary. "Bail should be one buck."

It's now 6:30 on the Friday before the Labour Day weekend. Anyone who can get to a cottage has already left. Humphrey is not prepared to make a decision on bail until he has had a chance to examine the German application more carefully. He adjourns the court until Tuesday morning. The police lock Schreiber's hands behind his back one more time, and he is taken off to the detention centre for the next three days.

When Schreiber returns to the courthouse on Tuesday morning, he's wearing a fresh shirt and a tie and a jacket to match the grey plaid pants. His hair is combed and his face has lost the pallor of shock and fear. With help from the Canadian government, his German enemies have humiliated him before the world, kept him in a jail cell for nearly a week, and portrayed him as a fugitive from justice. Today, he hopes, things will change. His friends have come to his aid.

Seated beside Barbara Schreiber in the back row of the courtroom is Elmer MacKay, probably his best friend in Canada. MacKay has been reclusive for years, ever since he left politics in 1993 to return to his country house in rural Nova Scotia. In the front row on the left sit three men, strangers to the reporters here, who turn and smile at Barbara Schreiber.

Greenspan wastes no time in his pitch for bail, and the court hears no more about the Schreibers' assets. "People are here to offer sureties," he declares to Justice Humphrey. "You would be well advised to call your witnesses, then," Humphrey responds grimly. Clearly he has read the lengthy German warrant over the weekend; his earlier chummy attitude to Greenspan has evaporated.

The first man up is John Harding, one of the strangers in the front row, a thin man of medium height with glasses and short, greying hair; he's wearing a blazer, a flowered tie, and a plaid shirt. While Harding is making his way to the witness box, Greenspan announces he has some big guns in waiting. One will be "Mr. Elmer MacKay, who has come from Nova Scotia...and there is Marc Lalonde in Montreal, who is prepared to be a surety." The reporters buzz. Barbara Schreiber smiles. Another, continues Greenspan, enjoying the excitement he's just generated, will be Hans Reichert, who controls the North American franchises for the Mövenpick restaurants.

Under Greenspan's guidance, Harding tells the court he has returned early from a holiday trip to his son's wedding in Whitehorse to put up his surety – his Ottawa house, worth $250,000. He is, he explains, an interior designer with a degree from McGill University and training at the Parsons School of Design in New York. He's fifty-three, married with three grown children. Harding joined the Department of External Affairs in 1970. With embassies and diplomatic residences all over the world, External Affairs needed designers and property managers; by 1990 he was director of the facilities and installations offices at External's Ottawa headquarters. He retired that year and opened his own design business, called Interiors by Harding; six years later, he tells the court, he sold "the retail end" of his business and began doing private design consulting only.

Harding's been living off the interest from the sale of that retail business, he confirms – although not entirely. Under questioning from Beveridge, he admits that he's also been an employee of Schreiber's since he left External Affairs. It turns out the men met in the late 1980s, around the time Schreiber bought his condominium in Ottawa's Rockcliffe Park. In 1992, Schreiber purchased another Ottawa property, a small parcel of commercial real estate on Beechwood Avenue. Within this parcel is a row of two-storey buildings that house what Harding describes as a "low-end" restaurant, a couple of shops, and two apartments overhead. One of the shops is Interiors by Harding.

Schreiber set up a company called Rockcliffe Enterprises Inc., or REI, as owner of the Beechwood Avenue real estate. Harding is not a shareholder in REI, but he has been its president since 1993. In effect, he is Schreiber's Ottawa property manager. For $12,000 a year, he says, he pays the bills on the condominium, makes sure the utilities are working, picks up the Schreibers if they're visiting, and generally looks after the place. It's not a business relationship, he states; it's friendship. But it seems the Schreibers rarely come to Ottawa; in the last four or five years, he says, he can't remember their staying at Bittern Court at all.

13

That changed in May 1999 when the couple let him know they would be using the condo. Harding met them at the airport and drove them home after a short stop for groceries. They left soon thereafter but were back in Ottawa a few days later and again stayed at the condo. But on a third visit they stayed at a hotel because they were afraid of being bothered by reporters. It seems someone had seen them at Bittern Court and squealed to *Frank*, the well-known satirical magazine. Harding doesn't know, he says, why Schreiber left Switzerland so abruptly in May.

Gathering credible bail guarantors has kept Eddie Greenspan busy all weekend. He talked to Marc Lalonde twice, and now he's ready to tell the judge that Lalonde will put up a surety of $100,000. Lalonde's guarantee is a major coup for Schreiber. During the sixteen years Pierre Trudeau was the country's prime minister, Lalonde was one of his most powerful cabinet ministers, ending his political career in 1984 as minister of finance. Now sixty, he is a partner at Stikeman Elliott in Montreal, a law firm famous for its tax experts. He can't be here today, says Greenspan, but he's prepared to come in a couple of days; in the meantime he'll read Lalonde's statement into the record.

Reporters mutter to one another as their pens scribble across the pages of their steno pads. It seems Lalonde and Schreiber have known each other since 1986 and he's been acting for Schreiber for years, representing his business interests to the Liberal government of Jean Chrétien. But the relationship with Schreiber is more than just business, suggests Greenspan. "He sees him frequently and knows him well."

Finally Greenspan calls Elmer MacKay. Tall and broad-shouldered, MacKay has a smooth bland face and looks younger than his sixty-three years. He is retired, though he says he still does a little pro bono work to keep up his standing in the Nova Scotia bar. He doesn't need to work; he's a wealthy man and owns more timberland than any other private individual in the province. Like Lalonde, he is prepared to put up a surety of $100,000.

First elected to Parliament in 1971 as the Tory member for Central Nova, in Pictou County, MacKay gave up his safe seat in 1983 so that his leader, Brian Mulroney, could run in his stead in a by-election. In the 1984 general election, Mulroney moved to his home riding in Quebec and MacKay took back his seat. His reward was the cabinet job he had always wanted: solicitor general, the man responsible for policing in Canada.

He has known Schreiber for about twenty years, he tells the court, prompted by Greenspan's matter-of-fact questioning. "And I went over to see him in May or June and suggested he come back to Canada. He has some property in Newfoundland, and I suggested he spend some time in Nova Scotia."

It's established that in fact Schreiber arrived in the first week of May and that he stayed with MacKay, who loaned him a car and a cellphone and introduced him to his circle. "I introduced him as my friend, Karlheinz Schreiber."

Greenspan makes the point that the former cabinet minister had no hesitation in offering hospitality to Schreiber or in introducing him by name, nor was there any attempt to hide or conceal his identity.

"I contributed to his delinquency by taking him to a casino and we played the slot machines," MacKay deadpans. "It was not a success." The judge chuckles and Greenspan grins happily. This is going very well.

"If the truth be known," MacKay says, "[Schreiber] is as hard to find as a basketball in a phone booth. And yes, I let him use my phone, and he may not have returned it – but he was my guest. It was his choice to keep the phone."

"Are you still paying the phone bill?" Beveridge asks.

"Yes. I do not object to paying the phone bill."

Now another element of Greenspan's strategy appears. Schreiber is in Canada not in order to hide from German prosecutors, and he didn't flee Switzerland a step ahead of the police; he's here to interest investors in a new enterprise.

"Mr. Schreiber owns a company that manufactures a high-quality spaghetti machine," explains MacKay. "I'm not here as a shill for Mr. Schreiber, but Mr. Schreiber hopes to do for spaghetti what Starbucks did for coffee."

Under Beveridge's questioning, MacKay says he's seen Schreiber only five or six times since he left politics in 1993, and each time he went to Zurich to visit his friend, he stayed only a day or two. Schreiber wasn't preoccupied with his legal problems, MacKay testifies, although he mentioned them occasionally: "A lot of it was hearsay, of course," he says dismissively. MacKay can't remember where he stayed in Switzerland on his overnight visit four months earlier, nor even the name of the town. Under pressure from Beveridge, he finally recalls the name of the hotel: "I think I stayed at the Schlosswald, a small hotel in a semi-rural area." He arrived on Friday, May 7, he testified, with tickets for himself and Schreiber to fly to Toronto the next day.

"Why were you so insistent he return with you?" Beveridge asks.

"I like to reciprocate," replies MacKay, suggesting it was simple hospitality.

"How long did he plan to stay?" Beveridge asks.

"It's not clear," MacKay says calmly. "It was understood he would be travelling around."

As soon as they arrived in Toronto, Bobby Hladun flew in from Edmonton to join them at the Sheraton Hotel so that he and Schreiber could talk. The next day they all flew to Halifax and spent a couple of days there. After that MacKay took Schreiber to his country home near the small city of New Glasgow, where they spent a week together. Barbara Schreiber followed her husband to Toronto ten days later, and MacKay tells the court he went with his friend to Toronto to meet her plane.

Schreiber had another reason to be in Toronto, and that was to talk to Greg Alford and others about his spaghetti machine, MacKay continues. "He's absolutely indefatigable about this machine."

What about you? presses Beveridge. Are you involved with the machine yourself? MacKay says he's not.

Then, perhaps remembering he is giving sworn testimony in a courtroom, he amends his answer. "Uh, previously on his behest I went to see Harrison McCain and some of the Irving interests on his behalf. There was no fee. It was strictly as a friend."

MacKay has opened some interesting doors for his friend: Harrison McCain of Florenceville, New Brunswick, is one of the wealthiest food producers in Canada, outstripped only by the New Brunswick Irvings, who, with a $7-billion fortune, are one of the wealthiest families in North America and are in the oil, shipbuilding, and timber business as well. MacKay admits that he was giving some thought to investing in the device himself, but he says he was really there "as a long-term friend. If a business opportunity arose – well, maybe, but I was not there as a supplicant."

Strangely, this "long-term friend" doesn't know where Schreiber is currently living in Toronto. "I had no occasion to know," he tells Beveridge.

Is Schreiber still using his phone?

"Dunno. He has several phones – he lives on the phone."

What does he know about Schreiber's circumstances in Germany?

"Very little. He has sometimes spoken of his matters in Europe but I am not his confidant nor his lawyer." He does know about the arrest warrant but can't remember whether Schreiber told him in Canada or in Switzerland.

"I had nothing to do with his decision to leave or not to leave Switzerland," declares MacKay. "He said Germany was a very tough place to do business."

At this comment, Schreiber, in the prisoner's box, shakes his head sadly.

The next witness is Hans Reichert, a short, dapper man with a loud tie and deep bags under his eyes, who says he did some tests with the spaghetti machine in one of his restaurants fifteen months ago. There were problems with it. "But I always thought it had potential," he adds quickly. The idea behind it is that it should be able to cook large quantities of spaghetti in a minute and a half. When Schreiber arrived in Canada in May, Reichert was pleased to meet him in person for the first time and talk further about the equipment. They had a nice dinner, he says, and discussed setting up a showroom in some vacant space he owned on Richmond Street in downtown Toronto. Here Mr. Schreiber could offer demos and training on the device. Although Reichert has never visited the Schreibers at their Toronto apartment, they've had at least ten meetings since May and have developed "a sort of friendship." And yes, he knows about the German arrest warrant, but there is enough amity between them for Reichert to put up a bail surety of $25,000.

Why, Beveridge asks, would you do this without knowing him better?

17

"He likes the machine!" quips Justice Humphrey, to scattered laughter in the court.

"I think it's a fair thing to put up – I'm interested in the spaghetti concept and the sauces," says Reichert.

Greg Alford is the last of the witnesses called by Greenspan. He's forty-three, tall and pleasant-looking with dark hair greying around the temples; he's wearing a dark summer suit, blue shirt, and glasses. Questioned by Greenspan, he explains that he's known Schreiber since about 1984, when Alford was a lobbyist at Government Consultants International in Ottawa. In 1988 Alford became vice-president of Bear Head Industries Limited, one of his GCI clients; Schreiber was the company chairman.

After he left Bear Head in 1996, he too saw the spaghetti machine. "I realized its potential," he says with a straight face. He and Schreiber set up a new company called Spaghettissimo North America Inc. and brought the equipment into Canada in 1997 for testing – with mixed results. They haven't been able to get it off the ground. Maybe soon. Everything is registered and run out of his home.

"I have been urging him to come to Canada to address this market," adds Alford.

He sees the Schreibers three or four times a week in Toronto. What Beveridge wants to know is why Alford, like MacKay, loaned Schreiber a cellphone. And why didn't he have one listed for the spaghetti machine company? "It's a start-up company," responds Alford quickly. "We don't have any credit cards or an office. We're not making any income."

So how has he been supporting his wife and two children since 1996?

"With personal savings." Alford tells the court that a European branch of Schreiber's spaghetti machine company paid him some consulting fees as well.

Why did you rent the apartment for the Schreibers?

"It was a company expense," Alford answers. "I signed the lease."

Were you instructed by Mr. Schreiber to sign the lease under the name of Hermann?

"We discussed this and talked to the lessor – he said it was done all the time, especially for entertainment people to avoid media lineups. It's intrusive to be asked constantly for interviews."

Were you aware he was giving a press interview when he was arrested?

"Yes."

And that he's given interviews in the past?

"Yes."

Alford confirms that he gave Schreiber an envelope of cash before the arrest. His explanation is simply that it came from Schreiber's account, for which he had signing authority in order to pay Schreiber's phone bills, his condo fees in Ottawa, his taxes, and other expenses. He doesn't explain why he seems to be doing the same odd jobs for which Harding is paid $12,000 a year, and Beveridge doesn't ask him.

Justice Humphrey wants to think about all this and dismisses court for the day. Another night in jail for Schreiber. On Wednesday morning everyone is back to hear whether the German prosecutor's plea for detention without bail has succeeded. Humphrey tells the court he has gone through the application for arrest and considered the testimony. Only the fact that a former minister of justice and a former solicitor general of Canada have spoken up for the prisoner and have laid their reputations and their money on the line has convinced him, he says. After the Schreibers put up $200,000 of their own cash and give sureties on their Ottawa properties, the prisoner is free on $1.2 million bail.

When Schreiber finally emerges from the courthouse, Barbara is smiling joyfully at his side, as if they have been given a not guilty verdict. Television crews cluster around to grab sound bites for their evening newscasts.

One reporter asks Elmer MacKay why he was prepared to guarantee bail. "He is a man of his word," replies MacKay. "I have known him for some time and I find him to be a good friend – that is as far as it goes. I don't desert my friends."

With Greenspan at his side, Schreiber acknowledges MacKay's faith with a promise. "It is, I think, a great pleasure to have friends. I have always had friends in my life. And I will never let a friend down. So they came here to get me out. I will never do anything to harm them."

Then, just before stepping into a taxi, he directs a few sympathetic words to the swarm of reporters around him. "I started out very poor.

In a small village. Nine hundred people. Poorest parents. I know what it means to work every day hard – this is what you do to feed your families. I admire you. Have a good day."

By this time, no one is paying attention to MacKay. He leaves the throng surrounding his jubilant friend and finds a quiet corner. Pulling a cellphone out of his pocket, he dials a number and says softly, "Mission accomplished." He snaps the phone shut and walks away.

On January 25, 2000, dozens of reporters, photographers, and camera-men are again gathered outside the courthouse in Toronto. It is a bitterly cold day and the press people are bundled in parkas and scarves, stamping their feet and blowing into their hands as they await the arrival of Karlheinz Schreiber and Eddie Greenspan. Nearly five months after Schreiber was granted bail, the formal hearing of Germany's extradition application begins today with a brief private discussion between Greenspan and Tom Beveridge concerning sched-uling matters. Normally there would be no reporters here at all. Most of the journalists in this crowd have come from Germany.

A pale grey Mercedes van slides up to the curb and the pack rushes forward, the reporters shoving to reach the car door first, the televi-sion crews using their large cameras to push through the mass. Long boom microphones hover over the heads of the crowd. Eddie Greenspan emerges first, looking sour and serious, wearing only his shirt, barrister's collar and bib, and trousers held up by wide black suspenders. He's carrying his court gown and a briefcase. Then comes the man of the hour, Schreiber himself, small and dapper, grinning and waving to the cameras like a pop star. As the two men advance towards the courthouse, the journalists push backwards in a rolling scrum; some stumble and trip over metal gates while they shout ques-tions at Schreiber and swear at one another.

Gretchen Drummie is the *Toronto Sun*'s court reporter, a ten-year veteran. She's more accustomed to rape and murder trials than she is to corruption cases, and this unruly melee astonishes her. "Man!" she breathes. "This is the biggest pig-fuck I've ever seen."

The German reporters swarm closer. Their bosses have told them they must get an interview with Schreiber, but only those who are appropriately deferential are getting an audience. "Herr Schreiber! Over here! Herr Schreiber!" His eyes dart around the crowd, searching for allies. He has told reporters that if they describe him as an arms dealer, their calls will not be returned. The arms-dealing angle comes as a surprise to most of the Canadian journalists, who have only ever heard of Schreiber as a "businessman." One German reporter took the trouble of phoning a Canadian colleague earlier in the day. "Don't speak to me at court today," he ordered. "Schreiber doesn't like you, so I don't want him to know we're friends."

The knot of people and cameras and boom mikes moves up the escalator and down the corridor towards the courtroom. Greenspan stops suddenly and wheels around to scold the group. "It is illegal," he growls, "to bring cameras into the courthouse. It is *illegal*. If you don't leave, you could be arrested." The television crews slink away and the reporters, chastened, enter the courtroom. But Greenspan himself does not stay; his private discussion with Beveridge is elsewhere, and he leaves his client sitting in the courtroom with his wife, Barbara.

Immediately, Schreiber is up and working the room. He waves to reporters and gives short statements here and there. Reporters beg him for interviews. "Ask Eddie," he suggests. "He's getting two hundred requests a day."

This new phase of Schreiber's remarkable career – from humiliated prisoner to strutting media star – began on November 4, 1999, almost two months after he was released on bail in Toronto, when the German police issued another arrest warrant. The warrant, which caused an uproar in Germany, is for Walther Leisler Kiep, the former treasurer of the Christian Democratic Union, a powerful backroom political leader and one of the country's most prominent business-men. The warrant states that Kiep received DM1 million, part of a commission Schreiber earned on a 1991 deal in which Thyssen Industrie AG, a giant German manufacturer, sold tanks to Saudi Arabia. Kiep admitted accepting the money but said he turned it over to the party, which deposited it in a secret account. As more of the story came to light, Germans were shocked to learn that the CDU, which had governed Germany for much of the postwar period, main-tained secret accounts and routinely accepted illegal contributions.

Eventually Helmut Kohl, chancellor for fifteen years until his defeat in 1998 by the Social Democrats under Gerhard Schröder, was implicated. Under fierce attack from the German public and politicians from his own party, Kohl, bitter and furious, resigned as honorary chairman of the CDU a week before this hearing.

After half an hour or so, Greenspan and Beveridge return to the courtroom and tell the judge that there will be another court hearing in a few days; it's over for today. Once again the insistent scrum gathers outside, and Schreiber and Greenspan answer a few more questions before heading to the van.

Eddie Greenspan is getting two hundred interview requests a day because his client has ignited the worst political scandal in Germany since the war, and he's playing it for everything he's worth. Schreiber's threats to tell all and damn the consequences to politicians in Germany are explicit: "I feel like a cat sitting on a cage full of mice," he tells the reporter from *Stern*, "and I don't know which one to eat next."

2

Making Friends

The reporters who had crowded around Karlheinz Schreiber's taxi as he left the courthouse on bail in September 1999 were mystified by his parting benediction. "I started out very poor... I know what it means to work every day hard – this is what you do to feed your families. I admire you." Was he goading them with heavy-handed irony? Was he cultivating their favour with a show of sympathy? Or was the newly released prisoner flushed with gratitude and beneficence and honestly expressing his feelings? Schreiber has no trouble speaking English and understands nuance. His words suggested a vision of journalists as toilers in the field, poor as church mice, struggling to put food in their children's mouths. Indeed, not an unrealistic portrayal for some, even those left snorting in disbelief at the curb as his cab pulled away.

Perhaps he viewed them as people who would like to have the kind of money he enjoyed – a reasonable assumption. That is how he always regarded those less well off, and that is how he treated them. He paved his way in life and business with flowers, chocolates, and presents for secretaries, with fine meals, trips, and gifts for businessmen, bureaucrats, and politicians. It's the way to get ahead and for him, it worked. Perhaps Schreiber's greatest strength was his uncanny ability – or desperate need – to make friends and keep them. For this man the world revolved around personal relationships, and his success, such as it was, can be attributed to this single talent. He had little else to rely on: no business degree, no legal training, not even a university education. But he could remember birthdays and anniversaries, and he was a generous host and a convivial socializer. "The King of Schmooze" was how one Toronto reporter described him. From humble journalists to powerful judges to ambitious politicians, Schreiber could legitimately claim he was a close friend to dozens of people. He worked harder at nothing else.

And he was right about his origins. He was poor. Friedrich Karlheinz Hermann Schreiber was born in 1934, in Petersdorf, a town in the Harz Mountains close to the old border with East Germany. Now known as Hohegeiss, it is a popular ski resort area today, but in the 1930s it was just another part of rural Germany. Schreiber described his parents as devout members of an evangelical Lutheran community who once ran a small store selling paint and furniture. His mother also worked as a cook and his father did upholstery.

Adolf Hitler had become chancellor the year before Schreiber's birth and, like any other youngster growing up in Germany during those years, Karlheinz did not have an easy childhood. His father went off to serve in the German army when the boy was five years old and was gone for seven years. Karlheinz's schooling was interrupted by the war; as he told a reporter for *Stern*, from the time he was eleven years old, he was interested in business, and soon he began trading cigarettes for eggs. His family left the Harz Mountains in 1950 and moved north to the much larger city of Braunschweig, where he briefly attended a trade school. He quit when he was sixteen and moved north to Hamburg to work in a department store.

Schreiber had grown up short and stout and, as he acknowledged himself, plain. He loved music and learned to play popular songs on his accordion; no one had to ask him twice to perform at a party. He was gregarious, aggressive, and restless, and after a few years he decided to move south, to Bavaria, to start his own business importing carpets from Iran. Although building a carpet business in a war-ravaged country where few people had money for luxuries was a daunting prospect, Schreiber did well.

Then a better opportunity came his way. He was offered work with a paving and road-marking company in Landsberg, a small city near Munich. As soon as he arrived, he knew he was home at last. Landsberg was a historic and picturesque Bavarian town with a beautiful, clean river, the Lech, running through it and an old town square at the heart. Mellowed brick and stone buildings crowded the streets, and fine views with the mountains in the background were easily found. Above the town on a hill is the prison where Hitler was incarcerated for thirteen months after his failed putsch in November 1923. Part of this time Rudolf Hess was a fellow prisoner, along with a less famous figure, Emil Maurice; with their help, Hitler wrote the first volume of *Mein Kampf*, which was published in the fall of 1925.

But Landsberg was the dark site of more than Nazism's beginnings. North of the town is the suburb of Kaufering; it was here that Hitler's engineers designed an infamous airplane production plant, code-named Wood Pigeon and staffed almost entirely with slave labour. It was supervised by the administrators at Dachau, about 40 kilometres to the northeast. To withstand Allied air raids, this concrete factory was built into the hills and half buried underground while its workers, in an ugly echo of the design, lived in primitive huts also half buried in the dirt. There were eleven workers' camps housing at least 30,000 people, mostly Jews, and three times that number would have been held there as slave workers if the war had not ended before the facility reached its planned capacity. Almost 14,000 people died at the plant. Only ruins remain today and the site is now a cemetery. A memorial stone commemorates the prisoners who lie in unmarked graves.

When Schreiber decided to settle in Kaufering, the place had not yet recovered its original charm; the ravages of the war were still evident in the concrete rubble of the factory and the wild tangle of destroyed huts and overgrown bushes around it. But he liked the area and felt he could make a home there, helping to restore prosperity to a community blessed by natural beauty. He loved Bavaria and its people, and he was fortunate in his new job. The road-marking company, Bayerische Bitumen-Chemie Ferdinand Heinrich GmbH, not only had room for him to advance quickly, it had a unique product he felt he could sell anywhere. Instead of simply painting lines on the road, the crews cut a groove in the pavement and filled it with liquid asphalt studded with reflective beads. The result was a luminescent, slightly gravelly material that could be seen at night, and felt, too, as tires passed over it. It was safer and more resilient than any other road-marking product. Before long Schreiber was running the company, and when the owner died in a car accident, Schreiber bought out his widow's share and gained control. By this time he was married to Christiane, a young woman from East Germany; they had two children, Viola, who was born in 1960, and Andreas, born in 1962.

Schreiber understood early on that road-marking contracts were awarded by governments; if he wanted his business to thrive, he had to meet the politicians and bureaucrats who made the contract decisions. He had to sell himself as well as the product. In hopes of a golden future, he set up in 1965 a holding company called Kensington Anstalt and registered it in the tax haven of Liechtenstein, a tiny principality southwest of Munich, just a few hours' drive away. Schreiber used Kensington as a shell to hold other companies.

Vaduz, Liechtenstein's capital, is home to hundreds of thousands of shell companies. Most are nothing more than a box in a post office or a brass plate on a building. These companies don't manufacture or trade any product or employ any individuals. They are simply paper companies designed to own or hold other companies, for legal liability and tax reasons. They also obscure the identity of those who own or control these other companies. Foreigners with shell or "letterbox" companies appoint trustees to run them and to represent their interests. Shell companies go hand in hand with tax havens, jurisdictions where there is little or no taxation. Many people use tax havens and shell companies to hide assets from family members – ex-wives, for example – or from business partners or law enforcement agencies. In the most secure tax havens, bank secrecy is the law; it is illegal to disclose information about account holders to tax investigators or police from any other country, or to other individuals.

As tax havens go, Liechtenstein, with only 30,000 citizens, remains one of the safest; its government is stable and its economy is dependent on the offshore banking business. Although it has a policy of cooperating with authorities from other countries on serious criminal investigations, it is almost impossible to breach bank secrecy there.

By 1969, Schreiber's road-marking company owned a subsidiary company in Lugano, Switzerland, run by friends of his. The subsidiary had sustained some losses in recent years, arousing suspicions of fraud among his German investors and the company's insurer. In 1969 an audit was ordered. One of the insurance company's directors knew an auditor and accountant in Lugano who agreed to do the review; his report concluded that the Lugano subsidiary's losses were not associated with any fraud. Schreiber was relieved and delighted with the report and just as pleased with the accountant who did the review, a young man named Giorgio Pelossi.

"He was happy with my work," Pelossi recalled, "and from that moment in 1969 I worked for him on all his foreign companies and foreign investments." Pelossi was helpful in many ways, becoming a conduit for investors in Schreiber's projects and bringing in cash infusions from his own clients. It wasn't long before Pelossi was working almost exclusively for Schreiber.

Two men could not be more dissimilar than Schreiber and his new associate. Soft-spoken, unobtrusive, and quiet, Pelossi was born in 1938 in Bellinzona, the capital of Ticino, an Italian-speaking canton in Switzerland. He went to high school in Lausanne, where he perfected his French; then he worked while he studied accounting at night. At twenty-one he moved to Zurich to continue his studies; there he met his future wife, Christa Duclos, a fashion designer who specialized in fur coats. In the early 1960s, while he completed his accounting degree, Pelossi worked as an auditor for a man who owned two companies in Zurich; in 1966, because his boss, like Schreiber, had a subsidiary company in Lugano, Pelossi took his bride back home. It was like a foreign country for Christa, who spoke only German, but her husband was glad to be back in Ticino.

Not long after he returned to Lugano, Pelossi completed a second business degree and decided to go into business for himself, working alone as an auditor, accountant, and business and tax consultant. In short, he said without any self-consciousness, he became an expert at helping people put their money beyond the reach of the tax collector, usually by tucking it safely inside shell companies in Liechtenstein.

The couple were happy in Lugano, business was good, and, like the Schreibers, Pelossi and his wife were raising two children, a boy, Michael, and a girl, Raffaela.

Pelossi worked with Schreiber to erect new shell companies under the parent Kensington. In 1972, for example, they registered Interleiten SA under Kensington. Assisting Schreiber during this time was a young woman called Dietlinde Kaupp, who began working for the road-marking company as a translator in 1971 and was soon promoted to his secretary. She would stay with him for the next twenty-five years.

Despite the complexity of his growing business empire, Schreiber never left the details to Pelossi and Kaupp alone. Wherever he travelled, he carried a three-ring binder. At meetings, he would pull out his binder, go to the index he'd made, find the reference, then turn to the proper page and begin to take notes. He also kept an appointment diary, recording every bit of business in a few abbreviated words – telephone calls, banking transactions, dinners, even groceries to pick up. He was similarly meticulous in his personal habits. An associate who later travelled with him around Alberta recalled that even if they were staying in a hotel for only one night, Schreiber would empty his entire suitcase, carefully putting the contents in their proper place – shirts and underwear in the dresser, pants hung up in the closet, toilet kit carefully laid out in the bathroom. This ritual would be repeated at every destination.

Through the 1960s and early 1970s, Schreiber pursued the rich and powerful who could help him in business. First among these was Franz Josef Strauss, a prominent Bavarian politician, like Schreiber strong-willed, outgoing, hugely ambitious, and patriotic. Born in 1915 and a soldier in the German artillery during World War II, Strauss also came from humble parentage; his father was a butcher in Munich. Young Strauss grew up determined to bring his state into the modern age and make it prosperous.

Where he was different from Schreiber was in his achievements as a young man; he was a talented athlete – a German cycling champion – and a brilliant classics scholar at the university in Munich. In 1949 he was elected to the Bundestag (the lower house of parliament), and in 1956 he became the minister of defence. Strauss was the architect of

Germany's rearmament in the 1950s and 1960s; one of his most controversial accomplishments was the relaxation of post-war legislation that impeded the sale of arms to other countries. Another was his rapprochement with the government of East Germany. In 1961 he became chairman of the Christian Social Union in Bavaria, the more right-wing sister party of the federal Christian Democratic Union, a post he held until his death.

His career was nearly destroyed in 1962 when he ordered police to search the offices of *Der Spiegel* after the magazine published an embarrassing article about leaked NATO documents. The furor that erupted after this interference with the press forced his resignation, and it took him four years to get back into the federal government. When he did, however, he enjoyed great success as minister of finance.

Strauss was determined to see Germany develop, especially his part of Germany, the Bavarian heartland around Munich. He believed that as Germany rebuilt its economy after the war, Bavaria could match the rest of the country as an industrial engine. Alliances were necessary and he didn't let old wartime grievances get in the way. In 1970, Strauss stood strongly behind the creation of an ambitious aircraft manufacturing enterprise, in partnership with France, called Airbus Industrie. At first Germany and France were equal shareholders. In 1971, Spain joined the consortium with a 4.2 percent share; Great Britain became a partner in 1979, taking a 20 percent share. The German participants included Messerschmitt-Bölkow-Blohm GmbH, a company that built helicopters and other military hardware such as fighter planes, missile systems, and space platforms. MBB created a separate company, Deutsche Airbus, for the Airbus program, and Strauss became one of four "fathers" of the consortium, along with Roger Beteille, Airbus's technical manager, Felix Kracht, senior vice-president of sales and production at Deutsche Airbus, and Henri Zigler, president of France's Sud-Aviation. (The French company merged later in 1970 into a group called Aerospatiale SA, which carried on its interest in Airbus.) The chairman of both Airbus Industrie and Deutsche Airbus was the Bavarian minister of state, Franz Josef Strauss. Airbus was to build passenger aircraft in competition with the world leaders, McDonnell Douglas, Lockheed, and Boeing, all American giants.

Strauss's heart was always in the regional politics of Bavaria, and in 1978 he would step down from federal politics to run for premier. After a decisive victory at the polls, he ruled the state for the next ten years and saw it grow in wealth and influence. Strauss intended to build his family's fortunes along with his political career, and he did not hesitate to forge relationships with the businessmen and industrialists who could help secure the Strausses' future.

For Schreiber a man like Strauss could be both role model and mentor. According to Giorgio Pelossi, Bayerische Bitumen-Chemie "had all the state contracts." Schreiber could not have won them without support from Strauss. While Strauss was busy with matters of state, he delegated his family's affairs to the person he trusted more than anyone else, his son Max, a Munich lawyer. Max Strauss and Karlheinz Schreiber became close friends.

Schreiber was pleased that his road-marking business was doing well, and he had the growing friendship with Franz Josef Strauss to thank for much of his success. His carpet-selling days were in the past. In the early 1970s, for the first time in his life, Schreiber was making decent money. And he didn't squirrel it away: he lived well and entertained extravagantly. He loved to welcome people to dinner and parties at his four-storey home and business complex at 22 Lechstrasse. Over the years it became a gathering place for visiting industrialists and politicians, a haven where they could relax in private and share their common interests.

Schreiber was a perfect host. "Come to my place," he'd urge, after a long day of formal meetings in Munich. "We'll have a great time." And they did. He would pull on a pair of Bavarian lederhosen, thick socks, and an open shirt, and fire up the custom-built barbecue. Dinner would be a loud and cheerful affair; beer was plentiful, wine flowed, jokes and gossip and cigar smoke filled the air. In high spirits, he'd pull out his accordion and lead the party in beer parlour songs or set up the pins in the bowling alley in his basement party room.

Such lavish hospitality was, to a great extent, a show of bravado. His marriage to Christiane had ended in 1967, adding personal financial pressures to those of his business. By this time, though, he was besotted with another woman, Renate Rauscher, who was much younger than he was and extremely attractive, with dark hair, large expressive eyes, and a wide, full mouth. They started living together when she was still a teenager, Christa Pelossi said, "but she wouldn't marry him. She's smart." When he introduced her as his wife, she would correct him every time; her name was Rauscher, not Schreiber.

Mad about her as he was, Schreiber was also jealous and refused to allow Renate to go on a holiday without him. On one occasion when she wanted to vacation alone at the apartment he rented on the Riviera, he asked Christa to go with her; when she refused, he sent his secretary along instead.

"The only mistake Renate ever made," Giorgio Pelossi observed dryly, "was to leave Schreiber before he made a lot of money."

In the winter of 1973, Schreiber met an interesting group of Canadians on an official visit to Munich. One of them was Horst Schmid, a fast-talking fire plug of a man and an up-and-coming politician from Alberta. Born in Munich in 1933, Schmid had emigrated in his late teens to Canada, where he'd studied accounting. He described himself in the *Canadian Parliamentary Guide* as an "exporter," although he had spent most of his pre-political life working as an electrician. A member of Edmonton's German-Canadian businessmen's association, he was first elected to the provincial legislature in 1971 when the Progressive Conservative Party won a landslide victory over the long-governing Social Credit Party. Schmid and his fellow Tories owed their triumph to their young and charismatic leader, Peter Lougheed, who founded a new political dynasty in Alberta. Lougheed promptly appointed Schmid minister of culture.

His musical taste was a little more highbrow than Schreiber's – Schmid had served on the board of the opera in Edmonton – but the two men hit it off immediately when they met at a reception hosted by Franz Josef Strauss. Schmid was on a goodwill mission to his homeland, a trade initiative paid for by the Alberta government to foster business investment in the province. He had brought along some of his Alberta buddies, among them Erwin Zeiter, a building contractor who owned several apartment buildings around Edmonton. Zeiter remembered the trip well, especially a dinner held in honour of the Canadians at the Villa Hiegel, the home of the wealthy Kroops family.

"Schmid introduced me to all kinds of industrialists who were way above my level," recalled Zeiter. "They were people who move $100 million a year, $200 million, big people...But they didn't know the difference between a minister from Alberta and a minister from Canada." Franz Josef Strauss knew the difference, but he encouraged the local businessmen to connect with the Albertans, telling them how well Schmid had done in Canada and extolling the opportunities there.

The Albertans were just as keen. You should try your luck in Canada, they urged Schreiber later over steins in the party room at Kaufering. Your road-marking business would do well. The OPEC oil crisis, which had driven up the world's oil prices, was hurting the economy everywhere but in Alberta. There the thriving oil and gas industry underpinned a provincial economy growing at 40 percent a year. We're paving the province. Come on along. This could be the answer, Schreiber thought. These fellows are well connected; Schmid is a cabinet minister.

In 1973 Pelossi and Schreiber gave serious consideration to taking a chance on Canada. The Strauss family had holdings in Canada, including interests in shopping centres and other real estate ventures. Some were in Alberta, where many Germans had settled – about 14 percent of Albertans were of German descent – and the Strauss connection would open doors. The more Schreiber thought about it, the more he was enchanted with the idea of a new frontier, a place where men still rode horses and branded cattle on vast ranches dotted with oil wells. It would be like Texas, and it would be an adventure. And with men like Schmid on side, he had contacts in high places.

Once he'd made up his mind, Schreiber set up an Alberta company and arranged, through a lawyer, to have it incorporated in Edmonton on October 15, 1974, some weeks before he arrived there himself. It would become one of Schreiber's principal companies in Canada, under which several others would be grouped. Pelossi came up with the name MLE Enterprises; he said MLE stood for Maple Leaf Enterprises.

In November 1974, Schreiber and Pelossi were ready to make their first exploratory trip, and they did it with a splash: ten days in Canada with stops in Toronto, Regina, Calgary, and Edmonton. There were eight or nine in the party, including several employees of Bayerische Bitumen-Chemie who would be involved in establishing the road-marking company in Canada, the first step in introducing the system to North America. Along as well were Bavaria's deputy premier and the minister of economy and trade. They were joined by a couple of other enterprising businessmen.

"We tried to set up a company in Moose Jaw," Pelossi remembered. Schreiber had arranged a press reception in a rented hall to announce his intention to establish a road-marking company in partnership with a local businessman. Schreiber preached enthusiastically about the Bitumen system, a safer solution, he told them, than simple paint on a road. Unfortunately, the man Schreiber chose to lead the venture soon wound up in jail on an unrelated smuggling charge, and the Moose Jaw company never materialized.

Not all was lost: he made at least one good contact in the province. As always, Schreiber was on the lookout for a friendly power-broker in the government, preferably a cabinet minister or the premier himself. Saskatchewan offered slim pickings for a right-wing newcomer from Germany, given that the party in power was the decidedly left-wing New Democratic Party under the leadership of strait-laced Allan Blakeney. But during his stay in Regina, Schreiber met John Messer, a hard-nosed cabinet minister to the right of his party. Messer was involved in the Saskatchewan Mineral Development Company, a Crown corporation that had received about $200 million from an Alberta company for exploration. They promised to stay in touch.

The convoy moved on to Alberta and during the few days they were there, Schreiber and Pelossi fell in love with the province. It was their idea of heaven: a stunning landscape with the soaring mountains and splendid ski resorts of their home regions, plenty of transplanted Europeans to make them feel comfortable, a place where a man could still be a pioneer but do it in style.

Schreiber himself waxed lyrical about Alberta. "I was impressed about the province since I am a mountain guy and farm boy," he told an Edmonton judge during a public inquiry in 1981. "I loved the country and as you know, sir, you are from Calgary too and you might understand, that people when they are born in the mountains, they like to stay with what they know and what they love." There was more to the attraction than scenery, he added. "The other thing is that the premier [Lougheed] very well advertised the minister for culture, Horst Schmid, who was born in Bavaria as you know...and [Schmid] told us a story about what he has done before he became a minister and that it could be a very comfortable way to do business with us, to contact him and ask him for help, so therefore the government is available."

Europe was old and set in its ways and didn't appreciate real entrepreneurs. Alberta was the promised land. They had come to the right place at the right time, and once Schmid was named Alberta's minister of trade in 1979, it was even better, Schreiber enthused. "It is very comfortable to work with people which know both situations, the European situation, especially Bavaria, speak the language, so from there came a real close kind of relationship, no doubt about that."

3

Wild Rose Country

Once back in Europe, Schreiber and Pelossi spent the next few months preparing for their move to Alberta. They had to find investors and arrange for apartments, offices, and company structures in Canada. Neither Schreiber nor Pelossi intended to relocate permanently or even for a few years; each wanted to maintain his European residence and keep the existing businesses running back home. Still, as long as they were spending several months a year in Alberta, Schreiber decided he and Renate would buy a modest apartment in Calgary and set up the road-marking business there under the name of MLE Enterprises. Pelossi expected to spend less time in Canada than Schreiber, but he brought Christa, Mike, and Raffaela to Calgary in 1976 to see how they liked it. Mike, who adapted well, moved to Edmonton a year later to attend a private high school.

Calgary was tailor-made for Schreiber. Built along the banks of the Bow River, it was a brash and brassy city of modern skyscrapers and sprawling suburbs spreading out over the surrounding low hills. The see-saw nod of oil-well pumps punctuated the landscape in every direction. Only a few disreputable taverns and a small pocket of Victorian housing hinted at the city's true frontier past. The faux-cowboy fashion – thick felt Smithbilt hats, hand-tooled cowboy boots, large silver belt buckles, and black string ties – was as romanticized as it was ubiquitous. In law offices, banks, and corporate boardrooms, it was not unusual to see a pair of gleaming and pointed leather boots peeking out beneath crisp suit trousers. Oil and gas might fuel modern Calgary's prosperity, but people were sentimental about the early days of cattle ranches and stockyards, of Blackfoot, Sarcee, and Stoney Indian settlements, of vast herds of bison roaming their river valley. It was a town where newcomers felt at home, even if they were aware that Calgary did have a quiet upper class of old money, old land, and old blood. They presented no obstacles to the ambitious and the hard-working.

Those who could afford to bought what they called "acreages" around the city, modest parcels of land where they could build spacious ranch-style homes, raise a few head of cattle, keep a horse or two, and drive into town in half an hour. Others made the most of the fast highway to Banff, the Rockies resort town an hour and a half north, where they could ski, climb, or hike. For Schreiber, it was paradise. "Alberta is Canada's Bavaria!" he would exult.

But Schreiber and Pelossi aspired to a wider territory than Calgary and its suburbs. The provincial government and its politicians were based in Edmonton, the largest city in the province, set close to its geographic centre. This was where MLE was registered and where its lawyers were located. It was a short hop on a commuter plane or a three-hour drive straight north from Calgary, and they were constantly back and forth between the two cities. Like Calgary, Edmonton had obliterated most of its pioneer traces, but it lacked Calgary's impatient energy. Divided by the deep and winding North Saskatchewan River, this was a city of academics and bureaucrats, people who were far more liberal than the folks to the south. Calgary was exuberantly pro-business and right-wing; Edmonton was home to left-wing activists and politicians, very few of whom wore cowboy boots or Smithbilt hats.

Schreiber immediately went to work making contacts, beginning with the local German community. He promoted his road-marking enterprise to everyone he encountered, but he was eager to spread his wings, and he discussed other opportunities with the German

Canadians he met on his daily rounds. One of these was Erwin Zeiter, a wealthy Edmonton property owner who was to become Schreiber's partner in several ventures. Zeiter said that around 1973 he invested a million dollars in MLE, and that he was startled by Schreiber's pursuit of political connections. "He always tried to get immediately in with the politicians. And I have been telling him that is not the way you do business in this part of the woods." According to Zeiter, Schreiber claimed that paying kickbacks was a normal business practice all over the world, Alberta included. Zeiter could not believe what Schreiber was suggesting. "I have been in business here for quite some time and I have... never had an idea to go to some city mayor or some roads department manager and say, 'Okay, you give me a contract to do the roads between here and Red Deer... and I give you some money or I do something for you.' Never happened, I never done that."

Zeiter said he told Schreiber, "Then you do whatever you have to do, but I do not understand how it's done and I have no desire to get involved in this." Zeiter wanted no knowledge of Schreiber making illicit payments to anyone – and he got none.

On November 27, 1976, Schreiber and Pelossi were flying back to Calgary from a business trip to Toronto. Schreiber took a piece of hotel letterhead out of his briefcase and sketched an organization chart of the companies they had set up together. At the top of the chart was his parent company, Kensington, the Liechtenstein shell company he had created in 1965; below were a dozen boxes with names scrawled in them. One was Interleiten SA; two others were subsidiaries of MLE, called MLE Sask and MLE – USA. What purpose these companies would serve was probably unclear even to Schreiber at the time, but the overall plan was to bring German investors into Alberta's oil and gas industry and into real estate development. Then Schreiber proposed a deal that recognized Pelossi's contribution to his ventures past and future, one that would have the added benefit of creating more distance between himself and the Liechtenstein shell companies.

"Giorgio, you will get 20 percent of everything Kensington earns while you work with me," Pelossi remembered Schreiber offering expansively. Schreiber added a note to the bottom of the page: "Giorgio becomes a millionaire for he gets 20% of everything. KHS

Toronto 27 Nov. 1976." Then he passed it to the man he fondly referred to as his "brother." Pelossi tucked it away in his briefcase – and kept it. Thereafter Giorgio Pelossi would take over the management of Kensington from Schreiber, though he would continue to act only on instructions from Schreiber.

Yet it was Pelossi who landed the biggest deal they had yet seen, along with an opportunity to make their fortune in Alberta real estate. Among the clients Pelossi had retained after he went into business with Schreiber was the German heiress Barbara Flick, a widow who lived a quiet and very private life near Lucerne. Flick was wealthier by far than any of the other Germans they knew and one of the wealthiest women in Europe. In the early 1950s she had married Otto-Ernst Flick, son of the industrialist Friedrich Karl Flick, who had built a steel and coal fortune in the 1920s. One of Hitler's financial backers, the older Flick had used Jewish and Gypsy slave labour during the war. After serving three years of a five-year sentence handed out at the Nuremberg war crimes trials, Flick returned to business life and made another fortune through the family's holding company, which owned, among other properties, the automaker Daimler-Benz. In 1966, after much family bickering, his younger son, also named Friedrich Karl, became the heir apparent to the Flick empire, and Otto-Ernst and Barbara left with a huge cash settlement.

An army of advisers, including Pelossi, were summoned to counsel the couple on the best investments and tax strategies. Some of their money went into Swiss bank accounts, and some went to investments; some went to land in Europe and North America. In Edmonton, for example, they owned a large office building next door to the landmark Macdonald Hotel. In 1979, Otto-Ernst died. Karl Raabe, Barbara's brother, began advising her on financial affairs and purchased a parcel of downtown Calgary land on her behalf for about $400,000. Not long afterwards, Raabe discovered that the city planned to rezone the land for a park. This was disturbing news.

Raabe came to Calgary that same year and called Pelossi for help; Pelossi brought along his partner, Karlheinz Schreiber. Schreiber didn't hesitate. If he could have the zoning changed and sell the property for a profit, he told Raabe, he and his associates would expect to take half the profit on the deal. Raabe and Flick agreed. "Schreiber got the land rezoned for development," said Pelossi. "The land was then sold to a company called Nova for $2 million." At that time the energy giant Nova was known as Alberta Gas Trunk Lines Ltd., and the company used the land to build a thirty-seven-storey office building.

Barbara Flick needed no more proof of Schreiber's talents. When he suggested he could arrange more deals like this one, she was happy to jump into a partnership with Schreiber and Pelossi. With her money and Schreiber's connections, the reasoning went, they could sell more land for profit.

Those connections were not insignificant. In 1976 Schreiber met a former Lougheed cabinet minister, William Dickie. Dickie had been minister of mines and minerals from 1971 until he left politics in 1975. He became a director of MLE (renamed MLE Industries Ltd.) in 1977; Schreiber was president and chairman, and his companion, Renate Rauscher, was listed as vice-president. Pelossi's wife, Christa, was named secretary, as she was to almost all the companies he set up in Alberta. Dickie became a director or officer of thirteen of the fourteen Alberta companies Schreiber incorporated between 1977 and 1981, with a small shareholding in each. In December 1977, Schreiber set up Bitucan Holdings Ltd., the most important company he would register during the years he spent in Alberta, and folded MLE into it.

Most of these companies existed only on paper, though Dickie and Schreiber had grandiose plans for energy and real estate ventures. As a former politician and lawyer, Dickie had the experience and the expertise Schreiber needed, and the ability to arrange meetings with cabinet ministers with a single telephone call.

Schreiber already had access to one of Alberta's most senior politicians. Hugh Horner was a doctor who also ran a working ranch near Barrhead, 190 kilometres north of Edmonton. As the deputy premier in Peter Lougheed's cabinet, he was the second most powerful politician in the province. After serving in Ottawa as a federal member of Parliament from 1958 to 1967, he resigned, moved into provincial politics, and was re-elected three more times. He served as Alberta's minister of agriculture, then transportation, while at the same time holding the office of deputy premier. With the sixth sense he had for such vulnerability, Schreiber learned that Horner was short of cash to pay off some debts on his ranch. He offered to arrange a loan for $150,000 from a Swiss bank; it arrived in the form of a mortgage on November 16, 1978, three years before Horner left the government. Years later, when the loan became public knowledge, Horner shrugged it off.

"It was a straightforward banking transaction, as far as I am concerned," Horner told the *Toronto Star* reporters Darcy Henton and Bill Schiller, who broke the story in 1995. "It was not anything out of the ordinary." Horner told the press he thought he'd paid back more than half the money, but he had lost touch with Schreiber and eventually obtained a court judgment to cancel the debt in 1993. "Karlheinz didn't say it was his [money]," Horner said in the interview. "I never knew it was his. He said he would get it from a Swiss bank, that's all." Horner excused his failure to repay the loan in full by saying he'd done consulting work for Schreiber and never been reimbursed.

But Giorgio Pelossi knew the money came from Barbara Flick and from Schreiber himself. Under Schreiber's direction, Pelossi had drawn up papers stating that the money was a loan from a man named Emilio Grossi. Grossi existed – he was the uncle of one of Pelossi's friends in Lugano – but he was a lender only on paper. The money was funnelled from Schreiber and Flick, $75,000 provided by each, but untraceable to either. Bill Dickie confirmed the details of the loan years later, telling an Alberta court in 1993, "Barbara Flick and Karlheinz Schreiber arranged a loan in the amount of $150,000.00 and provided the funds." Pelossi claimed that Horner paid back no more than $2,000 or $3,000.

The company Schreiber and Pelossi established with Barbara Flick was ABS Investments Ltd., incorporated on February 3, 1978. Bitucan owned 64 percent, Flick contributed $3 million for 26 percent, and Dickie held 10 percent. One of the directors of ABS was William Skoreyko, a former Alberta PC Party president and another habitué of Kaufering get-togethers, who had been the member of Parliament for Edmonton East.

Flick's involvement with Schreiber aroused the ire of another Calgary businessman, Christian Graef, who thought he had the inside track with her. Graef enjoyed a prominent role in the city's diplomatic set as the honorary consul for his home country of Finland. He had spent forty years advising foreign investors – especially German investors – on where to put their money in Alberta. He, too, had worked with the Flicks; he was the agent involved in the purchase of the office building in Edmonton, and every once in a while he would phone them in Switzerland to bring them up to date on their investments or to suggest new opportunities.

One day Graef bumped into Erwin Zeiter on a Calgary street corner; Zeiter introduced him to Karlheinz Schreiber. "Schreiber was trying to make his way into the Alberta highway department with road-marking equipment," Graef said. "At the time, they were optimistic. Mr. Zeiter had personal connections with the Alberta government that were useful to Schreiber."

Not long afterwards, Graef was in Munich and ran into Karl Raabe, Barbara Flick's brother, and Horst Schmid, who were staying at the same hotel. Graef introduced the two men, who had not met before. "The next thing I know," he recalled, "I am back in Edmonton and on my way into the Flick building when I see Barbara Flick, Bill Dickie, Karlheinz Schreiber, and Giorgio Pelossi together. I am dumbfounded. Mrs. Flick looked at me, I looked at her." Embarrassed, Flick stammered that Schmid had spoken to Dickie and they talked to Schreiber and...well, now they were going to be selling her building for her. Not Graef. Sorry.

The acquisition of land – and a plan far more sophisticated than a simple property transaction – now became Schreiber's main obsession. Gossip was circulating about Edmonton's intention to annex land around the city in anticipation of future growth. Until the mid-1980s, in fact, Edmonton grabbed more land than it would ever need. (Today, it is the second-largest city in Canada in acreage but only the tenth largest in population.) Once the city annexed hundreds of acres of farmland, its value would skyrocket because it could be sold to housing developers. Schreiber knew he had to acquire the right vacant land and quickly, and he hoped his intelligence on the city's plans was sound. He also knew that the provincial cabinet would have to approve any land annexation. He was grateful for the advice and expertise of Steven Kurylo, who had served as executive assistant to Horst Schmid and was working by then in the private sector.

Land deals were not Schreiber's only pursuits; he was also attracted to the glamorous, high-stakes world of aircraft sales. His entree was provided by Franz Josef Strauss, chairman of Deutsche Airbus and Airbus Industrie. In 1977 Pelossi, Schreiber, and two German partners set up a company called Miliar SA, headquartered in Lugano, Switzerland. Through it Schreiber signed his first commission contract with Airbus to sell A300 aircraft in Alberta and British Columbia. He made an early sales call on Rhys Eyton, the president and chief executive officer of Pacific Western Airlines Ltd., a regional carrier based in Calgary and owned at the time by the Alberta government.

Eyton, a good-looking chartered accountant from Vancouver in his early forties, had ascended the corporate ladder quickly, becoming a specialist in the airline industry. In 1967 he joined PWA, a small but strong airline serving the four western provinces and the North out of its Vancouver base. The Alberta government bought the airline in 1974; Eyton became president two years later and moved the company headquarters to Calgary. Despite his position as one of the province's most influential businessmen, Eyton acknowledged he was an outsider himself, and he viewed newcomers with good ideas as people to be welcomed. There was something about Schreiber, though, that made him cautious.

Thanks to Eyton's friendship with Hugh Horner, Schreiber won an appointment and a chance to make the pitch. No cigar. "We came too late," said Pelossi. "Eyton had already signed with Boeing."

That didn't deter Schreiber. He told Eyton the new Airbus 300 was perfect for the commuter service between Edmonton and Calgary during the week and ideal for weekend cargo flights north to Fort McMurray. In fact, Alberta could be the North American base for an Airbus fleet. Bill Dickie and Hugh Horner supported the idea, Schreiber later revealed in an interview. "They were interested to do something," he said, "and since they bought Pacific Western it might be a good idea to have a base for Airbus in the North American continent. This could really have gone to Alberta."

He had come up with a way to sweeten the deal even more. He

proposed to bring in another Alberta airline, Wardair International Ltd., the successful charter company founded by the legendary aviation pioneer Max Ward, and another aircraft manufacturer, de Havilland Aircraft of Canada Ltd., which was based in Toronto and manufactured small Dash 7 commuter planes. "In those days I had a consulting deal with de Havilland," said Schreiber, "and the idea was, more or less, to take four Dash 7s for each Airbus. And then use the Dash 7s for Wardair for Arctic tours." It was a complicated scheme, to say the least. Max Ward, Schreiber recalled, wanted to take charter tourists to the Arctic for wilderness tours, just the kind of trip he was sure Germans would love. And he knew they would love the Canadian west, too. So why shouldn't Max Ward have some Dash 7s to take small groups of sightseers to the Canadian Arctic? If Airbus could sell one plane to Ward and buy four Dash 7s, he was sure Airbus would help de Havilland sell the commuter planes in Europe...By the time he finished explaining this grand design, most listeners were thoroughly confused, although it seemed to make perfect sense to Schreiber.

He couldn't sell the idea or any part of it to Rhys Eyton. Patiently, Eyton again explained to Schreiber that PWA had signed a contract with an Irish leasing company and had just acquired a new fleet of Boeing 737s. He was not in the market for Airbus aircraft, nor was he interested in any co-venture deals. The meeting was, by all accounts, not friendly and it ended badly. Schreiber did not offer any special inducements to Eyton, but he was uncharacteristically rude when Eyton turned him down. With no encouragement to linger, he left abruptly, long before their scheduled hour was up.

By the late 1970s, Schreiber was describing himself as an "industrialist" with thirty companies around the world, and he did not like being rebuffed. This kind of thing didn't happen often; usually people were delighted to see him. He might not have been the shrewdest of businessmen, but he could always count on getting through the right doors. He was able to make most people laugh and relax and feel comfortable in his company. For his part, he felt comfortable in Alberta.

Pelossi, on the other hand, missed Lugano and spent more and more time back home. By 1980, Christa and Raffaela, homesick from the start, were back there for good, while Mike, who loved Edmonton, stayed to finish school. The men remained close, however, and in 1979 Schreiber arranged for Pelossi to be his trustee, giving him authority to act on his behalf in matters relating to their various companies. And, as always, they had fun together. Whenever he was in Alberta, Pelossi got a kick out of his partner's enthusiasm for the mountains. Schreiber had taken up horseback riding and brought friends over from Germany, including Max Strauss, for a taste of the cowboy life: riding, hunting, fishing, and songs around the campfire. Schreiber would play his accordion, offer a few choruses of "Wild Rose Country," and keep everyone in stitches.

And periodically he'd invite his Alberta buddies to Germany to play there just as hard, Bavarian-style. Each January, on the last Friday of the month, he hosted a carnival party. As he described it, "People are invited from around the world, normally between fifty and seventy guests including politicians, premiers, princes, whatever you want, and a lot of Albertans." At one of these carnival parties, he donned a clown outfit while Pelossi wore a dancer's costume with fancy pants and ruffled sleeves. Their Canadian guests joined in, dressing in equally silly outfits and horsing around like schoolchildren, throwing bowling balls with abandon, drinking the way they hadn't done since they were youngsters at university. But there is a telling photograph of Hugh Horner, wearing a ridiculous hat and hurling a ball down the long alley, his hawk face and grim expression showing his discomfort.

In 1981, however, three pieces of bad luck brought the Alberta idyll to an abrupt end: a serious recession, a messy land scandal, and a furious premier.

4

The Premier
Is Not Amused

Although Schreiber drew as many provincial cabinet ministers into his orbit as he could, there was one prize that eluded him: the favour of Alberta's premier, Peter Lougheed. This failure irked him. After all, as he told everyone, he was bringing big business and important investors into the province. On one occasion, during a visit by a Bavarian government official, Schreiber was somehow able to wangle the use of a government plane for a trip in the Rockies. Schreiber, Pelossi, and Steve Kurylo were on board with the visiting Bavarian. This was getting close. Why he could not take the last step, through Lougheed's door, was a mystery to him, but he never stopped trying.

A lawyer with a master's degree in business administration from Harvard, Lougheed was one of Alberta's aristocrats. His grandfather, Sir James Lougheed, had been a leader of the Conservative Party in the Senate and a cabinet minister in Ottawa in the early 1900s. Peter Lougheed played professional football for the Edmonton Eskimos before going into business; in 1965 he entered provincial politics and in 1971 he became premier. By the time Schreiber moved into Alberta, Lougheed was western Canada's leading spokesman, a major presence during the never-ending constitutional negotiations with Quebec, and one of the most respected politicians in the country.

In January 1980 Schreiber heard from Bill Dickie that the premier would be in Switzerland to meet with banking officials at the time of the annual Kaufering carnival party. Dickie intended to arrive early for the party and ski afterwards with Schreiber at the modest condominium Schreiber had recently purchased in Pontresina, four kilometres from St. Moritz. His visit would overlap with Lougheed's, scheduled for the first week of February. It was a happy coincidence and a great opportunity, Dickie thought. It was high time Lougheed and Schreiber got to know each other.

According to Schreiber's version of the story, the premier was hoping for a day or two of skiing on the weekend. Schreiber believed Lougheed would be interested in the resorts around Pontresina, attractions that might inspire ideas for similar developments in Alberta. "We had the feeling the people in Banff and those places could do a little bit more for après-ski," Schreiber said, "[so] they would know what to do when they come back from the mountains, from the slopes." Schreiber arranged a dinner in Pontresina for Lougheed and the others in his party, including Lee Richardson, Lougheed's executive assistant, and Joe Dutton, his executive secretary.

"I was surprised... he was so well informed about what I am doing with my road marking," Schreiber said, "though I told him it should be better for the government of Alberta. It is the smallest customer we have. The cities do much more work with us."

Lee Richardson recalled the evening differently. Richardson had a political career of his own, after working for Lougheed and later in the Prime Minister's Office in the early years of Brian Mulroney's government. In 1988 he was elected to Parliament for the riding of Calgary Southeast. Interviewed in October 1999, a month after Schreiber's arrest in Toronto, Richardson remembered he had met Schreiber twice, once in Europe with Lougheed and again in Ottawa at the parliamentary restaurant in 1991 with Elmer MacKay. Of the first encounter, he said that Lougheed's party had arranged to spend the weekend near St. Moritz. Dickie tracked them down and phoned Lougheed at his hotel to invite the group for dinner.

"We said no about eight times," remembered Richardson. "We were chased around until we finally gave up. Finally we went for dinner." Schreiber was over-friendly and embarrassingly persistent that night in his attentions to Lougheed, a man with an air of reserve that discourages most people from pressing too hard or too close.

"Schreiber was name-dropping like crazy," said Richardson. "He told us everyone he knew in Alberta. He talked about his friends in Germany and he talked about Strauss. He was so gushingly outgoing . . . Peter was particularly uncomfortable. I think Schreiber was talking about ministers in a way that would suggest that they were palsy-walsy. Well, that just wasn't the style of Lougheed's government in the least. He's offended that people even talk like that. So he just says, 'We're getting out of here.'"

Lougheed signalled for Dutton and Richardson to accompany him as he left the restaurant. He was staying at a different hotel, but he wanted a meeting in his room before they parted company. Dutton dropped Richardson and Lougheed at the premier's hotel, then went to find a parking spot. Lougheed uttered not a word while they waited for Dutton. As soon as he rejoined them, Lougheed erupted. "What the hell went on there?" Before they could answer, he told them he was suspicious and wanted some answers. Exactly who was Karlheinz Schreiber? Neither man seemed to know; they had arranged the dinner only after Dickie's repeated pleas.

On his return to Edmonton, Lougheed sent out a crisp directive to his most senior officials, warning that he would not put up with any of them doing business with Karlheinz Schreiber. "Frankly," said Richardson, "Peter Lougheed said if this guy ever does call, we're not home."

Although it was frustrating for Schreiber to meet such hostility from the premier's office, it didn't slow his pace. On September 9, 1980, he incorporated a new company, ABB Investments Ltd., as a subsidiary of ABS, to manage real estate and energy projects in western Canada. As the parent company, ABS would control the financing of the deals while the new subsidiary would handle all the administration. Schreiber named himself chairman of ABB, with Dickie as president and Horner as vice-president.

Six weeks later, John Messer, minister of mineral resources in Saskatchewan, who had impressed Schreiber during his first trip to

Canada in 1974, resigned from the Blakeney cabinet. "Mr. Messer, 39, said he wanted to quit while still young enough to pursue another career," reported Donald Humphries for the *Globe and Mail* on October 28, 1980. "He says he will rest up and 'deprogram' himself from Saskatchewan politics before pursuing any business offers." Several months after his resignation, Messer joined the ABB board; soon afterwards he became a director of ABS as well as of Pelalta Investments Ltd., another Schreiber company, in which he was given a 5 percent stake.

Resting up was not part of the plan for Schreiber and his partners. Every few weeks, Pelossi would incorporate yet another company to serve another group of his various investors. Many of the companies owned pieces of one another, creating an intricate web. Before long his investor list included twenty individuals and four companies. According to Pelossi, aside from his obliging friend Erwin Zeiter and the trusting Barbara Flick – whose $3 million went to buy about 1,200 acres of land south of Edmonton – there was a well-to-do German businesswoman, Lotte Pabst, who owned a Volkswagen dealership in Munich and invested about $2 million. Jöst Hurler, who controlled a supermarket group, put in about $8 million. Ludwig Huber, president of the Bayerische Landesbank and a former chief prosecutor of Bavaria, invested his bank's funds. (He and Schreiber set up a separate company, DLH Holdings Ltd., at this time as well, although Huber has said he invested only DM700, about C$450, in the firm and it was never active.) Heinrich Riemerschmid, vice-president of the Bavarian chamber of commerce, was another ABS investor; so were Kurt Ladendorff, a Hamburg accountant, Peter Arndt, Schreiber's tax adviser, Franz Josef Dannecker, the legal adviser to the Christian Social Union in Bavaria, and Harald Giebner, one of Schreiber's German lawyers. A few small private holding companies, controlled by friends in Liechtenstein, Panama, and Germany, also came on board.

The Canadian associates included John Messer and, of course, Dickie and Horner. Jürgen Hanne, a builder from Berlin who had emigrated to Alberta, where he invested in the oil business and home construction, gave money to Schreiber as well; he was represented by the name of his secretary, Erika Lutz. (Hanne was convicted by a

Berlin court in April 2000 in a case of real estate fraud and sentenced to eighteen months in prison.) And finally, the most important investor, if not the wealthiest, was the family of Franz Josef Strauss.

In 1980, Schreiber registered a holding company for the Strauss family called FMS Investments Ltd., which stood for Franz Josef Strauss and his wife, Marianne. The original shareholders of FMS were Marianne Strauss, with 48 percent, and ABS, with 52 percent. By 1982 the Strauss family (including the children, Max, Monika, and Franz Georg) owned the whole company. The Strausses used FMS to own shares of other companies set up by Schreiber: BLA Investments Ltd. and PLS Investments Ltd., for instance. FMS also went into joint investments with ABS.

By the end of 1980, Schreiber had set up the following Alberta companies, listed by incorporation date.

October 15, 1974: MLE Enterprises Ltd.
(renamed MLE Industries Ltd. in 1977)
May 2, 1977: HLP Holdings Ltd.
December 22, 1977: Bitucan Holdings Ltd.
February 3, 1978: ABS Investments Ltd.
May 24, 1979: PA Equities Ltd.
December 29, 1979: Pelalta Investments Ltd.
May 1, 1980: BLA Investments Ltd.
May 1, 1980: BHP Investments Ltd.
September 9, 1980: ABB Investments Ltd.
September 11, 1980: FMS Investments Ltd.
November 6, 1980: EPD Investments Ltd.
December 5, 1980: DLH Holdings Ltd.
December 5, 1980: PLS Investments Ltd.
December 5, 1980: PSW Holdings Ltd.

At the new year, it was time to relax in Bavaria. Invitations to the annual carnival party in Kaufering at the end of January 1981 attracted a few closely connected newcomers. One of the guests was Walter Wolf, an Austrian oil and construction company millionaire who had moved to Montreal in the 1960s to develop a construction business. Schreiber and Wolf had already met in Calgary, where Max Strauss, a mutual friend, had introduced them.

Wolf arrived at Kaufering with his Montreal lawyer, Michel Cogger. There Cogger, the Quebec Tory, met up with Dickie, the Alberta Tory. It was one big happy family of conservative business-men, all together in Schreiber's basement, with ideas and experience and insights to share. For his part, Cogger would benefit from his friendship with Wolf and Schreiber. Both men knew Franz Josef Strauss and his children, and Cogger ended up handling some of the legal work for the family's Montreal shopping centre.

Pushed by his mentor, Strauss, Schreiber had worked hard to bring more German investment into Canada and to secure contracts for a number of Strauss's pet industries. One was Airbus Industrie; another was Messerschmitt-Bölkow-Blohm, the huge Bavarian-based company that owned Deutsche Airbus, the German partner in Airbus Industrie. A third was Thyssen Industrie, the enormous Ruhr Valley conglomer-ate, which manufactured, among other things, tanks and military vehicles. Strauss, the former West German defence minister, wanted to sell into as many markets as possible. Schreiber urged his influential friends to support these companies in Canada, but there had been few tangible signs of progress. In Alberta, Peter Lougheed belonged to the right political party, but he had made his feelings clear where Schreiber and his projects were concerned. In Ottawa, the wrong party – the Liberal Party – was in power.

Schreiber had been part of the lobby effort to convince the Trudeau cabinet to purchase Airbus passenger planes for Air Canada, said a former adviser to Trudeau. Trudeau instructed one or two senior officials to meet with Schreiber because he was interested in opening new trading relationships with the Europeans and was well aware of Strauss's clout. In the end, the Air Canada board of the Trudeau era scuttled any thoughts of an Airbus acquisition. It chose six Boeing aircraft in 1979.

Schreiber confided his frustration to Cogger and Wolf. They offered a hopeful prediction. You know, he was told, Trudeau isn't going to be in power much longer; the people of Canada are fed up with the Liberals. The Conservatives are rising and they will win the next election – if they can get rid of the current leader, Joe Clark. He's a wimp, a closet Liberal, and he has no charisma.

None of this was news to Schreiber. He knew all about Clark, the Tory leader who represented Alberta's Yellowhead riding and who had defeated the Liberals in 1979. Alas, almost as soon as Clark was sworn into office, his policies and ministers suffered one mishap after another, and no one appeared clumsier than Clark himself. His government was defeated in a dramatic budget vote on December 13, 1979, only nine months after being elected to power. Clark had carelessly thrown it all away, thought many Conservatives; everything they'd dreamed of for so many years was gone again. Now Trudeau and his despised Liberals were back in power, laughing at them. The sting of ridicule was worse than defeat.

The federal Tories could take the next federal election, they agreed, with a new man at the helm. That man, Wolf and Cogger said, was Brian Mulroney. Schreiber had heard about Mulroney many times; he knew he was a Montreal lawyer and the president of the Iron Ore Company of Canada, that he was tall and attractive, a charmer who loved a good time. He was a man who lived and breathed Tory party politics and who was looking for a chance to make up for his humiliating defeat by Clark at the party's 1976 leadership convention. His campaign to gain the leadership was quietly but solidly under way. Wolf had been introduced to Mulroney by Michael Meighen, another Tory lawyer who served with Cogger on one of Wolf's company boards, and Wolf was an unabashed fan. Cogger was one of Mulroney's oldest friends.

Schreiber listened eagerly. It sounded promising. He'd struck out with Lougheed, he'd failed with Trudeau, but Mulroney and the possibility of a federal Conservative government offered fresh opportunities. Schreiber began to spend more time in Montreal, and by 1981 Cogger had introduced him first to Frank Moores, the former Conservative premier of Newfoundland, and then to Brian Mulroney. "I must say that in those days Karlheinz had a great deal of interest in the Tory leadership ... He was interested to see what was going on. So he was courting very much the Mulroney campaign or people therein," recalled one of Mulroney's friends.

In truth there was no official Mulroney leadership campaign. Not yet. Joe Clark was the leader of the party and would remain so unless he lost a leadership review vote; the next one was scheduled for the last weekend in January 1983. Mulroney had to be careful to distance himself publicly from those plotting to undermine the leader, but it was an open secret that Mulroney's Quebec supporters were working day and night to defeat Clark. Mulroney himself attended some of the crucial tactical meetings at Montreal's posh Mount Royal Club, beginning in late 1981. Most of the dump-Clark group were among Mulroney's closest friends. In addition to Cogger and other Quebec Tories, there was Peter White, an Ontario Tory, and Ken Waschuk, a Tory party employee from Saskatchewan. Fred Doucet, a friend of Mulroney's from their years at St. Francis Xavier University, was one of several Nova Scotians who joined the crew. Elmer MacKay turned up once at the Mount Royal Club but Fred von Veh, his close associate from the Toronto Tories, became a regular. Bob Coates, a Nova Scotia MP, was not a member of the Mount Royal Club group, but he too campaigned against the current leader at every opportunity. Their captain was Frank Moores. He raised the money for the cause and relished the coming fight.

Schreiber, always generous and full of promises, became welcome within the small circle of people working to unseat Clark. The group was impressed with his ambition, his German connections, and his utter dedication to conservative causes. "Schreiber was an active, busy little guy," said one member of the circle. "And very much to the right. I remember Frank [Moores] and I would joke that in Karlheinz's philosophy, anybody who didn't own a car should probably end up in jail: if someone didn't own a car, they weren't contributing enough to society."

Schreiber liked the Montreal crowd around Mulroney. They often gathered at the Ritz-Carlton Hotel on Sherbrooke Street, in the genteel comfort of its Maritime Bar. He was invited to their exclusive men's clubs, where the rooms were panelled in oak and mahogany and waiters served the best Scotch on silver trays. He liked the fine cuisine of Montreal's French restaurants and the chic shops with so many beautiful women hurrying in and out. This city, far more sophisticated and worldly than Calgary or Edmonton, felt familiar, a little like Munich.

And these new friends were real conservatives. He was far to their right, of course, but that was fine with them. Moores, in particular, clicked with Schreiber; he became a frequent guest at Kaufering and Pontresina.

"Schreiber was not the type to attend a Wednesday-night church basement meeting," confirmed one of the Mulroney cadre, referring to the riding association gatherings where delegates were elected for the upcoming convention, "but he would stay in touch through Frank, or through me. He always wanted to know what was going on and who the players were."

Schreiber made sure the Canadians met the right people whenever they came to Germany or Switzerland. On one occasion, Michel Cogger asked to see the Messerschmitt-Bölkow-Blohm helicopter factory about 40 kilometres from Munich, not far from Schreiber's house. Schreiber toured him through the factory, introducing him to senior research and administrative staff who treated Schreiber with respect, even deference. At least 7,000 employees worked at MBB. Cogger caught Schreiber's enthusiasm for the work being done there; it was an impressive facility and the helicopters were wonders of technology. Cogger wasn't sure what Schreiber's role was at MBB and thought he might be a marketing adviser. But he was in no doubt about his influence.

Schreiber needed to impress people like Cogger, since it was clear to him that the Conservatives were on their way to power in Ottawa. The federal government was a potential customer for MBB products – most of all, helicopters – and Cogger might soon be an important contact in that government. Schreiber could report back to Strauss that he was laying the groundwork for greater trade between Bavaria and Canada.

Much as he enjoyed being part of the elite crew of supporters behind Mulroney's clandestine leadership campaign, Schreiber had other projects on the go. As he boasted before a public inquiry in 1981, "I have thirty-six companies around the world. They all have different businesses, strange to say." Dickie spoke of travelling with Schreiber to Saudi Arabia, Mexico, Germany, France, and Switzerland, but Alberta was high on the list. The land assembly project was still to be completed in Edmonton, where the precise location of the city's planned annexation remained a mystery. Some developers were lobbying for expansion to the south of the city in the 14,000-acre Heritage Valley development. Others hoped for the annexation of the communities of St. Albert and Sherwood Park, on the north and west sides of Edmonton respectively. But rumours soon surfaced that Royal Trust was gobbling up land to the northeast, possibly discreetly banking land on instructions from the government. Using Steve Kurylo as its agent, ABS Investments started buying in the same area. In mid-May, Horner resigned from the provincial cabinet to become vice-chairman of an Alberta Crown corporation called Business Assistance for Native Corporations, and Skoreyko resigned as an MP and as the provincial party president to become chairman of the Alberta Liquor Control Board.

In late May, Kurylo had lunch at the Edmonton Club with Lorne Day, a local real estate speculator, to ask him to bid on a piece of land in the northeast sector for ABS. Day later told a public inquiry that Kurylo had told him, "We've got the politicians in our company and we know where to buy." When Day made the offer, however, it was turned down. Day later heard that Kurylo had hired another agent to make an offer on the same property, an offer that was accepted. It left Day out of a $40,000 commission, and he called Kurylo in a fury. When Kurylo spoke before the inquiry, he said that he was uncomfortable with Day, because he thought Day drank too much during their meeting, and that it was Day, not Kurylo, who had suggested he had insider connections.

ABS had also teamed up with a company called West City Land Management two years earlier, in June 1979, to buy two parcels of land totalling 240 acres in the Heritage Valley area; ABS took a 75 percent share. (On its own, ABS owned a further 480 acres in five parcels in the same area.) West City hired Jim Foster, a former Alberta attorney general, to lobby the twenty-nine-man cabinet on the land annexation plans, and he worked hard. As he admitted himself, he spoke to at least half of the cabinet – "as many Tory ministers as I could get my hands on."

Between May 21 and June 5, 1981, ABS bought nine more parcels of land, for a total of 1,270 acres northeast of Edmonton. When the Alberta government passed an order-in-council on June 11, 1981, allowing Edmonton to annex 80,000 acres of land, Schreiber was thrilled to find himself one of the lucky holders of new city land: thirteen of his sixteen parcels had been annexed.

It was a good guess, smiled Schreiber, when anyone asked him about the deal. But behind closed doors, gossip swept through Edmonton. Many people didn't like the smell of the thing, and when the *Edmonton Journal* published a story about an expensive celebration party Schreiber threw at Walden's Restaurant, the suspicions of inside knowledge became public. The *Journal* reported that Schreiber had been entertaining one of his investors, Heinrich Riemerschmid, who was prepared, Schreiber later said crossly, to bring more business to Alberta. "We had a lot of fun," Schreiber told a public inquiry. "I called the waiter, [said] give me the bill and I paid. A lousy example of Albertan hospitality the press did, showing the bills." The difficulty was the *Journal*'s story that Steve Kurylo had asked one of his former colleagues in the office of Horst Schmid, the trade minister, to make the reservation. It came in on government letterhead and requested that the bill be mailed to the trade minister's office. The inquiry heard that only an alert waitress stopped this from happening; she reminded the party that there was a mail strike on. Schreiber reached into his wallet and pulled out his own credit card. But Schmid's secretary testified that she remembered the episode differently. She said she had called the restaurant before the dinner to make it clear that the government would not be paying the bill.

By July 8, Peter Lougheed was so concerned by the stink rising from the annexation issue that he announced a public inquiry under Justice William Brennan of the Alberta Court of Queen's Bench. Although Schreiber wasn't the only one under suspicion, he needed a good lawyer. The counsel he used for most of his business dealings in Edmonton was Bobby Hladun, who had come recommended by Horst Schmid, another client. But Hladun did mostly criminal and real estate work; he didn't have the expertise to take on a commission of inquiry. After asking around, Schreiber hired one of Alberta's top lawyers, John (known as Jack) Major, a partner at Bennett Jones, the firm where Sir James Lougheed himself had once been a partner.

When Schreiber testified before Justice Brennan in September, he was unrepentant about involving three former cabinet ministers, Dickie, Horner, and Messer; an ex-MP, Skoreyko; and a former executive assistant to a minister, Kurylo. Of course he hoped they could sway opinion – that's what they were there for. He recruited them for his company because of their positions, he said, and through him, they'd made many business contacts in Germany. These relationships helped bring German money to Alberta.

"It was necessary," he told Brennan, "to have people over here for our investors which they know, which they trust, which have credibility. I don't know whether people over here know this so well, but many investors have been really unsuccessful in Canada. It might be they didn't have the right people who supported them over here, it might be that they have funny ideas. So I think the best thing I could do is to get lawyers like Mr. Dickie for the energy fields. Mr. Dickie is the retired minister for mines and minerals, like Mr. Messer, agriculture. Mr. Messer was minister for agriculture and labour and for economy and trade, later on for resources. So we have really experts around us."

He plowed on relentlessly, emphasizing how much money his Bavarian associates had brought into the province. "It is around one billion bucks, most of them high-risk money...And we have some serious problems with the German revenue fellows on that, and therefore again, ex-ministers and ex-politicians are very helpful finding out the ways here with Revenue Canada to get support, seeing the government in Bavaria and I can tell you they are very well respected and even our very very famous prime minister of Bavaria, Franz Josef Strauss, is supporting them wherever they can. I think they do a tremendous job for the province of Alberta."

J.R. Smith, a Calgary lawyer and the commission's chief counsel, listened patiently to this and much more. With formal courtesy he took Schreiber through his deliberate pursuit of ex-politicians, noting dryly "the unquestioned talents of the men who form your board." But, he questioned, "if one were of a suspicious nature, would you agree that one might feel that their duties might involve negotiations with government or obtaining information from government sources?"

Schreiber was unapologetic. "In the international business world, it is quite normal. When you speak with people who do not know anything about that, it might be strange, but I cannot change that and I will not. We will have some more cabinet ministers in the near future from other provinces in Canada to where we have some other big financing projects. And who should know – from the standpoint of investors, who should know better the law, how to handle governments, how to represent companies and investors over here than these people?"

With this spirited defence, he took another tack. He was nothing less than a dedicated patriot, a warrior fighting for conservative values against a dangerous opposition. "I am straight conservative," he said proudly. "You can see the communists and the socialists doing a job I don't like too much. And as I choose Alberta as my future homeland, I have to do something about it and I will." He saw nothing wrong with hiring former politicians. "These people should have a job. What should they do when they retire? Four years in cabinet and then hang around as peddlers?"

Smith had heard enough. Stiffly, he responded that he wasn't sure any one of them was placed in quite that desperate a situation.

It wasn't easy to rebuke Schreiber. "When they take government jobs, they say, oh *ja*, the friends get the jobs, one gives it to the other one. When they go to the free enterprise world, they are lobbyists. We have to live with that and I am prepared to."

Under Smith's questioning, Schreiber elaborated on his theme that he was making Alberta richer and better able to compete in the wider world, and that it was simply naive not to understand the realities of doing business in that world. When Smith talked about conflict of interest, Schreiber refused to see it as a problem. He agreed with Smith's suggestion that he felt wounded by a lack of cooperation from the Lougheed government.

"To be honest," he confided, "sometimes I have the feeling they are a bit too careful."

When Justice Brennan released his findings in the late fall of 1981, he noted that enough people knew about Royal Trust's activities in assembling the land north of Edmonton that others could reasonably conclude the government had shown an early preference for that location. He decided there was not sufficient evidence of wrongdoing on the part of former or current cabinet ministers, nor was he convinced that anyone had received inside information from the government. As for Schreiber's ABS Investments, however, Brennan said its activities were "suspicious," citing the well-connected Tories linked to the firm. He also warned that senior government officials should take better care in the future and stay away from investing in projects that required government decisions. Otherwise an "ugly cloud of suspicion of impropriety on their part will almost certainly descend on them." The decision was a pyrrhic victory for Schreiber and his fellow investors. An ugly cloud had descended upon them – and most heavily on Schreiber himself. Doing deals and winning friends was more difficult now, especially with Lougheed's opprobrium common knowledge.

Then came fresh calamities: a deep recession in 1982 and a complete collapse of the booming real estate market in Canada. Schreiber's road-marking company won fewer and fewer contracts. Erwin Zeiter lost the million dollars he'd invested in the business, and that blow led to others. Receivers eventually grabbed the fourteen apartment buildings Zeiter owned as well as the condo he'd bought in Switzerland on Schreiber's advice. The value of the land acquired by ABS and all its subsidiary companies slid lower every week, and the German investors began to panic. Eventually the plans to develop the newly annexed land fizzled; visions of shiny new suburbs and shopping malls evaporated. Much of the property returned to farmland. Heinrich Riemerschmid lost DM256,000, Lotte Pabst lost $2 million, the Strauss family lost at least a million and Jöst Hurler, said Pelossi, lost $8 million. It took several years for these disasters to surface completely, but as they did, Schreiber did pay back some of his Bavarian friends.

As for Zeiter, he was completely out of luck. Years later, when he was making a living with a bagel shop in downtown Edmonton, he said, "I am no friend of Karlheinz Schreiber."

5

Greener Pastures

After six years of aggressive effort in Canada, Karlheinz Schreiber's record was spotty. He'd alienated Peter Lougheed, struck out with Rhys Eyton at PWA, lost a fortune in Alberta real estate, seen his road-marking business fail, and been rebuffed by Pierre Trudeau's people in Ottawa.

Schreiber understood there would always be something of the outsider about him as he tried to make his way into the inner circles of Canadian business and politics, so in 1981 he made what was to be one of the smartest moves of his career: he became a Canadian citizen. Michel Cogger, acting for him in Montreal, helped him with the process. Giorgio Pelossi, who maintained a residence in Canada through his son, Michael, and continued to visit Canada regularly, also took out citizenship. And Schreiber made another interesting move that year. On August 10, he and Cogger incorporated a Quebec company called Démarcation Routière Indélébile (DRI) Inc., with headquarters registered in Montreal. It was another road-marking company, but it never amounted to anything. Eventually Cogger would find that Schreiber didn't need him as much as he once did. He didn't know what had happened to his friendship with Schreiber; the two just seemed to drift apart. As it happened, Schreiber had a five-star friend even closer to

Mulroney than his Laval University buddy Cogger. That was Frank Moores.

Moores was tall, charming, and reckless as a pirate; women found him irresistible. He came from old money in Newfoundland, where his father had owned a food processing company that was later sold to the British frozen food conglomerate Birdseye. As a boy Moores attended St. Andrew's College, an expensive private school in Aurora, Ontario. Too impatient for the university education his father wanted for him, he dropped out in his first term and entered the family business. By the time the company was sold, he had developed a taste for the brawling blood sport that was politics in Newfoundland. He ran federally and won; at thirty-five, he was a Conservative member of Parliament, and a year later he took the presidency of the party as well. But Ottawa was too tame and he had too little power. He took a run at the Newfoundland Tory leadership in 1970, won, and quit federal politics to lead the Tories in the provincial election in 1971. By 1972 he was the premier of the province.

His next seven years in office were wild, marked by scandals and controversy from the first day. Once he was in trouble for accepting a free television set; another time he was charged with hunting too much game and doing it out of season. The opposition attacked him constantly for awarding untendered contracts to his political allies. He liked to drink and party, and he had an eye for the girls, not exactly the behaviour expected of a man with a doting wife and seven children. He didn't care. "I think the voters liked me better for it," he chuckled.

Moores resigned from office in 1979 and moved to Montreal. He bought a large, semi-detached house at 403 Clarke Avenue in Westmount and, helped by a lucrative consulting contract from the Iron Ore Company of Canada, became active in the dump-Clark movement. Moores and Mulroney had been close for years. Iron Ore was the biggest employer in Newfoundland while Mulroney was president, and the men had come to know each other well through business and pleasure, taking fishing trips together, partying, and bar-hopping. It was Moores who put Mulroney's name in nomination for the Progressive Conservative Party leadership in 1976, a vote he lost to Joe Clark.

Karlheinz Schreiber and Frank Moores understood each other

immediately. Business was one shared passion, politics another, and the two were closely related. Their relationship was consummated with a business partnership involving a tiny Montreal company known as NBM Land Holdings Ltd. The company was officially incorporated in 1981 by Michel Cogger, who established its office on the twelfth floor of 500 Place d'Armes in Montreal. Documents reveal that the company was owned by Schreiber's ABS Investments, which had a 52 percent share, with the balance held by the Strauss family's FMS Investments. Cogger and Bill Dickie were installed as NBM's original directors. About a month later, it made an overture to Birchpoint Investments Ltd., a company owned in part by Frank Moores.

In 1979 Birchpoint Investments had assembled large parcels of land around Shearstown, Newfoundland, about five kilometres from the eastern coast. Moores and other investors had planned to build warehouses stocked full of supplies for present and future offshore oil projects. Oil rigs often need equipment, fuel, and other goods in a hurry, and Moores expected to capitalize on a ready market. And the location seemed prime: there was a modern harbour in nearby Bay Roberts. The next year Moores helped set up two more companies, both of which began buying up land around Shearstown. The first was Avalon Pioneer Ltd., which was incorporated in Toronto by a Stikeman Elliott lawyer, Dick Pound, but soon moved its offices to Montreal. The second was Port Atlantis Ltd., in which the giant engineering firm Lavalin Ltd. was a partner. Lavalin's president, Bernard Lamarre, and Moores were both directors. Port Atlantis quickly purchased parcels of land from Moores's Birchpoint Investments.

But months dragged on and the offshore oil industry remained stagnant. Moores had yet to build any warehouses, and one of Moores's partners was growing tired of waiting. Moores still saw its potential, however, and so, it seemed, did Schreiber. In January 1982, Schreiber put together financing for a substantial interest in the Newfoundland company, instructing NBM officials to issue a cheque to Birchpoint for $369,000, the price of a 50 percent share in the Shearstown land.

Since it had no assets of its own, NBM had to borrow the money from three other Schreiber-related companies, ABS Investments, Bitucan Holdings, and FMS Investments. Two of the companies lending money to NBM – ABS and FMS – were the same companies that owned NBM.

Walter Wolf recalled the involvement of FMS in particular. "I bumped into Schreiber and Max [Strauss] and Frank Moores in an airport in Dallas," said Wolf. "Max invested money with Frank Moores in the harbour [project] in Newfoundland." Wolf had used one of his own helicopters to fly with Schreiber, Strauss, and Moores into the area to view the property.

Cogger had already persuaded Wolf to invest $500,000 in a company called East Coast Energy, also designed to cash in on the projected boom by refuelling and supplying offshore ships and rigs working in Atlantic Canada's oil and gas fields. It too was owned by a consortium of Mulroney friends, headed by Fred Doucet and his brother Gerry. A facility at Shearstown seemed to make sense and looked like a good fit with East Coast Energy.

As it turned out, NBM's $369,000 investment appeared to be another failed venture for Schreiber. No warehouses were built at Shearstown. Still, there were some intriguing mysteries about the company. None of the participants would say what NBM stood for. At the time the $369,000 changed hands, Moores was running the dump-Clark movement out of Montreal as its key fundraiser. Whatever NBM was, it was no secret that the players involved with NBM were also some of the key players involved in the campaign to replace Joe Clark with Brian Mulroney.

Years later, NBM was reconfigured as an Alberta company; Cogger was dropped as a director and its new address belonged to Bobby Hladun's law firm. Schreiber would appoint only one new director, an obscure office clerk named Gordon Livingstone, who said he did not even know what the initials stood for.

While Schreiber was investing hundreds of thousands of dollars in Newfoundland real estate, he was still troubled by developments closer to home. The Edmonton lands fiasco had his investors grumbling: they wanted to know how development of the land was progressing – what was happening? Nothing, was the short answer. The real estate market across Canada was flat and dry, thanks to usurious interest rates that were running between 18 and 22 percent. Not surprisingly, demand had screeched to a halt, and people simply were not buying houses. This was not what Barbara Flick expected to hear. In the spring of 1982 she made up her mind that she would put no more money into ABS.

Schreiber was beside himself. The company still had to come up with $15 million to complete its purchase of the land. Her withdrawal would be disastrous, and he had to make it clear to her that if she didn't honour her commitment, an already shaky project would collapse. It was good money after bad, she believed. Besides, at this point Flick didn't care; she was just as angry as he was, and she wouldn't budge. With nowhere to turn, Schreiber launched a $119-million lawsuit against her, a tedious and difficult case that took years to wind its way through the Alberta courts. Its chief value at the time, explained Pelossi, was that Schreiber could use it to comfort his other investors. "[He was saying,] 'Okay, we have lost the money but we now have a chance to recover the money through this lawsuit.'"

This would be a crucial test for Hladun who, as the lawyer for ABS, worked as much for Flick as he did for Schreiber. In Schreiber's world, friendship and loyalty were everything, and Hladun had a decision to make: would he support Schreiber or Flick? There really was no question. He chose Schreiber. In 1986 the court appointed the auditors Clarkson Gordon to investigate the affairs of ABS. Hladun was found by a judge to have "misled" these auditors, and he was ordered to pay certain costs. But in 1981, Schreiber knew that whatever else happened here, he had a faithful retainer in Bobby Hladun.

During this period, Schreiber parted company with another woman in his life. He might have been a man with many secrets, but if there was one thing everyone knew about him, it was that he adored Renate Rauscher. He was jealous and possessive and crazy for her.

By this time, Rauscher was in her mid-thirties. She'd been working in his company as a kind of executive assistant, and they travelled everywhere together. But she was unhappy in a confining union and the relationship began to unravel. Soon she was spending more time in Europe, where she worked for other Schreiber concerns.

"He gave her everything, furs, jewellery, money, but she was kept as a slave," said Giorgio Pelossi. "Perhaps she opened her eyes and thought, 'Why should I stay? Perhaps I can build my own life.'"

Another person who came to know Rauscher well was Joan Kurylo. Joan's husband, Steve, spent so much time on Schreiber's business that the two women were often thrown together and a friendship grew. Rauscher was a trophy wife for Schreiber, Joan decided; but it wasn't as rewarding for Rauscher. "She had a sad soul," she thought. She knew Rauscher wasn't happy in the relationship. Maybe she was also fearful of the lifestyle they found themselves leading. Walter Wolf had told people he carried a handgun around in Europe to protect himself, which caused a sensation in the Tory crowd. What they didn't know was that Schreiber and Rauscher did so too. According to friends, they carried Beretta handguns most of the time in Europe, although not while they were in Canada. Were the weapons for show? No, said Kurylo, they were genuinely worried about their security. With their reputation for wealth, they feared kidnappers.

The final rupture was sudden and brutal. In 1984 Schreiber ordered his business manager in Kaufering, Albert Birkner, to take her off the payroll (although he continued to pay her some money as late as 1986). Renate was hurt and furious; for the next ten years they would barely speak to each other. Schreiber began courting an elegant, much younger woman, Barbara Schubert, Ludwig Huber's secretary at the Bayerische Landesbank in Munich.

At the end of 1982, when Schreiber felt at home with the Tories who were gathering around Mulroney in Montreal, he developed another friendship that was to become even stronger than the bond he shared with Frank Moores. It was at this time that he met a lanky Nova Scotian named Elmer MacKay. While Schreiber and Moores were two born schemers impatient with conventional rules, MacKay seemed a straight-arrow type, a country lawyer whose ambition was to become Canada's solicitor general, the person responsible for the country's police forces.

MacKay had been invited into the charmed circle around Mulroney because he'd been the original ringleader of the anti-Clark forces within the PC Party. In late 1981 he had even organized a campaign among his fellow Tory MPs to encourage them to write personal letters to Clark, asking him to step down and make way for a new leader. He succeeded in gathering forty-eight of these "Dear Joe" letters before the scheme became known within Clark's circle and was stopped.

Maybe it was their sense of being outsiders that pulled MacKay and Schreiber together. Neither lived in Montreal, where all the plotting began; MacKay came to the city for strategy meetings, and Schreiber turned up occasionally to talk about the financial support he could offer. Certainly the two men could not have been less alike. What had interested MacKay during his long years in opposition was a good scandal, especially one involving stolen or mismanaged money, political favours for friends of the government, or anything that smacked of corruption. Mounties whose investigations of powerful politicians or their friends had been derailed were among his best sources. Hardly a good fit for the cheerful Bavarian who considered *Schmiergelder* – literally, grease money – a driving force in politics. But the connection worked because of MacKay's determination to rid the party of Clark, the leader who had failed to give him the solicitor general's job during the Tories' brief flutter with power. When Clark allowed the Liberals to defeat his government on the unexpected budget vote in 1979, MacKay's contempt knew no bounds, and he surprised his friends by moving far to the right of his party. He also became, some said, a bitter person, as if his faith in the political system had been undermined by the failure of his party to hang on to the prize that had been so hard won. Schreiber understood his man.

Schreiber shared his ambitions for Canadian-German business development with MacKay, which would eventually include his dream of a Canadian manufacturing operation for Thyssen Industrie. Here the company could build armoured military vehicles for sale to the United States and other markets not open to military exports directly from Germany – Saudi Arabia, for starters. Such an arrangement would work to the advantage of Canada, Germany, and the United States, Schreiber often said, and he claimed to have the support of Germany's CDU for the plan. What would it take to get a plant up and running in MacKay's home province, where unemployment was severe and high-tech manufacturing was desperately needed? It would take substantial provincial and federal support. Nova Scotia's Tory premier, John Buchanan, would undoubtedly rejoice in the development. Bob

Coates, a Nova Scotia Tory MP, would support any initiative that brought business into his home province.

Schreiber, MacKay, and all the other dump-Clark stalwarts were counting down to the day they could get rid of the former prime minister. Clark was not about to step down voluntarily, but he would have to endure a leadership review vote at the upcoming annual meeting in Winnipeg at the end of January 1993. Mulroney's friends had been busy. The name of the game was to ensure that more anti-Clark partisans attended the delegate selection meetings in church basements and community halls than pro-Clark supporters. And in the province of Quebec, the battle was most intense. In Winnipeg, one of Mulroney's Quebec lieutenants arrived at the convention reception desk with almost 200 delegates in tow and cheques totalling $56,000 to pay the registration fees for them all.

The story travelled quickly around the convention. Concerned party staffers heard rumours that many delegates were "instant" Conservatives, who were given spending money and free hotel rooms so long as they voted against Clark. Dalton Camp, the long-time Tory adviser and former party president, told a CTV interviewer that "offshore money" had helped finance the dump-Clark movement. Walter Wolf eventually admitted he had contributed to the effort (not more than $25,000, he said, given as directors' fees to Michel Cogger and Michael Meighen).

Soon there were stories that Schreiber had put "big money" into the campaign to topple Clark, and he admitted his role to the German journalist John Goetz in 2000. "We organized the delegates, put them up in a hotel in Winnipeg for three nights," Schreiber boasted. "We paid for their flights and gave them a little shopping money, so they could bring their wives… And that is how we won the election." He said that Franz Josef Strauss "was fully involved, he knew everything."

In fact, the dump-Clark forces did not "win" the vote. Clark received the support of 66.9 percent of the delegates, a clear majority, but not enough, said Clark. He called a leadership convention for June 1983. He would be a candidate himself, but now Brian Mulroney was free to run against him. Schreiber says he contributed money to

Mulroney's official leadership campaign as well, a fact corroborated by Walter Wolf. "I knew that Schreiber, he paid cash for the leadership for Mulroney," Wolf stated.

Mulroney never revealed the names of those who gave money to his leadership campaign, and the records of the donors were stolen during a mysterious burglary in the Montreal offices of one of his key organizers in September 1984.

To no one's surprise, Mulroney took the leadership from Joe Clark on June 9, 1983. Elmer MacKay gave up his seat in Central Nova to allow Mulroney to run in a summer by-election, and by September the Mulroneys were at Stornoway, the official residence of the leader of the opposition. Although Pierre Trudeau didn't announce his decision to resign as prime minister until February 1984, the Tories smelled victory all through the winter of 1983–84. The country was tired of the Liberals, and a lot of Liberals confessed they were tired of themselves. They had no fresh ideas, no new programs, no inspiring leaders. Mulroney's people watched the polls closely, raised money for the coming election, sent several of his top MPs and their aides out to study each government department carefully, and nominated candidates in all the federal ridings.

Schreiber used this period of political phony war to press his advantage with Mulroney; he visited him in Ottawa several times. Max Strauss was a frequent guest of Walter Wolf in Montreal during these years, and the two often travelled to Ottawa together. Strauss also accompanied Schreiber to the capital. Mulroney had time for Schreiber and also for Max Strauss.

Pat MacAdam, a pal since university days who worked for Mulroney in his Parliament Hill offices at the time, remembered Schreiber's visits well. "I met him when he used to call on Mulroney," MacAdam said on CBC Television in fall 1999. "He was looking after the Franz Josef Strauss interests. The father, Franz Josef, was a good friend of Mulroney's in years gone by. The son used to call on him as a courtesy call. I was the gatekeeper then, and kept the appointments, and he'd come in with Max Strauss ... oh, maybe five, six, seven times a year."

MacAdam himself was smitten by Schreiber and didn't hesitate to say so. "My eyes light up when I see Karlheinz Schreiber... Karlheinz could light up a room when he entered it, because he was so friendly. He's gregarious... charismatic. Fun-loving. Generous. He was good to his employees. I've never ever heard anyone say an unkind word about him. And he always came calling with a good product. He wasn't selling influence, he was selling quality goods. I don't know any dark side to him."

In July, John Turner, the former Liberal minister of finance who had succeeded Trudeau as prime minister in June, sent the country to the polls. Turner had been out of politics for several years and was a rusty campaigner; his election team was fractious, unprepared, and up against a slick Tory machine, primed with plenty of money and the best advice they could buy from American consultants. Mulroney's victory was a foregone conclusion; what no one could have predicted was the strength of it. On September 4, 1984, he won the third-largest majority government in Canadian history, with 211 seats. The once-mighty Liberals were reduced to a shocked rump of forty.

The Conservative triumph changed Ottawa and Canada forever and marked a turning point in the fortunes of Karlheinz Schreiber. Without this victory and the connections he had solidified, Schreiber could not have achieved the wealth and success he so openly craved. He would have been nothing more than a glad-handing Bavarian running around looking for road-marking contracts, always dreaming of the big score.

6

Man in the Shadows

Hans Reiter examined the printouts of Karlheinz Schreiber's company bank statements with a sinking feeling. Had he made a dreadful mistake? As the credit manager at the Sparkasse Landsberg (the Landsberg Savings Bank), he had advanced large sums of money to Schreiber, who had always assured him that the loans were manageable. But look at these statements! The debts were large and they were growing. Still, Schreiber had been a man of his word. He may have been late with the occasional payment, but so far he had never defaulted, even when the business forecasts were grim.

"In 1982, I took on the task of arranging credit for Schreiber with a considerable amount of skepticism," Reiter said many years later. "The credit commitment could be regarded as very problematic. My attitude changed in the course of the year, because Mr. Schreiber's declarations always came true. I would like to cite an occurrence in this context which still remains in my memory today. Mr. Schreiber referred to a Mr. Mulroney, who was unknown to me at the time, and told me, 'My friend Mulroney will be prime minister of Canada next year.' This prediction actually came to pass. Similar declarations, which were in themselves not to be characterized as mundane, proved also to be true. From these experiences, combined with

assurances I already had, I had trust in Mr. Schreiber's statements."
And yes, the patronage of Franz Josef Strauss was like a paid-up Visa
card in his wallet.

But those were the only crumbs of comfort Reiter could take from
the worrisome state of Schreiber's affairs. First, there was the real
estate meltdown in Alberta. The road-marking business in Calgary
had been shaky and eventually the company ceased operations.
Schreiber sold the equipment to Lafrentz Road Services Ltd., which
also bought some of his German operations. At least the sale provided
a much-needed cash infusion. It wasn't enough, though, to ease
Reiter's concerns.

Reiter may not have had the courage to comment on his client's
personal expenditures, but they too were mounting. Schreiber travelled constantly, stayed in the finest hotels, and loved to entertain in
expensive restaurants. An accomplished cook himself, Schreiber was a
discriminating and generous host. For himself, he collected cars, and
several Mercedes-Benzes cluttered the driveway in Kaufering. How
many were there now? Seven? Eight?

But Schreiber assured Reiter that the good times were just around
the corner, that he was going to make more money than he had ever
dared to hope for. In the 1970s Schreiber had believed Canada would
be his economic oasis, but now he thought the small Central American
country of Costa Rica could serve his interests as well.

Schreiber might not have embarked on his adventure in Costa
Rica if it had not been for a chance meeting in Calgary with a man
named Serge Noghaven. An Argentinian by birth, Noghaven lived in
Montreal, but he was also, quite improbably, an emissary-at-large of
the president of Costa Rica, Luis Alberto Monge Alvarez. Although
his 1972 wedding certificate from a Montreal synagogue stated that
he was a "waiter from Argentina," he referred to himself as
Ambassador Noghaven. The name might have evolved too; the same
wedding certificate said he was the son of David Goldman and Eva
Faierman.

When President Monge first met Noghaven in the early 1980s, he
was impressed. "Noghaven was highly intelligent," he related. "He
brought trade missions from Czechoslovakia and Romania to Costa

Rica." Before long, Monge had provided Noghaven with a coveted diplomatic passport.

Fluent in several languages, Noghaven was sophisticated, dapper, even elegant, and certainly mysterious. He happened to be in Calgary in early 1982 on a trade mission sponsored by the Canadian government. Federal officials hoped a local manufacturer of prefabricated housing might win some orders from Costa Rica.

Schreiber was always on the lookout for potential business leads and attended the prefab housing meetings in hopes of making the right contacts. There was no mistaking the suave Noghaven as the most important official in the Costa Rican delegation, and Schreiber was quick to approach him about business opportunities in Central America. Their conversation eventually turned to Cold War politics and the current international hot spot, Nicaragua, on Costa Rica's northern border, across the San Juan River. Nicaraguan politics, like those of most Central American countries, pitted extremists from the left and right against each other. Since 1979, the left-wing Sandinistas had been in power.

U.S. President Ronald Reagan had been trying for some time to topple the Sandinista government of President Daniel Ortega, but Fidel Castro and the Soviet Union had been quietly supporting him. During the early and middle 1980s, secret service agents on both sides were especially busy in Central America, involved in one clandestine activity or another. But the Costa Rican government tried its best to stay out of the war. All President Monge hoped for was to act as a mediator between East and West in efforts to cool the tensions in the region.

When Schreiber spoke to Noghaven that day in Calgary, he bragged, as he almost always did, about his friendship with Franz Josef Strauss. Noghaven was intrigued. If Schreiber was telling the truth, he thought, perhaps Schreiber could introduce him to the Bavarian premier. Noghaven told Schreiber he had always believed that Strauss could play an important role in mediating in Central America; Strauss was friendly with Reagan and, at the same time, was well connected to Eastern-bloc nations.

"Could you introduce me to Strauss?" Noghaven asked Schreiber bluntly. Of course, Schreiber replied. Before he knew it, Noghaven was on a plane to Munich, there to meet the premier. For Noghaven, the introduction was crucial. He believed it would allow him to make contact with senior officials around Soviet president Leonid Brezhnev. He also believed Strauss could speak with Reagan about softening his anti-Sandinista views. Noghaven arranged to bring Monge to Bavaria, where he too met Strauss. Strauss favoured the Contras but was not nearly as hawkish as the U.S. president, or so Monge and Noghaven believed. Certainly he was interested in Costa Rica, but it wasn't just politics. There were business opportunities in this little country for German companies.

Monge made a side trip to Kaufering, where Schreiber held a dinner party in his honour. "Schreiber was a very powerful man, close to Strauss, who was dealing with helicopters and arms," said Monge. "He invited me to his house, where he had an impressive wine cellar."

At the time that Schreiber was hunting for business in Costa Rica, the country's political system was in a fragile state. Nestled between Panama to the south and Nicaragua to the north, Costa Rica stretched across the isthmus between the Pacific and Atlantic Oceans and had become an agricultural oasis, exporting its coffee and bananas around the world. By 1978 it had evolved into a healthy social-democratic state with a strong economy, governed by the elected National Liberation Party. Everything changed abruptly in 1980 when a toxic combination of inflation, declining banana and coffee prices, currency devaluation, and high oil costs created an economic crisis. But the catalyst for a real emergency in Costa Rica was the vicious civil war being fought to the north. Most Costa Ricans hated and feared Nicaragua's right-wing rebel army, the Contras; some had joined the Sandinista forces.

Although President Monge, who was elected in 1982, had favoured the Sandinistas, he hoped to maintain a neutral stance. He was under enormous pressure from the Reagan administration to support the Contras, and when he resisted, U.S. foreign aid became contingent on meeting U.S. demands. Monge believed he had no choice. When he appointed two right-wing ministers who were known to work closely with the U.S. Embassy, millions of American dollars arrived to bolster the police forces and millions more for economic aid. Although he capitulated on many fronts, however, Monge refused to reverse his declaration of neutrality in the Nicaraguan war, and he refused to support the Contras.

It was only when Monge made a trip abroad that his public security minister invited U.S. Special Forces personnel into the country and allowed them to begin training 750 local civil guards as highly armed special army units, all with the purpose of supporting the Contra army. Monge had no warning, and when he returned, the country was in crisis. Later it came to light that the CIA's station chief in San José, José Fernandes, was working with Costa Rica's director of intelligence and security and with other key contacts in Monge's office.

Years later Monge said he was between a rock and a hard place. "I was under tremendous pressure: on one side the Latin American left, the Europeans, and some Costa Ricans wanted me to support the Sandinistas and openly oppose supporting the Contras. On the other side, there was internal pressure to support them and lend them our territory, and the hawks from the Pentagon and the National Security Council paid me several visits, asking me if we needed help to face the Sandinistas. They showed me pictures of Sandinista troop movements in our border, gave me names of Costa Ricans working for the Sandinistas."

This was the situation in Costa Rica when Schreiber began exploring business opportunities there with Noghaven. Their first foray was into the coffee market. Coffee might seem a step backward for Schreiber, who had always been more interested in high technology than in agricultural products. In reality, the import and export of coffee was highly regulated by the International Coffee Organization, a London-based regulator of imports and exports. Anyone who could cut through the red tape stood to make a fortune, and Schreiber and Noghaven had an idea to do just that.

The ICO was created in the 1960s to find a way of stabilizing wildly fluctuating coffee prices around the world. Some years coffee farmers made enough to enjoy a decent living; other years they could barely feed their families. In the early 1980s the ICO decided to solve the problem by controlling the flow of exports, thereby controlling prices. Countries like Nicaragua and Costa Rica, who were members of the ICO, agreed to accept export quotas. The ICO issued certificates known as coffee export stamps to its members. Once a country used up its annual quota of coffee stamps, it could export no more coffee for that year.

In Nicaragua, Contra rebels were burning coffee crops in an effort to destabilize the economy, while across the San Juan River, Costa Rica had far more coffee than it needed. Coffee stamps were scarce in Costa Rica but plentiful in Nicaragua. Middlemen like Schreiber and Noghaven saw an opportunity in the misfortune of the war: if the Nicaraguans were not able to use their stamps, why couldn't Schreiber and Noghaven export the extra Costa Rican coffee as Nicaraguan coffee? The plan was irregular but clever. "The coffee deal was very peculiar," Monge said.

In Costa Rica, Schreiber and Noghaven contacted the coffee baron Ramon Aguilar, while in Nicaragua they enlisted Henry Ruiz, a Sandinista leader. The affair became even steamier with the entrance of Rita Santalla, a stunning Cuban-born aide to Monge who worked with Schreiber and Noghaven to make the coffee deal happen. But Monge, who was very close to her, says she was stiffed on the deal. According to one insider, neither he nor Schreiber made any money either, although Schreiber did pay Noghaven significant expenses, costs that ran through Bayerische Bitumen-Chemie, his company back in Kaufering.

Rita Santalla was born in Havana in 1955 and educated in Costa Rica and Puerto Rico, graduating in administration and business management in 1975. Fluent in English, she took further courses in North-South relations in Washington and Paris. In May 1982, the Costa Rican foreign ministry made arrangements for her to go to Canada as a commercial attaché, but the move never happened; instead, she became an aide to Monge and a consultant to entrepreneurs like Schreiber. She and Noghaven helped Schreiber organize a trade delegation from Alberta, which included Schreiber's old friend Horst Schmid. "A few of my ministers met with [Schmid]," remembered Monge. "I am sure Rita was able to pull off this visit through Schreiber."

Soon Schreiber, Noghaven, and Santalla were involved in various ventures together. Schreiber lent Noghaven DM600,000 to scout for construction business in Costa Rica for Liebherr-Holding GmbH, a giant multinational conglomerate and manufacturer of industrial cranes, earth-movers, and other sophisticated engineering equipment. And he was constantly alert to opportunities for MBB, Airbus Industrie, Thyssen, and another client, a German military gun manufacturer, Heckler & Koch.

But Schreiber was not just doing business. During this period, he helped develop a Costa Rican presence for the Hanns-Seidel-Stiftung, a Bavarian foundation which promoted Christian Social Union policies in Germany and abroad. The HSS was a well-known arm of the CSU, and in Costa Rica its main job was to promote "Christian humanism" and a conservative ideology. Other German political parties had already established foundations in Costa Rica, and President Monge said he not only supported the move, he had extended an invitation through Strauss. He reasoned that Costa Ricans should be exposed to all sorts of political philosophies, including the CSU's.

The Costa Rican offices of the Hanns-Seidel-Stiftung were opened officially in July 1983 by Fritz Pirkl, the head of the organization. Schreiber, who helped create the HSS, stood proudly at his side. Schreiber also made sure to invite his friend Kurt Pfleiderer, the president of Messerschmitt-Bölkow-Blohm's helicopter division. The presence of an MBB executive at the event made perfect sense. The two organizations were closely linked. MBB was partly owned by the government of Bavaria. The company had its own "political" officers who belonged to the HSS. Two of MBB's board members were CSU politicians, including Franz Josef Strauss. The HSS was not just a right-wing think tank, it cultivated business opportunities for Bavarian companies, forging commercial links with governments of all ideologies. Schreiber, acting for Pfleiderer, was soon lobbying President Monge to purchase MBB's helicopters. Schreiber, however, never won Monge's confidence.

"We don't have an army," the president would protest.

"But Costa Rica needs to arm itself against Nicaragua," Schreiber would respond.

"That's when I started to get suspicious," Monge recalled. "Rita told me later he was a key man in the arms trade."

Schreiber's activities in Costa Rica allowed him an entree into the secretive but romantic world of espionage. He was in fact moonlighting for the Bundesnachrichtendiest, or BND, the German intelligence agency, and he took his duties seriously, even adopting a code name, Hanne. His involvement was not as mysterious as it might seem. Many foreign businessmen became active on behalf of their nations' secret services in Central America in the early 1980s. Schreiber signed on in 1983 after being recommended by Franz Josef Strauss. That same year, he said, he attended a meeting between Strauss, Monge, and former U.S. secretary of state Henry Kissinger, who was then heading up a commission on Central America. He hinted that the encounter took place "at the height of the Nicaraguan crisis" and involved instructions to the BND, the details of which he would not reveal. Schreiber later claimed that he helped fund the Contras, though it is unclear exactly what he did or on whose authority he acted.

Early in Schreiber's career as a BND agent, Rainer Gepperth, deputy director of the Hanns-Seidel-Stiftung, introduced him to Werner Ströhlein, a senior West German spy who had acted as the BND's station chief in Costa Rica until he was assigned to Mexico in 1983. Ströhlein and Schreiber would eventually go into business together to win contracts in Costa Rica and elsewhere in Central America, and Schreiber introduced Ströhlein to Max Strauss. During a visit to Mexico City, Ströhlein snapped a lopsided photo of his friends – Strauss at over six feet and Schreiber closer to five – wearing identical tan suits and dark sunglasses.

Whether he was playing spy or serving as one, Schreiber's talents as a middleman could have been extremely useful to the BND. His road-marking business and connections in the construction industry with companies like Liebherr gave him a good cover for travelling to foreign countries and meeting government officials. Especially at this time, in 1983 and 1984, with Germany still divided and the East German intelligence service, the Stasi, extremely active and dangerous, the BND remained a strong international force. Certainly the BND collaborated with the CIA in support of Reagan's efforts to eliminate left-wing forces in Central America, especially in Nicaragua. After 1982, when Congress passed the Boland Amendment, which forbade giving aid to the Contras, these efforts involved covert operations. Reagan wanted help from other countries and West Germany wanted to oblige.

Schreiber declared that his business activities in Costa Rica over-lapped with his work for the BND and that he was so friendly with Monge's successor, Oscar Arias Sanchez, who won the Nobel Peace Prize in 1987 for bringing peace to the region, that he received a Costa Rican diplomatic passport. But Schreiber's pipeline to the government had opened two years earlier, when Monge was still the president, and it was Monge who gave him the diplomatic passport. (The Costa Ricans cancelled it in October 1996.)

Schreiber had become very attached to Santalla and enlisted her as a part-time BND agent, collecting useful political information for him and for German intelligence. One man who had been involved in security and intelligence in the country remembered her well. "She was a beautiful and dangerous woman," he said reflectively. Other people in Monge's office did not trust her and were always suspicious of her intentions. They knew she had to be working for someone else – not just for the president.

When Schreiber told Hans Reiter about his interest in Central America, he mentioned only the possibility of street repair contracts in Costa Rica and sales of Liebherr's road construction machines. He hoped for a total of DM55 million in contracts for Liebherr and had made a promising start with a contract from the Costa Rican govern-ment for DM14.5 million worth of machinery on which he had been promised a 5 percent commission, or DM725,000. The financing for the contract was to be provided by the KfW (Kreditanstalt für Wiederaufbau), the development bank that helped underwrite German projects abroad.

But by December of 1984, Schreiber had little more to show for his efforts in Costa Rica, and he was completely fed up with Noghaven. He had advanced him thousands of Deutschmarks, but they weren't getting anywhere with their plans for Liebherr or any other clients. He had Albert Birkner write Noghaven a letter at his Montreal address: "Because of your urgent requests and promises, we again and again tolerated the delays in paying back your loans. During a recent telephone call you told Mr. Schreiber that end of November the latest, you would come back to Europe to pay back your loans out of the profits you were expecting from a coffee deal which you were in the process of finalizing."

Unfortunately, Noghaven's deals were collapsing around him. He was trying to barter coffee and bananas for Skoda cars and Bohemian crystal, but nothing worked. And that wasn't all. Noghaven had been living part-time in Colombia when President Monge began to hear rumours about his shady dealings between the two countries. "Noghaven is a dangerous character," he was told. Monge summoned Noghaven to an early-morning meeting and demanded the return of his diplomatic passport. Noghaven would later set up shop in Panama, where Schreiber would continue to do business with him.

Schreiber seemed untroubled by his lack of success in Costa Rica; by then he loved the country and its people, and he believed that sooner or later he would land a big deal. Costa Rica felt like home, almost as appealing as Kaufering. He often invited Canadian friends to visit, and one year when he discovered that a couple of Elmer MacKay's children were planning a holiday in Costa Rica, he insisted they stay with him. They were uncomfortable with his pressing hospitality but did not know how to say no.

During these months, Schreiber travelled back and forth between Costa Rica and Canada. So too did Serge Noghaven. He had rented an expensive townhouse at 9 Redpath Court in Westmount, where he lived when he was in Canada with his wife and young daughter. People on the quiet cul-de-sac normally minded their own business, but Noghaven created plenty of curiosity. His house was like a fortress, the upstairs bedroom windows covered with black boards. He did not allow his daughter to play with the neighbourhood children, and when she did appear she was always surrounded by bodyguards. He led people to believe that he was involved in the coffee business in Costa Rica.[1]

Over the next few years, Rita Santalla remained on Schreiber's Bayerische Bitumen-Chemie payroll, earning US$2,000 a month (described as "expenses"), and, as his diaries show, they were in frequent contact. Schreiber's secretary, Dietlinde Kaupp, later claimed that the Liebherr group loaned Santalla DM80,000 through Schreiber's company. An undated letter from a business associate shows her dependence on him.

"Her financial difficulties are alarming," the letter stated. "Without your monthly transfers she would be out on the street. Maybe you should think about waiting to help her with her financial situation for a little while, at least until you know for sure whether the receipt of commission for the DM14.5-million project will come through."

In the summer of 1984, Schreiber found himself in Mexico to meet with Ströhlein about various business ventures. In particular he hoped to close a helicopter deal in the Chiapas region for MBB. The Mexicans could not afford to purchase the Bavarian-made machines, but Schreiber had arranged for a lease financed by German banks.

Schreiber decided he needed a shell company to funnel the commission payments he expected to receive. He instructed Pelossi, who had returned to Lugano permanently, to begin the paperwork. On August 4, Pelossi incorporated International Aircraft Leasing (IAL) Ltd. in Liechtenstein, with himself and Edmund Frick as trustees. Frick, one of Liechtenstein's most prominent citizens, was also one of the best-known trustees of shell companies in Europe. It has been estimated that he and other members of his family served in this role for at least 10,000 companies.

IAL was the second shell company Schreiber formed in 1984. Earlier he had incorporated ATG Investments Ltd. in Panama; Pelossi was its sole trustee. Both ATG and IAL were controlled by Kensington Anstalt, the original parent holding company that Schreiber had set up in 1965.

Pelossi administered all the companies from his office in Lugano. It was a sign of Schreiber's trust in Pelossi that he was given sole signing authority over IAL. Although the Chiapas deal fell through at the last minute, Schreiber would find two more uses for IAL in 1985, for projects he hoped to promote in Canada.

7

Useful Expenditures

No one can deny that Ottawa is a lovely city. Its traditional industries are government and tourism, the former housed in tidy office buildings, the latter a guarantee of manicured parks and clean canals. The old stones and spires of the Parliament Buildings, with their dark green copper roofs and glowing mullioned windows, are a splendid sight in every season. Behind them, to the north, are the low mountains of the Gatineau, a well-loved region of cottages, deep lakes, and thousands of acres of parklands laced with walking and ski trails. Among the city's glories are its rivers: the Ottawa, which flows wide at the bottom of a steep cliff behind the Parliament Buildings; the Gatineau, which flows south from the mountains; and the Rideau, which flows north from the St. Lawrence through the old town. The three rivers join in a wild convergence just below the prime minister's residence at 24 Sussex Drive to form a magnificent waterway that flows east for 150 kilometres to Montreal. Broad avenues and drives curve along the rivers' banks, and fine homes perch on the banks to take advantage of the views. This is a historic city, to be sure, but there are also scores of modern office complexes crowding the downtown streets and spreading into suburban communities, particularly Kanata to the west, which has become the centre of Canada's high-technology business.

In all of this there is only one piece of real estate that matters to the politicians, bureaucrats, diplomats, military brass, lobbyists, and reporters who dwell in Ottawa's power hothouse. That is the long block of Parliament Hill itself, straddling Wellington Street. On the north side are the Parliament Buildings, with the offices of MPs and senators; across the street, on the south, is the Langevin Building, which houses the Prime Minister's Office and the offices of the country's top civil servant, the clerk of the Privy Council. The prime minister and his staff have the use of two office suites, one in the Centre Block of the Parliament Buildings and one in the Langevin Building. If one were to distinguish between the two, one might suggest that the political work – patronage, contracts, fundraising, press relations, and the like – takes place in the privacy of the south side's Langevin Building, which is off-limits to the public, while the parliamentary work – legislation, speeches, Question Period, official visitors, and ceremony – takes place on the north side. For those who want access to these precincts, it is essential that they find office space of their own as close by as possible.

That's why Frank Moores wasn't content with the shabby offices he found himself occupying at 130 Albert Street in Ottawa in the fall of 1984. The building was functional, twelve storeys without style, five full blocks from the Hill. It was the kind of place where you park while your party is in opposition, not an address for friends of the new prime minister. It would do until Moores had his team in place, but then he intended to find something more suitable.

Well before the votes were counted in September's election, Moores had been preparing to move from Montreal to Ottawa, where he expected to cash in on what the polls were telling him would be a spectacular election victory. On September 15, while the country's political junkies and 211 anxious Tory MPs waited to hear who would be in the new Mulroney cabinet, Moores purchased a small lobbying firm, Alta Nova, from four Conservatives. Pat Walsh, Jamie Burns, Peter Thomson, and Fred von Veh had worked for Alberta MP Don Mazankowski (once Moores's flatmate when both men were rookie MPs) when he was transport minister in the short-lived Clark government.

Expecting Mazankowski to reclaim Transport and invite them aboard again as aides, the partners were happy to turn over their company, space, and client list to a new owner.

Moores eyed the workers still tiling the lobbies and painting the walls at 50 O'Connor, a luxury complex closer to the Hill and kitty-corner to the Four Seasons Hotel. The Ottawa establishment's famous Rideau Club was moving into an upper floor, and a new Hy's Steak House was opening on the ground level. Lang Michener, the Toronto law firm brought to Ottawa by Jean Chrétien when he lost the Liberal leadership to John Turner, was among the new tenants. That's where Moores wanted to be too.

Two days after he signed the papers for Alta Nova, Moores watched with pleasure as Brian Mulroney, beaming his famous grin, was sworn into office as prime minister of Canada. At his side was his new cabinet of thirty-nine men and women. Among the ministers were Bob Coates, the minister of defence (with Rick Logan, another dump-Clark alumnus, as his chief of staff), Elmer MacKay, the solicitor general, and Don Mazankowski, the minister of transport. Mulroney's aides included Pat MacAdam, who was in charge of caucus liaison. Fred Doucet, considered by insiders to be Mulroney's most trusted friend but too abrasive to become his chief of staff, was named senior adviser. All had supported the prime minister's campaign for the party leadership. His old rival, Joe Clark, was appointed secretary of state for external affairs.

Within a few months Moores had another partner. He was Gerry Doucet, Fred's brother, a lawyer from Halifax who had been a Nova Scotia cabinet minister. He would spend part of every week in Ottawa and the rest of his time in Nova Scotia.

Before long they had signed up some former Alta Nova clients, including Mercedes-Benz Canada, and many new ones including American Express Canada, Honeywell, Nabisco Brands Canada, Gulf + Western, Bombardier, Inc., the Iron Ore Company of Canada, and the Pharmaceutical Manufacturers Association of Canada. Karlheinz Schreiber's Bitucan Holdings signed on. The partners acquired a no-nonsense name, Government Consultants International (GCI), and a reputation for playing hardball. They demanded huge retainers and they wanted, as they said bluntly, "a piece of the action" – contingency fees, as they were known. This was the kind of arrangement one heard about in Washington, but it was a novelty to Ottawa.

With a contingency fee, the lobbyist involved is paid little or nothing if the sale doesn't happen but extremely well – usually a percentage of the sale – if the contract goes through. That win-at-all-costs scenario can test even the most ethical of parties, and some say it encourages chicanery and under-the-table payments. One of the most respected public affairs consultants in Ottawa refused to accept contingency payments, and for good reason. Bill Lee, a Liberal, had set up a lobbying firm several years earlier with a well-known Conservative, Bill Neville. "We have never accepted contingency fees and we never will," Lee said in an interview in 1989. "If our livelihood depends on getting the contract, there is a terrible temptation to do whatever is necessary to get it, like cashing in some political chips. We're in for the long haul and we can't do it."

That wasn't all. The GCI partners had no patience with bureaucratic protocol. Their man had won the biggest election victory anyone could remember, and things were going to change in this town. If Frank Moores wanted to attend a meeting of bureaucrats to discuss a contract that one of his clients was pursuing – well, hell, he'd be there. If Moores or Gerry Doucet wanted to speak to the prime minister, he'd better not find some flunky standing in the way. The partners were famous for their charm, but they soon became infamous for their total disregard of propriety. Assuming Mulroney as their protector, they got away with it, even when the press ran story after story about the firm's questionable activities.

"Frank is running an escort service," one of Ottawa's long-established lobbyists told the *Globe and Mail* during this period. "He packs the client's bag, carries it through the right door, and then makes his case for him. Frankly, he's marketing his connections, and if it doesn't stop, this whole profession is going to be under a cloud."

Moores shrugged off the charge as "completely unfair and untrue," and added, "I've never had so much fun in my life." Erik Nielsen, the new deputy prime minister, was stunned to discover that Moores had far better access to Mulroney and far more clout in government than he did, after his thirty-three years in politics.

Schreiber knew that Moores was his pipeline to government, and he could hardly wait to set up deals to sell German goods to Canada. None was more important – nor more timely – than selling Airbus jets. His first contract to sell Airbus in Canada, signed in 1977, had failed miserably, but now he simply *had* to succeed. Airbus Industrie's survival was at stake.

Two years earlier, in 1983, Airbus Industrie officials at the Toulouse headquarters could look out their windows and see a dozen brand-new planes, A300s, sitting on the tarmac like wallflowers at a party. These were the original Airbuses, mid-size aircraft with seating for 266 passengers inside a wide-bodied, two-aisle configuration that made them more comfortable than their competitors and ideal for long-haul routes. They cost between US$88 million and US$92 million each, and Airbus had been trying to sell them for two years. Unfortunately, there were no buyers.

"In 1983 we had a crisis in North America," admitted Patrick Croze, who was then president of Airbus North America. "That was a very difficult time for us because we were trying to launch the A320. We really needed to establish our presence in the market here." The new A320s were designed as workhorses, Airbus's answer for shorter, regional routes. They boasted the same wide-body comfort as the A300s, but they were smaller, with a single aisle, and cheaper at about US$53 million each.

The difficulty was that Boeing, based in Seattle, had a stranglehold on the passenger aircraft business worldwide, a dominance the Americans had enjoyed for two decades. Boeing, McDonnell Douglas, and Lockheed had been the industry leaders; Lockheed got out of passenger aircraft in 1981, and McDonnell Douglas was small compared with Boeing.

In the late 1960s European airframe manufacturers lost business in their home markets to Boeing; they couldn't compete with Boeing's planes or its prices. According to Airbus Industrie's official history, the European founders of Airbus "realized they would disappear if they were to continue competing against each other. Their task was a daunting one. Never before had Europe worked together on such a large – and truly cooperative – scale for a civil aircraft program. Each participating country would have to make compromises, putting aside national pride and working hard to overcome difficulties posed by different languages, cultures and even systems of weights and measures."

And they knew they would have to subsidize production ruthlessly until they drove the Americans out of the European market. As the *New York Times* has pointed out, "The stakes were huge – an estimated [US]$1 trillion or more in orders" by 2007. By the early 1980s Airbus had poured US$10 billion into developing the A320, designed to serve the short-haul European market as well as the lucrative charter market so thoroughly dominated by Boeing. The key to long-term success would be a march into North America itself, but the Airbus partners never dreamed how difficult this would be. They could sell aircraft to one another – Spain's Iberia bought a few planes, as did Air France – but these were modest orders. Rightly or wrongly, Airbus was seen as a second-rate manufacturer, and during the 1970s all it could do was sell planes to the Middle East and Third World countries.

To revive its efforts in the United States and Canada, Airbus president Bernard Lathière sent Patrick Croze to New York in 1983 as president of the North American region. Lathière had to move the unsold planes off the Toulouse tarmac, and he counted on Croze to make it happen. Croze found a mess waiting for him: the Washington public relations firm hired to promote the A320 had failed, and territorial wars were raging between the Airbus people in Toulouse and the staff in the United States. And he found that there was a generally unfavourable attitude towards Airbus among airlines throughout North America. As Croze remembered it, people would say, "It's a fly-by-night operation. And it's not going to last very long. They have no money anyway. It's an operations risk and it's a financial risk."

Croze settled his people down and got to work to sell the planes. He recruited a sales team of young, eager individuals to crack the Canadian market first. In this Croze had some experience. He had worked on the early attempt to sell Airbus planes to Air Canada in the late 1970s. Pierre Trudeau had been interested, but the historic links between Boeing and Air Canada were too strong to break. "They were not ready to take the risk at the time," says Croze. He realized his mistake had been to rush things; he had been in too much of a hurry and should have done more homework on Air Canada's organization. In 1981, Airbus succeeded in making a deal with Max Ward in Alberta to sell him half a dozen A300s for his charter company. Ward made the down payment but had to cancel the deal after his financing collapsed. The Wardair aircraft were among those still sitting on the Toulouse tarmac. Airbus was gracious about the Wardair disaster, telling Ward it would keep the deal open for a later time.

By 1983 Croze thought it was time Airbus Industrie had a formal presence in Canada. He appointed a German salesman, Gert Landrock, to manage the Canadian marketing campaign out of new offices in Montreal's Place Ville-Marie, just blocks from Air Canada's corporate offices. Airbus made its representations to the Air Canada board and to Transport officials, trying a line that had worked for them in Arab countries: "Are you going to remain forever a dependant of the American industry?" But the Canadians, in those Liberal days, didn't bite.

By the winter of 1984–85, with the new Conservative government in power, Air Canada had begun to take a serious look at modernizing its fleet. Airbus, Boeing, and McDonnell Douglas all suspected a major purchase was only a few years away. Here was a major opportunity for Airbus to gain the foothold it needed in North America. Patrick Croze geared up again, as did Strauss, Schreiber, and Moores. In 1985 Gert Landrock was visited by Schreiber and Moores, who told him they were exploring a financing arrangement between Airbus and Air Canada. They invited Landrock to attend a meeting with a senior airline economist. "Schreiber and Moores were thinking, 'To get the deal we have to have a financial package attractive to Air Canada,'" said the economist. "They came to me and said, 'Could you do a financial package that we'd take to Air Canada?' They said they knew nothing about how to do it." Moores and Schreiber ultimately gave up the notion of special financing for Air Canada; they would try something else.

Franz Josef Strauss knew better than anyone that the company had come perilously close to collapsing in the early 1980s. He never again wanted to see unsold planes sitting on the tarmac in Toulouse. In Schreiber Strauss saw an opportunity, an advantage, and one more weapon in the war to win orders away from the archrival, Boeing.

Envious Airbus officials had long complained that the Americans were unfairly subsidizing the Seattle-based aerospace giant, in particular with lucrative Department of Defense contracts. Now it was time for Airbus to retaliate. As Schreiber said in a 1995 interview with CBC-TV, "My friendship was with the chairman. And wherever I went, if I could support something, I did. And so the Airbus people in those days – Jesus Christ, it was a struggle. No business, and Boeing fighting them like hell."

In effect Airbus launched a do-or-die war against Boeing; the very survival of the company hung in the balance. One troubling signal was the restlessness of the British partner over the company's lacklustre sales record; it was making threatening noises about cutting back on its financial support.

In early 1985 Strauss shocked the industry by firing Bernard Lathière, who had been the president of Airbus for ten years, and replacing him with Jean Pierson of Aerospatiale, the French Airbus partner. Strauss and others did not like the concessions Lathière had made to some customers in his efforts to get the planes moving. Strauss also brought in a new German executive vice-president, Johann Schäffler, the first time the consortium had seen an MBB manager in a top job. Up to then, the senior positions had always been filled by the French.

Pierson told reporters he wouldn't be making any radical changes: "I prefer the word 'adjustments,'" he said. "We are not revolutionary people."

Just before the management shuffle, Schreiber held discussions with Pierre Pailleret, the Airbus vice-president, commercial (in charge of sales and marketing), and the company's top salesman. Pailleret told him Airbus was prepared to set up a potentially lucrative contract with his shell company International Aircraft Leasing to sell planes in Canada. In return, Schreiber had to promise to make the sale happen. IAL wouldn't see a dime unless planes were sold. The contract would have nothing to do with Airbus's North American operation. After his conversation with Pailleret, Schreiber called Giorgio Pelossi, who was at home in Lugano. Pelossi would play a crucial role in the arrangements that were to follow; he would, in fact, sign for IAL. To the outside world, Schreiber had nothing to do with the ownership of IAL. And it was true that for practical purposes, Giorgio Pelossi was in charge of all its banking and paperwork. Yet behind the scenes, the entire contract had been orchestrated by Schreiber.

Schreiber told Pelossi to get in touch with another Airbus official, Roger Bailly, who worked in the contracts division at the Toulouse headquarters, and to settle with him the details of the Airbus contract. On March 7, 1985, Bailly and Pelossi met at the Savoy Hotel in Zurich. Over lunch they discussed the final draft. Pelossi had seen earlier drafts of the agreement, but now, as Bailly waited, he studied it again carefully.

Contract AI/CC-L-573-3/85, an escrow agreement between Airbus Industrie and International Aircraft Leasing, stated that IAL would receive commissions of up to 3 percent for each Airbus 300, 310, or 320 sold in Canada. If Wardair, PWA, or Air Canada bought new Airbus planes, Schreiber would get a piece of the action on the sale of every aircraft. Even at 2 percent, the commissions could climb into the tens of millions. The potential was mind-boggling.

The commission payments would be generated automatically on delivery of each aircraft to the customer and deposited into the Banque Française du Commerce Extérieur (later merged into Natexis Banques Populaires) at 21 Boulevard Haussmann in Paris's Ninth Arrondissement. Pelossi would instruct the bank to forward it to another institution. Bailly did not need to know more than that.

There were several interesting aspects to this contract. One clause stated that if there was a "major political change" in Canada – presumably, if the Conservatives were no longer in power – the agreement would be terminated "automatically." The contract also stipulated that Schreiber would keep Airbus informed of his work in Canada and write up "periodic reports on his activities." Though it could have gone without saying, the contract spelled out the obvious: Schreiber promised to "exert his best efforts to promote the sales" of Airbus aircraft in Canada.

After lunch Pelossi headed for 225 Zollikerstrasse to meet Peter Kurer, a lawyer at one of the city's most prominent firms, Homburger, Achermann, Müller & Heini. As planned, Pierre Pailleret also came to the law firm for the afternoon appointment. The three men looked carefully over the final contract again before Pelossi signed the agreement for IAL and Pailleret signed for Airbus.

There was only one signed copy, and it would stay behind for safekeeping. Kurer's colleague Peter Widmer, a partner at Homburger, Achermann, put the contract in a safe and gave Pelossi a certificate of deposit he signed on the same day. The agreement would be amended four times over the next four years.

Why was the only signed contract in a safe in a Zurich law office? The deal was confidential, all right, but this precaution seemed downright paranoid. Or maybe not. Airbus executives were not unfamiliar with this kind of contract. They understood that despite the best intentions of all sides, there had been occasions when someone with a loose tongue had revealed the details of a secret commission or when police investigations in faraway countries had sniffed out the information. But Airbus always had a comeback: "Where's the signed contract?" Since Airbus knew no unauthorized person could ever have it, the question not only was safe, it was the undoing of the curious.

Pelossi returned to Lugano with a copy of the agreement for IAL's files, but his papers were not signed in case they ever fell into the wrong hands. He would eventually issue instructions to the Paris bank to wire the money, when it began to flow, to IAL's account 235.972.037 in the VP Bank (Verwaltungs- und Privat-Bank) in Vaduz. From there Pelossi arranged for it to be transferred into the Paradeplatz branch of the Swiss Bank Corporation branch, across the street from where he had sat with Bailly. (The branch was later taken over by the Union Bank of Switzerland.) Once it was safely tucked into Schreiber's account 18679 there, Pelossi's role in the transaction would be over, and Schreiber himself would arrange any further disbursements.

Airbus Industrie was engaging in a time-honoured tradition in the airline industry when it signed the contract with IAL. Under German law, paying a middleman to facilitate a sale was not illegal, nor was it illegal to pay bribes or to offer *Schmiergelder* to foreigners, or to claim *nützlichen Abgaben* or NAs ("useful expenditures" or "necessary expenses") – the quaint euphemism by which they were known on German income-tax forms – for cozying up to foreigners. But such practices could certainly be seen as unethical or immoral or just plain sleazy. It was sensible, therefore, to keep such contracts hidden, and that's what both Airbus and MBB tried to do in their dealings with Schreiber.

It was especially prudent in the case of any transaction involving Canadian Crown corporations, agencies, or government departments. With few exceptions, the government prohibited contracts in which the seller paid commissions to a third party to make the sale to the government. Like contingency fees for lobbyists, the practice was susceptible to abuse. An agent motivated solely by a lucrative commission cheque might resort to whatever measures were necessary to close the deal. But more important, the government wanted to pay the lowest possible price for its purchases. It reasoned that third-party commissions artificially inflated the overall costs on a contract, and that a supplier who paid such commissions could just as easily reduce its price to the taxpayer by the same amount. In effect the government argued that a company that paid third-party commissions secretly and in contravention of its normal prohibition would be defrauding the taxpayer.

How to construct a deal to avoid practices that were actually prohibited while engaging in some that were merely frowned upon or simply best hidden from prying eyes? It was all in the mechanics and in the use of an intermediary or middleman. "Both sides need something to ease their discomfort," explained one German expert on secret commissions, bribery, and fraud. "That's why trusted third parties do it. You base their payment on the completion of the contract. It's pure business." The company talks only to the middleman to arrive at the amount to pay and perhaps whom to pay. The person accepting the money also talks to the middleman, negotiating only with him. "This way no one has a bad conscience."

For a businessman who decides that bribing public officials is the only way to win a contract for the firm, the fact that bribery as a practice is an undesirable element of business would be only one part of the challenge. The second would be ensuring that once you decide to pay such bribes in the form of secret commission fees – a marketing expense, after all – you could find the right facilitator. An employee is usually not the answer; the risk is too great. A better option is a freelance middleman who comes well recommended.

The most notorious middleman at this time was Adnan Khashoggi, a Saudi arms broker and influence peddler who specialized in setting up the kinds of deal Schreiber had just struck with Airbus. Lower-profile candidates would include certain law and accounting firms who are prepared to handle such delicate briefs. Another option is simply to hire one of those companies whose sole purpose is to establish and manage this sort of relationship between willing parties. The "administrator" provides a necessary distance from the unsavoury transaction. It does not negotiate the bribe, it only administers it; it does not know where the money comes from or whether the recipient is guilty of a conflict of interest. The ethical or legal impacts are, to an administrator, irrelevant.

Schreiber called himself an adviser or troubleshooter, and it was a role he was proud of. It's all about understanding human nature, he explained, and about doing favours for people in the expectation that they will return them. As he told Bruno Schirra in a rambling interview for *Die Zeit* in February 2000, anyone who thinks middlemen don't perform a necessary service is naive.

"The important thing is always, always the human, personal contact," Schreiber said. "You know this idea of how corruption happens, or what one understands to be corruption, is, in general, childish."

Schirra reminded him of a previously reported remark of his: "Corruption is as old as prostitution and fulfills a comparable or similar function." Schreiber didn't back away.

"That won't stop," Schreiber said flatly. "Corruption and prostitution – I don't believe that it will ever stop." Human beings are driven by certain needs and desires, he added.

"There is this fairy tale of the fisher and his wife, eh? Who was never satisfied, who always wanted more. There are such wives, that drive their men like crazy... [They say,] 'Look what the neighbour has,' and so on. And then they [the husbands] cannot fulfill that any more, no? And somewhere they try to get additional income or a better job." It is at this point, he explained, that they are vulnerable to a bribe.

Schreiber pointed out another kind of corruption, that of the politician or government bureaucrat who wants more power and a higher position. "Is it corruption, in government or politics, to help people there get ahead? To get a higher position or to become a minister of state or to get onto committees or boards? It can't be said that everyone that you help to become something or to improve his own life and income situation and that of his family – that it is a bad thing."

Once the middleman has helped someone improve his lot in life, the middleman should be able to expect a benefit in return, he said. "You don't have to go to him and say: 'Here's an envelope with ten thousand, now do something for me.' He has already been morally forced into a dependency relationship. Maybe over the next five or eight or ten years, he will want to say to himself, 'Now I can finally do a favour for him too,' no?"

Schreiber had observed politicians for decades and thought he understood their motivations. His thesis was that most had little money and came from a working-class or middle-class background. They were union leaders, say, or schoolteachers. These were just the people who, out of pure envy, would often discourage successful businessmen from going into politics and making the changes a country needs. And it's frustrating for an entrepreneur in politics to be treated this way. "He will be shoved aside to the back benches and shoved into the committees that are meaningless. And then the huge frustration will begin of an entrepreneur who wants to move things forward." This, insisted Schreiber, is what true political corruption is, not the use of necessary expenses to make a deal happen.

When Schirra steered him back to the subject of how politicians can be influenced, Schreiber had several ideas. The informal drink at a bar when the middleman can remind his guest about a call for tenders. "When leaving he pockets an envelope, no?" Or maybe the middleman arranges for the money to go to the man's wife, suggested Schreiber. "His wife works somewhere, maybe does work at home for something – and receives above-average pay."

The middleman might attend a fundraising dinner and throw what Schreiber called "five hundred big ones" into a hat, or he can transfer money offshore so the politician avoids taxes. There are money transfers without records, he added, "and a certain special system with which this is done. There are a thousand ways this can take place. It won't go away."

While it might be "morally reprehensible or punishable," as he put it, in other countries, Germans can't concern themselves with such rules; in fact, people who object to such practices are, as he put it, "Neanderthals" who know nothing about how business is really done. The international revulsion against corruption is driven by Americans trying to secure their own economic dominance. But corruption is now so sophisticated, said Schreiber, "that those who do it have long since developed systems which are no longer touchable, are absolutely unable to be seen through. The 'useful expenditures' system has reached a perfection in international business which is amazing."

When Schirra asked Schreiber if it was true, as one newspaper had reported, that he had withdrawn DM3.4 million from a Swiss bank to pay useful expenditures, Schreiber admitted it was "thoroughly possible." And he added, "Wherein lies the problem?"

"So these 3.4 million were 'useful expenditures'?" Schirra asked.

"Yes, clearly. The – all of the money is for that. What do you think it's for?"

"And who did it go to?"

"I wouldn't tell you that."

"But you understand that I ask that?" Schirra persisted.

"We won't even talk about that. I'm not an information service."

Schirra pushed for more. "I'll put it into plain language and please correct me if I make any mistakes. That means that politicians expect to receive *nützlichen Abgaben*, thus *Schmiergelder*, from consultants such as yourself, if it's necessary?"

"Of course."

Schreiber made it clear to Schirra that what made him so angry was the hypocrisy of some German politicians. "It could be that the Bavarian finance minister meets with the Canadian minister of trade or of transportation, smiles at him, and says how wonderful the relationship between the two countries is, when just a half hour ago he was granting or permitting 'useful expenditures' with which politicians or bureaucrats in the country of the guest will be bribed. Great, huh?"

"So you're talking about Canada now," asked Schirra, "or anywhere?"

"I'm talking about... I'm talking about examples. That goes for any other country as well."

Sometimes useful expenditures take the form of goods instead of money. A Rolex watch is as good as cash. Almost any type of luxury goods works well – antiques, fine carpets, nice furniture, or good paintings. Wherever there are tax havens, there are people swapping possessions instead of cash. They are far harder to trace.

None of the German corporate officials in question chose luxury commodities as their currency, nor did they engage the services of lawyers, accountants, or specialized administrators as their middlemen; they chose Schreiber. The reason was simple. Some of the top people authorizing the arrangements with Schreiber also wanted a share of the cash. And the person who recommended him was Franz Josef Strauss.

Strauss had plenty of experience with this kind of agreement. One of the most interesting partnerships he enjoyed over the years was with the powerful East German fixer Alexander Schalck-Golodkowski. Schalck ran a government agency called the Kommerziale Koordination, popularly known as "KoKo," and had billions of marks at his disposal to pay bribes for the East German government when he thought it necessary. Before reunification, he masterminded the GDR's acquisition of hard currency by literally selling political prisoners to West Germany. To cover his tracks, Schalck used a sophisticated network of letterbox companies in Switzerland, Liechtenstein, Panama, and elsewhere. According to *Man Without a Face*, the 1997 autobiography of Markus Wolf, the legendary former chief of the Stasi, East Germany's foreign intelligence service, "Between 1964 and 1990 the GDR released over 33,000 political prisoners and over 215,000 citizens to reunify families, and received payments from the West of more than 3.4 billion deutschmarks. Schalck administered much of this money." Schalck set up dozens of shell companies as covers for different businesses, explained Wolf, "from importing cars to clandestine shipments of art sold to Western dealers from state collections."

Schalck's greatest challenge was nothing less than saving the

floundering republic from bankruptcy in 1983, and he did it by broker-
ing a deal with Strauss. The Bavarian premier arranged a government-
backed loan of DM1 billion for the GDR in return for better travel
arrangements for Germans visiting their families in the East.

Wolf alleged that other deals were made, "multi-sided deals," as he
called them in his book, to bring in hard currency. Given that the Stasi
routinely tapped the telephones of German leaders, Wolf knew a great
deal about payoffs that might have gone to certain people, and he
acknowledged as much in a recent interview.

"We had some different knowledge of corruption," he said, "especially of the Strauss family. There is proof in some of the materials
[documents]. We knew there existed a big corruption, especially with
military equipment and production." In particular, Wolf pointed to a
public scandal in the late 1960s and early 1970s when Strauss became
involved in discussions for the purchase of Star Fighter jets from
Lockheed. "Strauss earned a lot of money with military production,"
said Wolf.

Schreiber had been canny in designing a system for gathering and
dispensing the commission payments in utmost secrecy. Fortunately,
he had established his Liechtenstein network years earlier. German and
Canadian authorities could not easily investigate his activities there.

Plenty of people still use Switzerland as a haven for hiding their
money. Not only does the country's wealth depend, to a great extent,
on its banks' reputations for security and discretion, but its administrative structures reinforce these virtues. Some of Switzerland's poorest
cantons, such as Nidwalden, Uri, Schwyz, and Obwalden, have become
tax havens because they have no budget for the investigative policing of
white-collar crime. With twenty-six cantons, each with its own laws on
how to administer the country's criminal code, a Swiss prosecution
that begins in a canton like Nidwalden can be almost impossible.

"A Nidwalden trustee acts like a firewall on a computer," joked one
financial expert on Swiss trusts. Still, as he acknowledged, if there is
enough political pressure in Switzerland, the authorities can get
through into Nidwalden. Money is safer in Liechtenstein.

Yet even in Vaduz, Schreiber was cautious. He had three gatekeepers to hold the curious at bay. The first was Edmund Frick, his

Liechtenstein trustee. The second was Giorgio Pelossi, the other IAL trustee and his trusted partner in Lugano. The third was his Swiss account in Zurich. All served to disguise his involvement with Airbus Industrie and with others when they came on board. If there was any weakness in the system, it was on the other side. Airbus did not develop a comparable system of gatekeepers, although it did instruct the Banque Française du Commerce Extérieur not to identify Airbus as the source of its payments to IAL. To match Schreiber's measures would have meant engaging intermediaries to parcel out the cash payments – a task Airbus management reserved for itself. Perhaps they believed they were invulnerable; perhaps they thought Schreiber's precautions were enough. It was a risk they decided to take.

In the airline business it is not difficult to find an airline economist or salesman who says he has paid third-party commissions for sales in Africa, Asia, and the Middle East. "What's the story?" confused airline officials would ask reporters on the trail of the Airbus commissions. "This happens all the time."

Perhaps, but when the question was about secret commissions paid on the sale of airplanes in Canada, even jaded sales agents raised their antennae. "Canada? Are you sure?" To hear some describe it, there is an invisible anti-*Schmiergelder* blanket covering most of North America, where airplane contracts are won, or lost, on merit alone. If that is the case, it may have to do with the fact that most airlines in North America are privately owned, not government-run corporations. Still, the Airbus strategy, involving secret contracts and a middleman on commission, represented a departure from and a contravention of the rules.

On March 12, 1985, five days after Pelossi signed the Airbus contract with IAL, Prime Minister Brian Mulroney fired the board of Air Canada. "We just felt that we had to get a better grip on the board," said Tom Van Dusen, the press secretary for Transport Minister Mazankowski, in response to reporters' questions. No one was surprised or even particularly disturbed. The board had been made up of old Trudeau appointees, and an Air Canada directorship, with its first-class travel pass, was one of the most coveted patronage appointments in the government's purse. Seats on the board almost always went to bagmen and top party supporters.

This time it was no different. On March 15, Mulroney appointed thirteen new board members to Air Canada, with predictable reaction from the party's critics.

"Tory hacks, flacks, and bagmen," yelled an NDP MP, Nelson Riis, in the House of Commons.

Mazankowski responded affably that the appointments were just fine. "They are all very distinguished and well-qualified Canadians that represent all regions of the country," he told the House. "They will do tremendous service to Air Canada and a tremendous service to Canada."

While the board positions were technically within the gift of a minister of transport, they were in fact rewards dispensed by the prime minister to selected favourites. Every one of the new directors in this round had a PC Party background, and almost every one had been a Mulroney leadership supporter and fundraiser. Eyebrows went up when people saw Frank Moores's name on the list, and he didn't help matters when he turned up at the Ottawa Press Club after a press gallery dinner and swooped around the room like an airplane, laughing wildly. Also appointed was Gayle Christie, a Toronto Tory fundraiser who had once claimed she was qualified to join the Air Canada board because she had a driver's licence.

David Angus, another appointee, had been part of the Montreal gang leading the Mulroney leadership drive and was chairman of the PC Canada Fund, the party's main fundraising organization. Ken Waschuk, another ally from the dump-Clark days, won a seat. Fern Roberge was the manager of the Ritz-Carlton Hotel in Montreal, a close friend of Mulroney, and a Quebec Tory organizer. Another novice director was James Ross, a businessman from Fredericton, New Brunswick, who had been an important bagman in the Maritimes. Also new to the board was Fred Dickson, a Halifax lawyer who was close to Premier John Buchanan and who had run the Tories' campaign in Nova Scotia.

Schreiber watched with satisfaction as Mazankowski announced the new Air Canada board. He knew of most of the directors from the dump-Clark days. He was also pleased that Moores's lobby firm would be strengthened that same month with the addition of another influential recruit, Gary Ouellet. A Quebec City lawyer and PC Party organizer, Ouellet had come to Ottawa to set up the offices of the new junior transport minister, Benoît Bouchard. He had left that post and quickly joined GCI; before long he would be running the day-to-day operations. Ouellet's other passion, besides politics, was magic – he had written several books on the subject – and he had been part of Mulroney's inner circle during the long march to the leadership.

Not long after Ouellet joined GCI, Schreiber invited Giorgio Pelossi to the GCI offices in Ottawa to meet the partners. It was a good group, thought Pelossi. Gerry Doucet had none of his brother's sour demeanour and was sunny and pleasant most of the time. Gary Ouellet was the same – a charmer with a great sense of humour and a quick mind. Of course, no one liked to have a good time more than Moores himself; this was a man who partied harder than men half his age. Pelossi had the impression they were all working on Airbus. It was rare for Pelossi to attend this kind of meeting – he never set foot in GCI's offices again.

For Schreiber, on the other hand, meeting and greeting had become a full-time occupation since the election. Everywhere he went in Ottawa, people were welcoming and spoke of opportunity. Yet, surprisingly, Schreiber remained under the Ottawa press corps's radar. None wrote about him, very few knew about him. No one noticed him scurrying around town, lunching at the Château, chatting over drinks at the Four Seasons, always with MPs or lobbyists, always grinning, always hurrying.

8

Secrets and Lies

The handful of casual acquaintances in Ottawa who did recognize Karlheinz Schreiber believed his sole preoccupation was the construction of a Thyssen plant in Nova Scotia. Thyssen was the only project about which he could talk openly, the only one for which he had a legitimate business plan. It gave him reasons to be in Ottawa, where he could go quietly about his covert work on various matters. The murky projects in Costa Rica were never mentioned, and the Airbus arrangements were highly secretive. The nature of his relationship with Messerschmitt-Bölkow-Blohm was understood by very few, but it was in fact the project that was the furthest advanced.

Schreiber and Moores had moved quickly after the election to arrange meetings with the new industry minister, Sinclair Stevens, and the defence minister, Bob Coates, laying the groundwork for future dealings between MBB's helicopter division and the Canadian government. Schreiber reported to Kurt Pfleiderer, who had become vice-president of the marketing division of MBB, that these initial sessions had been a success and that further meetings were scheduled for November 8, 9, and 10. Pfleiderer noted Schreiber's optimism in an internal memo dated November 5, 1984, suggesting that Schreiber appeared to have clinched the deal that would demonstrate his value to the Germans.

"Cooperation with members of the new Canadian government was already tight before their election victory" and has contributed to the "winning" of a contract to supply helicopters to the Canadian Coast Guard, Pfleiderer wrote. His claim of success for MBB would have come as a surprise to most government officials, since the contract was still, at least publicly, at the discussion stage only.

Government documents reveal that the Canadian Coast Guard had been planning since 1979 to purchase a substantial number of new helicopters. Three years later, the decision-making process was well along: an analysis of eight possible helicopter types in May 1982 put two MBB models at the top of the list. In 1983, MBB enhanced its chances by announcing a joint venture with Fleet Industries Ltd. of Fort Erie, Ontario, to manufacture a new rotor system and the next generation of MBB's existing twin-turbine helicopter, the BO 105, using Fleet's production facilities. The federal and Ontario governments expected the project would generate three hundred jobs and develop a product that could be sold in the export market. By May 1984, MBB Helicopter Canada Ltd. (MCL) had been formed, with MBB holding 95 percent and Fleet 5 percent. The two governments agreed to contribute $34.9 million to the overall estimated cost of $69.3 million for a plant and for research and development.

But as yet there was no commitment from government to purchase anything that might come off the assembly line. MBB hoped it would eventually secure the Coast Guard contract, and until Schreiber entered the picture, it had energetically promoted the virtues of its product to the federal bureaucrats at Transport Canada, who were expected to make the decision. Schreiber and Moores had apparently convinced Pfleiderer that whatever the deliberations of these senior managers, it was political pull that would win the deal, and that their efforts in this direction had begun even before the Tories came to power.

The early-November meetings between MBB officials and Coates and Stevens went smoothly, the Coast Guard contract being only one of several agenda items. Also discussed were the export potential of the BO 105 (the Germans intended to circumvent their own laws by exporting helicopters from Canada to Chile and Iraq, among others) and the possible replacement of the Canadian Forces' Sea King helicopters.

By the end of the year, Pfleiderer understood what had to be done next. In a confidential internal memo dated December 22, 1984, he noted, "The expectations of the visits to both ministries in connection with... Frank Moores and Mr. K. H. Schreiber were fully met." Recording his meeting with Coates and his chief of staff, Rick Logan, Pfleiderer wrote that Coates had made clear "it was the personal wish of the Prime Minister to hire Mr. Bob Shey [sic] from Boston, an American industrialist." Robert Shea was an American-born insurance broker and financial consultant who had been a close friend of Mulroney's since their university days together at St. Francis Xavier in Nova Scotia; in 1983 he had raised funds from American corporations for Mulroney's leadership bid. Moores later appointed Shea to GCI's new advisory board.

Over at Sinclair Stevens's office, Pfleiderer was told that the Conservatives viewed the bureaucracy differently than the previous government. "Here was demonstrated with total clarity the line of the new government, which differs from actions to date in that political decisions are to be made above all, and that the reigning bureaucracy is reduced to a minimum. Accordingly, the new ministers are surrounding themselves mainly with party friends," he wrote.

Pfleiderer's memo concluded with recommendations for further action: first, MBB was to seal a consulting contract with Frank Moores's lobbying firm at a rate of C$6,000 per month, or C$72,000 annually, plus later "success fees." Second, Bob Shea was to be appointed to the supervisory board of MCL, MBB's new Canadian company.

On the last day of January 1985, senior managers from the Canadian Coast Guard met to discuss the helicopter project. Documents show that the bureaucrats regarded the BO 105 as best equipped to meet their needs for performance and safety, and they concluded that the department "should proceed" with the acquisition. Now, they believed, they had only to persuade their political masters. MBB believed their political masters had already been convinced.

That same month, GCI began receiving its monthly retainer from

MBB's head office in Munich, much against the wishes of its Canadian executives. "My advice [to head office] was that Canada is not a crooked country," said one senior manager. "Lobbyists are working for everyone and you should use our own people."

Schreiber's blunt style occasionally offended the MBB officials. Helge Wittholz, the president of MCL, remembered an embarrassing scene at the Ottawa airport. "He made – in very loud German – a bad comment about a very fat woman. A lot of people speak German. I was ashamed, I walked away."

In February Giorgio Pelossi, on behalf of IAL, negotiated an agreement with Kurt Pfleiderer concerning the commission arrangements on sales of MBB helicopters in Canada. MBB would pay IAL 8 percent of the invoice value of every helicopter sold in Canada, plus 15 percent on sales of spare parts and other hardware. MBB would deduct GCI's retainer from the eventual commission payment to IAL. With all the extras factored in, Schreiber and Moores stood to earn close to C$200,000 for every helicopter sold.

There was one unhappy development in these weeks. Bob Coates, one of Schreiber's best cabinet contacts, ended his political career abruptly by resigning on February 12 after the *Ottawa Citizen* published a story about a visit he had made to a German strip club in November with Rick Logan. The men had been on an official trip to a Canadian air base in Lahr, and the indiscretion cost both their jobs.

On February 23, Sinclair Stevens and a large entourage arrived in Munich for talks with Franz Josef Strauss and his officials. A group that included Bob Brown, the assistant deputy minister for capital and industrial goods in Stevens's ministry, Don McPhail, Canada's ambassador to Germany, and two aides to Stevens, Effie Triantafilopoulos and Phil Evershed, were whisked away to the Bavarian Alps almost immediately aboard BO 105 helicopters. Schreiber and his Kaufering office manager, Albert Birkner, were along for the ride.

It was public knowledge that Stevens and Strauss were to discuss the proposed Thyssen plant in Nova Scotia, but privately they were also talking about the sale of Canada's publicly owned aircraft assets, Canadair Ltd. and de Havilland. The government had announced its intention to privatize them; might MBB be interested?

The idea wasn't new. Around the time of Stevens's conversation with Strauss, Moores had called on Cliff MacKay, the director general of electronics and aerospace at the Department of Regional Industrial Expansion (DRIE). MacKay was involved at that time in promoting aerospace projects in different parts of the country. Moores wanted to test his reaction to an idea. GCI was already representing MBB on the Coast Guard helicopter deal, explained Moores. But MBB made more than helicopters – it was a large aerospace company. Here was Moores's pitch: If MBB undertook to purchase Canadair, would the government get Air Canada to commit itself to buying planes from Airbus?

MacKay, a chain-smoking, plain-talking bureaucrat, said he'd think it over and get back to him. Airbus salespeople made calls on MacKay every three or four months, just to let him know they were there, trying hard. The visit from Moores was different. MacKay knew Moores's status in Ottawa. He knew how close he was to Mulroney. And he knew that a negative response might be career suicide, but he understood immediately that no matter how many times Moores raised the idea, it was a non-starter, for three reasons.

First, it didn't make sense financially. Everyone was aware that Air Canada was going to make a major fleet purchase, and it didn't take a genius to figure out that Boeing and Airbus would offer their best prices only if there were competing bids. The second reason was that it would alienate Boeing to grant a contract without a competition – not a smart idea when the company had established itself as a good corporate citizen in Canada. And third, it would probably cause serious diplomatic problems with our neighbour to the south. However one judged it, the cost was too high.

MacKay eventually told Moores that he would happily talk to him about a possible purchase of Canadair or de Havilland, but the government would not be interested in doing business if it has anything to do with Airbus. Airbus can't be part of the deal. MacKay unequivocally separated the two matters; Moores had baldly revealed their connection.

By May 1985, Schreiber was corresponding directly with the president of MBB, Hanns Vogels, on the issue of MBB's export desires. "I can tell you that our efforts to loosen export restrictions in Canada for particular products that are of interest to you are proceeding exceptionally positively," Schreiber wrote on May 31. "I will be able to report more detail to you after my return [from Canada]." At the end of his note, he reminded Vogels of the importance of engaging Moores on future projects. "Use the contact through GCI (Frank Moores), also for other projects which are connected to the Canadian government. The use of this contact not only makes sense but is expected from the other side for many reasons."

A month later, on June 26, MBB in Germany sent a telex to Schreiber, updating him on MCL's wish list for export approval. MBB claimed its Canadian subsidiary had received export licences for Peru, Dubai, and Saudi Arabia but had been denied them for Iraq. It was in the middle of applying for licences to export to Pakistan and Egypt, and was considering applications for Bahrain, Venezuela, Colombia, Taiwan, Tunisia, Sudan, and South Africa.

In the summer of 1985 MBB and GCI formalized their relationship with a consultancy agreement on the BO 105 and BK 117 helicopters, one that would become null and void if Frank Moores ever left the lobby firm. As well, MBB and GCI recognized that IAL would be MBB's "sales representatives" in Canada for these helicopters.

A couple of months later, there was some disappointing news for Schreiber and the German executives at MBB: Canada had decided not to allow their requested export permit for Chile. Schreiber was not completely dismayed at the news; the next month he was talking to Pfleiderer about selling helicopters to Nigeria.

Albert Birkner, the business manager of Bayerische Bitumen-Chemie, Schreiber's Kaufering company, sat facing the firm's unhappy bankers on July 16, 1985. Revenues were down, the overdraft was rising, and Shell Oil had just cut him off. The business needed fuel oil, but Shell refused to deliver more than a token amount unless it received a substantial payment on account.

As Schreiber had instructed him, Birkner laid out a statement of his boss's financial prospects, emphasizing the expectation of imminent cash infusions. Jöst Hurler, one of Schreiber's German investors, had agreed to market their real estate properties in Alberta, assuming all of the related costs. Thyssen Industrie had made promises to Schreiber for help in winning contracts in Canada, and he expected some healthy commissions very soon. A third source of fresh income was the Liebherr crane contract for Costa Rica; Schreiber's payment should arrive any day. The bankers were not impressed.

Schreiber had other financial pressures at this time. He had recently married Barbara Schubert, and he wanted to make her feel secure and happy. The rest of his family was also very much on his mind. His son, Andi, lived in Kaufering, and Schreiber was grooming him to take over some of his business interests. Viola, his daughter, was near Augsburg, northwest of Munich. There were his aging parents to look after; he was close to them and they encouraged his visits. He entertained as generously as ever at Kaufering and Pontresina, and he travelled constantly between Europe, Canada, and Costa Rica. Hans Reiter was snapping at his heels about debts owing to the Sparkasse Landsberg. Schreiber needed to make a lot of money, and he needed it quickly. The MBB commissions were not due for several months, so he concentrated on the Airbus and Thyssen projects. Neither was proceeding as smoothly as he'd hoped.

In midsummer the media reported that GCI was lobbying for two of Air Canada's competitors, Nordair and Wardair. The story suggested a clear conflict of interest. How could Moores lobby for two airlines competing with Air Canada while serving on Air Canada's board? Moores issued a defiant statement saying he was doing nothing unusual; the Nordair and Wardair accounts were handled by others at GCI, not by its president.

On July 22, Michael Harris of the *Globe and Mail* took the story a step further, reporting evidence that pointed to a potentially more serious conflict. Harris had learned that Moores himself was representing Messerschmitt-Bölkow-Blohm, "part of a consortium interested in selling the A320 passenger aircraft to Air Canada when it replaces its aging fleet of 35 Boeing 727s."

Reporters on Parliament Hill could smell a scandal. The Montreal *Gazette* reacted strongly: "If Prime Minister Mulroney is to retain any credibility as a foe of patronage sleaze, as he portrayed himself only a year ago in his first election debate, he will have to deal swiftly and convincingly with the matter of Frank Moores," the paper declared in a July 23 editorial. "In all the years of Liberal patronage, it is hard to recall any appointment that raises quite the same smelly questions as those raised by Moores' membership on the board of directors of Air Canada."

The press coverage was too much for Air Canada's chairman, Claude Taylor. He liked Moores and found him an effective board member. Moores attended the meetings, read his briefing notes, and participated intelligently. None of this was enough, however, and Taylor decided it was time to confront him. He told Moores he should remove any appearance of conflict by leaving the board.

Moores reluctantly decided to drop Nordair and Wardair as clients, but he was mistaken if he thought the controversy would end there. Claude Taylor decided it was time to take the matter to another level. He called Transport Minister Don Mazankowski and told him Frank Moores had to go. He also spoke to Mulroney. Both men agreed Moores should resign. Pierre Jeanniot, the airline's president, was consulted. It wasn't a moment too soon.

The press and the opposition parties now understood that MBB was a major stakeholder in Airbus. Under fire, Moores denied he was lobbying for Airbus; all he was doing, he claimed, was lobbying for MBB and its helicopters.

Moores weighed his options; surrendering the Air Canada patronage plum would not be easy. One of the people he called for an opinion on whether he should step down from the board was Cliff MacKay. MacKay knew that Moores was acting for MBB, which was actively considering the purchase of Canadair. He also knew, at first hand, that Moores had been lobbying to sell Airbus planes to Air Canada. MacKay didn't mince his words.

"I don't think it's going to do your business any good," he said. "You should resign from Air Canada. Because the allegations will be that somehow you're influencing something... That'll be the allegation and there's no way to prove or disprove it."

That summer MacKay casually told a few reporters what he knew, that Moores had visited his office and had made it clear that Airbus

Industrie wanted to sell its planes to Air Canada. In August Moores heard that a Canadian Press reporter, Bob Fife, was about to reveal even more details about his involvement with Airbus. Fife would raise the issue of an Air Canada board member talking to government officials about Airbus selling its planes to the national airline.

On September 6, 1985, Moores decided he'd had enough. He called Fife into his office and handed him a copy of his letter of resignation, submitted that day. In return for the scoop, Moores said, he'd appreciate it if Fife didn't mention his relationship with Airbus. No deal, Fife said with a smile. For once Moores let his anger show. He was tired of being hounded, he snapped, and the directorship just wasn't worth it.

Pierre Jeanniot later told reporters that once Moores's involvement with Airbus was known, his fate was sealed. "We knew he was the lobbyist for Airbus," Jeanniot said to Jonathan Ferguson of the *Toronto Star*, in a story published December 13, 1995. "That's why he had to step down from the Air Canada board."

Moores had been at the centre of the criticism of aggressive lobbying tactics ever since Mulroney came to power. Ironically, his departure from Air Canada came just weeks after the controversy had forced a response from the government. In August Mulroney promised lobbying legislation, including a registry office that would compel lobbyists to list their clients. "I feel that it's important," he told reporters, "that you know who's sitting across the table from you and who he's representing, who's paying him and how much." The message was that the prime minister intended to have that information.

While this tempest blew in Canada, Airbus was negotiating another major contract, in India. A year earlier, in July 1984, Indian Airlines had sent Boeing a letter of intent to purchase several Boeing 757s, securing the deal with a payment of US$900,000. At the end of August 1985, however, Prime Minister Rajiv Gandhi, a pilot himself and the country's aviation minister, abruptly cancelled the contract. With the approval of the Ministry of Civil Aviation, Indian Airlines signed a US$1.47-billion contract for twenty-one Airbus 320s. The formal announcement was made on September 23. Boeing executives at the Seattle headquarters were first stunned and then furious. They were convinced that the German company had paid bribes to Indian

107

politicians. Although Moores had nothing to do with these events, the controversy around Moores's activities made the Boeing people deeply suspicious and alarmed that they might lose sales in Canada as well.

For years the top people at GCI denied they lobbied for Airbus or claimed their recollections were foggy. "We did not act for Airbus," said a senior executive a decade after Moores's resignation from the board of Air Canada. "People thought we did, but in fact we were acting for . . . uh, I can't remember, it's so long – a helicopter manufacturer." Could it have been MBB? "Yeah . . . They had a Canadian plant in Ontario somewhere and they were in trouble of some sorts. I don't even know if they're still there. Shows you how long I've paid attention to all this."

Moores always denied that he lobbied for Airbus. "I don't know where the hell the rumour came from," Moores said in 1994 and many times thereafter. As early as the fall of 1985, however, Boeing executives believed otherwise. "Moores's outfit was under contract to MBB, so Frank would go around telling people he never represented Airbus," said one Boeing executive. "But he represented one of the big partners, and he had pressure on him from Strauss and the West German group."

Schreiber and Moores hoped the heat would die down quickly and, except for the nervousness of Boeing, it did. It was a relief to turn to the one deal that was out in the open, the Thyssen project. By now, Schreiber had a proposed location for the Thyssen plant, a site arrived at by the Nova Scotia Tories working with Premier John Buchanan. The province was willing to donate a large parcel of land on Cape Breton, on the Bear Head Peninsula, near the island's biggest town, Port Hawkesbury.

A four-hour drive northeast from Halifax or two hours southwest of Sydney, Port Hawkesbury is an awkward place to get to. And once there, visitors find a small, down-at-heels, industrial town with only the Swedish Stora pulp mill to keep the local economy going.

It's not surprising that Cape Bretoners love their picturesque island with a passion, but it's also understandable that they nurse a grudge for the poverty that clings to so many corners of this place. When the Bear Head project was on offer, the coal mining that supported hundreds of working-class families was nearly gone, the fishing had been restricted, and the population was too small to sustain much manufacturing. For generations, people there counted on government regional development programs to keep their community afloat.

Undoubtedly its politicians wanted to do something for the area. When Gerry Doucet, a member of an Acadian family from Grand Étang on the island, was a Tory cabinet minister in the provincial government, he had represented Port Hawkesbury. The provincial member in the mid-1980s, Conservative Billy Joe Maclean, the minister of tourism in the Buchanan government, was another strong supporter. Mulroney wanted to help the area too; he'd won his first parliamentary election in the neighbouring riding of Central Nova, for the seat vacated by Elmer MacKay. Not only was the land for the plant provided, but Schreiber was confident that he could negotiate generous subsidies with both the Buchanan and the Mulroney governments. With his influence, he expected a cornucopia of grants, loans, tax credits, concessions, and contracts to pour out of Halifax and Ottawa.

In September 1985, Greg Alford, a young protégé of Frank Moores who had worked as his executive assistant and had become the president of GCI, wrote to Industry Minister Sinclair Stevens's assistant Phil Evershed, enclosing a package of information about Thyssen's defence program and the types of vehicles it wanted to manufacture at Bear Head. On October 8, Schreiber was flying from Canada to Germany when he spotted an article in the newspaper *Die Welt* concerning a deal between Saudi Arabia and Germany to make weapons with the help of Thyssen. The story mentioned that Saudi Arabia had purchased three hundred battle tanks from the Americans, as well as aircraft from Britain. The next day Schreiber wrote Sinclair Stevens a personal letter from Kaufering, drawing the Thyssen plans to the minister's attention. The message was clear: Canada would miss the boat on opportunities with Thyssen if it didn't move quickly.

Of course, Schreiber, too, needed to close one of his deals quickly. A week after his note to Stevens, on October 16, he received a letter from his bank reminding him once again of the sorry state of his account balance.

On October 21, Schreiber wrote to Winfried Haastert, a member of Thyssen's executive board, to suggest that the two of them meet soon in Munich with Max Strauss about business prospects in Saudi Arabia. Strauss had excellent contacts there. In his letter Schreiber mentioned there were internal discussions in the External Affairs Department in Ottawa about the Bear Head project, but he added that he was optimistic that when Prime Minister Mulroney returned from a trip abroad, a decision would be made in its favour.

People believed him. Certainly the managers at Thyssen did, because on October 31, 1985, he received a letter from Haastert confirming a decision to advance him a C$30,000 consulting fee through Bitucan and to pay a further C$4 million for the successful completion of the Bear Head deal, this fee to be paid through IAL in Vaduz. Thyssen granted him signed authorization to negotiate for the company on Bear Head. Schreiber was to become chairman of the new Bear Head Industries Ltd.; Jürgen Massmann, the director of defence technology at Thyssen's large-vehicle division, Thyssen Henschel, would be president. Schreiber was the active executive in Canada while Massmann carried on in his duties in Germany.

9

The Swiss Accounts

Nearly eleven months had passed since Giorgio Pelossi had last found himself in Zurich, signing the contract between IAL and Airbus Industrie. On the morning of February 4, 1986, he was back again, summoned from Lugano to meet with Schreiber and a Canadian friend.

Until now, Schreiber had been cautious to the point of paranoia; although he trusted Pelossi, he still kept many secrets from him, sharing information on a need-to-know basis only. Pelossi was part of the camouflage Schreiber had put in place, so it was counterproductive for Pelossi to see the whole picture. Pelossi was quite comfortable with the arrangement; they were partners, but partners needn't know everything, and he did not envy Karlheinz his constant travelling, the hush-hush conspiracies, and the financial high-wire act.

Because Pelossi was a trustee of the Liechtenstein and Panama letterbox companies, he certainly knew about the agreements in place with Airbus, MBB, and Thyssen; in fact, he had signed two of them. He even knew, in general terms, what Schreiber planned to do with the commission money once it started to roll in: he intended to share it with some of those who had helped achieve those agreements and whose efforts had made them so lucrative. Some was to go to Schreiber, the German interests, and perhaps other players in Europe, and the rest was earmarked for Schreiber's Canadian friends. Pelossi didn't know the identity of the recipients; his job was simply to transfer the commissions to Schreiber's Zurich account. After that, Schreiber would handle the individual payments.

On this day, however, Schreiber would break his rule about keeping Pelossi one step removed from the distribution scheme. He and Pelossi had been doing business together for fifteen years, and as far as Schreiber was concerned, Pelossi was family. As the two men settled into a restaurant near Zurich's Old City, Schreiber explained why he had called Pelossi to Zurich. It was to make sure that, if necessary, his friend would know how to divide the commission money among the main recipients. Couldn't the sources of the money manage the distribution of payments? No – the Thyssen, Airbus, and MBB executives involved could not and would not do it; they didn't want to know the clandestine details of Schreiber's arrangements. Their safety was in distance, in ignorance. That's what they were paying Schreiber to handle.

This, Schreiber told Pelossi, is the formula: half was to go to the European associates, including Schreiber himself, and half to the "Canadian friends."

Schreiber did not elaborate on who was in the European group, but Pelossi suspected it had to include Franz Josef Strauss, the only man who could have ordered the contracts between Schreiber and Airbus and MBB. As for the "Canadian friends," Schreiber told Pelossi they were to arrange those details today. Schreiber said they would soon be joined by Frank Moores, whom he had also summoned to Zurich. According to Pelossi's statements to German and Canadian investigators, he and Schreiber would help Moores open two bank accounts: one for Moores himself, and the other to hold commissions intended for Brian Mulroney. Schreiber explained that the commission money was to be split between the two accounts.

Pelossi did not bat an eye. He had been hiding and transferring money for a variety of clients for years. "It is normal all over the world in such business. It didn't surprise me," Pelossi says. "It is what he told me – but I can't prove it." And Schreiber later denied telling Pelossi that any of the money was destined for Brian Mulroney.[1]

Soon enough Frank Moores appeared and they all left the restaurant, walking down the street to the Paradeplatz branch of the Swiss Bank Corporation. The three men were directed to a small office where they met Paul Schnyder, assistant to André Strobel, the senior manager who normally handled Schreiber's accounts. Schreiber made the introductions and Pelossi was handed one of Schnyder's business cards with the bank's Paradeplatz address and telephone numbers on it.

As Schreiber had said, they attended to the details of opening two new accounts. The first was number 34107 and the second 34117. Moores asked Schnyder if he could assign a name to the second account, so as to remember which was which. "Of course," replied Schnyder, who asked him for the name. "Devon," said Moores.[2]

Pelossi, the careful accountant, made a note of which account was for which man. Retrieving Schnyder's business card from his pocket, he turned it over and wrote, "F. Moore + B.M." Below that he wrote, "34107," and in a third line, "34117." Beside the second number he added "DEVON." Paul Schnyder was to leave the bank for another branch eight years later in 1994, but Pelossi kept his business card tucked away in a safe place for many years.

Schreiber, Moores, and Pelossi left the bank and went off to a good restaurant in the Old City for a celebratory meal. Although Pelossi was eager to get home to Lugano, he felt good, he said later, that Schreiber had trusted him with this information, and he had no worries about carrying out any transfers Schreiber might order. Dinner was pleasant, and over drinks Moores told Pelossi all about the fiasco with his Air Canada directorship and why he had to leave the board. "He told me he had to quit," Pelossi said, "because he couldn't be a lobbyist at the same time."

It was the press that had exposed Moores's conflict of interest, precipitating his resignation from Air Canada's board and creating the first crisis for Schreiber's small circle in Ottawa. Ten days after the Zurich meeting, the press reported another, potentially far more damaging story. On February 14, the *Globe and Mail*'s Jeffrey Simpson wrote that the cabinet was deeply split over Thyssen's plans for the Bear Head plant in Nova Scotia.

Thyssen wanted to sell a variety of armoured vehicles, including tanks, to the Canadian and U.S. armed forces. But as part of the bargain, Thyssen was insisting on a five-year export permit allowing it to conduct marketing campaigns in and ship military vehicles to Saudi Arabia, Kuwait, Pakistan, Bahrain, Algeria, and the United Arab Emirates – all normally forbidden to buy from its factories in Germany. Thyssen faced the same domestic restrictions as MBB, but its designs were held up to greater public scrutiny in Canada.

Canada had a policy prohibiting the export of arms to most countries in regions of conflict, notably the Middle East; businesses in both countries were required to apply for permits to export military equipment. But the Germans were particularly sensitive, for understandable historical reasons. The Germans had developed not just a policy but tough laws. Indeed, the strict controls on military exports were often called the "Holocaust laws." That was why Thyssen looked to Canada for a way to circumvent its home country's restrictions. Fortunately for Thyssen, the prime minister and a number of cabinet ministers – especially Sinclair Stevens and Elmer MacKay – strongly supported its proposal. Those against it were led by Joe Clark, the secretary of state for external affairs, and his opposition could not be dismissed easily. It was his department that would have to issue the export permits Thyssen needed, and he would not budge. The *Globe* story said the cabinet had debated the issue twice without coming to a resolution.

Senior federal bureaucrats had anticipated problems even before the *Globe* article appeared. While Simpson was writing his story, the deputy minister of defence, Robert Fowler, was preparing a detailed briefing note to Paul Tellier, the clerk of the Privy Council, to warn him of trouble ahead. Thyssen's request for an export permit would be, he wrote, "a departure from standard government policy." He also explained that Thyssen was moving into Cape Breton to get around West Germany's laws.

As soon as the *Globe* story appeared, Tellier briefed Mulroney on questions that might be asked in the House of Commons and provided him with background information, sent over by Sinclair Stevens's office, on the number of jobs at stake. More pressure was exerted from Nova Scotia; by February 17, both Premier Buchanan and Billy Joe Maclean, the local MLA, were protesting to Ottawa.

In a passionate letter to Stevens and other cabinet ministers who supported Thyssen, Maclean argued that Canada's export policy hadn't been changed since 1923 and was now under review; it wasn't reasonable to reject Thyssen's proposal out of hand because it violated outdated doctrine. Do not allow opposition from Quebec and Ontario politicians who are claiming political interference to deter you, he cautioned; they may be protecting the interests of their own manufacturers. "Members should not be allowed to interfere in the creation of desperately needed jobs for Cape Breton."

Tellier's briefing for the prime minister had contained considerably more information on the Thyssen proposal, much of it in a fact sheet provided by DRIE. It noted that Thyssen had two other operations in Canada: the Budd Company, in Kitchener, Ontario, with 1,400 employees, was 78 percent owned by Thyssen and produced large auto parts; Temro, a division of Budd, was based in Winnipeg, employed several hundred people, and also produced auto parts. The memo made it clear that Thyssen's plan for the first phase of Bear Head's production was to manufacture military vehicles to sell in the Middle East. In the future, it added, the company hoped to sell in other markets, including the United States. Thyssen was prepared to invest $58 million in the first phase and to hire about 450 people. The Germans wanted the Canadian and Nova Scotia governments to kick in $27 million in infrastructure costs. But there was a possible second phase, one that would expand the range of products and Thyssen's investment to $100 million with a projected workforce of 2,000.

As the politicians argued, another organization began mobilizing opposition to the Thyssen project. Sidney Spivak, a Winnipeg businessman, was the head of the Canada-Israel Committee, one of the country's most powerful Jewish lobby groups. Spivak was also a well-liked former politician. He had been the Conservative leader in Manitoba in the 1970s and had many friends in the federal party. On February 14 he issued a tough press release, saying the proposal "would hamper efforts to bring about peace between Israel and the Arab states." Any sale to Saudi Arabia would be particularly offensive to Israel, he added. Five days later he wrote to the prime minister to say he was "profoundly disturbed by this proposal," and to urge him not to let it happen.

Another senior Conservative, Douglas Roche, a former MP who had been appointed Canada's ambassador for disarmament in 1984, added his voice to Spivak's. His letter to Mulroney also opposed the plan. "An affirmative decision by the Government will set off protest across the country," he wrote. "In my view, Thyssen will become a high-flag item around which will be developed a sustained attack on the government... A negative decision on Thyssen... will make it easier to have concerned Canadians accept the slight loosening of restrictions on the export of military and strategic goods outlined in the contemplated new policy."

The uproar was a setback for Schreiber, and it could not have come at a worse time. His bank was barking at him for money, and he was in the middle of a legal battle in Alberta with Barbara Flick. Cash was tight. He owed money to Heinrich and Renate Riemerschmid, from whom he had borrowed DM1 million. Heinrich Riemerschmid, vice-president of the Bavarian chamber of commerce, had put some money into Schreiber's Alberta real estate investments, but this loan was for some other purpose. On March 17, Schreiber had Pelossi sign an agreement with the Riemerschmids on IAL's behalf, promising to turn over DM1.15 million of the MBB earnings to repay their loan with interest as soon as the MBB money arrived.

Tellier had initially told Mulroney that all Thyssen wanted from the government was $27 million in infrastructure costs – land and services, essentially – but it soon emerged that the company wanted more. In fact, Thyssen began to play hardball. In an undated memo, only a third of which could be examined following Privy Council Office censorship, Tellier informed Mulroney that Thyssen was asking for a $425-million untendered contract to supply the Canadian Forces with 250 light armoured vehicles. Thyssen believed a deal of this scale would help the company to penetrate the U.S. market. A second undated memo from Tellier to Mulroney makes this goal more explicit: "One of Thyssen's conditions is that it be chosen as sole-source contractor for one-third of DND's [the Department of National

Defence's] requirements for light armoured vehicles. Thyssen expects to export to the United States as well."

Meanwhile Schreiber incorporated and registered Bear Head Industries in Canada. His lawyer in Nova Scotia was Edmund Chiasson, Gerry Doucet's law partner in Halifax, but it was a Quebec City lawyer, Ghislaine Levasseur, Gary Ouellet's former partner there, who first registered Bear Head in Quebec City.

Late April brought a fresh blow. A few weeks after a *Globe and Mail* story raised uncomfortable conflict-of-interest questions for Sinclair Stevens, the paper published a devastating follow-up report saying that the industry minister's wife had negotiated a $26-million loan for the couple's failing business from an executive at Magna International Inc., an auto-parts company that had received $64 million in federal government assistance for two plants in Cape Breton. Day after day, ferocious questioning by opposition MPs hammered the hapless minister in Parliament and more embarrassing revelations about his personal business deals came to light. With Mulroney on an Asian tour, Deputy Prime Minister Erik Nielsen had the unpleasant task of dismissing yet another minister, and on May 12 Stevens rose in the House of Commons to announce his resignation.

Schreiber had now lost two of his strongest allies in cabinet, Bob Coates and Sinclair Stevens. Elmer MacKay was still in cabinet, but he had lost much of his power months earlier after a number of bad judgment calls. He had been demoted from solicitor general to revenue minister. The speculation around Ottawa was that the Thyssen project was doomed.

In early June 1986, Schreiber appealed to Don Mazankowski, now filling in as industry minister temporarily. Slowly, hope returned. By June 19, Joe Clark's people at External Affairs were grudgingly allowing that the deal could go ahead, but Thyssen would have to make a major concession. If the company would remove battle tanks from its export permit request, the government might look again at its proposal. Rainer Wollman, speaking for Thyssen in Ottawa, said the demand was not a problem. "Tanks were never at the centre of our proposal," he told the *Globe*'s Patrick Martin. "It is the armoured personnel carrier we would particularly like to export." Schreiber breathed a sigh of relief.

But Schreiber took nothing for granted. Whether it was shrewd-
ness, experience, or just native cunning, he had decided to buy himself
a little insurance. The Mulroney government was just two years old
and there were no guarantees it would win another election. Schreiber
had too much riding on his plans to lose his influence with the decision-makers, whoever they might be. He asked Frank Moores if he
could put him in touch with a prominent Liberal. Moores called Marc
Lalonde – a brilliant choice. Lalonde had served Pierre Trudeau as a
minister in several cabinet posts, including Justice and Finance. He
was now a senior partner at one of Canada's leading law firms,
Stikeman Elliott in Montreal, and he was a much-respected figure
without a shred of scandal to his name.

When Moores contacted him, Lalonde had no idea what he could
offer Schreiber, but he agreed to see him anyway. The meeting went
well; almost as soon as he arrived in Lalonde's office, Schreiber had
Lalonde in stitches, laughing at his anecdotes and enjoying his
company. "Schreiber certainly appeared to be a man who was a
wheeler and dealer, a man who had many irons in the fire as we say,
and seemed to be able to find his way very well," Lalonde recalled.
"And he was a very outgoing and jolly individual. Charming. He is a
great storyteller."

Schreiber told Lalonde about Bear Head and his efforts to win the
federal government's support. All Lalonde's political clout in Ottawa
had evaporated once Mulroney came to power, but after Schreiber
persuaded him that he needed his legal and general policy advice,
Lalonde agreed to join the Bear Head team. Later, when he heard the
criticisms that the project was an attempt by Thyssen to get around
German export laws, his response was practical and matter-of-fact.
"Yeah, maybe, but so what?" he said. "You have that all the time –
multinational companies establishing subsidiaries in other countries
for all kinds of purposes."

Schreiber also told Lalonde he was a lobbyist for Airbus Industrie,
and he wondered whether Lalonde could point him in the right direction. "So far as I discussed Airbus with Mr. Schreiber," Lalonde said,
"this is what I would have told him... That our experience was – my
experience, having been in the government before – that Air Canada

would make its choice on the basis of the merits of the deal" and would brook no interference from government. Schreiber did not ask Lalonde to work on the Airbus file, but on occasion he spoke to him about the challenges involved. "One thing he told me, this was a very tough fight. Boeing had a very strong lobby, but they were playing a very, very rough game."

Although Lalonde said he could only speculate about what Schreiber was doing for Airbus, he added that Schreiber was probably gathering intelligence on Air Canada and the federal politicians in Ottawa for Airbus executives in Toulouse.

Anthony Lawler, hired in January 1986 by the Airbus sales department in North America, took a serious look at its Canadian operations. He dismissed Gert Landrock. Lawler took over the Air Canada account himself from his base in New York, and by March he had closed the Canadian office. Lawler decided that at least two salesmen were needed in Canada, one for PWA and another for Air Canada, since the two airlines were vigorous competitors. Tony Morse took over the PWA and CP Air accounts.

No sooner had Lawler immersed himself in the Air Canada file than he received a call from someone named Karlheinz Schreiber, offering to help him sell Airbus planes. The two met at Schreiber's condominium in Calgary. Lawler soured on Schreiber immediately. He didn't think Schreiber would be helpful, and he believed Air Canada might resent a newcomer's involvement. "I would not touch the guy with a barge pole," he told people back at the Airbus office in the U.S. Lawler had no idea Airbus had signed a contract with a Liechtenstein company under which Schreiber would receive commissions.

In the spring of 1986, Pierre Pailleret, the Airbus vice-president with whom Schreiber had negotiated the secret commissions agreement for IAL, was replaced by Stuart Iddles. A former British Aerospace executive who had once worked in Manitoba for Saunders Aircraft, Iddles was named senior vice-president of sales and marketing for Airbus Industrie. He took over where Pailleret had left off. Soon he was on his way to Canada, meeting publicly with Air Canada and PWA executives and privately with Schreiber.

Early that summer Moores met up with an old fly-fishing buddy named Keith Miller at the Château Laurier in Ottawa. Miller, a no-nonsense Australian, was a pilot and airline economist who had been president of Eastern Provincial Airlines. Eastern flew into New-foundland, among other destinations, and Miller knew Moores from the time of his premiership. Miller also knew most of the players in the airline business; more recently he had been president of Air Atlantic, founded by the Newfoundland entrepreneur Craig Dobbin.

The meeting had been arranged by John Lundrigan, another former Newfoundland MP who had moved to Ottawa and become a lobbyist. Lundrigan told Moores he should hire both himself and Miller to help him lobby for Airbus. Lundrigan demanded that Moores pay him a commission of some sort, but Miller said he would be involved only if he was hired as an employee. Miller wanted no part of any commission deal. Lundrigan, for his part, eventually went to work for Boeing.

Moores wanted to enlist Miller's expertise. As an airline economist with a stellar reputation, Miller would be a prime candidate for the Airbus team. The two men talked for several hours and agreed to meet again the next time Stuart Iddles of Airbus was in Canada.

Miller met Schreiber only once, on a visit to the GCI offices, where he was told Schreiber represented Franz Josef Strauss, though it was unclear exactly what that meant. Schreiber seemed to have little inter-est in Miller, although he gave his blessing to any potential relation-ship: "If you are recommended by Frank, that's okay with me." For his part Miller was not keen on Schreiber. "He was your typical 10 percent man," Miller later told friends. He nicknamed him "Herman the German."

Eventually Miller met with Moores and Iddles over breakfast at one of the anonymous hotels on the airport strip. Iddles, who knew of Miller and would have been delighted to have him on board, did not need to be convinced that Miller could play an important role in persuading Air Canada of the economic benefits of choosing Airbus. He told Miller to get a lawyer and draw up a contract, and he invited him to Toulouse for a full briefing. Then, late for his next appoint-ment, Iddles rose to his feet. He told Miller he was seeing Max Ward.

Miller never did go with Airbus, but became a consultant for Boeing instead.

Schreiber was juggling the three Canadian projects: Thyssen, MBB, and Airbus. The MBB deal bore fruit in June with the opening of the new MCL facility at Fort Erie, an enterprise to which the federal government alone had contributed $42 million, and the official confirmation of the company's largest sale: twelve BO 105 helicopters to the Canadian Coast Guard. On behalf of the Canadian government, the Conservative MP for Erie, Girve Fretz, proudly signed the contract for a projected cost of $24 million, though the final tally would be considerably higher. Transport Minister Don Mazankowski issued a press release trumpeting the purchase a week later.

In any other circumstances, Jim Grant, MBB's senior marketing executive in Ottawa, could have rightly congratulated himself for a job well done. He had been an energetic representative of MBB's interests for years, knew every minister and bureaucrat who could affect his employer's fortunes, and had steadfastly adhered to a straightforward sales pitch. But Grant knew there was something afoot with Karlheinz Schreiber and Frank Moores. For starters, he had never felt comfortable with the MBB head office's decision to hire Moores's firm at $6,000 a month to do exactly what he himself was doing. And Schreiber's apparent status with his bosses, not to mention an imperious manner with MBB employees, grated. In early July Schreiber even asked Grant, a vice-president, to make travel arrangements for him, requesting reservations at Vancouver's high-priced Westin Bayshore. He told Grant to have a helicopter ready in Vancouver, as he had some "important friends" he wanted to impress.

Grant's unease was shared by Helge Wittholz, the president of MCL. Wittholz had worked with Kurt Pfleiderer at head office in Munich and was rewarded with the plum appointment to Canada in 1984. Wittholz and his family enjoyed Canada so much that they vowed to become Canadian citizens as early as they could. Only two weeks after the signing of the Coast Guard deal, he learned about a secret contract between the head office in Germany and IAL in Liechtenstein to pay commissions on the helicopter deal he had signed. Wittholz was horrified since he had already promised, in writing, that no commissions would be paid. He believed the agreement was illegal and quickly called the head office in Munich. During an 8 a.m. telephone call with Munich, one of the company's lawyers told Wittholz that the IAL contract "was not illegal if they did not pay money here" – that is, if the money didn't come from MCL's budget. Wittholz was not convinced. Neither was Grant.

But their concerns did not register with the Germans. On July 22, 1986, Kurt Pfleiderer confirmed that MBB would send a down payment of C$767,283 to IAL at the end of September – provided that MBB had received its initial payment from the Canadian government. It was a red-letter day for Schreiber.

Giorgio Pelossi was also pleased that the first of the secret commissions from Canadian deals were about to flow into IAL's accounts in Liechtenstein. His job was to forward the funds to Schreiber's personal account in Zurich. Unfortunately he would not get the chance. On September 11, Pelossi was arrested by Swiss police and detained without charge. He was suspected of swindling money from a bank account belonging to someone laundering drug money for the Mafia.

No one knew how long the authorities would keep him in jail, so in early October he asked his secretary, Myriam Clara, to write to MBB to arrange for the commissions to be deposited directly into Schreiber's account 18679 in Zurich. Pelossi's arrest was troubling news for Schreiber, but not completely surprising. Possible links to the Mafia went with the territory of hiding other people's money. Schreiber kept Pelossi on as his trustee.

On October 7, MBB wired C$641,283 to Schreiber's Zurich account 18679, having deducted $126,000 to cover GCI's share. All of it would go to repay the Riemerschmids' loan.

Wittholz continued to stew and on December 17 he called a meeting to discuss the commissions. Heinz Pluckthun, the president of the helicopter and military division of MBB, Pfleiderer, the vice-president of marketing, Wittholz, and Hans Mülhloff, vice-president of finance, gathered in Munich. Wittholz let it be known he believed the commissions were "illegal and unnecessary." Pfleiderer, who fully supported the commissions and thought they were absolutely necessary, strongly denied they were illegal. There was an unresolved discussion as to which company would pay them – the branch plant in Canada or headquarters in Munich – and the question of how the commissions had affected the price charged to the Coast Guard was raised. For his part, Pfleiderer was beginning to think his old friend Wittholz had spent too much time in Canada. It was as if the Canadians thought they owned the company. The colony was becoming a headache.

Wittholz had liked and admired Pfleiderer, but he was not prepared to buckle under the pressure from head office. He couldn't think of a single reason why MBB should pay these commissions. "It doesn't make any sense. Why is this being done?" he asked Pfleiderer again and again. "What is this all about?"

In October 1986, Patrick Croze, the president of Airbus Industrie's North American operation, resigned his high-profile post. Airbus had hired Croze in 1983, impressed by his charm, energy, and ideas, but the chemistry between Croze and Jean Pierson had never been good since Pierson's arrival in Toulouse the previous year. The final split, which was particularly acrimonious, came when Croze argued against Pierson's plan to move the U.S. headquarters from New York to Herndon, Virginia.

Croze, the man in charge of marketing Airbus in North America, knew nothing about the agreement between IAL and Airbus for commissions on sales of the A320 in Canada. In fact, he knew nothing about Schreiber at all. As one airline insider explained, "You would think that if such an agreement existed he would know about it. But if such an agreement existed, the organization might want to take particular precautions so that he would not hear about it. He was the guy most exposed – as the company president in the United States, the only part of the world where such an agreement would be totally illegal."

As Christmas approached, the Airbus play accelerated. Lucien Bouchard, a lawyer from Chicoutimi, Quebec, one of Mulroney's closest associates, was then Canada's ambassador to France and, not surprisingly, was well versed on Airbus. According to one airline executive, he agreed to meet with Moores and Ouellet in the PMO, where the GCI partners hoped to set the internal game plan on how to persuade Air Canada and the government to buy the planes. Their cause would be helped if Airbus could secure a sale to another Canadian carrier. The likeliest candidate was Wardair: Max Ward had recently been negotiating with Boeing for the purchase of twelve Boeing 767s. If he could be sold Airbus 310-312s instead, Airbus would gain priceless credibility with Air Canada.

At about the same time, Brian Walker, a senior executive at Wardair, was in a meeting with Max Ward when a call came in from someone at Airbus. Ward, who had already given Boeing a deposit for US$1 million, told his caller, "We've made a deal, we can't go back on our deal. I am sorry." His caller kept him on the phone, and Ward rolled his eyes at Walker. After he rang off, he said that Airbus was still determined to get his order.

So determined that, according to Schreiber himself, he knew he had to go straight to the top. He called Franz Josef Strauss. Max Ward needs help with his financing, he said. "Can you give assistance to Wardair?" Schreiber didn't hesitate to tell this story; he wanted people to know how far his influence reached. He said he had been a friend of Ward's since the Alberta days. "From there started a relationship," said Schreiber. "I really tried to help him. I look at him as a friend. Yes, I like the guy a lot because he impresses me, what he did. And yes, I must say he is a good man."

Despite Moores's repeated public assertions that he did not lobby for Airbus, Schreiber himself stated that Moores was very much involved in the Wardair effort, as did a Wardair insider who described Moores's aggressive lobbying as "a hard sell." However, Ward denied it. "I didn't meet Karl Schreiber until we had made the deal and everything was done." And Moores? "We hardly knew him . . . He had nothing to do with it at all." Ward was surprisingly candid on another matter, though: what he had to do to be successful in the airline business in the Far East or Central and South America.

"We used to fly to Mexico, and we had to have a little something in the pocket to get our landing rights and all those good things. But it was chicken feed. It wasn't big money."

Once Strauss had been briefed on the problem, the strategy was sharp and swift: give Ward a deal he couldn't turn down. Stuart Iddles met Ward in Toronto just before Christmas and took the price of a dozen A310-312s down so low that Ward had to think hard about his commitment to Boeing.

"Max wasn't a guy to go back on his word," said Brian Walker. "But it's not just the price of the airplane. It's all the other stuff they throw in with it... But from a price point of view, Airbus was just determined Ward was going to buy it."

When Walker found out that Ward had finally decided to ask Boeing to return his US$1-million deposit, he was not pleased. "I was not in love with the plane," he recalled. He believed the Airbus 310-312 was overengineered for the sort of charter business that had been Ward's strength, and that it would require extra maintenance, a significant consideration given that Airbus's after-sales service was deemed less satisfactory than Boeing's. "It was totally wrong for what we were trying to do," Walker said.

Boeing executives agreed to return Ward's deposit, but they were dismayed. They were more concerned than ever about the Air Canada contract. Stories were floating around that GCI was quietly lobbying senior officials in the Prime Minister's Office to support an order. One tale involved Charlie McMillan, a senior economic adviser in the PMO (his brother Tom McMillan was a cabinet minister). McMillan confided to a friend that Gary Ouellet of GCI had approached him privately to convince him that the Airbus proposal was better than Boeing's. McMillan would later deny it.

Moores's annual Christmas "Screech-in" was a notorious event in Ottawa, a crowded, noisy party held in the GCI offices at 50 O'Connor. Tory MPs, senators, chiefs of staff, Progressive Conservative Party apparatchiks, members of the Prime Minister's Office, a few bureaucrats, other lobbyists, and a handful of journalists (they had to be careful; Moores was considered "mad, bad, and dangerous") would stream in and grab a drink, hoping to avoid the lethal Newfoundland brew being handed around. People traded information like hard currency, swapping, hinting, and begging, snatching the details of contracts and deals, patronage appointments, or bureaucratic plums, people in trouble, or people on the make. The Air Canada contract was the talk of the party. Was the sale going to Boeing again? Or was the gang at Airbus in the lead?

Transport Minister Don Mazankowski held a Christmas party too that year, and many of the same guests were in attendance, along with an extra layer of airline, railroad, shipping, and trucking executives. The talk at this gathering was Wardair. They knew Max Ward had put a million dollars down on a dozen new Boeing jets for his growing charter business. But with no public announcement yet made, there was a story on the wind that he had just changed his mind, that he had second thoughts about the noise of the Boeing air-conditioning systems – and that he had jumped to Airbus.

Merv Cronie, Boeing's Ottawa representative, was slightly combative at the best of times. That night he was livid. He regarded Airbus's tactics to win Ward's business as despicable, and he didn't hesitate to share his views with anyone he could buttonhole. One of the people he told, again and again, on their morning jogs together was Tom Niles, the American ambassador to Canada. Those Germans will stop at nothing, he'd complain. Niles was extremely concerned; he was getting the same information from other sources.

Schreiber, grinning and gloating, was at the minister's party that night, and so was Mazankowski's air transportation adviser, Fred von Veh, one of the original partners in Alta Nova before it was sold to Frank Moores. Max Ward showed up too, looking sheepish but pleased. When Keith Miller, who had made his move to Boeing and come to Ottawa from Florida for the affair, tried to weave through the crowd to speak to Ward, Elmer MacKay and some of his friends blocked his way. Miller didn't know until then that MacKay had gone to the airport to pick up Ward and would drive him back to the airport later. The Airbus lobby would give no one the chance to persuade Ward to return to Boeing.

Finally Miller got through to Ward. "Any chance you'll change your mind again?" he asked the embarrassed businessman.

"No," Ward replied.

On Boxing Day, Thyssen transferred C$1.5 million to Schreiber's bank account in Zurich to cover any costs he might incur in arranging the Bear Head project. Thyssen agreed to loan him this C$1.5 million personally, not through IAL or any other Liechtenstein shell, and it would be unrelated to the contingency fees.

If he could pull off the Thyssen deal, the rewards would be sweet. But he still had a big job ahead of him. Thyssen wanted him to open markets for its military products in Canada, the U.S., and the Middle East, and Schreiber first had to guarantee a production facility in Canada, one that would be heavily subsidized by the governments of Canada and Nova Scotia.

10

Flying High

The worst-kept secret in aviation circles became public on January 16, 1987, when Wardair officially announced the purchase of a dozen Airbus 310-312s for its charter fleet. The deal, valued at US$675 million, was unveiled during the two-day visit to Edmonton of the French foreign minister, Jean-Bernard Raimond. To pay for the planes, Wardair planned to sell seven airliners from its current fleet, run a public share offering, and borrow from European banks.

The Canadian public paid no attention to any of this; they were avidly following yet another federal cabinet scandal, this one involving the junior transport minister, André Bissonnette, who was fired on January 18. Bissonnette was involved in $3 million worth of land flips when the Swiss arms manufacturer Oerlikon Aerospace announced it was building a plant in his riding. In February, Roch LaSalle left the cabinet over smelly contract deals during his tenure as public works minister as well as his ties to organized crime figures in Montreal.

These eruptions cost the Mulroney government its popularity at the polls and led to speculation about the Conservatives' chances in the next election. In the offices of MBB Helicopter Canada (MCL), they aroused nervousness: if the government changed, might the details of some of its procurement deals come up for re-examination?

Barbecuing Kaufering-style:
An experienced cook, Schreiber loved to
dress in traditional Bavarian lederhosen
and prepare barbecue treats for friends.
(Private collection)

Clowning around: Schreiber invited friends
from around the world to his carnival party;
here he dons a clown outfit while former
Alberta cabinet minister William Dickie opts
for the Mexican look. (Private collection)

Winding up: Wearing a party hat, Alberta cabinet minister Hugh Horner takes aim in
Schreiber's private basement bowling alley. (Private collection)

Not amused: Premier Peter Lougheed, shown in 1985, forbade his senior staff from doing business with Schreiber after a disastrous dinner in Switzerland. (*Alberta Report*)

Bavaria forever: Horst Schmid, a former Alberta cabinet minister and fellow Bavarian, shown in 1985, became one of Schreiber's strongest allies in Lougheed's government. (*Alberta Report*)

Flying high: Schreiber and his business partner Giorgio Pelossi aloft in an Alberta government jet – without the premier's knowledge. (Private collection)

Day trippers: Proud new Albertans, Pelossi and Schreiber show their friend Max Strauss some of their adopted province's best scenery at Château Lake Louise. (Private collection)

The Lion of Bavaria: Schreiber's mentor, Franz Josef Strauss, was a butcher's son but became a wealthy, powerful politician determined to help German business win contracts in Canada. (Bonn-Sequenz)

Ever faithful: Alberta lawyer Bobby Hladun has acted for Schreiber for more than twenty years, stickhandling his business affairs in Canada and in Europe. (CP)

Assignment Mexico: Schreiber, here with Max Strauss, did a little business for the BND, Germany's intelligence agency, in Central America. (Michael Stiller)

A powerful ear: Luis Alberto Monge, president-elect of Costa Rica, and his wife, Doris, on inauguration day in 1982. Monge encouraged Schreiber's business and political interests in his country. (AP)

Matchmaker: Michel Cogger, brushing past reporters, met Schreiber through his clients, the Strauss family. He introduced Schreiber to the Mulroney crowd in Montreal. (CP)

At the top of his game: Former Liberal finance minister Marc Lalonde, seen in 1984, began working for Schreiber in 1986 and tried to persuade Prime Minister Jean Chrétien to go ahead with the Bear Head project. (CP)

In control: Claude Taylor, then president of Air Canada, sits at the controls of a Boeing 767 in Montreal in 1982. (CP)

Kings of the Hill: (left to right) Gary Ouellet, Gerry Doucet, Francis Fox, and Frank Moores of the infamous lobbying firm GCI stroll in front of Parliament Hill in 1985. Fox, a former Liberal cabinet minister, became a member of the group that year. (Private collection)

No way: Paul Tellier, clerk of the Privy Council in Ottawa, seen in 1994, engaged in an acrimonious exchange of letters with Schreiber over the Bear Head project in Nova Scotia. (*Maclean's*)

Banquet in Bonn: On June 13, 1991, Helmut Kohl hosted a state banquet for Brian Mulroney at the Schaumburg Palace. Although his name was not on the guest list, Schreiber was there – at the far left of the picture, on the side opposite Mulroney, near the end of the table. (Bundesbild)

So rattled was Jim Grant in the early months of 1987 that when he received a call from CBC Television's business show, *Venture*, he made a note in his files. *Venture* simply wanted to interview Grant about how companies such as his successfully conduct business with government, how the tendering process works, and so on, but Grant was alarmed by the interest. MBB had outside lobbyists, he wrote in his memo; it also had a "friend of the PM's on the board of directors." In fact, MBB "have not had a contract that was let for tender"; the Coast Guard deal was a "directed contract." He believed that the cost of the commissions paid to Schreiber would have been factored into the cost to the Coast Guard.

At the end of February, Grant and Wittholz together prepared and signed a memo to their German bosses that recorded their concerns about the entire Coast Guard deal and how it might affect their company's future. They relayed the stories they were hearing that money from Bavaria had somehow ended up in the secret campaign to install Mulroney as leader of the Progressive Conservative Party; in their minds, the issue was becoming increasingly serious. "The areas that are most dangerous at this particular time are . . . associations with patronage friends of the Prime Minister; retention of the friends of the Prime Minister on boards of directors; any indication of foreign involvement; any indication of foreign money that goes into party funds, directly or indirectly."

Their memo continued with a sweeping warning: "It is strongly recommended that we have a supportable position correct in legal, moral and business terms to deal with our ongoing relationships. Any sort of scandal at the present time, even of a minimal nature, could prejudice the Sea King Programme, the CFLH [Canadian Forces Light Helicopter] Programme, the Coast Guard programme, any Airbus sales, any other business ventures that would be tried by MBB. The mood of the business community is becoming more negative to the government. It is quite probable that Boeing will be extremely aggressive in any future Airbus sales and it will go to all means to determine any relationship that exists, whether it is through Germany or France, in connection with any lobbying efforts on behalf of Airbus." Grant and Wittholz understood very well how closely MBB and Airbus were linked. Both were partially owned by the Bavarian government, and Franz Josef Strauss was a senior member of both companies' boards of directors.

Eventually the picture was made even clearer to the Canadian executives by Kurt Pfleiderer: Schreiber's secret commissions had more to do with events prior to the 1984 election than with his connections after it to the victorious Conservatives. Schreiber had been involved in the effort to wrestle control of the Tory party away from Joe Clark and into the hands of Brian Mulroney; it had been an expensive undertaking and there were debts to be settled.

Wittholz, a relative newcomer to Canada, knew nothing about the dump-Clark movement and needed to have the story explained slowly. Schreiber had donated serious money to the cause, funds that paid for anti-Clark delegates to travel to Winnipeg by chartered jet, that provided a bit of spending money while they were there, that ensured they voted Clark out as leader. Where did Schreiber's money come from? According to the story, it came from the Hanns-Seidel-Stiftung, the foreign branch of the CSU. Wittholz was told that the funds had been sent with the knowledge of Franz Josef Strauss, with whom Schreiber was close. The Bavarians' expectations were simple: if Mulroney came to power, they anticipated that business from Canada would flow their way. And with that business would come secret commissions that would, in part, find their way back to the CSU. Pfleiderer did not say if he knew where the rest of the commission money would end up. It was a story for which neither Grant nor Wittholz had any proof, but it made sense, at last, of the commissions MBB was paying.

While MBB's BO 105 helicopters were being delivered on a steady, almost monthly schedule to the Coast Guard throughout 1987, the two men grew more angry than nervous. They intended to challenge Kurt Pfleiderer at a breakfast meeting at the Château Laurier in Ottawa on October 4, 1987. Jim Grant and Heinz Pluckthun had settled themselves in the "gold key" floor's dining room when Pfleiderer and Helge Wittholz joined them. Grant got straight to the point and said he was considering leaving MBB altogether. Wittholz expressed his personal disappointment with Pfleiderer. Pfleiderer could stand it no longer. "If you don't like what we're doing, then you should go sell ballpoint pens!" he shouted.

They were never going to agree, and the moment passed. Grant and Pluckthun returned to their Ottawa office. Wittholz and Pfleiderer joined Moores for a speedy drive to Montreal, where they would meet with Don Lowe, a vice-president of Canadair. They travelled in Moores's limo. While Moores busied himself with his radar detector, Pfleiderer sat in the back with Wittholz and tried to patch up the spat. "This kind of thing goes on all over the world," he told Wittholz, adding that he had been involved in such secret deals many times, in other countries.

Public scandals like the Bissonnette and LaSalle affairs, along with others involving fundraisers and party backroom organizers, disturbed many senior Conservatives, and they began blaming the prime minister's staff. Even Frank Moores was telling Mulroney that he'd made a bad mistake in appointing so many old friends to senior jobs in the PMO when they had no political experience. Mulroney was loath to turn anyone out but finally bowed to pressure, and before long several individuals had departed. They included Peter White, who had been responsible for running the patronage and appointments machine; Fred Doucet, who had alienated half of Ottawa with his abrupt style and was rewarded with a newly created post, ambassador of international summit planning; the economic adviser Charlie McMillan, who returned to university teaching; the communications director, Bill Fox, famous for his combative style and hot temper, who became a lobbyist; and the caucus liaison chief, Pat MacAdam, was sent to a senior job at the High Commission in London.

When a reporter asked Moores if Mulroney could fix all the problems before the next election, Moores replied, "I'm not sure. I don't know really. At this stage I have severe doubts."

In later years, this exchange would be cited by Mulroney's allies as evidence that he and Moores had quarrelled and their friendship had been irreparably fractured. It was said that Mulroney never completely forgave him for his comments. Still, it is the case that Mulroney continued to include Moores in private social gatherings of his intimates. Fully two years later, Moores and his wife, Beth, were among the celebrants at Mulroney's fiftieth-birthday party on March 20, 1989.

A falling-out, however slight, between Mulroney and Moores might have presented a problem for GCI, a company that billed itself as tight with the government. In reality it wasn't an issue. Moores was spending less time running GCI anyway, and Gary Ouellet became the company's chairman. Ouellet and Mulroney respected and admired each other, and unlike Moores, Ouellet kept his cards close to his chest. Whatever had really happened between Mulroney and Moores, one thing was clear, according to a Tory insider: increasingly the contact between the PMO and GCI was "through Gary."

In early 1987 another Schreiber associate ran into difficulties in Bonn. Jürgen Massmann, the senior Thyssen Henschel official who was involved with him in Bear Head Industries, was in serious trouble. On February 3 and 4, following a tip from moles in the German Ministry of Defence, the ministry's security service searched Massmann's office and found fifty-four sensitive Ministry of Defence documents, all concerning federal defence projects, all documents that Massmann, as a supplier soliciting contracts from the ministry, should never have seen. Another search, this one at the offices of Heinrich Grosser, head of a department called Pre-development of Military Vehicles in the Ministry of Defence, uncovered another cache of confidential documents. Massmann was questioned about the documents on February 26, 1987; he answered with reluctance and as briefly as possible.

Over the next few months, suspicious investigators tried to find out more, but neither Massmann nor his colleague Winfried Haastert, a Thyssen director, would talk. Finally they interviewed Schreiber. He defended Massmann as an honourable man and said they were working on a deal together which could be worth US$100 billion in tank orders for Bear Head. The investigators remained wary, and Massmann was forbidden by the Defence Ministry to work on any of its projects.

By March 1987 many familiar faces were gone from the Prime Minister's Office, replaced by a team chosen by Derek Burney, the new chief of staff. The prime minister made another senior appointment at this time: Donald McPhail, Canada's ambassador to West Germany, was named president of a new federal government agency called the Atlantic Canada Opportunities Agency (ACOA), with its own subsidiary granting agency, Enterprise Cape Breton. It seemed like a puzzling shift for a career diplomat, although McPhail's German experience gave him the right background to consider the Thyssen deal.

Things began to fall neatly into place. For starters, Giorgio Pelossi was released on March 11 from the Swiss jail where he had spent six long months without ever being charged. Also that month, Cliff MacKay, recently promoted to assistant deputy minister at DRIE, met with Schreiber, Greg Alford, Jürgen Massmann, and Klaus Sonneck, in charge of sales and marketing for Thyssen Henschel, to discuss the Bear Head project. And at the end of March, Schreiber met with the ever-patient Hans Reiter at the Sparkasse Landsberg to report that Thyssen would shortly pay him between C$2 million and C$3 million for his efforts in Cape Breton.

Back in Ottawa in the summer, Schreiber's years of plotting and manoeuvring and hustling began to pay off. On June 3, 1987, Airbus amended its contract with IAL to increase certain commission rates and extend the agreement. The total commissions for the much-hoped-for Air Canada deal could pile up to as much as US$30,340,000. Then, a little over a month later, on July 7, MBB paid another C$130,478 directly to Schreiber's Zurich account and sent C$353,403.52 to Moores at GCI from the helicopter sale to the Canadian Coast Guard.

But Schreiber and his associates in Germany could not afford to be complacent. For nearly a year Boeing had known the Air Canada contract would be a nasty fight; now Thyssen's competitors also began to wake up. In an August 27 briefing note for the minister of national defence, Perrin Beatty, deputy minister Bev Dewar pointed out that the Thyssen armoured personnel carrier was unlikely to appeal to the U.S. government. There were other competitors, Dewar said, who were better qualified; and as if to prove his point, the next day two worried officials from General Motors, Bill Pettipas and Bill Kienapple, visited DND officials to explain why their products were superior.

On October 30, 1987, Schreiber's Bear Head project took an important step forward when the Nova Scotia government, under Premier John Buchanan, committed itself to the Bear Head project with offers of free land, free servicing, and other inducements.

Although Schreiber received a letter on November 12 from Winfried Haastert confirming a payment to IAL of C$4 million as soon as both Canadian governments signed a "letter of intent" – which is an agreement in principle to proceed with a deal – there were hints of trouble between Thyssen and federal officials. Thyssen wanted even more land, more infrastructure costs, more guaranteed contracts; Ottawa wanted more jobs and more investment. The parties couldn't come to a resolution and Schreiber grew impatient. He needed funds from Thyssen immediately, and he directed Pelossi to write to a company director, Ernst Höffken, requesting his promised advance of C$1.9 million. They were sure the letter of intent would be in Thyssen's hands early in the new year.

On December 22, Schreiber looked after some corporate house-keeping, informing his contacts at Thyssen that he had sold Bear Head Industries to them and they owed him C$100,000 for it. This was a long-planned move, with payment built into the C$4-million fee, that had avoided complications when Bear Head was first established; it had been simpler for Schreiber to incorporate a company in Canada under his ownership. The next day Thyssen transferred C$100,000 directly to him, and Haastert and Höffken initiated the transfer of the C$1.9-million advance to him through IAL as an "honorarium."

"If we have decided therefore to meet your request to accelerate the release of payment on account," Haastert said in a letter to Pelossi dated December 28, "it is only done realizing that you expressly guarantee that the remaining prerequisites will be met in the near future."

A day or two later, Haastert saw that he'd made a serious mistake. His December 28 letter mentioned the payment of contingency fees to IAL, and specifically to Schreiber. This could be a damaging admission, should it be discovered; Schreiber had worked hard to hide his connection to IAL. Haastert quickly pulled the offending page and substituted another in the files that mentioned only IAL. But he kept his word about the money. On December 30, Thyssen sent C$1.9 million to IAL in Vaduz as an advance on the contingency fees for the Bear Head deal.

According to Pelossi, Schreiber also kept his word. "I had a phone call from Schreiber just before Christmas and I made a note of it," Pelossi explained. "In that note it says, '$500,000 for Winfried Haastert.' I didn't give Haastert the money personally. Schreiber gave it. I just withdrew the money... on January 3, and then I went with Schreiber and put it into a safety deposit box at the LGT Bank in Liechtenstein. Two days later he told me Haastert would come to Vaduz in the next two or three days to pick up the money. It came from the first two million we got from Thyssen."

Haastert used his funds, Pelossi discovered, to buy an apartment in Lugano. The rest of the Thyssen payment, Pelossi said, was divided further: $100,000 went to Max Strauss as a forgivable "loan," which Strauss turned over to a company in Munich called Dieter Klein Elektronik. There was $50,000 for Bobby Hladun, paid through Bitucan in Calgary, and $50,000 for Pelossi. Another $100,000 went to pay off a loan at a Schweizerische Kreditanstalt branch in Bellinzona; $75,000 was for Schreiber directly. And $1 million went to pay Schreiber's debts with Hans Reiter's bank.

It was a very happy New Year for a lot of people. Moores surprised Ottawa by persuading the top civil servant in the Department of Transport, Ramsey Withers, to join GCI. Withers, who as deputy minister had reported to Don Mazankowski, was a great catch. Moores and his wife, Beth, celebrated the New Year with the Mulroneys and a group of close friends at the prime minister's official country house at Harrington Lake in the Gatineau Hills. Gary Ouellet was there, as were Lee Richardson and Bill Fox, both now lobbyists in the capital. Schreiber returned to Germany to be with his family.

But 1988 would present challenges to all these men. Mulroney's mandate was running out, and the Tories would have to fight a federal election within the year. There was real concern that they could lose their parliamentary majority and a chance that they would lose power altogether. In Schreiber's view, it was essential that the current government approve the Air Canada contract and the Thyssen project as soon as possible. His cabinet allies, the people around Mulroney, and the men at GCI had the same goals. He redoubled his efforts.

In Ottawa, information is gold, and those hungriest for it are opposition politicians eager to reveal, usually with much feigned indignation, any evidence of government wrongdoing. By February, the opposition was well briefed on lobbying efforts by Airbus and even better informed on Ramsey Withers's move to Moores's shop.

John Crosbie, the new minister of transport, lumbered to his feet to tell the Commons that Withers had had nothing to do with Air Canada's fleet replacement plan while he was deputy minister. This was a man, he told the House, "of complete integrity, honour, faithful service, and rectitude," who was not privy to Air Canada's secrets.

Unfortunately, this wasn't the whole story; Withers had been aware of Air Canada's impending fleet purchase. In fact, on December 27, 1987, Withers wrote a letter to Ian MacDonald, an aerospace industry consultant, describing MacDonald's understanding of Air Canada's fleet plans as "inaccurate in some areas." He was far more familiar with the Air Canada situation than Crosbie suggested.

Crosbie himself drew unwelcome scrutiny for his relationship with Moores. A fellow Newfoundlander, he was a frequent visitor to Birch Point, Moores's weekend home near Chaffeys Locks, a resort area about an hour and a half's drive southwest of Ottawa. He was there so often with his family, a neighbour told the *Toronto Star*, that people thought he was related to Moores. When the newspaper asked Crosbie about the visits, he was furious.

"It has no relevance," Crosbie snapped at the reporter. "Frank was smart enough not to make any representation directly to me." In the same exchange Crosbie said he knew Moores was an Airbus lobbyist. A few days later he called the *Star* to say he'd made an error: Moores was not lobbying for Airbus.

As Air Canada's decision approached, Schreiber and Airbus agreed to another amendment to the IAL agreement that ruled out any commissions to Schreiber on the Wardair sale. In doing so, Airbus stated that on its own it had made "substantial financial efforts" to win the Wardair contract and to persuade Max Ward to cancel his Boeing order.

Still, Schreiber wasn't unhappy. The latest amendment broadened the scope of the original agreement: instead of receiving commissions

France launches Airbus fraud probe

French authorities have opened a preliminary investigation into **Airbus Group SE** over allegations of fraudulent practices in selling planes and arranging financing.

The probe by the Parquet National Financier follows steps by Britain's Serious Fraud Office in August, 2016, to look into possible fraud, bribery and corruption in Airbus's civil-aviation business related to third-party consultants, the company said. The two authorities will co-ordinate with one another, Airbus said. Airbus said it will co-operate fully.

The Toulouse, France-based plane maker had flagged to British regulators and the European Export Credit Agencies last year "misstatements and omissions" involving outside contractors in some export financing applications, which it found through an internal probe.

Bloomberg News

Natural Resources Canada pegged the

FROM PAGE 1

on just three types of Airbus aircraft, the A300, the A310, and the A320, he would now also receive commissions on sales of Airbus Industrie's two newest products, the A330 and the A340. The latest version of the contract was far more generous than the one Pelossi had first signed.

There was so much gossip about the negotiations that even within Airbus itself, some employees were nervous. It wasn't the executives in Toulouse who were concerned, but rather a group at the new four-storey chrome and glass building that housed the American Airbus headquarters in Herndon, Virginia.

The North American sales force was right to be alert. When a three-year Congressional investigation had reported that more than four hundred American companies had admitted to paying over $300 million in bribes to foreign officials, Congress passed the Foreign Corrupt Practices Act in 1977. The new act strictly forbade American companies from paying bribes to win contracts in other countries, but it didn't please everybody. Some American businesses complained that it put them at a competitive disadvantage. They argued, in effect, that they should be allowed to pay bribes like everyone else, or that international law should be changed to prohibit their competitors from paying bribes.[1]

For the moment, however, the reality was that American citizens could go to jail if they were part of an illegal kickback or bribery scheme in their companies. Simply the knowledge of a possible secret commission deal was enough to cause anxiety in the minds of some employees. And in the months leading up to the Air Canada purchase, that's exactly what happened at the Airbus offices in Herndon.

Anthony Lawler, the Airbus salesman responsible for the Air Canada campaign, had devoted himself to the effort for two years. Not only did he have to be familiar with the complex technical aspects of the aircraft, he also had to be pleasant and persuasive, willing to schmooze the dozens of Air Canada officials involved in the decision-making process.

Lawler had reason to be optimistic. Though Airbus might still be viewed as an upstart manufacturer by some, it was making noticeable inroads into North America with modest sales to smaller American airlines. It was also enjoying a more favourable press in the business pages. Industry observers tended to agree that Airbus's innovative technology produced a quieter, more traveller-friendly airplane than the Boeing alternative. The A320 was fuel-efficient; while it may have been slightly more expensive to buy, Air Canada would save money in the long run. Lawler was thrilled to be selling this plane, and he could tell from the reception at Air Canada that he had a reasonable shot at winning the order. He was in daily contact with Air Canada personnel, and he was frequently joined by John Leahy, Airbus's senior vice-president of marketing in North America.

But late in the game, on a trip to Montreal in the spring of 1988, Lawler heard a story that gave him a sick feeling in the pit of his stomach. An Air Canada vice-president told Lawler about a call he'd taken from Frank Moores. Moores purported to be a lobbyist for Airbus Industrie, but the Air Canada executive could not help laughing when Moores had to ask him the type of aircraft he was supposed to be selling. Recalling the incident years later, Lawler would not name the vice-president but said the conversation sounded more like the way deals got done in Africa, South America, and "the Arab world." Lawler said Moores never once called him.

Lawler also heard a rumour that Airbus money was being paid to Canadians to facilitate the transaction. If true, it was shocking news for Lawler, who knew nothing about any such scheme. *He* was the one who had worked on the deal since 1986, day in and day out, and now it seemed he had been out of the loop all along. If this rumour was true, Airbus had been acting on the edge of the law, or even over the edge. He worried about the North American operation – and about himself. If he was aware of possible criminal activity and appeared to go along with it, he could be in trouble too.

Lawler flew back to Washington, D.C., and, still upset, drove straight to Herndon, fifteen minutes away, with some questions for his boss, Tom Ronell. Ronell had worked at Northwest Airlines and then at McDonnell Douglas as a financial analyst before landing in a vice-president's corner office at Airbus. Until Lawler barged into his office, Ronell had no inkling that anything irregular was under way in the

Canadian market. He had heard a lot of stories about how planes were sold around the world, but never something like this on North American soil.

Lawler told him he was troubled by what he had heard. Ronell thanked Lawler for coming forward, but he wasn't sure what to do. Could Airbus really be paying people off? Uncertain what to do next, Ronell confided in his friend Jay Zito, another Airbus salesman who had gained his trust and often served as a kind of sounding board.

"This is heavy shit," Zito told Ronell; it was far too serious for staff at their level. They decided to keep in touch and share any information they heard. As the weeks went on, there were more rumours, one that pegged the secret Airbus payoff at C$34 million. If this number was accurate, Ronell knew that that much money didn't arrive in one person's bank account without the expectation that it would be spread around. Zito told Ronell he should pick up the phone and call Bob Woodward of the *Washington Post*. Ronell didn't call Woodward, but he did arrange a meeting with Allan Boyd, a former politician and former chairman of the Civil Aviation Board, who was then the chairman of Airbus North America.

At first, Boyd listened patiently as Ronell revealed that some of the staff were upset about the stories circulating in Canada. As he laid out his concerns, Ronell tried to be professional – but tact was never one of his strong points. Finally he gave up trying. "What the hell's going on?" he blurted. Boyd, the consummate politician, kept his cool and thanked Ronell for his concerns.

The next day was a different matter. Ronell was called into the president's office. Jim Bryan was furious about the end run to the chairman.

"Why did you go to Boyd and bother him?" Bryan snapped.

Ronell and Zito discussed what had happened and decided they had to protect themselves.

"Bury yourself in a bunker," Zito advised Ronell. "Let the others take the fall."

Fortunately for the two anxious salesmen, Airbus Industrie kept its North American employees largely in the dark. In effect, Airbus had orchestrated two quite different marketing campaigns. John Leahy led the official drive to sell Airbus to North American clients, but Stuart Iddles, his new boss in Toulouse – a man with whom he frequently clashed – ran the more discreet operation. Iddles had a public role, meeting frequently with the presidents and chairmen of the major airlines, but he was also Schreiber's contact at Airbus.

Gary Kincaid, an Airbus salesman who watched from the relative safety of the Canadian Airlines account (PWA had merged with Nordair, Eastern Provincial Airlines, and CP Air to form the new airline in 1987), commented, "Let's just say there was much that was different about the Air Canada sale, as opposed to the normal business that we did in the United States. There was an awful lot of involvement from Toulouse. People who normally didn't get involved in the sales campaigns in North America were involved in Air Canada. That is about as much as I can tell you."

If Airbus's American personnel were nervous about what their company might be up to, Boeing executives were furious at the possibility. Merv Cronie, the Ottawa salesman, didn't restrain himself. How did Boeing stand a chance if Airbus was throwing around that kind of money? he protested. What was Moores's role?

Moores simply smiled at the criticism. Who, me? How often do I have to tell people I'm not lobbying for Airbus? To some, Cronie looked like a poor loser.

But the Boeing people continued to complain to the U.S. ambassador, Tom Niles, whose job it was to fight for the Boeing proposal – or at least to ensure that Boeing lost the deal fair and square, not because of bribes or kickbacks or secret commissions paid by its competitors. Cronie began buttonholing Air Canada directors to tell them of his suspicions about Moores. Peter Bawden, a director from Alberta, was among those who relayed Cronie's comments to Claude Taylor. Cronie finally called Taylor himself. The gossip was unsettling and damaging, and Taylor knew Cronie was pushing too hard. "Pull this guy out of Canada," he warned Boeing's president. "He'll do you more harm than good. You've got an excellent product, but you've got the wrong guy selling it." It wasn't long before Cronie was back in the United States.

But Tom Niles had no illusions about Moores's influence on the Mulroney government, and he grew increasingly concerned about the

Air Canada deal. Niles was a career diplomat, a smart, quiet, and cautious man whose rise in the U.S. State Department had been rapid. He wasn't a backslapping, hard-drinking, singalong type, and he would have been just as uncomfortable in the basement in Kaufering as Peter Lougheed would have been. Niles was something of an anomaly. The U.S. Embassy in Ottawa was usually a political reward for one of the American president's fundraisers, the kind of man who, if confronted with rough tactics, would retaliate in kind. But Tom Niles would have to find another way.

In the end he went to see the top people at Transport Canada and Air Canada. Officials from the Office of the U.S. Trade Representative came to Canada to talk to John Crosbie; even the FBI was eventually asked to look into the allegations.

"We're not asking for favouritism and saying, 'Hey, buy American,'" Niles told the Canadians. All he hoped was that the decision would be based on the merits of the case. But Niles received only assurances that Transport Canada had nothing to do with equipment decisions, that the purchase was entirely up to the airline, and that the airline made these decisions on the basis of strictly commercial considerations. Niles believed he was getting the runaround.

The Americans scrutinized the picture from every angle and could foresee more unpleasant possibilities. Any contract as big as this one can include items called "offsets," a five-dollar word that means little to lay people. The fifty-cent version is "side deals," in which the seller of a product agrees to do additional business with Canadian companies. For example, Airbus could promise to subcontract certain tasks to a Canadian company in return for the Air Canada order. It sounds like a reasonable idea: Canadian companies enjoy more business, and more Canadian jobs are created as a result. However, offset agreements can be viewed as an unfair trade practice since they tend to distract the purchaser from simply ordering the best product at the best price. Consequently, offsets are highly regulated under the General Agreement on Trade and Tariffs (GATT).

U.S. officials were hearing stories that Airbus Industrie was secretly proposing to provide offsets to Canadair, recently acquired from the government by Bombardier in Montreal, provided it won the Air

Canada contract. At least that was the rumour. There was little the Americans could do: they had no evidence of such a proposal and therefore could not invoke the GATT. If there was a secret deal involving offsets, the government would have had to play a prominent role, negotiating between Airbus, Bombardier, and Air Canada. Officially, the government insisted there never was such a scheme.

Still, Cliff MacKay at DRIE confirmed that some Ottawa bureaucrats were worried, and he tried to make sure the two deals were not linked. If Airbus wanted to give Canadair contracts, so be it; if Air Canada wanted to purchase the Airbus jets, so be it. One had nothing to do with the other. "Canadair was competing very aggressively for some major subcontracts negotiated with Airbus... Our concern was that the waters not get muddied in that context and that the deals be kept quite separate." Later Airbus announced it would indeed provide subcontracts to Canadair, a fact that seemed only to confirm the worst fears of the American officials. When asked about the coincidental timing of the Air Canada–Airbus negotiations and the Canadair-Airbus subcontracts, MacKay said, "To the best of my knowledge, [an offset deal] never happened."

On March 11, 1988, the *Financial Post* published an unconfirmed story that Air Canada would purchase thirty-four Airbus planes and that the corporation had asked the federal government for a $300-million equity infusion in January to help pay for them. "In an era of fiscal restraint, only a handful of senior cabinet ministers – such as Transport Minister John Crosbie – appear willing to loosen the purse strings for the Crown corporation."

The story contradicted those who claimed the cabinet had nothing to do with the Air Canada purchase. For years afterwards this assertion was trotted out by spin doctors trying to persuade people that the cabinet hadn't been involved. And once again, journalists tried to link Moores and GCI to the story. "GCI doesn't work for Airbus," Gary Ouellet protested to *Toronto Star* reporters in a story published on March 14. "There is no dire plot to lobby anybody." Later he told the newspaper that he didn't realize MBB was a partner in Airbus Industrie.

Any decision to purchase new aircraft at Air Canada would involve a myriad of decision-makers. While technically the decision rested with Air Canada, a Crown corporation operating at arm's length from the government, an expenditure of this magnitude would have to be approved by the government of the day. Air Canada itself had three committees independently assessing the competing bids: a technical committee, a financial committee, and a marketing committee. Each had its own criteria. These committees reported their findings to the president, Pierre Jeanniot, who then made a recommendation to the Air Canada board. The board then sent its recommendation to the government for official approval.

Technically, at this point the government would have no say in which aircraft a Crown corporation could purchase, but it did have the power to deny Air Canada the money to buy them. The approval process began with the transport minister, John Crosbie, who formally signed off on the proposal before handing it over to Treasury Board. While a team of Treasury Board bureaucrats crunched the numbers, they also had to get approval from Finance Minister Michael Wilson. As soon as the proposal had worked its way through these stages, it ended up in a cabinet committee chaired by Treasury Board President Don Mazankowski. It was this team of Tory cabinet ministers who had the final say on the deal.

Some weeks later, Gérard Veilleux, the secretary to the Treasury Board, called Jeanniot with the news he'd been hoping for. The government had approved the largest civilian purchase of aircraft in Canada's history from Airbus Industrie.

11

Payday

Scrutiny and approval of the Air Canada–Airbus deal at successive levels of authority consumed the early part of 1988. At any stage, including the cabinet's review, the expenditure could have been questioned, the financial terms rejected, or the application declined altogether. Officially the process was cloaked in secrecy, but that only encouraged a continuous stream of speculation, denials, more gossip, and more determined but quiet protests by Ambassador Niles. Before the country was told about the Airbus purchase, however, Air Canada made the front pages with another long-rumoured event.

On April 12, Don Mazankowski announced the government's intention to privatize Air Canada. It would be done in two stages over two years, the first step being a sale of up to 45 percent of the airline to the public through a share issue. Sitting beside him at the press conference were Claude Taylor and Pierre Jeanniot, the chairman and the president of Air Canada. It was a triumphant moment for the Conservative government and for the Air Canada executives, who had wholeheartedly supported the move for some time.

The announcement caught some journalists off guard. The most recent signals out of Ottawa had suggested the Mulroney government was hesitant about privatizing Air Canada. A year earlier, in 1987, the government seemed ready politically and philosophically to turn the Crown corporation over to the private sector and had even scheduled an announcement during a meeting of cabinet ministers in western Canada. At the last minute the announcement was cancelled after an apparent change of policy. But now the government was prepared to move forward after all. What prompted it to act in 1988 and not the previous year?

No one knew for sure, but there was no disputing the fact that if Air Canada had been privatized the year before, the government would have had no say in the decision to purchase Airbus aircraft. As a Crown corporation the airline had to secure the government's approval of its $1-billion-plus purchase. The timing may have been pure coincidence, but it left some reporters scratching their heads. Why not privatize Air Canada first and let the private sector deal with it?

The question of timing was at the heart of a charge levied against Conservative premier Gary Filmon just days before the provincial election in Manitoba on April 26. During a television debate, Liberal opposition leader Sharon Carstairs told the audience that Filmon had known for weeks about an Air Canada deal that would hurt the province – but had kept it under wraps for fear of political damage.

"According to widespread reports from both government and industry," wrote the Globe's Geoffrey York on April 25, "Air Canada has agreed to spend $2-billion to purchase a fleet of aircraft from Airbus Industrie of France, to replace its old Boeing 727 aircraft. The new aircraft from Airbus would probably be serviced and maintained by Canadair Ltd. of Montreal. That would cost jobs at the Air Canada maintenance base in Winnipeg, which has traditionally serviced the 727s." The offsets deal raised its head once again, and in Manitoba it was an ugly sight. This was the province that had lost another lucrative maintenance contract to Canadair back in 1986, even though by all objective criteria, Bristol Aerospace of Winnipeg had submitted a lower, better bid. History was repeating itself and Filmon had no explanation; all he could do was insist that Air Canada had not yet decided on the fleet purchase or on the subcontract arrangements. These and other lost aircraft servicing contracts aroused howls from western Canadians, contributing not only to the plunge of the federal

Tories' popularity in the region but to the rise of a new political movement that called itself the Reform Party.

Ambassador Tom Niles was equally discontented. In late spring he
called a meeting with Derek Burney, the prime minister's chief of staff,
and raised the rumours of secret payments to lobbyists. Burney told
Niles to bring forward any evidence he might have. The *Toronto Star*
wrote some years later about American attempts to encourage a
Canadian police investigation at the time and quoted a senior U.S.
diplomatic source as saying that Burney's request was inappropriate:
Canadians would have been outraged by the notion of U.S. authorities
investigating their fellow citizens in Canada.

"It's very convenient to say give us the evidence," the official told
the *Star*. "Now be reasonable. How is [the ambassador] supposed to
have the evidence for a criminal investigation? The embassy... is not
in the criminal investigation business. We thought frankly... that a
heads-up ought to be enough. That's the normal way you do business
between close allies. You really don't want them to be embarrassed."

Perhaps not, but it wasn't long before James Baker, the U.S. treasury secretary, had been alerted, in large part by Niles. On April 22,
1988, Baker and Niles met privately with the prime minister, telling
him that they had heard disturbing reports and gently suggesting that
the situation might bear some examination by the proper agencies.
The Americans continued to suspect Airbus of paying secret commissions and of offering side-deal inducements that would benefit
Canadian manufacturers. It could not have escaped their notice that
on May 2, Henri Martre, chairman of Aerospatiale, the French Airbus
partner, announced at a Paris news conference that his company was
"within a few days" of awarding a contract to Canadair in Montreal to
build airframe parts for the Airbus 330 and 340 jets.

Ultimately, the "days" stretched to months – the contract was not
formally announced by Canadair until September, two months after
the Airbus purchase was made public – but it was worth the wait.
Canadair won a sixteen-year contract for fuselages and beams for
Airbus 330s and 340s and jobs for between 550 and 1,000 workers.
News reports carried denials from government and company spokes-
men that there was any link between the Air Canada purchase from

Airbus and the Canadair contract from Aerospatiale. Not surprisingly perhaps, Canadair's parent – Bombardier – was another GCI client.

On May 3, Dietlinde Kaupp, Schreiber's secretary in Kaufering, took a telephone message for him, one that was a warning sign that Schreiber's carefully hidden connections to the Airbus lobbying effort were finally surfacing. "Linda Deebles," jotted Kaupp in her daybook, alongside a Toronto telephone number. Linda Diebel, the *Toronto Star* reporter who had figured out that Ramsey Withers had indeed known about the Air Canada fleet negotiations when he was deputy minister of transport, was looking for Schreiber. But Schreiber was not interested in talking with Diebel; he had far more important calls to make that day, including several to Stuart Iddles in Toulouse.

The Airbus commission bonanza was almost in his grasp and anticipation turned his mind to practical matters, in particular to the transfer of some of these funds, subtly disguised, to Canada. There was a way, through Bitucan, one of his Alberta companies, a corporate entity that was little more than a file folder in a desk. He had tested this method with the earlier payment of $50,000 to Hladun for legal services.

In late April, Schreiber had instructed Erika Lutz to send a bill from Bitucan to one of his Liechtenstein shell companies, Merkur Handels- und Industrie AG. (Lutz performed only the occasional secretarial task for him while working full-time for Jürgen Hanne, one of his old investors.) In turn, Merkur would collect the sum owing from the various European bank accounts he controlled. Anyone poking into Bitucan's affairs wouldn't have a clue where the money was really coming from. Bitucan needed only a reason to bill Merkur, one that wouldn't draw undue attention. Schreiber invented an entirely fictional business venture which he christened "the Indonesian project." On April 22, 1988, Lutz prepared an invoice on Bitucan letterhead to Merkur Handels of Vaduz, Liechtenstein. "To invoice you for services rendered regarding your industrial project in Indonesia. Please remit Can. $50,000.00. Bitucan Bank account, 1012-765 Bank of Montreal, Calgary Standard Life branch. Bank Guiding Number: 25029001."

In comparison to the sums Schreiber expected, $50,000 was a drop in the bucket, but the route it followed was significant: it represented the method by which money could flow to Canada from Europe. Even the normally phlegmatic Giorgio Pelossi had to chuckle when he received Bitucan's invoice back in Liechtenstein. Schreiber had kept his sense of humour along the way, and Pelossi couldn't help but smile at "the Indonesian project." On May 11, Pelossi asked the VP Bank in Vaduz, home of IAL's account 236.972.029, to transfer the money owed by Merkur Handels to Bitucan. He told the clerk not to mention the name of IAL in the wire transfer back to Canada.

Although the banking records don't reveal what this $50,000 was used for in Canada, one week later Bitucan paid $50,000 to Bobby Hladun's Edmonton law firm, Hladun, Blakely.

That summer the Bear Head project came under heavy fire. Despite Don McPhail's assurances from ACOA – on April 19 he had written to Schreiber to say that as soon as a few concerns were addressed, he would recommend that the government proceed – other bureaucrats were throwing up obstacles. Admiral Ed Healey in Defence described the strategy paper on Bear Head prepared by DRIE as "naïve and simplistic." R.D. Gillespie, the chief of supply at Defence, also raised warning flags in a memo dated July 7, 1988. The officers knew that though Thyssen was insisting that defence contracts be included in the deal, their department wouldn't need Thyssen's kind of military vehicles for at least ten years. And even when it needed them, there were many suppliers to choose from; Thyssen was just one.

Schreiber turned to what he knew best, schmoozing. Frank Oberle, the federal minister of science and technology and a German immigrant himself, was visiting his homeland on official business in early June. Schreiber had met him years ago at the German Embassy in Ottawa; the two had kept in touch. Schreiber took Oberle to dinner in Munich on June 8, along with the Thyssen director Winfried Haastert, MBB's vice-president of marketing, Kurt Pfleiderer, and five others. The meal came to DM770 (about C$540); not bad for an evening of pleasant talk, good food, and a discussion of business opportunities in Canada. Oberle, however, insists he never participated in talks on Thyssen projects; he was there simply as Schreiber's friend. They spent another happy evening together bowling in the basement at Kaufering.

As far as Oberle was concerned, Schreiber was an international salesman who understood how business was conducted in faraway places. "Schreiber obviously worked with monies given to him by large industries to grease the skids and facilitate some of the sales... by paying bribes and doing things the way other countries deemed to be normal business practice," said Oberle. "We don't, obviously." While Schreiber felt comfortable paying bribes in other countries, Oberle admitted, he was sure this was something he would never do in Canada.

The negative reviews of the Thyssen project from men like Ed Healey were not timely, to say the least; Mulroney was hosting his first G-7 Summit in Toronto, and German chancellor Helmut Kohl had scheduled an informal pre-summit meeting in Ottawa. Schreiber had written to Kohl himself in May to encourage their discussions: "You must talk to Brian Mulroney about Bear Head – you must be enthusiastic." On the Canadian side, there was a bureaucratic scramble to smooth over any awkwardness caused by Defence Department naysayers. By June 15, the day Kohl was expected in the capital, Derek Burney had prepared a briefing memo on Thyssen for Mulroney's use with the press. Meanwhile, officials in Bonn were briefing Kohl to make sure he was well aware of potential Airbus sales to Air Canada. The Canadian government had yet to approve the sale, and the German bureaucrats were concerned that the Canadians might not allow the Crown corporation's decision to stand.

When Kohl and his wife, Hannelore, accompanied by seventy-five aides and thirty journalists, arrived at Ottawa's Uplands Airport, Mulroney's press aides handed out briefing notes to reporters on the agenda of the private talks between the two leaders. This list was predictable: agricultural subsidies, refugees, the large German population in Canada, and Canada's help in rebuilding Germany after World War II. There was no mention of Bear Head, Airbus, or MBB. Journalists didn't raise these items and Mulroney had no need of the talking points on Bear Head that had been part of Burney's memo.

Canadians took Kohl to their hearts; even the liberal *Toronto Star* couldn't resist lavishing praise on the chancellor. "'My biggest asset is that people would buy a used car from me without hesitating,' West German Chancellor Helmut Kohl once said. 'I am proud of that trust.' A slick, sophisticated politician the 58-year-old Kohl is not," the *Star* opined, "but he has earned a reputation as a dependable stalwart from his first days as a member of the Christian Democratic Party 41 years ago. He is perceived in his country as the down-to-earth German Everyman who typifies the importance of diligence, discipline, morality, order and optimism."

Cheered by the chancellor's popularity in Canada and confident that Thyssen was safe, Schreiber ignored the negative messages from the Defence Department's mandarins. Two days after Kohl left Canada, Schreiber cheerfully filled out an application for federal tax credits for the Bear Head project. On July 11, he was entertaining again, this time at one of his favourite restaurants in Landsberg. Around the table were Greg Alford, the president of GCI; Alford's boss, Gary Ouellet; Winfried Haastert and his wife; Schreiber and Barbara; and Schreiber's German business manager, Albert Birkner, and his wife.

On July 20, 1988, Pierre Jeanniot held a news conference to make the public announcement that Air Canada would purchase thirty-four A320s to replace its ageing Boeing 727s, for a price of US$1.8 billion. Delivery would begin in March 1990. The reason for choosing Airbus? Because it had a longer range, said Jeanniot.

The purchase agreement, in keeping with standard government practice, prohibited payment of commissions to third parties by either side, but Schreiber saw reason to celebrate. Five days after Jeanniot's announcement, Schreiber triumphantly sent photocopies of stories from the *Ottawa Citizen* and the Montreal *Gazette* to Giorgio Pelossi. He made an appointment with Hans Reiter to let him know the good news. As Reiter later recalled, "Schreiber told me that the Airbus sale came about through his negotiation and that he expected a commission of between three and six million dollars from it... At the time, [he] further indicated that this commission officially belonged to an IAL company from Switzerland or Liechtenstein. At my urging, Schreiber then said that the IAL company would confirm a transfer of commission revenues of over two million Canadian dollars from the Airbus negotiations, and would sign over the relevant claims [loan repayments] pertaining to these commissions. I asked Schreiber to give me some more detailed background on the IAL company. But

Schreiber did not want to respond and only shrugged his shoulders."

Schreiber may not have wanted to go into the particulars, but he did sign over C$2 million to the Sparkasse Landsberg.

"Dear Mr. Reiter," IAL's letter read. "We herewith confirm the irrevocable assignation to you of our claim to the $2,000,000 (two million) commission due to us from Airbus Industrie, as per the contract dated March 7, 1985. The commission claim is based on the completion of the transaction with the airline Air Canada in July 1988. The assignation will serve to secure loans which were guaranteed to Bayer. Bitumen Chemie, Kaufering. You may expect a payment on account of our commission claim by the end of August 1988. We trust you find this satisfactory." There would be no more worries about the bank, and once the money came in, Schreiber wouldn't have to work another day in his life.

Meanwhile, anticipating a fall election, the government rushed Air Canada's privatization bill through Parliament, securing royal assent on August 18. By the end of August, Air Canada had selected RBC Dominion Securities as the lead underwriter on the privatization of 45 percent of the company. The airline hoped to raise $300 million, capital that would help pay for the new planes.

The Conservatives feared the displeasure of the Canadian electorate after four years of cabinet resignations and firings, police investigations, and convictions. Mulroney and his strategists knew he was not popular enough on his own to defeat even the weak Liberals under their leader, John Turner. To win, the Tories needed an overriding national issue, and the one they had to hand was their support for free trade, an economic policy Mulroney had opposed just a few years earlier. The business community, both national and international, supported the free trade initiative with massive advertising dollars. Nationalists, labour leaders, and the Liberal left opposed it with rallies and rhetoric. Free trade gave the Tories what they desired: a diversion from their record.

Schreiber remained happily invisible, lobbying even harder for his pet project in Nova Scotia. The commissions due him from Thyssen were minuscule compared with those expected from Airbus, but Bear Head was about more than money. He had spent more time on this file than on any other; it was a project that would allow him to make a lasting mark in Canada.

On September 21, Colonel G.V. Porter, director of defence industrial resources and part of the Defence Department team evaluating the Bear Head deal, scrawled a brief comment on a confidential memorandum about Bear Head circulating among his colleagues: "If anyone is suggesting that this is a normal staffing exercise where options are being considered and time is available to keep all informed, they are badly mistaken... As you are aware, the... [deleted] has been a 'political matter' – largely a matter for legal staffs." Later, in an official document, Porter refers to the "stated need to proceed urgently." Urgently? Perhaps it wasn't surprising that this "political matter" was urgent. An election was imminent and even though there was little chance the Tories would lose, Schreiber wanted to get the Thyssen deal through while his friends were still in their familiar seats.

On September 27, the federal government finally signed an "understanding in principle" with Thyssen to support a manufacturing facility in the Bear Head region of Cape Breton. The agreement carried the signatures of Schreiber, Gerald Merrithew, the minister responsible for ACOA at that time, Perrin Beatty, then the minister of defence, and Robert de Cotret, minister of regional industrial expansion. The document was essential to Schreiber; he couldn't collect his full C$4-million fee without it.

Two days later, Bear Head issued a carefully crafted press release. The wording drew attention away from Thyssen's military production and emphasized the company's environmental products, especially wastewater recycling equipment. It mentioned industrial conveyor and transport systems before it finally tucked "light military vehicles for the Canadian and United States markets" into the list, followed by "machine tooling." There was no mention of sales to the Middle East, only the bland statement that "all exports of Bear Head Industries, including those outside of North America, will of course be in full accordance with the Government's export policy on export controls." And there was icing on the cake too: "Should the company win contracts in Canada for the next generation of light armoured vehicles," read the release, "a portion of the work would be carried out at the Trenton Works plant in Pictou County," an installation belonging to Lavalin, one of Canada's largest engineering firms.

To the few who even noticed the announcement, it seemed unimportant; what mattered then was that Mulroney's free trade campaign had caught fire, and the polls predicted another Conservative victory in the election called for November 21. Nonetheless, remembered Pelossi, "I was a little concerned and I asked Schreiber, 'What happens if your friends are no more in power?' And he told me, 'I have already set up other connections with the Liberal Party in case of trouble or changes in the politics.'"

Schreiber had made two excellent connections with leading Liberals; one was Marc Lalonde, who had been engaged by Thyssen for legal work since 1986; the other was Allan MacEachen, the formidable Liberal partisan and senator from Cape Breton who was in favour of the Bear Head project. How such prominent Liberals came to befriend a man as right-wing as Schreiber can be explained in part. Allan MacEachen always held Cape Breton's welfare dear, and as a finance minister and secretary of state for external affairs under Trudeau, he had met many of the German politicians supporting the deals in Canada.

Lalonde was a bigger puzzle. His friends suggested that after the Liberals' defeat in 1984, Lalonde was a double pariah in Quebec. Not only was he a strong Trudeau federalist – anathema to many Québécois at the time – he was disliked by many of English Canada's business leaders for what they saw as leftist disdain for their issues. The business Schreiber and Thyssen brought to him was welcome.

On October 1, 1988, Franz Josef Strauss was enjoying a day of deer hunting at the estate of Prince Johannes von Thurn und Taxis. The prince's five-hundred-room palace, St. Emmeram Castle near Munich, was one of seven castles in the family, a portfolio of land holdings that included thousands of hectares of land on Saltspring Island and Vancouver Island in British Columbia. Believed to be Germany's second-richest man, with assets worth about US$2.5 billion, the prince was one of his country's most eccentric citizens. He had married at fifty-four to produce an heir; his wife, Gloria, was only twenty, and she succeeded in adding three children to the line. The couple lived a life of unbridled extravagance and were known as "the Duke and Duchess of Decadence."

Strauss loved luxury and hunting, and Prince Johannes offered both in the grand style of European nobility. But Strauss was seventy-three and in poor shape. Although not a hopeless alcoholic like his chum Prince Johannes, he ate and drank too much and was seriously overweight. To the shock of those with him in the hunting party that day, Strauss collapsed suddenly and could not be revived. His panic-stricken companions rushed him by helicopter to the hospital in nearby Regensburg, 100 kilometres north of Munich, where he died on Monday, October 3, without regaining consciousness. Doctors ruled it a heart attack.

Strauss's passing was a major event in Germany, one marked with lengthy and respectful feature stories in newspapers around the world. If they mentioned his arch-conservatism or the scandals of his past, the references were perfunctory. Most newspaper editorial writers compared him to Konrad Adenauer and Willy Brandt, among the nation's greatest leaders. The Lion of Bavaria was dead and, love him or hate him, he had fought for his country's prosperity. His wife, Marianne, had predeceased him in a car crash four years earlier; those left to mourn him were his three children, Max, Monika Hohlmeier, and Franz Georg.

Schreiber was distraught by the death of his friend and mentor. He was among the mourners at the sombre state funeral but dissuaded Giorgio Pelossi from attending. Although Pelossi had been at Marianne Strauss's funeral a few years earlier, Schreiber told him it would be better not to come to Franz Josef's; there would be too many people there. Instead Pelossi stayed in Lugano attending to business. The day after the hunting party, he had sent an invoice on IAL letterhead to Thyssen, requesting the balance of the C$4-million contingency fee for bringing in the Bear Head deal. Thyssen had already paid Schreiber C$100,000 for the Bear Head company and an advance of C$1.9 million in December 1987. There was C$2 million still to come.

Ironically, two days after Strauss's death, on Wednesday, October 5, the first Airbus commission payment – US$5 million – arrived,

Schreiber's greatest triumph to date in his career as a middleman. The funds could have gone directly into Schreiber's personal account in Zurich, but instead the money had begun its convoluted journey in Paris, deposited by Airbus Industrie into the Banque Française du Commerce Extérieur. From there, it was transferred to IAL's account 235.972.037 at the VP Bank in Vaduz. Pelossi was waiting, and as soon as it arrived, he immediately sent US$4.5 million of it "upstairs" to IAL's parent company, Kensington Anstalt, through the Kensington bank account, number 235.971.021. The remaining US$500,000 was kept in the IAL bank account for the time being.

Schreiber himself sped to Vaduz. When the US$4.5 million landed in the Kensington account, Pelossi signed a cheque to Schreiber for the full amount and handed it over to him; Schreiber then signed a receipt for his accountant's records. The Airbus money had travelled through Liechtenstein in less than eight hours. At the end of the day, the cheque in his purse, Schreiber drove to Zurich, where Dietlinde Kaupp had reserved a room for him at the Savoy Hotel.

First thing on the morning of October 6, he bustled over to the Swiss Bank Corporation and deposited the funds in account 18679. Aside from half a million he would keep in the Zurich account, the money didn't rest there long. At the same time Schreiber instructed the bank to write him a cheque on that account for US$4 million, which he would take home to Kaufering. He left Zurich and on October 7, deposited the money into account 511618, his personal account at the Sparkasse Landsberg.

Five days later, on Wednesday, October 12, Schreiber transferred money from his Landsberg account to Interleiten, another of his companies in Vaduz. The amount was SF2,282,170 (about US$1.44 million), deposited to account 239.655.015 at the VP Bank in Vaduz. On paper, it looked as if Schreiber was paying back a personal loan he owed to one of his own companies. In less than a week, much of Airbus's original US$5 million had come full circle, back to the Vaduz bank.

Six days after that, Pelossi was back in Vaduz, withdrawing SF650,000 in cash from the Interleiten account for Schreiber. After getting the money from Pelossi, Schreiber and his wife drove to

Pontresina. The next day, October 19, they met Toni Kägi, an employee of the Schweizerische Kreditanstalt bank, and opened account 2227 for Barbara. Schreiber arranged to have access to the account as well.

The same day, Pelossi was still in Liechtenstein, transferring SF1.4 million from the Interleiten account back upstairs to Kensington, the parent company. Once again, he immediately transferred it to Schreiber's personal account in Zurich, 18679, where it had already been just days before. The money was going round and round, changing currencies and countries, and now it was back in Schreiber's favourite, most secure account in Zurich. On October 19, too, Schreiber transferred an additional US$585,500 – the remaining Airbus money still sitting in Liechtenstein – from Kensington to 18679 in Zurich. All this perpetual motion made sense in one way; it gave the appearance of activity and purpose to a set of obedient shell companies.

He wasn't finished. On October 20, Schreiber transferred US$500,000 into a new Canadian-dollar subaccount, 41391.0, that he set up under his main account, 18679. Subaccounts are perfectly normal in Swiss banking practice; they help to keep track of the source and destination of certain monies within a single bank account. Schreiber already had subaccounts in place to receive payments in various currencies. For instance, Canadian-dollar payments went automatically to subaccount 18679.1, and U.S.-dollar payments to 18679.4.

From 1988 through 1991, Schreiber would establish a series of subaccounts and assign to each a nickname or code name. The name was always attached to the subaccount number in his banking records; in his diary notes, he most often used only the moniker. The new Canadian-dollar subaccount 41391.0, for example, carried the name Frankfurt. Others set up in this period included 18679.6, called Stewardess, and 18679.7, labelled Master.

Frankfurt 41391.0 received its first deposit on October 20: the infusion of Airbus money converted to C$658,735. Six days later someone withdrew C$100,000 in cash from the subaccount. Years later it would be easy to prove that the money came from Airbus; what would be more of a challenge to establish was who made the withdrawals. Tracing a bank transaction is difficult enough, but following a briefcase of cash is virtually impossible.

If the Airbus money was starting to slosh around Schreiber's bank accounts in Europe, the Thyssen–Bear Head money was not far behind. On October 26, 1988, Thyssen Industrie sent the remainder of its promised C$4-million contingency fee – C$2 million – to IAL, money that Pelossi then transferred to Kensington. The next day Schreiber personally made two cash withdrawals from the Kensington bank account in Vaduz: one for C$150,000 and another for C$81,466.40. The day after, he wired C$1.1 million to his Zurich account and another C$500,000 to Barbara's account in Pontresina.

Schreiber was swimming in a sea of cash and it was delicious, it was balm in Gilead. For all his show of wealth, he had been insecure for most of his life, living on borrowed money and lines of credit, holding off the bankers with promises of imminent transfers of cash.

He even had money to spend on a new compound in Kaufering, moving his home and business to 27 Raiffeisenstrasse. Squatting low, brown, and beamy on a large corner lot and surrounded by a 15-foot-high fence that is monitored by security cameras, the house is several times the size of its more modest neighbours.

Now, at fifty-four, Karlheinz Schreiber was finally the success he had always believed he could be. He wasn't a brilliant businessman and his speech was often rough and rambling, betraying his lack of education, but fate had blessed him with different skills. He was a tireless networker who cultivated every contact. The favours he'd done, the secrets he'd kept had finally paid off. He believed he had finessed one of the most ambitious aircraft sales in history, perhaps even rescuing Airbus Industrie from failure. He had completed his task for his late patron, Franz Josef Strauss. He had also made a fortune – for himself and for others.

12

For Services Rendered

It was November 8, 1988, the day of the presidential election in the United States. The Republican candidate, George Bush of Texas, the vice-president under Ronald Reagan, was running well ahead of the Democratic contender, Michael Dukakis, the governor of Massachusetts. The election was no cliff-hanger, but it was still a great excuse for a party to the partners at GCI. Frank Moores, Gary Ouellet, and Gerry Doucet rented a downtown Ottawa hotel suite and invited guests to come and watch the fun: a conservative clobbering a liberal. Giorgio Pelossi was in town so Schreiber took him along, and the whole gang turned up to cheer Bush's victory.

Perhaps Schreiber took a moment to have a quiet word with the three partners and with Gerry's brother Fred; there were business successes as well as political triumphs to toast that evening. Each of these Canadian associates had just submitted invoices to Schreiber "for services rendered" – there was no elaboration – in the amount of C$90,000. One by one, they had sent their invoices to Bitucan Holdings Ltd., care of Jürgen Hanne's office on the twelfth floor of Calgary's Dome Tower. There Erika Lutz still managed Schreiber's Bank of Montreal account and paid Bitucan's bills.

Fred Doucet's invoice, dated November 2, arrived under the

letterhead of Fred Doucet Consulting International. Three months after stepping down as ambassador of international summit planning for "health reasons," he was setting himself up as a lobbyist. Gerry Doucet, a partner at GCI, sent in his invoice on November 2 under the letterhead of his law firm in Halifax: Gerry Doucet & Associates, Barristers and Solicitors. Moores's bill went in under his personal letterhead at 403 Clarke Avenue in Montreal, and Gary Ouellet's was under the letterhead of his personal company, Lemoine Consultants, named after the street where he lived in Sillery, a suburb of Quebec City. The "Canadian friends," as they were always called by Schreiber and Pelossi, invoiced Bitucan for a total of C$360,000.

GCI, the lobbying firm, billed Bitucan for a further C$250,000 at the same time. The sum paid to GCI and the friends added up to C$610,000. On U.S. election day, Schreiber transferred C$610,000 from Frankfurt 41391.0, one of his Canadian-dollar subaccounts in the Swiss Bank Corporation in Zurich, to his company Merkur Handels in Vaduz to cover these invoices.

To move the funds to Canada, Schreiber used the method he had set up with Lutz several months earlier. Lutz drafted a false invoice from Bitucan, billing Merkur for C$710,000, once again referring to the fictional venture in the Far East. "To invoice you for services rendered regarding your industrial project in Indonesia," she typed.

When the bogus invoice arrived in Liechtenstein, Schreiber transferred the funds from his Zurich account to the Merkur account in Vaduz. Most of it came out of his Frankfurt subaccount, but $100,000 appears to have been drawn from another Canadian-funds subaccount, 18679.1. Once the $710,000 arrived in Vaduz, Pelossi wired it to Bitucan's account at the Bank of Montreal in Calgary. Lutz sent out cheques to the Canadian friends on November 15.

In mid-November Canadair announced it had snared another Airbus contract, this one worth C$400 million, to supply high-tech wing components for A330s and A340s, bringing the value of its contracts with Airbus to C$1.6 billion. In a luncheon speech to the Montreal Chamber of Commerce on November 15, Jean Pierson, the president of Airbus Industrie, told his audience just how important the Canadian market was to his company. The sales to Air Canada,

Canadian Airlines, and Wardair, he said, would help to boost Airbus's share of the world commercial jet market from 16 percent to 35 percent by 2006. Pierson couldn't resist taking a swipe at his competition. Boeing says Airbus is unfairly subsidized by four governments, Pierson argued, but what about the US$23 million in subsidies that Boeing and McDonnell Douglas had received over the past ten years? American airlines had received far more government money than Airbus through military contracts.

"How can one speak of a market imbalance when those who accuse us control 84 percent of the present civil aircraft market?" Pierson asked. "What does one say about their policy to monopolize the market for long-range carriers?"

Pierson predicted that the world commercial jetliner market would be worth US$510 billion by 2006, and Airbus hoped to take US$180 billion of that for itself. "Over the past seven years," reported the *Globe and Mail*, Airbus had sold US$16 billion worth of aircraft, "[US]$13.2 billion of which came from countries outside the consortium, including Canada." In Canada, the potential orders added up to thirty-four A320s for Air Canada, fourteen A310s for Wardair, and seventeen A320s for Canadian Airlines. No wonder Boeing was looking for scapegoats.

By this time Niles had informed the Federal Bureau of Investigation of the controversy through its officer at the embassy. Boeing's director of security flew from the Seattle headquarters to Ottawa to meet with Rod Stamler, the assistant deputy commissioner of the RCMP, as well as with Niles and U.S. State Department officials. "Boeing did its own investigation, as did the FBI and the State Department," Stamler said later.

Boeing was convinced secret commissions had been paid but had no evidence. Nonetheless the FBI took the complaint seriously; so did the RCMP. They poked away at their parallel investigations for several weeks and the FBI did prepare a report for Niles; he, in turn, discussed it with Don McCutchan, a man he trusted, serving as senior adviser to Finance Minister Michael Wilson. McCutchan carried Niles's concerns to Wilson, but no action was taken at the political level. By 1990, the FBI investigation had fizzled out; the Mounties put their investigation on ice. Only the State Department and, latterly, the Central Intelligence Agency kept at it.

Nearly two weeks after George Bush rolled over Michael Dukakis, Brian Mulroney flattened John Turner for the second time. On November 21, 1988, even though the Tories did not win the popular vote – more Canadians voted against free trade and the government than for it – they did win the only thing that mattered: enough seats to form a majority government.

Back in Germany for the Christmas season, Schreiber had many errands to run and people to see, but one of his priorities was to withdraw more money in Canadian funds. On December 5, subaccount 18679.1 saw a cash withdrawal of C$503,000.

Schreiber had much on his mind and Hans Reiter recalls the period well, because he was making many of his financial arrangements at the Sparkasse Landsberg. As Reiter later told German authorities, "I can remember construction cranes – I believe it had to do with a deal of the Liebherr company in Costa Rica; helicopters, freight vehicles, Mercedeses, fruit juices, Airbus planes." A potpourri of deals. Reiter's interest was in seeing the bank's loans repaid; that happened on December 22 when Schreiber paid back about DM1.5 million out of his Thyssen contingency fees. As the year ended, IAL's fee income for 1988 added up to about DM11.6 million, well over C$8 million. It worked out to a total of C$116,250 from MBB, US$5,188,000 from Airbus, and C$2 million from Thyssen for Bear Head.

Michel Cogger had not kept in touch with Schreiber the way Moores had, but in late 1988, he had a visit from his old friend. Schreiber had set up an office for Bear Head in a suite at the Inn of the Provinces in Ottawa and asked Cogger to join the ranks of lobbyists working on the Nova Scotia project. Cogger politely declined. Greg Alford was ready to make a move; he left his job as president of GCI and relocated a few blocks east to become the new executive vice-president of Bear Head Industries. Jürgen Massmann was president, but as he was based in Europe, Alford would manage the Canadian operation and assist with the push to get the plant built. It was tough sledding. Despite the understanding in principle – which was not binding on either side –

enthusiasm was waning in Ottawa, pummelled by the mutinous opposition of the generals at Defence. Perhaps Cogger sniffed the wind and
thought this was a fight that couldn't be won. More likely, he was still
smarting at being sidelined when Schreiber had found more powerful
friends closer to the centre. "He has enough lobbyists," Cogger told
his friends.

Over the next few months, Schreiber hopped from project to
project in Ottawa, Germany, Costa Rica, and Austria. The details in his
diaries and correspondence suggest their scope. On January 31, 1989,
while Schreiber was in Germany, Werner Ströhlein, his old BND
associate, wrote to him about the financing of a deal in San José;
DM15.5 million promised by the German government had been
stalled, but he expected it would come through by April. A more delicate issue, Ströhlein added, was Rita Santalla, who, after five years on
Schreiber's payroll, was becoming an expensive luxury. Once the
government money arrives, he suggested, she should be dealt with:
"To prevent a bigger disaster, one should consider the question of
further helping her out financially in order then to settle her defi-
nitely." The next day Schreiber was in Vienna, discussing projects in
Austria over lunch with Massmann and Helmut Wieczorek, a former
Thyssen manager and now a Social Democratic member of the
Bundestag who had visited the Bear Head site in Nova Scotia. Albert
Birkner, Schreiber's manager in Kaufering, was with them.

It wasn't all business, of course; Schreiber enjoyed spending money
as much as he enjoyed earning it. In March 1989, he and Barbara paid
$375,000 in cash for a new condominium in Ottawa's Rockcliffe Park.
The Schreibers' top-floor unit faced tiny MacKay Lake in the middle of
the capital's toniest residential enclave. Frank Moores also decided to
buy some real estate. Almost fanatically devoted to salmon fishing,
Moores was familiar with all the finest rivers and salmon pools in
Newfoundland, Labrador, New Brunswick, and Quebec – areas
famous to fly fishermen around the world. For a few years he had
rented a camp in the Gaspé region of Quebec, and now he could afford
to buy his own. The property he chose came with the fishing rights to
an 18-kilometre stretch of the Cascapédia River, one of the best
salmon rivers anywhere. Moores says he paid between $150,000 and

$200,000 for the camp, sharing the cost with a friend; others say that might be what the buildings were worth, but the fishing rights alone would command about $2 million. Moores spent another fortune on renovations. He also made improvements at Birch Point, adding a two-bedroom guest cottage to his Ontario property.

By strange coincidence, or perhaps as an illustration of the small world occupied by Canada's business elites, it was fishing that brought Moores and an old nemesis together. Bob Perdue was the president of Boeing and no fan of Moores, especially as he knew Moores was working on the Airbus file. But Perdue, too, was a fly-fishing enthusiast who liked to spend time on the Cascapédia River. One day, well after Airbus won the Air Canada contract and Perdue had retired, he caught a fish in front of Moores's place. His boat was in some difficulty at the time and Moores, he said, immediately came out to help.

"That was the last time I saw him – really the only time I ever met him – and he was a very gracious host," Perdue said, smiling. "Very kind. A real gentleman."

With the successes of the previous year behind him, Schreiber's confidence was high and he was ready to tackle new projects in other countries. He had demonstrated what he could do for those companies willing to pay for his help in landing the big contracts. The death of Strauss had done nothing to diminish Schreiber's influence; he was running his own show and it felt good.

The next challenge was to try to repeat the Airbus victory in Thailand, where the Royal Thai Air Force and Thai Airways International Ltd. were in the market for new passenger aircraft. Again, his contact at Airbus was the chief salesman in Europe, Stuart Iddles, and together they began to negotiate with a contact of Max Strauss's, Pitak Intrawityanunt, a senior adviser to the Thai cabinet. But Iddles had a fright. On April 10, 1989, Jean Pierson received an urgent fax from Jean-Louis Terrier, the president of Nord Sud Export Consultants, a small firm in Paris offering advice to companies looking for business in developing countries like Thailand. Terrier published a newsletter for his clients, and his message to Pierson was that his sources told him there was a corrupt deal in the making between the Royal Thai Air Force and Airbus Industrie.

Worried, Pierson sent a copy of the fax to Iddles, whose response was swift and indignant.

"This is scandalous!" Iddles scrawled on the fax. "I will travel to Thailand to check this story. If true, I propose we <u>do</u> <u>not</u> <u>sell</u> rather than have a scandal of this kind. SI."

Iddles's professed outrage at seedy tales of payoffs was probably heartfelt; he and Schreiber must have hoped that their arrangement with Intrawityanunt would remain a secret. The three men had worked together to lay the groundwork for Airbus sales to Thailand. The contract they were to sign, AI/CC-L-2053-5-90, was similar to the one between IAL and Airbus for the Air Canada deal, with different fee schedules for different types of aircraft.

The contract called for the sale of five Airbus 300s to Thai Airways International at a commission of US$600,000 per plane, for a total of US$3 million; eight Airbus 330s to Thai Airways International at the same commission per plane, for a total of US$4.8 million; and one Airbus 310 to the Royal Thai Air Force, again for US$600,000. IAL's entire earnings on the Thai deal were projected at more than US$8 million. Iddles's theatrics notwithstanding, Schreiber had reason for optimism.

An unpleasant matter came to a head on April 10 when Schreiber told Albert Birkner to fire Rita Santalla. Blaming a "structural reorganization" in the Kaufering headquarters of Bayerische Bitumen-Chemie, Birkner gave her three months' notice in a brief and chilly note. Schreiber had kept Santalla on after Serge Noghaven left Costa Rica; she still had good contacts in government there although she had left the president's office when Oscar Arias succeeded Monge. She was also meant to act as Schreiber's liaison with Liebherr officials, who were still trying to drum up business in Costa Rica for their truck cranes and other hydraulic equipment. But the new business wasn't coming in, and the vivacious Rita had become an extravagance they couldn't afford. Birkner didn't know that Schreiber continued to pay her an allowance for another two years; she was a favourite of his. Schreiber was still trying to negotiate a DM14.5-million road-building project in Costa Rica, and perhaps he felt he needed Santalla as another set of eyes and ears in the country. The project never happened.

Serge Noghaven, who returned to Costa Rica from time to time, was another costly retainer. The expenses he claimed for work he did for Bayerische Bitumen-Chemie had "problems," Birkner complained. Noghaven had owed Schreiber well over DM600,000, but Schreiber told Birkner it had been paid back. Birkner was bewildered by his boss's faraway employees and their even more mysterious jobs; what they did, he had no idea.

As he said some years later, "I also recall a document signed by Mr. Schreiber dated July 6, 1989, in which Schreiber agrees to a settlement with Mr. Noghaven if DM600,000 is paid. Why this amount was then paid in cash to the Sparkasse I do not know. Neither do I know who paid this amount. I was not directly involved in talks regarding the settlement with Mr. Noghaven. I exclusively derive my knowledge from Mr. Schreiber."

Financial transactions and especially the transfer of funds across currencies and countries were among Schreiber's particular skills. When Moores sent another personal invoice "for services rendered," in the amount of C$60,000 to Bitucan's Calgary office on May 17, the payment took a slightly different route. Schreiber wanted the bill paid as before through one of his Vaduz shell companies, Merkur Handels, so Pelossi arranged to have the Merkur account, 239.239.030 at Schreiber's Vaduz bank, send C$60,000 to the Bitucan account at the Bank of Montreal in Calgary. Erika Lutz then wrote a cheque to Moores from Bitucan's Calgary account on May 22 and sent it to his account 639.740.0 at the Royal Bank branch near his office in Ottawa.

Schreiber worried that even this roundabout way of paying Moores was too obvious. "Destroy the invoice," he ordered on May 30. A week later Moores sent a fresh invoice for the money, but this time Merkur was billed directly, not Bitucan. The links between Moores and another Canadian entity that might draw scrutiny were thus obscured.

Not long after fixing the Moores bill, Schreiber agreed to yet another amendment to the Airbus contract. It confirmed that the company had paid IAL US$5 million as a "pre-delivery payment" – estimated by Airbus to be one-quarter of what he would eventually earn – and that future commissions would be made plane by plane as Air Canada took delivery.

By the summer of 1989, Fred Doucet had become a registered lobbyist for two of Schreiber's companies. The first was Bitucan, making him a lobbyist for a shell company; the second was Bear Head Industries. He was sitting in on meetings with Schreiber, Greg Alford, and senior government officials to explore all the tax credits, grants, loans, and contracts they might be able to extract from the government's coffers. Prosperity agreed with him and he too looked for a vacation property. A year earlier Gerry had purchased a condominium at the Silver Sands Beach and Racquet Club in St. Petersburg, Florida. On July 26, Fred bought a unit on the floor above his brother. Fred wasn't able to spend a lot of time enjoying his new property that summer. He was working too hard on the Bear Head file.

Few of the bureaucrats were happy about these meetings, but everyone knew that Schreiber and Doucet had to be taken seriously. They had the protection of the PMO, and they didn't hesitate to remind people of the fact.

Admiral Ed Healey didn't care. He sat through the meetings and evaluated the Bear Head proposal for the Defence Department. He didn't like it and he didn't back away. In one meeting with senior officials from the Prime Minister's Office, the Privy Council Office, National Defence, and DRIE, he warned that Bear Head would have to jump through the normal contracting hoops required of every company. "A message," he commented later, "that Schreiber did not want to hear.

"His argument was that this would be good for Cape Breton and this will create jobs," Healey said. "He was attempting to appeal to our sense of doing great things for the country, and in the bureaucracy, of doing great things which our political masters wanted done – which is to help relieve the unemployment situation in a depressed area of the country."

It was a questionable proposition for many reasons, Healey said. "Canada already had a capacity to produce military vehicles. External Affairs was never keen on exporting stuff that goes boom in the night."

Schreiber's suggestion that the plant would be making not just military vehicles but also environmental equipment – scrubbers to clean the sulphur emissions out of coal-burning industrial chimneys – struck Healey as ludicrous.

"We said, 'Well, how does that work, for God's sake? One minute you're producing a chimney scrubber and the next minute an armoured car's coming down the line?' It doesn't make any sense. They never got fleshed out, these ideas; it was just what would sell politically."

And Schreiber's style rankled. "Schreiber came to see me a couple of times. He was full of himself. He dropped some names. He was very persistent."

It was an uncomfortable time for Defence Minister Perrin Beatty. His officials' reports were negative, but the Prime Minister's Office and many of his fellow MPs were clearly on Bear Head's side. "Perrin was like a guy on hot coals," recalled Healey. "He didn't want any part of this." But as far as Healey and his colleagues were concerned, the whole scheme was suspect.

Schreiber was welcomed in some of the most important office suites in town, and no pipsqueak Canadian admiral was going to patronize him. Years later, he gave an interview to the journalist Bruno Schirra in which he boasted of his access to Ottawa's power-brokers.

"A small, round man storms into the neo-classic hotel lobby," Schirra wrote, describing their meeting at the Château Laurier Hotel, "like ball lightning in cold weather. A brown designer jacket, a white turtleneck sweater over brown corduroy pants. At his wrist a Louis Vuitton bag swings back and forth." Schreiber rushed Schirra outside and into his car; then they sped along the main downtown streets so that Schreiber could point out his old haunts.

"I went in and out of here," he said, pointing at the Supreme Court building, then the Parliament Buildings and the Prime Minister's Office, all strung along three blocks of Wellington Street.

"All doors were open to me. Always."

Mulroney wanted his advice, he bragged, as did the external affairs minister, Joe Clark, and their political advisers. At discreet meetings and intimate dinners he would explain the global arms business to them, its influence on the course of world affairs. Schreiber was not misleading Schirra. He did have access to the highest levels of the Conservative government. He had the prime minister's ear and he had the friendship of Fred Doucet, one of the prime minister's closest confidants. With this kind of leverage, surely he could overcome the fools in Defence.

The military brass weren't Bear Head's only detractors. Canada's Jewish community was keeping an eye on developments and had no lessons to learn from Schreiber about lobbying. The Canada-Israel Committee, led by Sidney Spivak, continued to protest. An internal CIC memo prepared in September 1989 was contemptuous of Bear Head Industries, calling it a "fly-by-night" operation. Jürgen Massmann, Bear Head's president, had no office in Nova Scotia and was "operating out of a briefcase and hotel room. The only tangible evidence of the proposed project being the press releases he issued."

Spivak learned that the federal cabinet was still divided on the issue of support for the Thyssen project. External Affairs under Joe Clark remained uneasy about it; Nova Scotia's politicians were all for it. To Spivak and the CIC, the mystery was why Thyssen wanted to operate this plant in Canada at all. Why hadn't Thyssen considered Brazil or Argentina, where the governments had no objections to arms manufacturers needing export licences to send goods to the Middle East? The CIC memo also noted, with some sarcasm, that every time the arms issue became sensitive, Thyssen would switch to promotion of its environmental products.

Despite the opposition in Ottawa, Schreiber remained confident and buoyant. At the same time, of course, he had to be extremely careful. IAL in Vaduz would not be receiving any more commission income until 1990, but distributing the bounty that had already accumulated gave Schreiber plenty to do. Pelossi and Lutz followed his precise instructions on moving it quickly into an intricate maze of companies and bank accounts. His friends in Canada and in Germany needed the same protection.

In 1989 there were a series of transactions in and out of his 18679 account, sometimes in small amounts. On January 24, someone withdrew C$40,000 cash from the Frankfurt 41391.0 subaccount, converting it to U.S. funds; then on March 31, 1989, someone withdrew a further C$91,455 from the Frankfurt subaccount in cash, again converting it to another currency. On June 29, 1989, there was another withdrawal of C$30,000, again in another currency. Schreiber's Deutschmark account, 18679.2, saw a credit of DM573,000 on July 6, and on the same day 18679.1, the Canadian-funds subaccount, was debited C$361,742, roughly the same sum. And on it went. In September there was a C$30,000 cash withdrawal from the Frankfurt subaccount and another transfer to the Master subaccount; on December 6, 1989, more than C$20,000 was transferred from the Frankfurt subaccount to another account.

As the year progressed, Mulroney's government was preoccupied by the troubled negotiations for the Free Trade Agreement with the United States. Chancellor Kohl had a more historic agenda – the growing rapprochement with East Germany and eventual reunification. Inspired by Mikhail Gorbachev's liberal reforms in the Soviet Union, Hungary's government began to relax its restrictions on visiting East Germans and was soon allowing them to slip across Hungary's border with Austria. By the summer, thousands of East Germans were using this route to the West. Others sought refuge in West German embassies in Prague and Warsaw. Border guards made no effort to staunch the flow of refugees, and by the late fall the new leader of East Germany, Egon Krenz, realized there was nothing his government could do to stop it.

On November 9, 1989, Krenz's government feebly announced new liberalized travel regulations, which, to most Germans, signalled a capitulation. That night thousands of East Germans demanded that the guards let them pass into West Berlin, where rejoicing crowds greeted them with tears and riotous celebrations. Around the world, millions watched these proud, emotional hours on television. Political observers were reassured by the presence of the man who would rise to the challenge of uniting the two Germanys. Helmut Kohl was more than equal to the task. Not only would he ensure the safety of a flood of refugees into West Germany, but he would draft a treaty between the two halves of the country, create a monetary union, and secure international support for the rebuilding of his nation.

Frank Moores, whose income was so dependent on German

companies, must have watched these momentous events with interest, but nation-building was of less interest to him at that moment than the acquisition of another house, the second property he'd bought in less than a year. He and Beth found a waterfront condominium in an exclusive gated community at River Harbour, in Jupiter, Florida, just a short drive north of West Palm Beach. Along with a private marina for fifty-six boats, the complex offered four tennis courts, a heated swimming pool, and several excellent golf courses nearby. There was even a resident celebrity: the movie star Burt Reynolds had his own unit and a park in the community named after him. Moores gave the owners a US$10,000 down payment; then he contacted Schreiber.

"Schreiber called me and said, 'I need a company to buy a condo in Florida for Frank Moores,'" explained Pelossi. Pelossi picked a handy shell company he'd set up a few years earlier for another client; it was called Ticinella Anstalt, named after Ticino, the Swiss canton where Pelossi was born. He sold the company to Schreiber for US$6,000.

"I had instructions from Moores directly about what to do with the money," said Pelossi. "He phoned me."

Schreiber withdrew the balance owing on the condo from the Frankfurt subaccount in the Swiss Bank Corporation in Zurich and moved it into a new Vaduz account for Ticinella. On January 31, 1990, twelve days after Air Canada took delivery of the first Airbus plane, Pelossi wired US$188,000 – which appeared on the surface to come from a Schreiber-owned company, Ticinella – to Florida to close the sale. The registered owner was Ticinella Anstalt, but the annual Florida tax bills and all the other property charges were sent to Moores at Chaffeys Locks.

13

Tanks for the Saudis

"Holy shit!" A big grin split Horst Schmid's face as he listened to the caller on the other end of the telephone. When he hung up, he turned to his visitor, Christian Graef, and chuckled in disbelief.

"You know, Schreiber really just did it."

"Did what?" Graef asked. He didn't need to ask who Schreiber was; he remembered him well, although it had been several years since he had seen him. Schreiber rarely came to Alberta any more. Schmid was now the commissioner general for tourism in Alberta, and Graef had dropped in for a visit. During their chat, the phone rang, and Schmid had taken the call.

Now Schmid was too busy to answer Graef's question. He pulled a calculator towards him and started to punch the buttons.

"Mmm ... one percent of that to this ... a billion dollars ... eight ... plus this ... That's a lot of money."

"What are you talking about?" Graef asked again.

"Well, Schreiber just made a deal with the Airbus people, or with the Canadian government," Schmid answered, looking up. "Holy God, he sure made a pile of money."

The first of the Air Canada planes had touched down on the tarmac in Toronto on January 19, 1990, and within days the Airbus money began winding its way from the Paris bank through Liechten-stein and into Schreiber's account 18679 at the Swiss Bank Corporation in Zurich. There Schreiber divided the money among his various subaccounts. There would be variations in the way he allocated the funds in the months and years ahead, but often he followed a simple formula: his Canadian-funds subaccount 18679.1 received half of the Airbus commissions; the Frankfurt subaccount, 41391.0, received one-quarter. The Master subaccount, 18679.7, received one-eighth, and the Stewardess subaccount, 18679.6, received the final one-eighth.

Bank records for March 26, 1990, reveal how Schreiber split up the first two Airbus commissions, a total of US$751,000, which had arrived in his American-dollar subaccount. Schreiber transferred a little more than half, US$377,000, into 18679.1, converting it to C$443,352. Another 25 percent went into the Frankfurt subaccount, converted to C$219,912; the Master subaccount received a further C$109,956, or 12.5 percent; and the Stewardess subaccount received the final 12.5 percent, still in U.S. dollars, US$93,500.

The German prosecutors and tax investigators would later scruti-nize the bank record and diary references to these subaccounts and their coded monikers as if they were the Dead Sea Scrolls. Schreiber's naming system was transparent: he attached a familiar first name to the account or, more frequently, he simply altered it slightly to make a new word. After following the evidence of his business connections and contractual arrangements, his travel itineraries and appointment diaries, and money transfers in and out of various accounts, the inves-tigators concluded that the subaccount nicknames were indeed easily deciphered. In several official documents prepared over the next few years, they would identify Frankfurt as representing Frank Moores and Stewardess as representing Stuart Iddles.[1] Master, they believed, was Franz Josef Strauss. Schreiber didn't give the Canadian-funds subac-count 18679.1 a code name; it held funds for many purposes, includ-ing for Schreiber himself.

According to Giorgio Pelossi's sworn statements, when he and Schreiber had met Frank Moores in Zurich in 1986 to open Moores's two Swiss accounts, Schreiber had told him that half the Airbus commission money was to go to the "Canadian friends" and the other half was to be split among the European associates, Schreiber among them. Pelossi had no idea whether in fact Schreiber was allocating the commissions this way, since he never had access to the Zurich bank accounts, but the bank documents do indicate at least one notable deviation from Pelossi's version of the procedure.

Pelossi said Schreiber at first intended to transfer the Canadians' half of the Airbus money in two portions to Frank Moores's two bank accounts, 34107 and 34117, the latter code-named Devon. Account 34107 was for Moores and other Canadian associates, while Devon 34117 was allegedly earmarked for Brian Mulroney. Or so Schreiber described it, according to Pelossi's statements.

Bank records obtained by the prosecutors do not show Airbus money going into account 34117; whatever the reason for creating Devon, it was never used for this purpose. Instead, it appears that Schreiber kept control of the money himself, creating his own subaccounts with his own code names. Why let Moores have all the fun? And while the money trail into Schreiber's subaccounts is clear, the money trail out is opaque. Over time Schreiber – or people acting for him – would withdraw millions of dollars in seemingly untraceable cash.

Also in March, Schreiber would have been reminded just how important it was to keep his activities secret. A damaging story broke about four Indian government officials who may have accepted kickbacks from Airbus Industrie. The story had its roots in the industry rumours that had circulated six years earlier involving Rajiv Gandhi. Investigators charged that these officials had reversed a government decision to buy Boeing 757 jetliners and purchased thirty-eight Airbus 320s instead, a deal worth about US$1.7 billion. It was alleged that at the request of Airbus, its salesman Ranjit Jayaratnam had paid commissions to various players. On March 29, the Indian government filed preliminary charges against Airbus Industrie, alleging bribery and corruption, but eventually the whole investigation was quietly closed. Airbus could claim it had convinced India to reverse its Boeing decision at the last minute thanks to effective lobbying, just as it had done with Wardair back in 1987.

If hints of a scandal in India caused Schreiber any concern, they did not slow him down. In May he met with Pitak Intrawityanunt in

London concerning the sale of Airbus jets to the Royal Thai Air Force and Thai Airways International. On June 20, Roger Bailly, the lawyer in the contracts division of Airbus Industrie who had drafted the contract for the Air Canada commissions, faxed a seven-page Airbus-IAL agreement to Pelossi, confirming an earlier discussion. The money would go into IAL's account 235.972.037 in Vaduz.

Now that Schreiber could count on a steady flow of commissions from Airbus Industrie, he devoted more of his attention to his beloved Bear Head project, a venture in desperate need of rejuvenation. He was attracting more opponents than converts, for several reasons. Part of it had to do with his style: he wasn't taken seriously by many of the businessmen and bureaucrats who counted.

One such businessman was Bernard Lamarre, the president of Lavalin. Schreiber had been trying for years to arrange a joint venture with Bear Head and one of Lavalin's subsidiaries, an engineering works in Trenton, Nova Scotia. Lavalin was even mentioned in the understanding in principle that Schreiber had signed with the federal government in 1988. In reality, Lamarre recalled, a business venture with Schreiber was never a possibility. "His project was so vague ... no business plan, nothing at all, it went nowhere." He added: "I thought, myself, that [Schreiber] was like a used-car salesman ... He was bragging about all kinds of things, but there was no substance behind anything. I always thought he was a buffoon."

In early February 1990, Schreiber prepared for a crucial meeting with senior Ottawa mandarins at National Defence Headquarters. He, Jürgen Massmann of Thyssen Henschel, and Greg Alford of Bear Head Industries had been promised two and a half hours with a who's who of defence procurement. Chief among them were Robert Fowler, the deputy minister of defence, and General John de Chastelain, chief of defence staff. Cliff MacKay was there from the Industry Department, as well as officials from External Affairs, Supply and Services, Finance, the Privy Council Office, and the Atlantic Canada Opportunities Agency.

Fowler was the senior mandarin and the toughest sell. "It was very obvious from both the tone and the comments given to me by the deputy minister that this was not a meeting that [Fowler] wanted," said Colonel Michel Drapeau, who also attended. "The meeting had been forced upon him." Fowler's reluctance appeared to have had as much to do with Schreiber as it did with his project. "The impression [Fowler] left me with was that Schreiber was a parvenu, and Schreiber had ... little class. Little education. [Fowler] was not very charitable nor very complimentary."

Even so, this was a stellar group and an important opportunity, and Schreiber showed up at Conference Room A of the Major General Pearkes Building in Ottawa on February 5, prepared to convince and cajole the officials whose support he so desperately needed. That same day, Paul Tellier, the clerk of the Privy Council, sent a memo marked "Secret" to Brian Mulroney. Tellier told the prime minister that "the international situation has evolved" since his government first pledged support for Bear Head in 1988; the Cold War was over and there was less need for armoured vehicles in the military. Referring to the gathering across town at NDHQ, he wrote, "It will be made clear to Thyssen Industries during the meeting that the acquisition of [armoured vehicles] is no longer being contemplated on the scale nor in the time frame that had been initially planned."

Robert Fowler's message was exactly that. Minutes of the meeting show the deputy minister was blunt: "The DM emphasized that no commitment of any kind would be given at this meeting ... The DM acknowledged Thyssen's expertise in the production of armoured vehicles and tanks but underscored the fact that Canada has no plans now, or in the foreseeable future to purchase tanks. DND does have plans to purchase Light Armoured Vehicles (LAV) but these plans are well in the future, and will depend on available financing ... Canada will not give investors a 'carte blanche' on exports." Already the meeting was tense and Schreiber had not even spoken. As Drapeau described it, the atmosphere was "glacial."

Fowler ended his remarks with an apology that he, the chief of defence staff, and the vice-chief of defence staff had to leave the meeting. He did add, however, that he thought the planned briefing by Thyssen would be "beneficial to those remaining." Fowler's abrupt departure was an insult, to be sure. Later Schreiber privately fumed about his treatment by bureaucrats. But he didn't give up. The civil servants may have been against him but the politicians were not. He believed Mulroney was on his side, and he bragged openly about Elmer MacKay's unqualified support. His team of well-connected lobbyists harangued the exasperated bureaucrats at one meeting after another for the rest of the year.

Schreiber continued to enjoy the time he spent with Mulroney, despite the Bear Head setbacks. The two men talked about more than tanks and light armoured vehicles. Schreiber complained often about his dislike of bureaucracy, but he also spoke to Mulroney about Germany's plans for reunification. Mulroney paid close attention to Schreiber's views and would draw on those conversations when the topic came up with his international counterparts, as it did in early 1990.

In February Chancellor Helmut Kohl and his interior minister, Wolfgang Schäuble, went to Washington for talks with President George Bush about Germany's reunification plans. Kohl and Bush spent a weekend at Camp David, the presidential country retreat in Maryland, and conferred with both British prime minister Margaret Thatcher and Canadian prime minister Brian Mulroney by telephone. Mulroney would say years later that Schreiber's views helped influence his opinion on the issue of German reunification, particularly at a time when others were opposed to it. On this occasion, Mulroney undoubtedly found Schreiber's contribution useful.

"On the infrequent occasions when I would see him on business, when he was promoting the Thyssen project, he would raise this German reunification issue and speak very knowledgeably about it," said Mulroney in 1996. "It was something that interested me a great deal, as a question of Canadian foreign policy, and as you may remember, ultimately, when Chancellor Kohl reported to the commission of the Bundestag on the achievements of the ... unification, he particularly thanked the United States, Russia, and Canada for our contributions to that objective ... I was of course impressed by anyone with good knowledge – a good knowledge base and the capacity to articulate it."

A day or two before the Camp David phone conference, Schäuble had met with Secretary of State James Baker in Washington. Security issues were at the top of all agendas. Kohl and Bush agreed that a united Germany should remain a member of NATO, and that NATO troops should remain in West Germany, but Kohl upset the Americans with a strong suggestion that the Conference on Security and Co-operation in Europe, a thirty-five-nation bloc that included the United States, should now run NATO's troops – which would effectively put the CSCE in charge of NATO itself. Mulroney and Kohl would have a chance to talk about this again in a few months because the Canadian prime minister was planning to visit Bonn in June.

Schreiber soldiered on with Bear Head, occasionally sending forlorn letters to Elmer MacKay, now the minister responsible for the Atlantic Canada Opportunities Agency. "For the last five years, Minister, our approach has been forthright at all times," he wrote on April 5, 1990. "You will appreciate that I am somewhat disturbed that our integrity has been questioned, and I am further upset that misinformation continues to circulate as regards this project."

Schreiber tried yet another angle on the people at Defence: if the generals would soften their opposition enough to buy just a few of Thyssen's Fuchs (Fox) tanks, he could use the sale to impress the U.S. army, which was calling for bids on a large tank contract. Thyssen could cooperate with an American company, General Dynamics Land Systems Divisions, to build the vehicles, but Canada would still get lots of jobs. The military brass responded with unhelpful questions about whether the tanks would be able to fit into transport aircraft for ferrying to war zones.

Following yet another meeting with Jürgen Massmann, Dick Gentles, a director general in the PCO, wrote a summary memo on April 19: "The information I received from our liaison officer in Tactical Command would seem to indicate that the option to purchase more Fox ... vehicles may be one of the many offerings placed on the altar of the peace dividend." In other words, there wasn't a hope in hell of a tank order from the U.S. army for Thyssen.

Three weeks later Laurent Beaudoin, the chairman and chief executive officer of Bombardier, complained to Mulroney that Schreiber's activities were threatening his business plans in Europe. Bombardier was one of Canada's international success stories, manufacturing railway and subway cars as well as its famous snowmobiles and winning countless lucrative contracts with foreign governments. When Bombardier took over Canadair, it went into the aerospace business with enthusiasm. It developed a surveillance drone – a small, unmanned, preprogrammed aircraft – called the CL-289, with two partners, Dornier, a German subsidiary of Daimler-Benz, and France's Société Anonyme de Télécommunications. In late 1987, Germany signed a C$410-million contract to buy the drone from Bombardier, and in 1990 it was about to sign a follow-up contract worth C$175 million.

"It has recently come to our attention," Beaudoin wrote to Mulroney with repressed fury, "that a Mr. Karlheinz Schreiber, of Bear Head Industries (Thyssen) in Cape Breton, has been encouraging German government officials and Ministers to not approve the CL-289 follow-on order unless a Light Armoured Vehicle project, directed by Thyssen, is approved by the Canadian Government. We have also been told that the Honourable Elmer McKay [sic] has been supporting Mr. Schreiber in these efforts."

While he had no direct knowledge of the Bear Head deal, Beaudoin told the prime minister, it was his understanding that there was little chance it would go ahead. "If this is the case," he added, "we need to find a way to delicately unwind an increasingly difficult situation."

Beaudoin's letter had to be handled just as delicately. Schreiber was seen as a friend of the prime minister. Paul Tellier understood something of Mulroney's dilemma and drafted a reply for him full of concern and diplomacy. After expressing pleasure about the success of the drone and the deal Bombardier had signed with the German government, the letter noted it would be "most unfortunate" if the contract were linked to Bear Head.

"The Government does not wish any connection to be made" between the two, Mulroney's response said. Adding that no decision had yet been taken on Bear Head, the letter suggested Beaudoin avail himself of the services of Canada's staff in Bonn to help market the drone and declared that Canada was ready to tell the Germans that the government unequivocally supported Bombardier in its effort to win the follow-on order. It was pleasant and meaningless and made no mention of

Schreiber or his campaign to tie the drone deal to Bear Head.

In the meantime Schreiber had managed to arrange yet another meeting with Paul Tellier, this time with Elmer MacKay at his side. Afterwards, on July 8, Schreiber wrote a "Dear Paul" letter to the nation's chief civil servant. "Thank you for taking the time to meet with me and the Hon. Elmer MacKay on the Bear Head project. I am very encouraged by the Prime Minister's support in this project ... Our experience also teaches us, however, that there are pockets of misinformation, either arising out of honest error or otherwise. Much of the last five years has been spent identifying and subsequently debunking this misinformation ... I am totally confident that a simple phone call to myself or Mr. MacKay, who is well aware of this file, will set the record straight should you ever encounter any such misinformation."

Perhaps there was some life left in Bear Head after all.

During the summer of 1990, Jürgen Massmann solicited Schreiber's help with a new Thyssen project involving the government of Saudi Arabia, one that would be far more lucrative than the struggling Bear Head deal. For a long time, Thyssen had wanted to sell military vehicles to Saudi Arabia but had been prevented from doing so by Germany's tough laws prohibiting the sale of arms and military equipment to regions of conflict such as the Middle East. It was one of the reasons Thyssen had looked for a redoubt in Nova Scotia and had spent so much money trying to make Bear Head happen.

Only the tiny country of Kuwait separated Saudi Arabia from its aggressive neighbour Iraq, and by 1990 it was eager to purchase matériel from Thyssen. In particular, it hoped to buy Thyssen's famous Fuchs "sniffer" tanks, the top-of-the-line model designed to detect nuclear, chemical, and biological contamination.[2] Saudi officials made delicate but pressing overtures to Thyssen executives. Everyone understood that money was not an issue; the Saudis spent billions of dollars on defence every year. Was there no way around these restrictive German laws?

Massmann and his colleagues believed a deal could be done, but they were realistic. To win the necessary federal export permit would require obtaining an exemption to the rule at the highest bureaucratic and political levels in Bonn. And there were the Saudis themselves to consider; nothing happened in this rich Muslim kingdom without the approval of those close to the royal family.

Massmann had started to pave the way during two days of meetings on June 26 and 27 in Paris with a wealthy Saudi businessman, Mansour Ojjeh, the owner of Techniques d'Avant-Garde, a Luxembourg-based company. Although consumers identified TAG with expensive Swiss watches, particularly TAG Heuer, the firm controlled aircraft companies, hotels, electronics manufacturers, construction companies, and oil concessions in Africa, the Middle East, and Asia. Through its car manufacturer, McLaren International, TAG invested millions in Formula One car races. But Ojjeh was more than a billionaire businessman, he was one of the most influential power brokers in the Middle East.

His father, Akhram Ojjeh, had been an adviser to the Saudi royal family and represented French arms manufacturers in the country; as Richard Norton wrote in the *Guardian*, Akhram Ojjeh was "widely believed to be a broker between the Saudi defence establishment and western arms dealers." His influence had been inherited by his son. Thanks to Mansour Ojjeh's connections in Germany – Max Strauss, for example, was a close friend – and his offices in Riyadh, he became a helpful facilitator for Thyssen's ambitions in Saudi Arabia. When Ojjeh met with Massmann in Paris, it was to figure out how to make the sale attractive to all parties. What it would take, both men knew, was money.

Interestingly, Thyssen Henschel already had an experienced operations and marketing manager, Jörg Bühler, who enjoyed excellent connections to Adnan Khashoggi. But Massmann stepped around Bühler and Khashoggi. Indeed, the whole process was so secretive that Ojjeh did not want to deal directly with Thyssen Henschel. They knew Saudi Arabia disallowed payments to third-party agents in any deal involving government purchases. Should such payments be discovered, the deal would be cancelled. Massmann and Ojjeh had to make their plans in complete secrecy, confining documents to a small group, and everything had to be done as quickly as possible.

But on August 2, 1990, the project escalated into an emergency.

Iraq's president, Saddam Hussein, ordered an invasion of Kuwait, and the war in the Persian Gulf began. The Saudis looked to the West for help, but no nation rushed to assist. U.S. president George Bush declared his country's fierce opposition to the invasion three days later and sent his defence secretary, Richard Cheney, to meet Saudi Arabia's King Fahd on August 6. The king asked Cheney for military support. Within two days, U.S. fighter planes had arrived in Riyadh, but the Americans were far too cautious to jump into combat; diplomacy and discussion came first.

At the same time, the Saudi ambassador to Bonn, Abbas Ghazzawi, was in touch with Holger Pfahls, the deputy minister of defence, looking for Germany's contribution. The answer was the standard reply: there were restrictions against the sale of military equipment in the Middle East. Pfahls himself thought the prohibition was ridiculous. Maybe we could give the Saudis some of our own Thyssen tanks and call it a loan, someone suggested. It was an idea worth pursuing.

Eleven days later, on August 13, Thyssen decided Jürgen Massmann was not to blame after all for the presence of sensitive documents concerning federal defence matters in his office in 1987. He was free to deal again with Defence Ministry officials such as Pfahls. On August 22, Massmann wrote to the Saudi defence minister, Prince Sultan Abdullah bin Abdul Aziz, to underline a piece of information that the Saudis already knew: that Thyssen Henschel's entire inventory of sniffer tanks had been sold to the U.S. armed forces (over the strong protests of U.S. tank manufacturers). If the prince wanted more information, Massmann would be happy to provide it. A copy of Massmann's letter to the prince was faxed to a number in France and to another in Munich, to the office of a local businessman connected to Ojjeh who had agreed to act as an intermediary between Massmann and Ojjeh. Among the documents the German prosecutors were to find years later was a fax of the contract between Thyssen Henschel and the Ojjeh group – sent by Max Strauss.

Massman also courted Colonel Ulrich Wegener, a legendary military figure in Germany, whose elite counterterrorist unit, Grenzschutzgruppe 9, had successfully rescued hostages after a Lufthansa plane was hijacked to Mogadishu, Somalia, in October 1977. Known ever after as "the hero of Mogadishu," Wegener had retired in 1990 to a career as a consultant on military issues and anti-terrorist measures. To the Thyssen executives, he was an ideal person to assist on the Saudi matter: his stature with the German military and the Defence Ministry would immediately open doors. His name began to appear frequently in Massmann's diary.

Massmann and his friends developed a complicated scheme but there was nothing subtle about it – money would grease the deal. They needed a middleman to pull it all together, and Schreiber was the ideal candidate. He thoroughly understood Thyssen's military vehicle program and the various products manufactured by the company. Even though he had not yet been successful in establishing a Canadian plant, Thyssen's executives knew how hard he worked and trusted him completely. Massmann knew too that Schreiber had the infrastructure in place – the Liechtenstein shell companies, the protective trustees, and the Swiss bank accounts – to manage money on the scale required by this deal. Schreiber enjoyed excellent contacts among Saudi Arabians, and he moved easily in the Thyssen crowd and in government circles. One of his tasks would be to help persuade the Kohl government to bend the export law. The man whose support they needed was Holger Pfahls.

If Karlheinz Schreiber understood one tenet of the middleman's creed, it was that every man has his price. Another man might be tall and handsome, possessed of a distinguished pedigree and an elegant home. That man might have the envy of his peers and travel in distinguished company and yes, he might look down on a plain man from a poor family, a fellow with coarse language and rough manners. But these men became equals when the rough man knew the other man's vulnerabilities. This was Schreiber's gift. He could calculate, to a fine degree, a man's price. He even knew when the currency of desire was not money but leverage, say, or information or simply friendship.

Schreiber clearly understood what it would take to secure Holger Pfahls's support for the Saudi tank contract. As a young man, Pfahls had been a protégé of Franz Josef Strauss, who recognized his drive, intelligence, and talent. Handsome and charismatic with a taste for luxury and adventure, he'd joined the CSU in Bavaria and quickly climbed the bureaucratic ladder, moving into security and intelligence areas. Before long he was the president of the Bundesamtes für Verfassungsschutz, or BfV, the federal government department that deals with right-wing and left-wing extremists and terrorists operating within Germany. Pfahls had served as deputy minister of defence under Minister Gerhard Stoltenberg since 1987. He was responsible, among other things, for the budget, armaments decisions, and procurement. If Pfahls were to approve an export permit for the tanks, Schreiber believed, the deal could go ahead. What, then, was Pfahls's price? Whether or not Pfahls agreed to accept an inducement, at this time or later, it is certain that he threw his support behind the Thyssen scheme.

On September 7, 1990, Schreiber welcomed a group of visitors to his home in Kaufering, among them Pfahls, a few senior Saudi officials chosen on the advice of Ojjeh, and representatives from Thyssen. The participants had decided Kaufering was the safest venue; no hotel or office could guarantee them the privacy they required. They had gathered to discuss the plan they now called Operation Fox.

The Saudis wanted thirty-six military vehicles, including several of the Fuchs tanks, and decided their best option was a "special loan" from the German army. Thyssen could refit the equipment for the Saudis' use and immediately begin manufacturing replacement vehicles for the German army. The price was steep: before it was over, Saudi Arabia would pay DM446 million for the deal, an amount that included millions in "consulting fees" – DM220 million (about C$300 million), as it happened, very nearly half the value of the deal. The bare cost of the equipment would eventually add up to DM226 million.

It was the management of consulting fees that took so much careful attention. According to German authorities who later investigated the plot, the money for the various players – bribes, kickbacks, and secret commissions – was held in three Panamanian companies: a shell called Ovessim that was registered in 1989, another shell called Linsur, and Schreiber's own holding company, ATG, set up in 1984. Schreiber wanted 6 percent of the value of the contract for himself and other close associates who would facilitate the final sale. Initially, the funds flowing to Schreiber were to be paid to Bayerische Bitumen-Chemie.

Before the project went ahead, however, Schreiber proposed a further payment of DM1.35 million, above and beyond the 6 percent, for his role as a mediator, assisting in establishing contacts with the Saudis and preparing Thyssen's proposal. According to Markus Dettmer in *Der Spiegel* on November 17, 1999, Schreiber insisted there be no written record of this part of the arrangement, and Massmann agreed; when an invoice for the DM1.35 million arrived from Bayerische Bitumen-Chemie on October 9, Thyssen paid it.

Three days after the meeting at Kaufering, Holger Pfahls met with the operations chief of the German army to broach the idea of a tank loan. The military men were not enthusiastic. Brigadier General Rainer Fell, Major General Norbert Majewski, Lieutenant General Hanns Jörn Boes, and Major General Karl Timm were all against it. If the tanks came from the German military's existing stock, they said, the army's strength would be seriously compromised. Thyssen couldn't supply replacements fast enough. Pfahls brushed away their criticism. We'll order more, he said, nonsensically.

Pfahls's next meeting with the Saudis included their ambassador and Saudi military brass. Germany's ambassador in Riyadh met with Saudi officials there to discuss the transfer of equipment, and on September 26, the Saudis invited a German team to Riyadh to explore an offer of ten used tanks from the German army. Pfahls went to his boss, Stoltenberg, for approval, but Stoltenberg sided with the generals.

One ministry bureaucrat who observed Pfahls's involvement in the effort to get the deal approved was Friedrich-Karl Kölsch. Kölsch later told prosecutors that Jürgen Massmann, Winfried Haastert, and Schreiber's accountant Lorenzo Wullschleger made frequent visits to Pfahls. Another former associate, Wilhelm Priegnitz, described Pfahls's meetings with Massmann, the Saudi ambassador, military attachés, and others. What was unusual, Priegnitz said, was that all the correspondence relating to the affair went straight to Pfahls, not to a more junior official.

On October 4, Pfahls wrote directly to Helmut Kohl, asking for approval of the tank deal with the Saudis. When he was slow to respond,

Pfahls pressed harder. He presented a plan for a three-way deal between Thyssen Henschel, the German government, and Saudi Arabia, one in which the army would turn over ten refitted tanks to Saudi Arabia and the government would order replacements. In the interim the German army would be left with just twenty-four Fuchs tanks.

By October 10, four senior Thyssen executives, led by Alfons Pannenbäcker, head of the corporate tax department of Thyssen Industrie, the parent company, had put their signatures to an internal memo outlining the proposal to the Saudis. Marked "strictly confidential," the memorandum from Thyssen Henschel and Thyssen's engineering division described the financial details of an arrangement involving military vehicles, communications equipment, and a maintenance and service facility. At this stage, the basic cost was projected at DM158 million. On top of this amount, the note said, there would be "not insubstantial commission payments" of 40 percent of the total contract sum. The document specified that these commissions could be paid to foreign nationals, who would not have to pay taxes in Germany. Thyssen would claim the commissions as deductible expenses on its own income-tax statements.

On October 19, Saudi army officers were able to see the Fuchs sniffer tanks in action at a demonstration on the U.S. military base in Dhahran, and they liked what they saw. Their impatience grew. But so too did the cost of the project.

While Schreiber waited anxiously for the deal to be blessed by the chancellor, Massmann worked to bring the politicians on side. On October 31, 1990, he wrote to Erich Riedl, the federal economics minister in Bonn, seeking his endorsement. Riedl, a Bavarian always considered on the right of his party, was in favour of sending the tanks, but his ministry acknowledged that even if on loan, they had to be classified as weapons of war. The prohibition of sales to the Middle East most definitely applied.

But to Massmann, Schreiber, and Pfahls, such a prohibition was not an insurmountable obstacle. On November 16, Massmann and Jörg Bühler, who had finally been brought on board, were in Riyadh for another meeting with the Saudis. Massmann left after just two days; Bühler stayed on to bargain over contractual details with Saudi officials.

The contract he was negotiating contained the customary prohibition against commission payments.

In late November, Massmann visited Lorenzo Wullschleger to confirm payment to Schreiber's ATG of 6 percent of the tank deal's final price. All the while Massmann kept Ojjeh's Munich contact informed of developments.

The details of the commission agreements were kept confidential and hidden to all but the players themselves. In the same way that the Airbus-IAL contract had been signed and deposited in a law office in Zurich, Thyssen's agreements with the various shell companies were secreted in a safety deposit box in the Swiss Bank Corporation's Paradeplatz branch, also in Zurich. Thyssen's lawyer Wolfgang Pigorsch saw to these arrangements, he later claimed, on Massmann's instructions.

The Thyssen-ATG agreement was structured as a consulting contract under which ATG would provide "marketing services," as the time-honoured euphemism described it, to Thyssen. The contract was not with Thyssen's Henschel division, the branch that would contract with the Saudis, but with Thyssen Industrie AG, a larger entity that comprised many parts. Who could tell to which budget or company division these marketing expenses were posted?

The various pieces of paperwork carried the signatures of one or more Thyssen executives: CEO Eckhard Rohkamm, Ernst Höffken, or Winfried Haastert. Once the official supply contract was approved by the Kohl administration and signed by the principals, the secret commissions contracts were to be removed from the safety deposit box and replaced by documents bearing later dates. It would be prudent to do away with the pre-deal paperwork: the Saudi prohibition against third-party agents would be circumvented by a technicality. (For some reason Haastert breached the security of that plan: he kept a copy of the original ATG agreement in his private safe at home, a copy that was eventually surrendered to the prosecutors.)

It had taken six months of careful manoeuvring, but by the beginning of December everything was in place. First, there was a final draft of a formal contract between Thyssen Henschel and the Saudi Ministry of Defence that required only the final signatures. Thyssen would supply the Saudis with refitted equipment: ten Fuchs sniffer tanks, fourteen armoured personnel carriers, eight ambulances, and four mobile command vehicles. Any tax wrinkles related to the contract had been smoothed out by Schreiber's friend Rolf Wegener (no relation to Ulrich Wegener), who served as a mediator and go-between with the Saudis. In late November he secured agreement that there would be no taxes payable in Saudi Arabia on the related services and training to be provided by Thyssen.

Thyssen's estimate of its profit was between 8 and 10 percent of the total value of the deal. The secret commissions payable had risen from 40 to 47 percent of the value. The details of these commissions, how much and to whom, were likewise confirmed among the parties. In the words of the investigating authorities some years later, "the bribes available had been fixed."

In November the Gulf War became an international effort against Iraq, led by U.S. General Norman Schwarzkopf. The United Nations had authorized the use of force to remove Iraq's army from Kuwait, and the international military coalition included thirty-six countries, Canada and Germany among them. But Helmut Kohl had still not granted approval. It was taking too long, and Schreiber and Massmann feared their carefully woven webs could come to nothing if the hostilities should end.

For Schreiber, these months were exciting but frustrating. His Thyssen schemes seemed to encounter one difficulty after another. He had not given up on Bear Head, and in late September it appeared he was floating a trial balloon to see if he could pressure the Canadian government into a positive decision. "Bear Head says it may cancel its $85 million military vehicle factory," blared the Canadian Press headline on September 29, 1990. The story quoted Greg Alford, Bear Head's vice-president, as saying the war in the Persian Gulf and delays at National Defence might force Bear Head to abandon its plans for a plant in Nova Scotia. The article also mentioned that the project had been in limbo ever since Canada slashed its defence budget in 1989.

The same day the Bear Head story ran, Gary Ouellet, one of Bear Head's lobbyists, opened an account at the same bank his friends patronized – the Swiss Bank Corporation's Paradeplatz branch in Zurich. He gave Schreiber full power of attorney over his account, number 45828.

During that year, while Schreiber battled the obstreperous Ottawa bureaucrats and plotted to sell tanks to the Saudis, another drama was quietly unfolding out of his sight. His partner in so many clandestine arrangements and transactions, the man who made everything run so smoothly and efficiently between banks and shell companies, was unhappy.

Giorgio Pelossi had never forgotten his friend's promise that some day, they would both be rich. He still had the contract Schreiber had drafted on hotel writing paper during a flight across Canada, back in their Alberta days. Now, as he processed millions of dollars, as he watched the Airbus commissions flow into IAL and then stood aside as Schreiber shipped them out again to men less deserving than himself, he brooded. Part of this windfall should have been his, he believed, but he didn't have the guts to confront Schreiber directly. His friend was always too busy; he couldn't pin him down. *I know he'll acknowledge what he promised*, Pelossi finally told himself, *but it wouldn't hurt to be proactive.*

On August 13, Pelossi arranged to have his own shell company set up by Edmund Frick, naming it the Erfel Anstalt. The next step was to create a contract between Schreiber's IAL and Erfel. From then on, Erfel was to take 5 percent of the money coming into IAL before it was sent to the Swiss Bank Corporation in Zurich. On August 16, Pelossi sliced off his first cut – US$200,000 – and tucked it into Erfel's new bank account. The next day, when US$140,000 rolled into Vaduz from Airbus Industrie, he saw to its distribution in the usual way. The only difference was that now some of the wealth stayed with him.

14

Cashing In

On the first day of 1991, Karlheinz Schreiber opened a new appointment diary to record the names, phone numbers, and bank accounts that he would refer to frequently in the months ahead. Much of what he noted was in a personal shorthand or code, but he kept it simple enough to be understood at a glance.

A marvel of meticulous record-keeping, his diaries captured hundreds of phone calls, money transfers, and important meetings. The telephone numbers included residences, car phones, and cell-phones; the names on his to-call lists were neatly ticked off when he reached them. Most men with the kind of agenda he set for himself would have relinquished these organizational minutiae to a secretary, but Schreiber seemed to have a passion for managing it all himself.

Just before the addresses section he listed ten names in neat and careful script. Seven of them were nicknames or codes, variations of the individuals' first names, as was his habit. All would be studied later by investigators and by a Swiss court, who, after examining the evidence, would connect them to Schreiber's associates.[1] Maxwell, which stood for Max Strauss, headed the list. Stewardess, for the Airbus vice-president Stuart Iddles, was next, followed by Jürglund, the code name for Jürgen Massmann of Thyssen Henschel. Pitak, fourth on the list, was Pitak Intrawityanunt, the special adviser to the Thai cabinet who had been befriended by Max Strauss and Schreiber in 1989. The fifth name, Holgart, was code for Holger Pfahls, deputy defence minister of Germany. Fred, the next name, was Fred Doucet; Frankfurt, the seventh name, stood for Frank Moores; and Winter, the eighth, was the code name for Winfried Haastert of Thyssen Industrie. Marc was number nine and represented Marc Lalonde, but Waldherr, the final name on the list, was in code; it was for Walther Leisler Kiep, the treasurer of the Christian Democratic Union.

As Schreiber organized his commission payment schedules for his various projects, he would open subaccounts at his bank for more of the people on the list: Lalonde (counsel for Bear Head), Doucet (lobbyist for Bear Head), Intrawityanunt, Massmann, Pfahls, and Haastert. For Kiep there would be a code name but no bank subaccount; he would be dealt with by another method.

Except for Kiep, the code names noted in his diary were the same names he attached to the subaccounts. Those for the Canadians – Fred, Frankfurt, and Marc – were set up in Canadian dollars, as was Maxwell, earlier called Master; those for the other Europeans – Holgart, Jürglund, and Winter – were all in Deutschmarks. The Stewardess and Pitak subaccounts were in American dollars. In anticipation of Thyssen's commissions for the Saudi tank deal, Schreiber got the new bank accounts organized as quickly as possible.

Meanwhile the Airbus money was flowing like Niagara. By November 23, 1990, the seventh plane had landed on Canadian soil. Schreiber's work was complete on this file; his only task now was managing the millions of U.S. dollars streaming from IAL into his Zurich bank account 18679.

Schreiber always moved the money expeditiously. Only four days after the November 23 aircraft delivery, for example, US$393,000 made its way from the Banque Française du Commerce Extérieur in Paris to an IAL account in the VP Bank in Vaduz; on December 5, another US$393,000 arrived. Airbus sent a further US$200,000 on January 3, 1991, to IAL in Liechtenstein. Pelossi sent all three payments to account 18679, bringing the total to US$986,000. It was almost time for another round of payments to his friends.

Schreiber looked forward to revenues from the Saudi tank contract, but matters seemed stalled. Schreiber spoke to Pfahls on January 6 and again the next day; no one would collect a penny until the export permit was approved.

The escalating crisis in the Gulf worked in their favour. On January 9, 1991, the U.S. secretary of state, James Baker, met Iraq's military leader, Tariq Aziz, in Geneva to seek a peaceful end to the standoff. The meeting was a failure. Three days later Congress approved the use of military force in the Gulf, and on January 15, the deadline set by the United Nations for a withdrawal from Kuwait passed with no action by Iraq. Tension mounted as the world waited for the United States to react. At 2:38 a.m. local time on January 17, Operation Desert Storm was launched without warning when an Allied strike force led by U.S. Apache missiles began bombing Iraq. Later that same day, the final contract between Thyssen Henschel and the Ministry of Defence and Aviation of the Kingdom of Saudi Arabia was concluded. Massmann signed for Thyssen; Jörg Bühler was a witness.

On January 19, 1991, Schreiber opened his diary to record reminders and some careful calculations. Precise little notes fill the spaces with to-do lists and calls to make. "Tel Fred," he reminded himself almost daily during this period. "Fax Stuart." And he devoted a few lines to simple arithmetic. First, under "Fred" he jotted the figure "30 000." Below it he noted the three most recent Airbus payments for Air Canada, and the total, US$986,000, in a column. He divided this amount in half, leaving "493" for what he labelled "CAN." He assigned a quarter to himself ("246") and one-eighth ("123") to Maxwell and Stewardess. And just below that math, off to the left, he wrote that Frankfurt was to get "246" – half of what was assigned to the Canadian side of the ledger. The remaining quarter? He did not name the designated recipient.

Schreiber had unwittingly provided an important clue: by designating half of the Airbus commissions as "CAN," he appeared to confirm what he had never committed to paper until now. As Pelossi claimed, Schreiber had indeed earmarked half the money for

Commissions on three Airbus 320s, paid November 1990 to January 1991

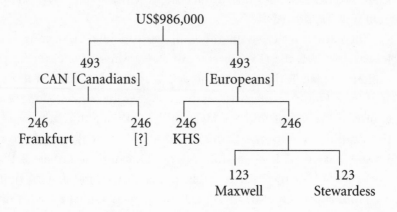

Canadians. And since the Frankfurt subaccount received half the "CAN" money, the real question was, Who got the other half?

Schreiber and Frank Moores appeared to be as amicable as ever. Early in 1991 they began to wonder if they were owed more money by MBB, on their commissions from the helicopter sale to the Canadian Coast Guard back in 1986. They made a request to the federal government under the Access to Information Act to find out exactly how many helicopters had been purchased, including spare parts. It was ironic that the lobbyists who were supposed to have made the deal were soliciting information from the customer to find out what it was they had sold.

On January 9, 1991, Frank Moores wrote to Schreiber. Marked "Personal and Confidential" and "For His Eyes Only," the letter was prepared by Frank Moores's loyal secretary, Nancy O'Neil.

"Dear Karlheinz," Moores began, "Please find enclosed... some calculations I have made." Moores and Schreiber agreed that MBB probably did owe them more than they had been paid. They gave the file to Pelossi.

"I had to fight with the people at MBB for about three months," recalled Pelossi. "We fought about this until May, and then they sent me a statement. In that statement was a small balance in MBB's favour. It wasn't correct, but eventually Schreiber told me not to pursue the matter any more." They probably had been underpaid, but they didn't want to make waves. They let it die.

Taking care of the spoils of the Thai Airways contract also required thought. On January 19, the same day he noted the Air Canada commissions in his diary, Schreiber recorded those from the Thai sale as well. He added commissions from the delivery of two planes – US$1,080,000 in all – and then subtracted US$600,000 for the man he called "Pit," Pitak Intrawityanunt. That money went into the Pitak subaccount, 46341.3. Schreiber sliced the remaining US$480,000 three ways, with one-third for himself, one-third for Maxwell, and one-third for Stewardess.

Schreiber's bank records mirror the diary notes. The Stewardess subaccount, for example, received both Air Canada and Thai Airways commissions in this period. The proceeds added up to US$283,000 – exactly what went into Stewardess. Later, on January 24, Schreiber transferred that US$283,000 into an unidentified account. Schreiber made a note in his diary at the time indicating that Stewardess had an account in Zurich at Lloyds Bank. Stuart Iddles would later pay for a US$1.75-million house in Puerto Vallarta, Mexico, from his account at Lloyds Bank in Zurich.

Schreiber's deposits to the Maxwell subaccount were identical to those to Stewardess, although Maxwell was in Canadian funds. When Schreiber transferred the US$123,000 from the Air Canada sale and US$160,000 from the Thai sale into the Maxwell subaccount, the exchange rate turned it into about C$142,000 and C$185,000 respectively. Unlike the other subaccounts, the Maxwell subaccount remained untouched. Schreiber never withdrew any cash from it, nor transferred any money out. If he really was building a nest egg for Max Strauss, he was keeping it in a safe place. Or so he thought.

The rest of the world may have been riveted by the televised bombardments of Desert Storm, but Schreiber was literally in his counting house during those exciting and dangerous days. On January 23, $112,400 in cash was taken out of his U.S.-funds subaccount in Zurich. A further $100,000 was transferred to an unidentified destination. Since he had already assigned funds for Stewardess, Maxwell, and Frankfurt, it is unclear who was to receive these two amounts. Were they for Schreiber himself? Possibly, since his diary note of January 19 indicates he was owed US$246,000. But also according to his diary, he appeared to owe an unnamed Canadian or Canadians US$246,000. On January 29, he transferred US$271,000 out of the U.S.-funds subaccount and into the Canadian-funds subaccount 18679.1, converting it to C$313,818.

On January 24, the Fred subaccount was credited with C$30,000. A diary note on February 8 read "Strobel 30 Doucet." On March 18, there was a withdrawal of C$30,000 from the Fred subaccount, 46341.2.

By the end of January there was more than C$1.4 million sitting in 18679.1, collecting interest. Certainly there had been some earlier cash withdrawals, notably the C$503,000 taken out in December 1988, and two others more recently. On March 31, 1989, there was a cash withdrawal of C$91,455 and on June 12, 1990, another for C$60,000. Was Schreiber slowly doling out money to its intended Canadian recipients? Or was he simply paying himself his share of the commissions?

While Schreiber filtered commissions into the various accounts, he remained preoccupied with his Thyssen projects. He visited Walther Leisler Kiep in Frankfurt on February 5 to talk to him about the Saudi proposal, and he prepared for meetings on Bear Head in Canada. His diary notes that month reminded him to get "documents" for "Brian," and to tell Bear Head vice-president Greg Alford to congratulate Don Cameron, the cabinet minister who had replaced John Buchanan as the new premier of Nova Scotia. On February 20 he made a note to call Jack Major, his lawyer from the Brennan inquiry days, who was soon to be appointed to the Alberta Court of Appeal. He also itemized calls to be made to Bobby Hladun, Fred Doucet, and Elmer MacKay.

Perhaps the most surprising meetings he had during these days were with Ilse Skorzeny, the elderly widow of Count Otto Skorzeny, one of Hitler's most feared SS commanders during World War II. Often called "the most dangerous man in Europe" by Allied military officers, Skorzeny took part in the invasions of Holland, France, the Balkans, and Russia and was awarded the Iron Cross. He was given an extraordinary assignment from Hitler: the rescue in 1943 of the Italian dictator Benito Mussolini from a resort hotel in the Gran Sasso mountains, where he'd been held for two months after his own party turned against him. It is difficult to know whether Skorzeny will go down in history for this daring and successful escapade or for a more brutal accomplishment. It was Skorzeny who hunted down the German generals who had plotted to kill Hitler.

Others believe his worst crime came after the war, when as one of the ringleaders of the infamous Odessa organization, he helped former SS officers, including Adolf Eichmann, to find safe havens in South America. Skorzeny was tried as a war criminal in 1948, but he escaped and fled to Argentina, where he became a crony of Juan Perón and Eva Perón's bodyguard; later he moved to Spain, and he died there in 1975.

Again and again, Schreiber's diaries reveal appointments and phone calls to Ilse Skorzeny, who was a business person in her own right, known to have strong sympathies with Germany's neo-Nazi movement. There is no evidence that Schreiber shared her views, but just the mention of the Skorzeny name aroused public comment.

By February 20, Schreiber was in Ottawa, using the Bear Head office at the Inn of the Provinces. There he took time to write a four-page confidential letter to Kiep, in which he asked him to use his influence as a CDU insider to persuade the Kohl cabinet to approve the tank deal. He expressed concern about changes he saw in German foreign policy with regard to Canada, the United States, and Saudi Arabia, and he told Kiep that the Saudi government was annoyed by the German government's "hesitant attitude" in supplying the tanks. Please inform the chancellor about this matter, he urged Kiep. He added that he would like to be remembered to Kohl, whom he last saw in Ottawa, when Kohl and Mulroney met before the 1988 G-7 economic summit.

A week later, on February 27, the cabinet finally granted permission for the export of the military equipment to Saudi Arabia. Now Thyssen needed the "borrowed" tanks from the German army, and an order for new replacements. It took until April 10, after much agitation from Pfahls, to obtain the army's cooperation. Schreiber was thrilled and relieved. Thyssen now knew he could manage a project of this complexity; his lack of success with Bear Head was less embarrassing, and he could return to it with fresh confidence.

The irony was that the Gulf War was over. On February 26, the Iraqis fled from Kuwait, and two days later a ceasefire went into effect. On March 3, General Schwarzkopf accepted the Iraqi generals' surrender at Safwan. Fortunately, the Saudis still wanted the tanks.

By March 11, Schreiber was back in Germany but keeping in touch with his Canadian contacts; on March 12, his secretary, Dietlinde Kaupp, reminded him to call "Ottawa" at "16" hours. On March 15, there was a cash withdrawal of C$84,745.76 from the Canadian-funds subaccount 18679.1, and a further C$100,000 in cash was drawn from the Frankfurt subaccount, 41391.0.

Meanwhile, officials in the Prime Minister's Office and the neighbouring Privy Council Office were bracing themselves for another of his visits to Ottawa.

"We understand Karlheinz Schreiber of Thyssen/Bear Head will be in Ottawa next week and may try to contact you," said an internal note from Paul Tellier to Norman Spector, then Mulroney's chief of staff. Tellier warned Spector about a "possible linkage between this issue and that of the import and export of automatic weapons," and added a cautionary note that "if the Thyssen project were to proceed, it would be a direct competitor of DDGM [Diesel Division, General Motors]." In other words, General Motors, which was fighting hard to sell light armoured vehicles to the Canadian army, wouldn't appreciate the Defence Department dancing with another partner.

Schreiber, still in Europe, was juggling several commitments. He had written the name "Brian Mulroney" above the March 20 heading in his diary; on March 18, he made a note to send "Brian" a "birthday telegram." He wouldn't be in Ottawa again for a few weeks, but he looked forward to seeing Mulroney personally at that time. On April 4, he met his Zurich banker, André Strobel, in the lakeside town of St. Gallen at noon "concerning Jadallah." The name of Sami Jadallah, a Palestinian-American businessman and fundraiser for Palestinian causes, appeared frequently in Schreiber's diaries. They shared an interest in opportunities in Saudi Arabia.

On April 5, Schreiber was once again calculating the split of US$400,000 in Airbus commissions coming down the pipeline. Following the customary formula, he transferred the money out of his U.S.-dollar subaccount. He directed one chunk of US$200,000 to his Canadian-funds subaccount 18679.1, another chunk of US$100,000 to the Frankfurt subaccount, 41391.0, and two further chunks of US$50,000 each to the Maxwell account, 18679.7, and the Stewardess account, 18679.6. If his January 19 diary notes reflect his practice, half of the US$200,000 directed to the Canadian-funds subaccount was for himself and half was for an unnamed Canadian or Canadians.

On April 7, Schreiber caught a flight out of Munich at 10:15 a.m. and landed in Ottawa at about 4:30 p.m. He called Elmer MacKay at 9 o'clock that night, and the next day he met with Fred Doucet all day, planning their Bear Head strategy. On the 9th he saw Doucet and Moores, and his diary indicates that he expected to meet with the prime minister at 4 p.m., only to have the appointment cancelled. He met instead with MacKay.

Finally, at 4 p.m. on April 10, Schreiber and Doucet won a rescheduled meeting with the prime minister and Paul Tellier. All they were asking for, Doucet insisted, was a modest order of 250 military vehicles from the Department of National Defence, and some infrastructure assistance. Following the session, Doucet wrote Tellier to say he hoped that they had overcome the final obstacles.

"Karlheinz Schreiber and I appreciated the time you provided us yesterday and the leadership you are prepared to give to the Bear Head Industries project," wrote Doucet. "We sincerely hope we were able to bring some clarity to what has been a very frustrating experience in trying to get this remarkable project kick started. In addition to the updated MOU [memorandum of understanding] that I left with you yesterday, I now enclose a brief review of the project prepared by Bear Head Industries. Again our sincere thanks and we eagerly await your call for the next meeting which you felt would be early next week." It sounded hopeful; one meeting this week, and another promised for next week. Finally they were getting somewhere.

Schreiber rushed off to Calgary to see Bobby Hladun and Erika Lutz. And he didn't forget to call Jack Major. But by the weekend neither he nor Doucet had heard back from Tellier. Schreiber called Doucet five times in one day, reaching him at 10 p.m. Doucet had no news to report.

The next day Schreiber, still in Alberta, attended to routine business, calling Kiep, Pelossi, and Strauss. There was a curious name in Schreiber's diary for April 15, that of Anwar Khan. Khan was a banker with the Ottawa branch of BCCI, the Bank of Credit and Commerce International. (BCCI soon collapsed under the weight of a massive international police investigation.) The next day Schreiber appears to have met with Walter Twinn, a native Indian Conservative senator from Alberta. Still no word from Tellier, and still Schreiber had to sit tight. He telephoned Lutz, reminded her to pay Hladun C$20,000, and then called John Harding, his Ottawa property manager, and Marc Lalonde. He flew back to Ottawa from Alberta, where he had a late-afternoon meeting with Doucet.

They couldn't know that Tellier's PCO colleague William Rowat was drafting a memo that would deliver another blow to their ambitions. In his "Analysis of the New Thyssen Proposal," Rowat wrote that Thyssen was being more flexible but still was not saying how the government's costs were to come down. Furthermore, Rowat reminded Tellier, Thyssen would manufacture the military vehicles several years before the Defence Department actually needed them.

Unaware of Rowat's views, Doucet and Schreiber persevered. The promised second meeting with Tellier did not materialize. The days turned into weeks, and Schreiber slowly realized that he was getting the cold shoulder from Canada's most respected and feared bureaucrat. How could Tellier treat him like this, Schreiber wondered. Didn't Tellier understand how close he was to Mulroney?

Schreiber spent much of April phoning Fred, Fred's brother Gerry, his Ottawa property manager, John Harding, and Greg Alford. He was as restless as a flea. On April 18, he wrote in his diary that he was seeing Elmer on Friday about Bob, presumably Bobby Hladun: "Elmer wg. Bob Freitag." He also wrote "Maz Brief," then, below that, "Brian Brief" – and across from both, he wrote "Fred?" *Brief* means letter; perhaps Schreiber thought about giving letters to Fred Doucet for relaying to the prime minister and Don Mazankowski, now the deputy prime minister.

The next day, April 19, he met with Anwar Khan at the Ottawa branch of the BCCI. He wrote another vague note about Mulroney: "Brief Brian 1+2." At 5:30 he was calling Hladun, and at 8:30 he spoke to Lalonde in Montreal. At 10 p.m. he had to catch a flight from Mirabel airport, just outside Montreal, to return to Europe. He hadn't had a second meeting with Tellier, but he hadn't given up.

Schreiber made a list of fifteen cabinet ministers in the Mulroney government. He would see them all if he had to. On April 22 he again wrote "Brian, 1+2," but added " = 40." The days crept by with no word from Canada. He kept in touch with Elmer MacKay, complained vociferously about the bureaucracy, and called Jim Fox and Jack Vance, two retired Armed Forces officers who were helping him lobby for Bear Head. On May 5, he caught a morning flight from Munich and was in Ottawa again by 2:30 p.m. He called Moores and Doucet. He made a note the next day to ask MacKay whether he thought it worthwhile to encourage Lavalin to get involved in their project, thinking again of its industrial facilities in Trenton, Nova Scotia. He made a note to call Strobel, the banker in Zurich, and then, in a corner of the page, he wrote a series of names: Fred, Elmer, Marcel (Marcel Masse, the new minister of defence), Brian, Jack (Vance). Was it a meeting? The diary is unclear.

What is clear is that Schreiber was at the end of his rope. He had expected to see Tellier again only days after their April 10 meeting, and almost a month had gone by. The happy-go-lucky hail-fellow-well-met had a nasty streak, and he aimed it straight at Paul Tellier in a letter dated May 7, 1991.

"This letter follows from my meeting of April 10 with the Prime Minister, yourself and Fred Doucet," Schreiber wrote, warming up. "It was understood that you would... chair a meeting between government and company officials... within one week's time. It is now nearing a month since that meeting."

He complained about calling three times and never being called back. He quoted Mulroney as saying in the earlier meeting how much he cared for the safety of Canadian soldiers. He then implied Tellier had misled the prime minister.

"A case in point is a statement which you made to the PM to the effect that a vehicle which meets the requirement of the MRCV [Multi Role Combat Vehicle] Program was available off the shelf for

$500,000. This statement is preposterous and I trust you have corrected the record." Schreiber added that he couldn't understand why the simple issues "are now so complicated," particularly when, as he claimed, the project had the support of Mulroney, Stevens, ACOA, External Affairs, the province of Nova Scotia, and Lavalin. He even suggested some of the words out of Tellier's mouth may have been "maliciously false."

For his part, Tellier was hardly worried about Karlheinz Schreiber, nor did he think much of him. On May 17, 1991, he fired back his own letter, much shorter, but much more to the point.

> Dear Mr. Schreiber,
>
> I acknowledge your letter of May 7th.
>
> There are many statements in your letter which are either inaccurate, untrue or with which I do not agree. I do not think any useful purpose would be served at this point in getting involved in a lengthy exchange of correspondence. However I do want to confirm with you that senior officials from the Department of National Defence will arrange a meeting at your mutual convenience, the purpose of which will be to review your proposal and formally reply to it. I understand that you feel you have never received a formal reply.
>
> I sincerely hope that this meeting will clarify, to your entire satisfaction, any confusion that may still exist.
>
> Yours sincerely,
>
> Paul M. Tellier

Schreiber had enough sense to understand that this scalding note – flatly dismissing his version of events – was not good news, but by now he wasn't surprised, only outraged that he, a friend of the prime minister, would be treated so rudely. His consolation was that he was making millions of dollars in other ventures and there would be another day to fight this battle.

With the Saudi deal consummated at last, the commission monies were flowing into Schreiber's shell companies. The ultimate value of the supply contract reached DM446,379,480; of this, approximately 47 percent, or DM220 million, was attributed to "consulting fees." Over the next two years, according to the prosecutors' later analysis, DM67.5 million was parked in Ovessim, largely for distribution as kickbacks to individuals on the Saudi side; DM116.3 million was passed through Linsur to persons or institutions not clearly identified in the records; and just under DM26.8 million – 6 percent of the total contract – was divided between ATG in Vaduz and BBC in Kaufering. The amount transferred to ATG was by far the greater: DM24.4 million would be hidden there, well away from the eyes of the tax authorities, and destined mainly for Schreiber's European associates. BBC received DM2.4 million, which Schreiber would declare as personal income, subject to tax. Finally, DM8.93 million found its way to another shell company, the Great Aziz, controlled not by Schreiber, the investigators believed, but by Rolf Wegener. He received 2 percent of the contract value for his efforts. Documents found in Thyssen's files suggest that Ulrich Wegener's contribution was worth 1 percent.

In May Schreiber twice made notes in his diary to instruct Strobel to credit the Marc subaccount with C$165,000 and the Frankfurt subaccount with C$50,000. These transfers were made, albeit three weeks later, on June 14. Aside from more shorthand notes about Airbus commission breakdowns ("202 Kh. 100 FRA 50 Stu. 50 Mx"), his diary suggests he was more excited about Brian Mulroney's upcoming trip to Germany.

"12 June London Brian in Germany," he wrote in his diary for May 31. Then again on June 4, "11+12 London; 13-16 Jun," in one line over the other with "Brian" joining the two lines. On June 12 he wrote, "Tel. BM wg. Viola"; what BM stood for was not shown. That day he took Lufthansa Flight 18 from Munich to Bonn, where he booked into a hotel.

The next evening he attended a banquet in Mulroney's honour. The prime minister was making an official visit to Germany, and Helmut Kohl hosted the dinner in the city's Schaumburg Palace. There were fewer than fifty guests in attendance, among them several influential German politicians. Schreiber's name was not on the official guest list and no one seemed to know who had invited him. Kohl said later he had never met Karlheinz Schreiber; perhaps the chancellor had forgotten that he was a guest at this event.

If dining with Mulroney and Helmut Kohl was the highlight of his month, a meeting with Alexander Haig, secretary of state under Reagan, wasn't far behind. On June 15, Schreiber treated Haig to lunch at the Königshof restaurant in Munich. Joining them were the U.S. ambassador, Vernon Walters, and Erich Riedl, the conservative cabinet minister from Bavaria. They toasted the occasion with a bottle of Moët et Chandon. Food seemed to be on Schreiber's mind that day; he found time to pick up some of his favourite *Weisswurst*, the specialty sausage that, legend has it, is best eaten before noon.

On Friday, June 27, he called Fred Doucet about yet another meeting with "Brian" on the Bear Head project. Judging by the diary entries from this period, Schreiber was thinking a lot about Mulroney. He genuinely liked him. But he couldn't understand why, if Mulroney was in favour of the Bear Head project, he didn't push it through the system. In every other way, the prime minister was a sympathetic personality. One man may have been a successful politician and the other a backroom boy, but in many ways they were similar animals. Both came from small communities as far from city life as one could imagine. If their parents were not poor, they were at least from working-class families who had never known financial security. Both men wanted to escape that life and make a better one for their families. Both had seen how the rich lived and were determined to be part of that world.

Schreiber wanted his friendship with Mulroney to survive even the Bear Head fiasco. Perhaps that explains why, on June 29, he noted in his diary a call to the Cartier jewellery store in Düsseldorf about "Knöpfe" – probably cufflinks or studs for a dress shirt – for "Brian." On July 2 he hopped on a plane to Düsseldorf at 10:30 in the morning; he made the purchase and was back in Munich by 6 p.m.

In Lugano, Giorgio Pelossi carried on his duties as usual but took silent comfort in his own fattening bank balance. For more than twenty years he had been the well-heeled accountant who helped Schreiber stickhandle his way past anxious bankers. But then, more recently, their positions had been reversed: Schreiber was rich and

Pelossi was the one in financial difficulties. He had made some bad investments and owed a lot of money in back taxes. The more he fell into debt and the wealthier Schreiber grew, the less tolerable it became.

He felt more closely tied to Schreiber than to any of his other clients. He wasn't just Schreiber's accountant; he was his partner. By May 29, 1991, Pelossi had withdrawn US$826,640 from his partner's companies. Schreiber's view of their relationship may have been slightly different by this time. It was Lorenzo Wullschleger who would sign the contracts on the Saudi tank affair; Pelossi knew nothing about it.

Several months had passed since Pelossi began skimming portions of the Airbus commissions, but it was not until June that Schreiber began to wonder if something was wrong with the accounting. The Zurich account was short and his antennae went up. What was amiss in Liechtenstein? On his own, he drove to Vaduz where he met with Edmund Frick, one of IAL's trustees, who was also, of course, Pelossi's trustee for Erfel Anstalt. To Schreiber's annoyance, Frick refused to give him any information about IAL or let him see any files, since Liechtenstein's strict business secrecy law forbade such a thing. Schreiber's system was so byzantine that even he couldn't gain entry to his own records. What he needed, explained Frick, was his share certificate – but Pelossi had the certificate back in Lugano. On July 3, he travelled to Lugano to confront his old friend.

"Why didn't you transfer all the money?" Schreiber demanded.

The extra money is in Erfel Anstalt, replied Pelossi, who was just as furious. He wouldn't give any of it back unless Schreiber signed a document agreeing to pay Erfel a portion of the commissions.

"I have a right to some of those commissions, Karlheinz," Pelossi protested.

Schreiber couldn't believe what his old friend was telling him. In Schreiber's eyes, Pelossi had utterly betrayed him, indeed he had stolen from him. He demanded the share certificate, and Pelossi knew he had to turn it over. Years before, the two men had dreamed about great riches from Canada. Now that dream had come true. Both men could have retired rich on the proceeds. But greed, envy, and anger would destroy their friendship. Schreiber stormed out; the brotherly relationship was definitely over.

Back in Liechtenstein, Schreiber combed the records for the money he believed Pelossi had stolen from him. There was the first withdrawal on August 16, 1990, for $200,000, followed by six more: September 24, 1990, for $100,000; November 22, 1990, for $100,000; December 13, 1990, for $176,640; January 2, 1991, for $100,000; March 12, 1991, for $100,000; and the final withdrawal on May 29, 1991, for $50,000. How could he have allowed this to go on so long? Why hadn't he seen it before? Schreiber eventually forced Pelossi to resign from IAL and tried to recover IAL's bookkeeping records. But Pelossi intended to hang on to those documents.

Schreiber knew he had to call Roger Bailly at Airbus Industrie at once and warn him not to send any further commission money to IAL in Vaduz for the time being. But where was it to go? Reluctantly, Schreiber instructed Airbus to forward it directly from Paris to his account 18679 in Zurich. On August 19 Airbus and Schreiber executed a transaction they had always tried to avoid and thereby established a direct link between the airline's bank and the account in Zurich. Only once before had such a connection been visible. In 1986, Pelossi's detention in jail had necessitated a direct deposit of MBB commissions into Schreiber's personal account.

15

Falling from the
Fourth Floor

On August 17, 1991, anticipating the arrival of the first of the commissions from Thyssen on the Saudi contract, Schreiber entered a new list of calculations in his diary.

2 Ho
1 Wi
1 L.K.
0.5 E.R.
0.5 Mx
0.5 W.B.
0.55 Lor. AT

German authorities would later claim in court documents that the numbers represented millions of DM or fractions thereof and that the initials represented some of the European friends of Karlheinz Schreiber: Ho, the letters beside the largest number on the list, stood for Holger Pfahls, Wi for Winfried Haastert, L.K. was Walther Leisler Kiep, E.R. was Erich Riedl, Mx represented Max Strauss, and Lor. was Lorenzo Wullschleger. W.B. could not be identified.

In June, Schreiber had opened an account for ATG at the familiar

Swiss Bank Corporation branch in Zurich; number 47252 would hold the tank money for himself and for the friends. (He also opened a second new account, number 47251, for a company called Primus, like ATG a Panamanian shell.)

In late August, Schreiber was in touch with Walther Leisler Kiep. He suggested they meet in the small Swiss border town of St. Margarethen, at the southeastern end of Lake Constance, where Austria, Switzerland, and Germany meet. Kiep drove in from his holiday home in Switzerland, telling Horst Weyrauch, the CDU's tax adviser, to join them there by noon on August 26. That morning Schreiber withdrew DM1,305,200 in cash from his ATG Deutschmark account 47252 in Zurich and packed DM1 million of the cash into a small suitcase. He drove to St. Margarethen and met the others in a pizza restaurant. There Schreiber, Kiep, and Weyrauch had a brief discussion before returning to their cars, at which point Schreiber passed the suitcase to Kiep.

Kiep did not take the suitcase with him; instead, he turned it over to Weyrauch. As reported by Stephen Grey in the *Times* of London, he deposited the money the next day in account 4115602403, with the note "CBN/891" (for CDU, Bonn, August 1991), at the Georg Hauck & Sohn Bank in Frankfurt, the bank used by the CDU. But the CDU's records never showed the deposit. Instead, Kiep split the money three ways. He took DM300,000 for himself, to pay fines levied two months earlier following his conviction for income-tax evasion in a case involving party funds in the mid-1980s. Weyrauch kept about DM420,000 for his services – he had helped the CDU with its debt problem – and the rest, about DM370,000, eventually passed to Uwe Lüthje, a party insider and friend of Kiep's.

Lüthje, by then in his seventies, had been a financial adviser to the CDU for over fifty years, ever since World War II. He knew who the party donors were, how much they gave, why they gave, and who asked them. He knew where the CDU's money was hidden, including a secret Swiss account holding over SF1.5 million, and he knew how to keep such funds off the party books. No one in the CDU knew more about the party's finances than Uwe Lüthje.

Years later, both Kiep and Schreiber would insist that the money was a gift to the CDU, and the timing of the donation so close to the Saudi tank affair was a simple coincidence. It was, they said, a normal, everyday donation to the party – but one that went unrecorded.

The next day Schreiber's long-serving manager in Kaufering, Albert Birkner, received a gift of DM50,000; Birkner later described it as a retirement bonus from his boss. With the fatal exception of Pelossi, Schreiber appreciated the need to spread the money around, to ensure that everyone was included. Kiep, too, agreed with that principle.

Schreiber had dated his first invoice to Thyssen for "marketing services" on July 25. Thyssen was to transfer payment directly to his ATG account, 47252, in Zurich. André Strobel, Schreiber's banker at the Swiss Bank Corporation, had been vigilant in his efforts to protect Schreiber's identity: "Do not mention payee on bank order!" the internal transfer order noted. The first payment of just under DM11 million from Thyssen arrived on August 13, and by early September, it was time to dole it out to his deserving associates. On Sunday, September 1, Schreiber recorded a second list of allocations in his diary.

Waldherr	1
Holgart	3.8
Jürglund	4.125
Winter	1 200
Maxwell	500

The total was 10.625 – that is, DM10,625,000. Kiep – Waldherr – had already received his DM1 million. On September 2, Strobel transferred the other sums into the subaccounts, according to Schreiber's instructions. He moved DM3.8 million into the Holgart account, DM4.125 million into the Jürglund account, DM1.2 million into the Winter account, and DM500,000 into Maxwell, converting it to C$327,439.

On September 3, he noted that Elmer MacKay was to meet Fred Doucet on September 6, presumably to devise new ways to nag the generals, but there was another note as well about "gospel services."

His diary revealed evidence of some new interest in religion. His secretary's diary indicated payments of C$65,000 for Frank Moores and C$35,000 for Greg Alford.

It was a busy month, as it turned out; a blizzard of calls to Canada about Bear Head, and a couple of fast visits to Ottawa. A regular routine was emerging with respect to his Canadian trips; they were often preceded by substantial cash withdrawals from his Canadian-dollar subaccount 18679.1 and from the various subaccounts that held commissions from the Canadian projects. In advance of his second trip to Canada that September, Schreiber made appointments with Alford, MacKay, and Doucet, and Dietlinde Kaupp noted in her diary for September 20 an amount of $60,000 with the name "Gayle" written beside it. The day following, Kaupp booked Canadian Pacific Flight 061 to Toronto for September 25. On September 24 and 25, Schreiber withdrew just over C$75,000 in Canadian currency from two of his Zurich accounts: $20,100 from the Frankfurt subaccount, then another $35,092.56 from the same account to change into $30,000 U.S. dollars, and another $20,100 from his other Canadian-funds subaccount. In addition, he took two separate amounts of DM451,350 and DM58,980 from his Deutschmark subaccount. On the 25th he flew to Toronto.

"Gayle" might have referred to a fundraising dinner that Gayle Christie, one of Mulroney's 1985 appointees to the Air Canada board, was helping to organize. When she was asked years later if she knew anything about the C$60,000, Christie said she had never met Schreiber, though she may have spoken to Greg Alford about the dinner.

Schreiber's next flight was to Halifax, where he had an appointment with Premier Don Cameron on the 27th to talk about Bear Head. Two days later he was in Ottawa and called Heike Pfahls, Holger Pfahls's daughter, who seemed to be using his Rockcliffe Park condo. His main objectives that day were to see Marcel Masse, the minister of defence, and to arrange meetings with Mulroney, Moores, MacKay, and others. He had yet another scheme to propose: a possible sale of ships to the armed forces from Thyssen's North Sea plants, for which he was promised a commission of at least DM6 million. What kind of ships these were is not clear in the documents, although there are some references to icebreakers.

On Tuesday, October 1, Schreiber's diary suggests that he was to call Fred Doucet at breakfast, about 7:30 a.m. Even though Doucet was now working with his brother Gerry in their new lobbying company, Fred Doucet Consulting International, he was still one of the prime minister's closest confidants, the individual who could most easily arrange those meetings with his former boss. When Schreiber needed to see Mulroney quickly, he didn't bother with the switchboard at the PMO; he called Doucet.

Schreiber's diary contains an entry for the same evening, at 10 p.m.: "Parliament Brian." Schreiber might well have desired the meeting at that time. Parliament Hill is quiet; Commons committees have usually finished their business and the members have departed, often gathering again informally at a pizza joint or a downtown bar. A few MPs may be working late in their offices; journalists, their deadlines passed, are all at home; a few security guards sit by the doors, gossiping and glancing at their monitors.

Schreiber's diary records a meeting with Doucet from 1:45 p.m. to 3:00 p.m. the following afternoon. And he noted on the same page meetings with Marcel Masse and Michael Wilson. The next morning at 8:30, he and Fred Doucet were with a large group of senior officials to discuss, once again, defence procurement. This was the kind of access to Ottawa's top politicians and bureaucrats that few enjoyed.

By Friday Schreiber was on his way back to Munich, excited by the prospect of attending a meeting of an organization he had just joined, Atlantik-Brücke (Atlantic Bridge), a powerful but little-known German–North American business association with the goal of promoting trade across the Atlantic. Walther Kiep was its chairman and Schreiber was a proud new member, recommended by Kiep. The organization's Canadian branch met in Canada and Germany in alternating years. On October 7 and 8, Schreiber attended meetings in Potsdam, with Kiep in the chair. It was an opportunity for Schreiber to mingle with other German leaders; one was Brigitte Baumeister, who was to become the CDU's treasurer and a good friend. A leading Canadian member was Allan MacEachen, a former external affairs minister in

Pierre Trudeau's Liberal government; he too developed a relationship with Schreiber.

Holger Pfahls must have been exhausted by the stress of the past year. Quarrelling with the generals, pushing the tank deal with Kohl, dealing with the aggressive middleman from Kaufering – all of it had worn him down and he decided he needed a change. On October 14, Pfahls checked into the Kursanatorium Hohen Freudenstadt, for a month's rest. He occupied an apartment there, with his own direct telephone line. He spoke to Schreiber several times, and they decided to get together next in December.

Schreiber needed no such respite; he was busy and life was full of satisfactions. He had worked behind the scenes on one of the largest aircraft deals in modern history. He had managed the commissions on a sensitive and important tank deal in the midst of a modern war. He was a deal-maker on the scale of a Khashoggi, and he was advancing the fortunes of German industry. His efforts were patriotic, even heroic. As he said more than once, he deserved a medal.

Instead, he was made to suffer the treachery of Giorgio Pelossi, an outrage he meant to correct. Pelossi would remember their next encounter well. "I was summoned by Schreiber on October 25, 1991, to the offices of the trust company Pagani & Wullschleger, in Lugano... [Present were] Dr. Lorenzo Wullschleger, ... Schreiber, his son Andreas." Schreiber had prepared a statement in which Pelossi would admit he owed Schreiber the money he had taken. In front of Andreas and Wullschleger, he demanded that Pelossi sign it. Pelossi refused. Schreiber threatened to call Carla del Ponte, Switzerland's chief prosecutor. At that, Pelossi's defiance dissolved; he didn't need any more trouble of that sort in his life. He signed the document and crept away, humiliated. Schreiber may have felt triumphant, but he had just made the biggest mistake of his life.

As winter approached, Schreiber ran the traps in Ottawa, speaking to Fred Doucet once or twice a day and to the rest of his circle almost as often. He was in touch with some of his old comrades from Costa Rica; Rita Santalla and former president Monge were noted in his diary frequently in early November, perhaps because they were still involved in Liebherr's activities in San José. Sami Jadallah popped up from time to time as well. On October 8, Schreiber's ATG account, 47252, was credited with DM5,030,000, and on November 5, the same amount was transferred to his Deutschmark subaccount, 18679.2. His diary for November 6 suggests that he instructed Strobel to make a number of transfers: US$50,000 to JA (Schreiber's code for Jadallah), C$35,000 to Marc, DM1.2 million to Winter, DM100,000 to Jürglund, US$400,000 to Pitak, and C$100,000 to Frankfurt.

Whenever possible, Schreiber liked to give the cash to his beneficiaries in person. It was safer and they wouldn't forget who had made it happen. This had been the case in early 1988, when Winfried Haastert met Schreiber in Vaduz to pick up DM500,000 from a safety deposit box, money that had bought his flat in Lugano. Schreiber decided their next rendezvous should take place in Zurich; Haastert arranged a flight for November 6. According to the prosecutors' records, Schreiber flew in from Munich the same day and withdrew DM1,210,000 from the Winter subaccount, 46341.7. Haastert returned to Düsseldorf the following day.

At the end of November, Schreiber made another quick trip to Ottawa; his diary shows a dinner date with Lalonde on Saturday, November 30, brunch with Mulroney the next morning, and dinner with Justice Jack Major on Monday. While he was in Ottawa, Thyssen transferred DM4 million to the ATG account in Zurich. After calls back and forth with Strobel, DM2 million was moved into the Jürglund subaccount, 46341.1. In early December, soon after returning to Europe, Schreiber called Pfahls, back home from his cure, and the next day he withdrew DM278,000 from the Holgart subaccount. On December 12, he met Pfahls, as arranged, close to Pfahls's country house at Tegernsee where, the prosecutors allege in court documents, he passed over the cash.[1]

His closest associates during this period were all Canadian, not German. Names of Strauss family members rarely appeared in his notes, and references to his Kaufering enterprises almost disappeared. Around this time, Schreiber seemed to become more introspective, more interested in his family. He wouldn't ever have to worry about money again, so perhaps it was natural that he began to think about his immortal soul. He began attending the 9:30 a.m. Sunday service at a local evangelical Protestant church. He believed he had been blessed after all, and the day after Christmas, he made a decision that for him was a powerful and moving experience. His diary records the commitment: "Join the evangelical church."

Frank Moores was also making a change. On December 23, he and Beth sold their house at 403 Clarke Avenue in Montreal. From then on, he meant to take life easy, play a lot of golf, and spend more time in Florida or at Chaffeys Locks. He could let the smart boys, led by Ramsey Withers, run the lobbying shop. As he turned the page on this part of his life, he made an indelible impression on one startled Montrealer, a prospective buyer, who came to inspect the house on Clarke Avenue. Moores was in an expansive mood and showed off the house's many amenities himself. He took the man down the stairs into a well-finished basement with a large television room. He showed him a room to the side that had been handsomely furnished as his personal office. Next to the office was a laundry room. And right across from the laundry room, in the farthest corner of the basement, was another small space that looked as if it had been designed as a wine cellar. He led the way in.

"Look at this," Moores urged, as he pulled back a corner of the rug. Underneath was a round metal plug, about eight inches in diameter, set flush with the concrete floor. It looked like a drain. Set into the plug was a small ring, just big enough to lift with a finger; Moores pulled and the metal plug lifted out, revealing a round metal safe sunk into the floor, sealed with a sophisticated combination lock. The visitor didn't know what to say; he wasn't even sure he knew what it was. Puzzled, he looked at Moores, who chuckled at his confusion. "This is where we keep the money!" he exclaimed.

He laughed even louder as he replaced the carpet and patted it into place.

Six months after kicking Giorgio Pelossi out of IAL and arranging payment of the Airbus commissions on the Thai and Air Canada deals directly to his account in Zurich, Schreiber reverted to the old method of running the money through the IAL shell first. Nearly US$3 million had streamed into Zurich from Airbus's Paris bank in the last six months of 1991, but with the former system restored, the money flow was so routine it was almost humdrum. The Maxwell, Stewardess, Frankfurt, and Canadian-funds subaccounts received their customary percentages. An Airbus commission of US$426,000 arrived February 14, 1992; a few days later the Canadian-funds subaccount 18679.1 received US$213,000 (C$252,192). The Frankfurt subaccount gained C$126,688, the Maxwell subaccount C$62,752, and the Stewardess subaccount US$53,000.

In late February and early March, however, there were several far more interesting transactions. On February 26, Schreiber moved US$107,000 in Airbus commission monies into his Frankfurt account, converting it to C$126,688. On the 28th, he arranged for the transfer of a neatly rounded C$127,000 into Frank Moores's personal account 34107 in Zurich.

On March 11, according to bank documents, C$100,000 was transferred out of the Frankfurt account and into Gary Ouellet's account, 45828. That same day, Ouellet transferred C$100,000 plus a small fee to another Swiss Bank Corporation branch.

Then on March 12, Schreiber sent an even C$1 million from the Frankfurt subaccount to Frank Moores's account 34107. Between March 16 and March 20, Moores bought a million dollars' worth of blue-chip stocks – Seagram, BCE, Molson, AT&T, and others – depleting the account to a near-zero balance.

Pelossi was out of IAL but not out of mind. Giorgio knew more of Schreiber's secrets than anyone else. Still, how much mischief could he make? He may have known the magnitude of the secret commissions, but he didn't have the details of the splits on the commission payments. Nor did he know much, if anything, about Schreiber's cash payouts – the useful expenditures – to various individuals. Besides, there were strict laws in Switzerland that forbade trustees and accountants like Pelossi from saying too much.

In February 1992, however, Schreiber knew Pelossi was up to something. Letters kept arriving from Pelossi's lawyer, Hans Kopp, proposing some kind of resolution to their dispute. Schreiber didn't say no, but he didn't say yes either. Sometimes he would reply to Kopp saying he was confused; he had nothing to do with these Liechtenstein companies. His strategy was to delay.

In the spring of 1992, Schreiber returned to Canada to push the Bear Head deal or some variation of it with renewed energy. Almost immediately the scheme suffered another setback. On March 17, 1992, R.D. Gillespie, the assistant deputy minister responsible for matériel at National Defence Headquarters in Ottawa, wrote an internal memo to the PCO, copying it to the chief of defence staff, John de Chastelain, and to Robert Fowler, the deputy minister. There was no mistaking its impact. The Defence Department had decided against new Multi Role Combat Vehicles – MRCVs – as they called the vehicles Thyssen Henschel wanted to sell. Defence intended to order, without competition, a limited number of replacement vehicles from General Motors.

Replacement vehicles! Without competition! From another company! The bureaucrats had tried to kill the Bear Head project several times since the heady days of 1988; surely the scheme was dead and buried now. But Schreiber wouldn't accept that verdict. He arranged yet more meetings in Ottawa, slated for the first week in May.

On April 29, 1992, there was a withdrawal of C$50,000 cash from the Marc subaccount, 18679.5. That same day someone withdrew DM500,000 from the Holgart subaccount, 46341.0. Dietlinde Kaupp had noted "Pfahls" on April 28 and April 29 in her personal organizer. On May 6, Schreiber had his bank transfer C$220,000 into his Canadian-funds subaccount 18679.1. The next day, his banker transferred C$179,000 out of the same subaccount to an unidentified destination.

By this time, Schreiber had abandoned the dream of a plant in Cape Breton altogether and was pinning his hopes on building a facility in Montreal, where he expected support from Mulroney's allies in the province. In early May, he met with Elmer MacKay, the perennial Thyssen booster, with Marcel Masse, the minister of defence, and with Mulroney. According to Schreiber's optimistic version of their conversation, Mulroney once again breathed life into the moribund project. Schreiber followed up with an appreciative letter.

Dear Prime Minister,

Subsequent to our meeting of last week and the meeting with the Hon. Marcel Masse, I am pleased to inform you that I have now had very encouraging meetings with representatives of the Premier and officials from the Province of Quebec, and with four senior Army Generals.

The next important step in the whole process is to have a meeting as early as possible with l'Hon. Marcel Masse to discuss the areas of his very important involvement. A letter to Minister Masse is attached which will inform you of that proposal.

I will keep you informed on our progress, and will request a further meeting when the situation is more fully advanced. I know that I can count on your continuing support, although I appreciate that all our activities are greatly overshadowed by the tragic events in Nova Scotia,[2] and Elmer's strong personal concern and involvement.

Sincerely yours,

Karlheinz Schreiber

Mulroney must have stared at the letter and wondered what to do next. His bureaucrats had been telling him for years that Thyssen's proposal was not acceptable, no matter where the plant was located or what new bells and whistles it offered. The bureaucrats were on one side; Schreiber was on the other. Now Schreiber wanted another meeting.

Schreiber's more detailed letter of May 13 to Masse ended with the prompt that he looked forward to meeting with him again, as they had all agreed, "to discuss the next necessary steps to bring this project to fruition." On May 20, Robert Fowler summoned Jürgen Massmann, Greg Alford, and Jack Vance, the retired general working for Schreiber, to a meeting at National Defence Headquarters. No one had forgotten the session two years earlier, in February 1990, when it had been painfully obvious that Fowler was seeing Schreiber only reluctantly. This meeting, dealing with the same dubious project, spoke to Schreiber's pull in Ottawa. Also present were de Chastelain and Gillespie.

They listened politely as Massmann, Alford, and Vance outlined the new proposal. The suggestion now was that a Thyssen facility be opened in the Montreal area to produce Multi Role Combat Vehicles for the ever-increasing number of peacekeeping forces worldwide. Thyssen Henschel was developing a new line of light armoured vehicles for NATO; Masse had acknowledged the growing need for peacekeepers on the international scene and pledged his support in an April 1992 statement on defence policy; and Schreiber and his colleagues even had the endorsement of four senior army generals. Here was Canada's opportunity.

The bureaucrats were not impressed. What had begun as an exercise to circumvent German laws governing the export of weapons of war was now being dressed up as blessing for the forces of world peace. The response was quick and firm: Fowler would not recommend DND support, he did not believe DND could avoid substantial costs under the proposal, he did not want his officials to become salesmen for an export product DND did not foresee purchasing itself, and he did not want DND becoming involved in an export program – it had never done so before, and was not about to start now. There was not a crumb of comfort to be found in Fowler's declaration, only the final suggestion that they go to the Industry Department and try their luck there.

When Schreiber received the summary of the meeting from Vance, he lost his temper. The year previous he had put up with the impertinent Tellier; now he had to take this rebuke from DND. Vance must have faxed his letter to Schreiber because the next day, May 22, he responded with a quick and forceful letter to Mulroney, one that began diplomatically but rapidly descended into a diatribe against DND and its "stone-wall" tactics.

Dear Prime Minister:
As promised I write to keep you informed of recent events which have occurred as I proceed to realize our project by the method which I agreed with you during our last meeting.
I am pleased to confirm the very positive support we have received for our proposal from the Hon. Jean Corbeil [minister of transport] as expressed through M. Richard Le Lay his Chief of Staff. Furthermore, I understand that it is intent [sic] of

Min. Corbeil to solicit the support of Min. Benoit Bouchard.[3]

More recently, as a result of my May 13, 1992, letter to Min. Masse, a delegation from our Company was invited on May 20th to discuss the involvement being requested of DND by the Company.

The outcome of that meeting was completely unhelpful and I am dismayed by the lack of co-operation and understanding of the important economic benefits which this proposal offers to Canada. You will see by the attached report of the meeting that the DND position has been to simply "stone-wall" the Company's proposal. Though not a complete surprise, it was even more negative than I expected.

I have travelled to Germany for this week but will be back in Ottawa on May 31st. to resume my activity towards our project.

Most sincerely,

Karlheinz Schreiber

The letter leaves no doubt that Schreiber thought he and Mulroney were in this together, referring to "our project" and keeping him informed "as promised."

On June 24, 1992, in a note marked "Secret," Tellier put the entire file in perspective. He reminded the prime minister that while his government did sign an "understanding in principle" with Schreiber in 1988, the sole commitment was to "consider participation" of the company in a procurement program. In other words, the understanding was worthless. Tellier went on to outline other obstacles, such as the lack of an export market. He gently reminded the prime minister that there could be serious public policy concerns over the project: "Exports of this type of vehicle would raise issues of foreign policy and armament sales."

At least the trip to Ottawa had not been a complete waste of time for Jürgen Massmann. While there he was able to make arrangements for his sixteen-year-old son, Sven, to attend Ashbury College, an exclusive private school for boys. For most families, the fees were prohibitive, but Massmann had nothing to worry about. Schreiber paid them on his behalf, transferring DM35,564.15 from his Jürglund subaccount, 46341.1, in Zurich in favour of Ashbury College on Mariposa Avenue in Ottawa.

As the summer wore on, Schreiber spent more time in Europe than in Canada. The Canadian adventure was nearly over. He was exploring fresh ventures and had formed a company called Industry Consulting International in Liechtenstein, hoping to get involved in a project in Moscow with the Liebherr group. It was this opportunity that took him to a yacht in the Mediterranean owned by a wealthy German industrialist living in Monaco, Herbert Leiduck. He couldn't resist the temptation to impress his host with stories of his exploits in Canada.

The two men were relaxing on the *Herbaro*, a floating monstrosity once owned by Prince Rainier of Monaco that dwarfed the other pleasure boats moored in the harbour. Schreiber had brought Barbel, but soon she and Leiduck's wife, Barbara, left the men alone to discuss business.

Their common interest was a construction deal with the Russian army, building housing for military personnel in Moscow. The Liebherr construction group had brought in Schreiber and had suggested he should meet Leiduck, whose companies would also be involved.

Schreiber knew who Leiduck was, but his host had never heard of Schreiber. So Schreiber described his business experience, mentioning his success with Airbus in Canada, with Thyssen in Saudi Arabia. He told Leiduck he had "very good contacts" in Moscow. Leiduck asked how he organized his businesses, and Schreiber outlined his structure, making it clear that he was as meticulous a businessman as one would find.

"How do you do it?" Leiduck asked Schreiber, looking for an explanation of his success in Canada.

To Leiduck's surprise, Schreiber immediately volunteered his "tremendously" good connections to political power in Canada.

"I've got most of the important Canadian politicians in my pocket," he told his surprised host. "I gave them a couple of million dollars."

Leiduck repeated the remark in an affidavit to the Augsburg prosecutors, filed in a German court.

For his part, Leiduck did not take any of it seriously and years later would insist he still had a hard time believing it. He figured Schreiber had a character flaw that led him to try to impress others with inflated tales.

For all his talk of his consulting services, observed Leiduck, Schreiber had no infrastructure to speak of, no network of offices or army of support staff. "So that throws up the question, What actually did he offer to those [governments] to buy aircraft from Airbus and to buy the German tanks? I think this is very important. Because he could only deal in – let's say, in the political area."

Leiduck actually came to admire Schreiber for the niche he found. "I think that considering how he worked himself up and he is in the business, in the huge international business – it is really an achievement . . . to be taken seriously by those people."[4]

In July 1992, Schreiber finally met with Pelossi's lawyer, Hans Kopp, in Zurich. By then Pelossi had reconsidered his leverage and become aggressive, telling his lawyer he would never pay back the money he had put into Erfel Anstalt. It was his, and further, he was owed millions more. Kopp told Schreiber that no one wanted unpleasantness. Pelossi would settle for an additional US$2 million, far less than what he said he was owed, and promised to end matters there. He would even sign a confidentiality agreement. Payment of the $2 million could be spread out over six years, an incentive for Pelossi to keep quiet.

But Kopp was prepared to be tough if he had to be. He told Schreiber that Pelossi would sue him if he didn't agree to the settlement. And, naturally, Schreiber was wily enough to realize that the civil suit could come to the attention of the Augsburg tax authorities, perhaps even an investigative journalist or two. Schreiber said he would consider the settlement. He needed more time to think about it.

In the fall of 1992, Walther Leisler Kiep decided to retire from his post as treasurer of the CDU. He wrote Uwe Lüthje, one of his closest colleagues, on October 16, thanking him for his twenty-one years of service to the party and telling him he would receive a bonus of DM370,000 for his contributions. Though the amount was significant, there was no hint that this was an unauthorized payment; Kiep indicated he would be sending a copy of his letter to Horst Weyrauch's office to handle the execution and taxation of the payment at source. Six days later Weyrauch closed the account he had set up at Georg Hauck & Sohn in August 1991 to hold the cash handed to him in St. Margarethen.

In November, when ATG invoiced Thyssen Industrie for a further DM3 million, Thyssen once again made sure its name was nowhere on the bank records. Just as Strobel had done earlier, Thyssen paymasters also wanted to keep Schreiber's name off the paperwork. "Do not mention payee on bank order!" the wire transfer indicated. Of the DM3 million, Schreiber would later transfer DM1,435,000 to the Jürglund subaccount.

Also in November, someone withdrew C$30,000 in cash from Schreiber's Frankfurt subaccount. And in Ottawa, Schreiber's friend John Harding became president of Rockcliffe Enterprises Inc., the little holding company that owns the property on Beechwood Avenue on the edge of Rockcliffe Park. Jack Major was named to the Supreme Court of Canada by the prime minister that same month, a high honour for Schreiber's old friend.

But two events in December should have rung alarm bells. On December 9, 1992, Schreiber was in Düsseldorf to answer questions from tax authorities. What interested them in particular were the loans and commissions he had received for Bear Head. After long discussion, Schreiber and the officials agreed on the following facts.

First, Thyssen, through Schreiber, had made substantial payments to a "third party" in his negotiations with governments in Canada. Second, Thyssen committed itself to those payments only after support came from those governments, and Schreiber believed he got that support in the October 30, 1987, agreement with the province of Nova Scotia and the September 27, 1988, understanding in principle with the federal government.

Additionally, it was Schreiber's contention that any payments given to IAL were for "useful expenditures" and that they went to Frank Moores, whom he called an associate of IAL who had agreed to distribute the money in Canada.

But the tax authorities had no way of verifying that the money went for "useful expenditures" – and was therefore not subject to tax –

unless Schreiber gave them more information. From now on, they all agreed, Schreiber would have to provide the names of the final recipients of "useful expenditures" from IAL. Schreiber also pledged to ensure that none of the money would flow back to any German citizens.

All in all, Schreiber barely got his knuckles rapped. But the point was made – if he was going to pay *Schmiergelder*, he had to name those who got the money. Otherwise he would have to pay tax on the commissions.

The next week brought another round in the dispute with Pelossi. For a moment it looked as if there might be a settlement in sight. Schreiber and Kopp had met in July, another meeting was held in November, and now they were holding a final session to iron out the details. Under the terms of the draft agreement, Schreiber was to pay Pelossi US$1 million, on top of the close to US$1 million Pelossi had already taken from him. For his part, Pelossi agreed not to release any of his documents, and to place them in his lawyer's office, in escrow. Once Pelossi received his final payment from Schreiber, all the documents and copies would be returned. There could be no mention of Airbus in the agreement, obviously, and so Schreiber was to pay US$1 million for an unexplained "T." business. The funds would be paid in three instalments in December 1992, December 1994, and December 1996. (Schreiber agreed to give Pelossi 26 percent of any award coming out of the upcoming Barbara Flick trial, which, as it turned out, was settled before it went to court.)

Now came the fine tuning. On one side of the table sat Pelossi, calm and composed as always, with Kopp at his side. On the other side was Schreiber, accompanied by Harald Giebner, a lawyer from Munich, and Bobby Hladun, who had flown in from Calgary. Perhaps it was inevitable that the fine tuning should turn into coarse argument. Each side argued for amendments. Soon Kopp was again reminding Schreiber that he had better settle, or suffer the consequences. Pelossi would go public with a fight Schreiber could not win. There was a silence around the table as Schreiber, Giebner, and Hladun, all of them steaming, listened to Kopp. If the agreement failed, Pelossi would make sure Schreiber's activities were exposed for all to see. "Giorgio Pelossi would fall from the first floor," Kopp said calmly, but "Karlheinz Schreiber would fall from the fourth floor."

What Bobby Hladun was doing at this meeting is known only to him and his client. The discussion concerned International Aircraft Leasing of Vaduz, Liechtenstein, and the secrets that lay inside the company, not Schreiber's Alberta companies. Pelossi later said he believed Hladun was brought in to claim that he was the president of IAL and to say further that IAL was owned by a number of Canadians. The ownership of IAL was not a minor issue; in fact, it was the only one that mattered to Schreiber. If no one could prove that he held control over IAL, then no one could prove that he had evaded taxes, or so went his thinking. If Hladun was the president of IAL, then his statements about ownership would carry some weight in a court of law.

Technically, because IAL was a classic Liechtenstein shell with trustees, it would be almost impossible to prove he owned it. But if he was the one appointing the trustees, if he was the one who had access to the share certificate, if he was the one who controlled the company, how could he say it wasn't his?

As for Hladun, he barely spoke at the meeting. Later, when questioned by a CBC Television reporter, Hladun would say only that he was at the Zurich meeting as Schreiber's lawyer, insisting that if he revealed anything more he would breach solicitor-client privilege. Pressed on the point, he conceded that "someone can be a president for a specific time and purpose and that's all."

Whatever Hladun's precise role in IAL, the meeting in Kopp's office failed. There would be no agreement on that day nor in the weeks and months following. The two sides were too far apart. Pelossi later concluded that Schreiber had no intention of settling in the first place, that the negotiations were just a ploy to stall for time. He consulted Kopp about his options. Swiss law seemed to prevent a trustee from speaking directly to the press or to the police, but a lawsuit against Schreiber might accomplish the same purpose.

16

Code Name Britan

What is it about easy wealth that turns men's minds to real estate? As soon as the secret commission funds made their way into various subaccounts, people started to buy themselves holiday getaways. Jürgen Massmann's idea of escape was the Swiss Alpine village of Zuoz in the Engadine Valley, some 25 kilometres north of St. Moritz and about 15 kilometres from Schreiber's weekend place in Pontresina. Not only was the skiing superb, with first-class hotels, but Zuoz was just as lovely in the summer when the mountain meadows were blanketed with wildflowers.

In early January 1993, Massmann rented an apartment in the village and began to furnish it. Sounds quite straightforward, but there was a little mystery here, and an arrangement not unlike the one that put Frank Moores into a Florida condominium. On that occasion, Schreiber transferred money out of the Frankfurt subaccount into one of his Vaduz accounts and then, with Pelossi's help, set up the ownership under a shell called Ticinella Anstalt, which was itself controlled by Kensington Anstalt. On paper Schreiber owned it; in fact, Moores paid for it.

Schreiber had deposited DM1,435,000 in the Jürglund subaccount, 46341.1, on December 21. In January, he bought Apartment 5,

House A, in the Lains Quarter of the village for DM1.3 million, taken from 46341.1. Schreiber purchased the apartment from his friend Edi Rominger, a St. Moritz businessman and a famous skier in his day who was in construction and luxury apartment development. Schreiber arranged to have the ownership registered in the name of another friend, the Saudi businessman Mahmoud Othman. On January 4, Massmann signed a rental agreement with a real estate company called Islas Immobilien. Six weeks later, on February 10, there was a further deduction of DM86,909.30 from the Jürglund subaccount to pay Rominger for furniture from his local store. On paper, Othman owned the apartment. On paper, Schreiber paid for it. On paper, the money came from the Jürglund subaccount – which was set up for Massmann. Whose is it? Some day a judge may decide.

In Canada, the pundits were predicting a defeat for the Tories; the country was in recession and the fallout from free trade was blamed for the shutdown of hundreds of companies and the loss of thousands of jobs. Almost a decade of high-profile debacles and scandals had cost the Mulroney team whatever goodwill it had achieved. Mulroney's own approval ratings were the lowest of any Canadian prime minister's since political polling had begun. It was time to award one final round of patronage appointments, find a comfortable role for himself in the private sector, and make a graceful exit.

His closest friends knew what was coming, and they too began to make plans. In February, Fred Doucet changed the name of his lobbying firm from Fred Doucet Consulting International to the Government Business Consulting Group Inc. He hired several prominent Liberals, including a former Trudeau cabinet minister, Jean-Jacques Blais, who was named the new president. Doucet's announcement of these appointments was a clear signal to the rest of Ottawa.

Frank Moores was also preparing to pack up and leave. Four of his top lobbyists, led by GCI's president, Ramsey Withers, left to start their own firm. Pat MacAdam had joined in 1989, but he was a contract employee, distracted of late by an investigation into his affairs for income-tax evasion. Moores was enjoying the links in Florida, playing frequently at the exclusive Loxahatchee Golf Club; Ouellet was profoundly bored and had no interest in returning to his Quebec City law practice. His dream was to become a professional magician, so one day he just ran away to join the international star David Copperfield in Los Angeles. Soon there was no one left in the offices at 50 O'Connor, so Moores sold what was left of the business and moved his files to his secretary's house in a suburb outside Ottawa.

Mulroney too was attracted to Florida, and he and his wife, Mila, were looking at real estate in Palm Beach, during their annual winter holiday. Maybe they couldn't afford the US$3-million pink and white house in a gated community that they were renting from a Maryland businessman, Buddy Jenkins, but local real estate agents confided to the *Toronto Star* that the couple had done some scouting for houses on Island Drive, where the average price was US$2.5 million. The Mulroneys had been visiting Palm Beach every winter for years and many of their closest friends were established there. They showed serious interest that January.

Schreiber's instincts were sharp enough to pick up the signals, but he told friends he wasn't worried; he had plenty of Liberals to pick from, and he already had Marc Lalonde as his lawyer in Montreal. But with the political future uncertain, there were few major contract initiatives under way; the government was strapped and there was no money for anything new.

On February 24, 1993, it was finally announced that Mulroney would step down as prime minister and leader of the Progressive Conservative Party on June 25. As Schreiber's power in Germany had depended on his friendship with Franz Josef Strauss, so in Ottawa he was feared and listened to because of his ready access to Mulroney. Though he may not have fully understood it at the time, there was nothing left for Schreiber in Ottawa. It was over.

In the first few months of 1993, Schreiber's attention was divided between the changing tide in Canada and events at home in Bavaria. Max Streibl, successor to his great mentor, Strauss, as chairman of the CSU and premier of Bavaria, was under fire over an aircraft deal worth nearly US$2 billion. The company at the heart of the affair was Grob Air & Space Travel GmbH, manufacturers of the Egrett D-500, a military plane designed to carry the new Lapas surveillance system. Even though test pilots had been lukewarm about the aircraft, Bonn had ordered ten of them. When reports surfaced in February 1993 that Burkhardt Grob, the company's owner and a major donor to the CSU, had paid for flights and holidays to his ranch in Brazil for Streibl and other senior government officials, there was an uproar. The Brazilian connection prompted references to Grob as Streibl's "amigo," and soon more revelations spilled out about Streibl's use of free cars and plane travel provided by other friends. As the affair broadened, the cozy group of businessmen around Streibl and many others who had been close to Strauss became known as the "Amigos." By May 1993, the Amigo scandal had forced Streibl to resign as premier.

Schreiber turned to the federal CDU in a last-ditch effort to enlist Chancellor Kohl's help for his Canadian project. On April 23, 1993, Schreiber wrote to Kiep, asking him to thank Kohl for his previous support on the Saudi tank deal. Schreiber emphasized that he was now interested in selling Thyssen vehicles through Canada for "peacekeeping" purposes. Schreiber admitted to Kiep, however, that he desperately needed some help from the chancellor.

"Though I have a close friendship with the Canadian Prime Minister Brian Mulroney," Schreiber said, "I have not yet been successful in convincing the Canadians of their own best interests in realizing this project with us." Schreiber asked Kiep if Kohl could approach Mulroney directly. Schreiber had heard that Mulroney would be travelling to Europe in the future and "possibly [to] Bonn."

Kiep passed on the message. On April 27, he wrote to Kohl, drawing his attention to Schreiber's Bear Head project. On May 9, Brian and Mila Mulroney visited Kohl and his wife, Hannelore, in the German countryside near Heidelberg. The following morning, Kohl and Mulroney met to discuss trade and other issues; records do not indicate whether Bear Head was raised. In what was being called Mulroney's "farewell tour" of European cities by the Canadian media, the Mulroneys continued on to London, England, for visits with Prime Minister John Major and an audience with the Queen.

For any party that has held power for nine years and twice been elected as a majority government, it must be hard to look reality in the eye. The polls told the Conservatives that they couldn't win again, but as the convention to choose a new leader approached, hearts started racing. The only problem was finding candidates; the party's wily old dogs were quietly backing away into law firms, university common rooms, book contracts, whatever they could find. The field was left to two leading candidates, Kim Campbell, a former justice minister who had replaced Marcel Masse at Defence, and Jean Charest, the environment minister. A bright and attractive woman, Campbell's only flaws were her lack of experience and an unfortunate tendency to utter ingenuous statements at the wrong times. At first she had Mulroney's support and that of most of his inner circle. The cynical would say that these men knew the Tories were doomed; why not run a sacrificial lamb this time and wait for a serious candidate to take over when there was a real chance of victory? Her opponent was a man who had as many problems as she did. Jean Charest was an appealing and clever lawyer from Quebec, but Canadians had had enough of clever lawyers from Quebec. At thirty-five, he seemed far too young and lacked a national profile.

As the weeks passed, Mulroney's friends began to regret their support for Campbell, and by the time of the leadership convention they were frantically trying to convert delegates to Charest. Schreiber, a Tory party member, had supported Charest from the beginning and made sure he was in Ottawa for the convention, which began on June 9. He wandered around the halls, visited the hospitality suites, and sat with Elmer MacKay in Charest's crowded section at the Ottawa Civic Centre while the votes were counted. Schreiber had expressed his approval of Charest in the time-honoured fashion with a donation to his campaign in the amount of C$13,000.

He had backed the wrong horse. Kim Campbell won the convention and was sworn in as prime minister on June 25. Mulroney was still a member of Parliament, but after his resignation as party leader and prime minister he did not return to the House of Commons again; in fact, he left Ottawa for good. He and Mila spent the month of July in France, and in early August, Mulroney became a partner at Ogilvy Renault, the Montreal law firm where he'd practised law many years before. He soon accepted invitations to serve as a director of several corporate boards.

Meanwhile, Schreiber spent most of his time in Kaufering. The Airbus commissions continued to sail through the system and into his account, the latest arriving on July 4, 1993, to the tune of US$354,000. That deposit joined a previous one for US$1,369,000 on May 7 and another before that on April 7 for US$480,000.

Zurich is populated by bankers and businessmen in July, but also by tourists who flock to its Old City to shop, to dine, to walk along the Limmat or meander through the cobbled alleyways. Schreiber never tired of Zurich, and he enjoyed the trips most when he could take Barbel and browse through expensive shops. Schreiber's favourite stop, of course, was the Swiss Bank Corporation on the Paradeplatz, where he would meet with his banker, André Strobel.

On Wednesday, July 21, his banking transactions were quite ordinary. He wired C$100,023.17 out of the Canadian-funds subaccount 18679.1 to an unknown destination, and on Thursday he moved C$50,023 somewhere else as well. On Friday the subaccount was debited another C$66,210, also transferred to an unknown destination. The following Monday, however, there was a new wrinkle.

Until then Schreiber could count nine code names on subaccounts, or *Rubriken*, in his bank in Zurich, each representing a specific individual, according to documents prepared by the German investigators.[1] But on July 26, Schreiber and Strobel made a transaction in a subaccount numbered 46341.5. Judging by its number, it would have been set up in 1991, and it was in Canadian funds, just like the ones he had created for Frankfurt, Fred, and Marc. On Monday, July 26, he transferred C$500,000 into this subaccount from the Frankfurt subaccount; the record of the transaction shows a new code name: Britan.

What was Britan? Why did Schreiber put money in it in 1993, long after the Airbus and Thyssen and MBB deals were in place? And why did the money come from the Frankfurt subaccount, the one set up in Canadian dollars to funnel "useful expenditures"?

Schreiber refused to tell investigators what or who Britan was, but he left a trail of interesting clues. All the other Zurich codes referring to Canadians were attached to Canadian-dollar subaccounts. Britan seemed to be for a Canadian, since it was also in Canadian funds. Only once – for the Master subaccount – did Schreiber devise a code name based on anything other than the individual's first name. A few names were altered in such a way as to become other words: Stuart became Stewardess; Frank became Frankfurt; Winfried became Winter. Though spelled differently, Britan sounded like Britain.

If Schreiber followed his usual pattern of slightly adapting a person's first name, then it would seem logical that the new subaccount represented a Canadian whose first name was close to "Britan." It wouldn't take a genius to see that Britan minus one consonant could be Brian. Add to this the fact that Schreiber's appointment diaries were filled with references to his meetings with "Brian" when referring to Prime Minister Brian Mulroney. It was not unreasonable to conclude that Britan stood for Brian Mulroney.

This was not to suggest that Mulroney knew anything about the coded account, nor that he received any of the money in the account. It was entirely possible that Schreiber was simply playing an elaborate game, pretending to be allocating payments when he was in fact keeping the money to himself. If he was paying it out as *Schmiergelder*, he wouldn't have to pay tax on it; that was what he told the tax authorities he had done with the money. He could even point to his Zurich bank accounts, ten of which bore rather obvious code names.

But Schreiber's Zurich accounts were carefully hidden, and the German tax collector would probably never see them. Why would he establish and maintain a bogus money trail that the authorities would never find? Perhaps he wanted to be extra careful. Perhaps it was just in case.

There was at least one more possibility: that Britan did refer to Brian Mulroney, and that Schreiber did earmark funds to give to Mulroney shortly after he left office. There was nothing to prohibit Schreiber from doing so: a gift is a gift. It was also possible that a large retirement purse for Mulroney was being assembled by friends who began collecting for it in the winter of 1992–93, and that Schreiber used the Britan account to contribute to a fund whose donors Mulroney was not even aware of. Mulroney emphatically denied, however, that he ever received a retirement purse from anyone.

Years later, the historian Michael Bliss put forward his argument in the wake of allegations that Mulroney may have received secret commission money from Schreiber. In the *Toronto Star* on December 15, 1995, Bliss contended that while Mulroney would never have agreed to a retirement gift while he was in office, it's possible that his friends resorted to a Plan B in the form of a retirement fund. The deposit to the Britan account would fit in with this theory, since it received the C$500,000 from the Frankfurt subaccount a month after Mulroney officially resigned as prime minister.

"[Stevie] Cameron's claim that a $4-million farewell purse was raised by Mulroney's friends in 1992-93 has been flatly denied by Mulroney," Bliss wrote. "But whether or not Mulroney was given or took any money from friends and admirers after his period of public service, it's quite possible that some of his friends who were doing well out of government contracts and contacts did set aside money that they expected to throw in the hat when it was finally passed. To make sure that talented people were rewarded for public service had, after all, become a Canadian tradition, almost part of the obligations incumbent on the well-to-do.

"If special commissions were paid in the Airbus deal – a not uncommon commercial practice in Europe – it is quite possible that the recipients, whoever they were, might have intended someday to give some of the money to Mulroney. By the same token, Mulroney would remain entirely innocent of any wrongdoing... His only guilt might be by association."

In Bliss's view, the Airbus-IAL contract was normal and above board, perhaps even commonplace. He may not have known that the contract stipulated it was to be cancelled in the event of a "major political change" in Canada, and that Airbus Industrie and Schreiber both denied the contract even existed. Still, Bliss's main point had some merit: Schreiber may have intended to give Mulroney money from the secret commissions without Mulroney knowing about it. Either way, there is no proof Mulroney received a penny from Karlheinz Schreiber.

On July 27, just a day after Schreiber deposited C$500,000 into the new Britan account, someone made a C$100,000 cash withdrawal. At the same time, the accumulated balance in Schreiber's Canadian-funds subaccount 18679.1 had reached C$5.8 million.

By September, Schreiber had summoned the energy to return to Canada to try to revive Bear Head with the new party leadership. Jean Charest expressed some interest – $13,000 would get his attention, and he wouldn't want to be rude to a fellow Tory – and before long Kim Campbell's office was considering the proposal. No one took it seriously and Campbell was preoccupied. Schreiber was so upset that no one was honouring the 1988 understanding in principle that he told Elmer MacKay he was thinking of suing the federal government.

Buoyed by an optimistic public opinion poll, Campbell announced that voters would go to the polls on October 26. Many of her former colleagues voted with their feet. John Crosbie, Marcel Masse, Michael Wilson, and Elmer MacKay were just a few senior Tory ministers who decided not to run again. They smelled disaster and they were not wrong. Campbell herself had a painful campaign, stumbling over one gaffe after another, and by the end of September it was clear the Tories didn't have a hope of being re-elected.

If you were Schreiber, you might be thankful that Marc Lalonde was a friend and on retainer. The former Liberal finance and justice minister was admired in the Liberal Party. If Jean Chrétien's crew were going to be running the government, Lalonde would have a pipeline right into the Prime Minister's Office. In the middle of the campaign, on September 29, Schreiber transferred C$500,000 out of the Frankfurt subaccount and into the Marc subaccount, 18679.5.

One week before the federal election in Canada, another US$480,000 in Airbus commissions came into Schreiber's U.S.-funds subaccount in Zurich, 18679.4. German prosecutors' documents filed in court would claim that the Airbus payments for the Strauss family ended with this deposit. The Augsburg authorities concluded that in all, US$5.2 million went to the Strauss family as its share of the Airbus commissions for Canada and Thailand, between October 3, 1988, and October 21, 1993. They theorize that the Strauss family had lost millions in Canada as a result of Schreiber's business misadventures, and that he had always wanted to make good their losses.

On October 26, the Conservative era came to an end. The Tories were reduced from a majority government to two lowly seats, and the party was virtually destroyed. Although Campbell had run an inept campaign, there was no denying that the results were a reaction to the Mulroney regime, a government that many Canadians regarded as arrogant, corrupt, and out of touch.

In the fall of 1993, Schreiber seemed to be transferring much more money out of his various Canadian-funds subaccounts than he had in the past. On November 3, for example, another C$100,000 in cash was withdrawn from the Britan account. Someone took C$66,520.79 in cash out of the Frankfurt subaccount, converting it to U.S. dollars, and then an additional C$50,000 in cash from the same account. The Marc subaccount also saw a cash withdrawal of C$50,000, as did the Canadian-funds subaccount 18679.1. That same month Schreiber transferred C$250,000 out of the Marc account to some unspecified destination, and on December 30, he debited the Frankfurt subaccount C$240,000.

Schreiber received the last of the Thyssen Saudi money in the fall of 1993, when the arms manufacturer transferred DM1.4 million via the account in Vaduz into 47252, the ATG account in Zurich. On December 10, Schreiber transferred DM700,000 of the ATG money into the Jürglund subaccount, 46341.1.

According to the prosecutors' later calculations, the total amounts from the Saudi venture paid to his associates through bank transfers or in cash were:

Jürglund	DM8,650,000
Winter	DM1,200,000
Waldherr	DM1,000,000
Maxwell	DM 500,000
Holgart	DM3,800,000

As the new year began, the activity in the accounts accelerated. On January 19, 1994, Schreiber transferred C$953,707.19 out of the Canadian-funds subaccount 18679.1. It was the largest single transfer of funds from the account. There was no clue as to its ultimate resting place, only a note on the bank file indicating that the money had been converted to another currency before it disappeared.

17

The Hounds at His Heels

Ottawa grew less appealing for the Schreibers in 1994; their Conservative friends had scattered to the winds, returning to home towns or moving to cities where the climate was friendlier. The smugness of the triumphant Liberals – especially their sanctimonious cant about ethics in government – was hard to take.

One of the few incentives for Schreiber to visit Canada at all was to see his friend Elmer MacKay, who had retired to his farm and wooded acres in rural Nova Scotia. Schreiber was so fond of MacKay's son Peter, a talented young lawyer, that he had arranged a job for him at Thyssen headquarters in Germany. Peter MacKay hadn't been happy at Thyssen, said family friends, and left after six months to become a Crown prosecutor in Nova Scotia. He was close to his father and saw a lot of Schreiber during this period. When their conversations turned to business and politics, Schreiber couldn't hide his frustration that the Bear Head project had failed, and he would tell the MacKays how he and Marc Lalonde were working hard to resurrect it.

His disappointments in Canada might have been easier to accept if the news stories breaking in Bavaria hadn't been so painful. Schreiber had idolized Franz Josef Strauss, but in the spring of 1994, his hero's reputation was crumbling under the revelations of one scandal after another. Suspicions of corruption had been confirmed the year before with Max Streibl's Brazilian indiscretions and had quickly spread to his predecessor. Germans were calling the whole network that had grown up around Strauss "Amigoland." It was all about the cozy relationships and favours exchanged among certain businessmen and members of Strauss's government. The old stories of Strauss's murky business dealings with the East German spy Alexander Schalck-Golodkowski resurfaced. In February, Peter Gauweiler, Bavaria's environment minister, had been forced to resign over a scandal involving legal fees.

These embarrassments could not have emerged at a worse time for the Christian Social Union; 1994 was a crucial election year, with state and general elections, as well as elections to the European parliament, on the calendar. Michael Glos, the CSU's parliamentary leader in Bonn, summed up the situation carefully when he told a radio interviewer, "We profited from Strauss, and we are naturally affected if his image is clouded and some negative aspects come to light."

The *Nürnberger Nachrichten* pointed out that what made the affair particularly awkward was that the CSU had tried to turn Strauss into a national icon. "After his death, streets, squares and even an airport were named after Strauss," the paper observed. "His successors are defiantly continuing to honour him, and this is what makes things so difficult."

"Everybody knew he wasn't a saint," admitted Theodore Waigel, a senior member of the CSU who was also Helmut Kohl's minister of finance.

The most damning story appeared in *Der Spiegel* at the beginning of April. The magazine reported that Eduard Zwick, a multimillionaire who owned one of the country's most luxurious spas, had fled to Switzerland just ahead of the tax authorities, who claimed he owed DM70 million in unpaid income tax. It became known that Strauss had accepted many favours from Zwick over the years, favours that included the use of a private plane, free holidays at Zwick's country home in France – even financial advice and helpful references at Zwick's own banks in Switzerland. And Strauss repaid him, so the story went, with a timely tip that he was under investigation for tax evasion and that he should leave Germany immediately, pleading ill health. If he could persuade the tax officials that he was seriously ill, there was a good chance they would drop the investigation. Or, failing that, perhaps the tax bite could be softened substantially.

The matter simmered for years and became public in 1994 when Streibl's successor, Edmund Stoiber – a man who campaigned on a platform of clean government – was credited with the arrest in January 1994 of Zwick's son Johannes, as an accomplice in the tax affair. Zwick Senior roared back to health and defended his son vigorously. Not only did Zwick accuse Stoiber and other leading Bavarian politicians of double-crossing him, he threatened to expose some of their secrets. It emerged that a former finance minister had borrowed money from Zwick and that Stoiber himself had been a weekend guest of Zwick in the south of France.

The conspiracy of silence around political corruption in Bavaria was broken and newspapers had a field day, especially the foreign press. "Something is rotten in the proud and prosperous Free State of Bavaria, once a byword for the post-war success story of the German federal republic," wrote Quentin Peel in the *Financial Times* of London on April 19. On June 7, the *Daily Telegraph* weighed in with a tough story on endemic corruption in Germany. "Everyone holds out his palm for greasing," the headline said. "Inside Germany, corruption is rife." The *Telegraph*'s Robin Gedye described a culture of corruption so strong that some British businessmen found it almost impossible to do business with German companies. He quoted from a new study of crime in Germany which stated that "organized corruption" and its growing acceptance was a dangerous phenomenon. "The top of the crop of current scandals," Gedye added, "are allegations that Franz Josef Strauss . . . was involved in extensive tax evasion plots."

While the Amigo scandals were splashed across the front pages of newspapers in Europe in the spring of 1994, Stuart Iddles left Airbus Industrie to return to British Aerospace. He didn't stay long. The pull of sunny days in stress-free climes was too enticing, and he began spending more time at his villa in Roses, Spain, or at his spread in Puerto Vallarta, Mexico. His real estate agent in Mexico, Brock Squire, recalled Iddles telling him that on one occasion he tried to take a briefcase full of cash out of Switzerland. Swiss authorities found the money in a routine search of his luggage and confiscated it; Iddles was outraged that he had to launch legal action to recover it. Squire, who had since had a falling-out with Iddles, said the former Airbus vice-president told him that the company often looked the other way if executives were involved in secret side deals. "I think that's where they made their serious money," Squire told a CBC-TV reporter in 1998.

Fortunately for Schreiber, his name never popped up in any of the Strauss scandal stories, but Pelossi's threats of exposure still hung over his head.

As it turned out, the first disturbing call he received that spring was not from a prying reporter or tax official but from the Royal Canadian Mounted Police. On March 3, 1994, Inspector Brian Retiff, an officer with the Commercial Crime Unit in Edmonton, phoned to ask Schreiber about the $150,000 loan he had made to Hugh Horner back in 1976. Retiff wanted to know what the loan was for and why Horner had repaid only part of it. Did it have anything to do with Schreiber's road-marking business? Schreiber gave him nothing of significance.

Mulroney had been out of office for ten months, but Schreiber remained in regular touch with him and with a few other Ottawa pals. On April 6, he reminded himself to call Marc Lalonde; below Lalonde's name he jotted "Manley wg. 2.Mai." Possibly he hoped Lalonde might arrange a meeting with Chrétien's industry minister, John Manley, on May 2. On April 7, he wrote "CAN-Brian?" in his diary, and on April 9 he flew to Ottawa from Munich. He met with Elmer MacKay and with Bobby Hladun. On this trip, he spent some time in Calgary as well and saw Erika Lutz. He had jotted down the name of the RCMP officer who had called him about the Horner loan. "RCMP 4.3. Insp. Retiff (Red) 495-6731." Whether he talked to Retiff or not while in Alberta, Schreiber certainly had him on his mind, aware that the RCMP was asking questions about a possible criminal investigation. After two days in Alberta, he flew back to Ottawa, where he met with Jack Major, his friend on the Supreme Court of Canada.

Schreiber was counting on Lalonde, who should have been able to take another run at the Bear Head project with the Liberal government. Lalonde seemed to have been helpful in many ways; a diary entry suggests Schreiber spoke to him not just about Bear Head but also about Air Canada and Airbus. He scheduled meetings with Industry Minister Manley, Transport Minister Doug Young, and Secretary of State for Finance Roy MacLaren. He called on Senator Allan MacEachen – a fellow member of Atlantik-Brücke – and recorded Finance Minister Paul Martin's name. His notes show he was hopeful of seeing Jean Chrétien.

On April 23, Schreiber took a limousine to Montreal; his diary doesn't reveal whom he saw there. The next day he was back in Munich. The Liebherr contract that he'd discussed with Herbert Leiduck in Monaco looked as if it might go ahead, so he flew to Moscow on May 4. While there he heard about a new Air Canada agreement with Airbus for twenty-five A319 passenger jets to replace its thirty-five DC 9s, a deal worth a billion dollars. Instead of buying the aircraft outright, Air Canada, now fully privatized, would lease them. Schreiber wrote notes about the order on the margins of his page for May 5.

7 sold to 2 leasing comp
Lease back to AC
Everything is paid
Kontrak Manager J. Besner
Fleet Manager / McRay
President Hollis Harris

The question arises, Was Schreiber still receiving commissions on sales of Airbus planes to Air Canada? Clearly this latest contract was of interest to him. Later, he jotted, "Albert 25 AB-AC," perhaps a reminder to talk to Albert Birkner in Kaufering about the twenty-five new planes going to Air Canada. (Even though Birkner had retired, Schreiber continued to consult him about his business affairs.) He made another notation to speak to Jean Pierson and Stuart Iddles.

While still in Moscow, he doodled this entry for himself:

Frank • Brian • Marc • Cretien [sic]
Jack M

The first names of Frank Moores, Brian Mulroney, Marc Lalonde, and Jack Major; only Chrétien went by his last name in Schreiber's notes. The Canadians were never far from his mind.

On May 6, his business in Moscow completed, he ordered a cab to the airport. En route, another car hurtled by and sideswiped his vehicle. "We went into a truck," he told CBC-TV six months later. "The damn bugger . . . just crossed the street from the right side to the left side and we were thrown to the opposite highway lanes in high traffic . . . I nearly died." Although he was badly shaken up, he recovered quickly and lost no time away from his ongoing projects.

That summer Schreiber was in touch with Iddles, Lalonde, Doucet, and Strobel and spoke to Leiduck about the Moscow project. He made several calls to the German ambassador to Canada, Hans-Gunter Sulimma. For a change there were very few money transfers, with one notable exception: on July 21, 1994, someone withdrew C$50,000 in cash from the Britan subaccount and another C$50,000 out of the Marc subaccount.

That summer his attention was caught by a business opportunity that was entirely different from his former interests. Given that he loved to cook, perhaps it was not so surprising to his family. The company was called Spaghettissimo, and the product was a machine to make and cook spaghetti, a sort of pasta equivalent of the bread-making machines for home kitchens that were the latest cookware fad. But the Spaghettissimo machine was designed for restaurant use, not home cooking, by engineers at Thyssen, where the patent resided. Schreiber had dreams of selling it to restaurants around the world. His partners were his son, Andreas, and Greg Alford, who was still hanging on as president of the floundering Bear Head Industries.

It was on Friday, July 29, during this period of planning for a new venture, that Schreiber jotted a couple of enigmatic notes in his diary. The first consisted of four short lines:

Maxwell –
Delta Int. EST. SBV
LO/234-986-1
D-200 St. Gallen

The second was simply a reminder: "# Tel. Ströhlein."

These entries were Schreiber's shorthand reference to a company involved in a daring and complicated business transaction – not one of his, but one that drew in many of the same players who were attached to his deals. Maxwell referred to Max Strauss, while Delta International Establishment was a holding company owned by a fellow German, Dieter Holzer, a highly placed middleman just like Schreiber, a sometime agent for the BND, and a member of Franz Josef Strauss's Amigo circle. Holzer, who lived in Monaco, and Strauss often travelled together on business and became close; when Max Strauss grew older, he too befriended Holzer and eventually received a great deal of money from Delta. Strauss's allies said later they believed it could have been for legal work.

SBV was an abbreviation for the Schweizerische Bankverein, the Swiss Bank Corporation; the number LO/234-986-1 referred to a bank account, and D-200 St. Gallen – given Schreiber's usual practice of dropping zeros from the end of cash transactions – suggested a transaction of DM200,000 at the St. Gallen branch. Werner Ströhlein, of course, was Schreiber's old friend from the German security and intelligence service. He was now pursuing private business interests.

By the summer of 1994, when Schreiber was entering this information in his diary, Elf Aquitaine, the giant French state-owned oil company founded by Charles de Gaulle in the early 1960s, had purchased the decrepit East German Leuna oil refinery, Germany's largest chemical plant before World War II, in a deal worth billions of dollars. When Elf took over the refinery in 1992, 18,000 people worked in a rusting plant considered obsolete and an environmental nightmare.

Elf had originally promised to invest DM4.8 billion in a new refinery, but when the smoke cleared from the deal, what Germans saw was a huge DM1.4-billion subsidy for Elf from the German government, plus the inclusion of the East German chain of Minol gas stations as part of the package. The deal had been structured by Germany's privatization agency, Treuhandanstalt, which arranged for Elf to take two-thirds ownership in Leuna and acquire 650 acres of land for the new plant. Rumours of *Schmiergelder* floated around the project, and there were muttered suggestions that both French and German politicians had been paid off. In 1994 Elf began construction of a new US$2.6-billion refinery that was trumpeted as state-of-the-art, but the 4,000 workers who had survived successive waves of cuts at the plant were dismayed to find that it would employ only about 700 people. That same year Kohl was up for re-election. French president François Mitterrand wanted the Christian Democratic Union back in power; Kohl was his ally in the fight to win a European monetary union. The history of the Elf-Leuna deal became an issue of politics as much as economic development.

In an arrangement uncannily similar to the one Schreiber had established for the Saudi tank sale, Dieter Holzer's company acted as the intermediary for massive payments to make the deal happen. Elf paid FF256 million, which travelled through Liechtenstein companies and Swiss bank accounts into shells controlled by three men. One was Holzer; it was his Liechtenstein shell company, Delta International Establishment, that was believed to have washed DM50 million in bribes on the Elf deal. The second was Pierre Lethier, one of Holzer's friends and a senior official in France's security services in the 1980s. The third was André Guelfi, a French businessman based in Switzerland, who funnelled some of the money through companies he owned. What was Elf paying for? The answer was in a letter written on September 12, 1991, by André Guillon, a senior executive at Elf, to the company's chief executive officer, Loik Le Floch-Prigent, a document that was obtained by the Paris newspaper *Le Parisien*.

"For the success of the project," Guillon wrote, "the intervention of one or several external consultants will be necessary. They should know German institutions well and especially the mechanisms of financial aid available." Their remuneration was tied to the amounts Elf eventually won in state aid and subsidies.

Along with the three middlemen, Holger Pfahls, Walther Leisler Kiep, and Max Strauss had their hands in the negotiations. Pfahls attended meetings in Kohl's office as an adviser. Even after leaving the Defence Department in the summer of 1992 for a job in Brussels with Daimler-Benz, he stayed close to the Elf-Leuna project. Kiep's assignment was to court Elf. "My job was to try to interest oil companies in the

Leuna project," Kiep told the *New York Times*. "I played an important role in bringing Elf on board as investor [sic]." True, said Munich's *Süddeutsche Zeitung* newspaper, but there was more to the story than this. Because Kiep was in the insurance business, Dieter Holzer and several of his companies bought policies from the insurance company with which he was associated. And when Elf needed insurance for Leuna, it bought it from Kiep's firm.

Max Strauss's part in all this? The Augsburg prosecutors began investigating him for allegedly diverting and laundering DM400,000 he received from Holzer through Delta. According to German Justice Ministry documents, Strauss and Holzer may have also used Delta to hide DM50 million in *Schmiergelder* supplied by Elf, some of which, rumour had it, went to Helmut Kohl's party, the CDU.

A deal of this magnitude would normally have created a massive paper trail, similar to that flowing from the Saudi tank deal, but something peculiar happened with the Leuna project. Most of the files disappeared. And within Elf itself, no one was talking; famous for its secrecy, its power, and its political networks, Elf was a company that did not hesitate to give millions of francs to support France's right-wing parties.

The Elf-Leuna saga illuminated a political and business culture that encouraged and endorsed the payment of millions of dollars in *Schmiergelder* to ensure contracts for government-supported industry and the donation of millions more into right-wing party coffers. Schreiber operated comfortably within that culture. Using shell companies and numbered Swiss accounts to mask such transactions was, quite simply, business as usual.

In August Anette Littmann, a business reporter based in the Hamburg head office of *Der Spiegel*, had a casual discussion with one of her sources, a lawyer in Frankfurt. As they chatted, he hinted that he'd heard an interesting story about a Swiss accountant called Giorgio Pelossi. This Pelossi might have a tale to tell. Why didn't she call him and check it out?

Intrigued, Littmann telephoned Pelossi; although he was friendly, he remained so guarded in his comments that she wasn't sure what his story really was. But after Schreiber's name came up, she phoned him too. Schreiber did not return her call. Littmann knew she didn't have much to go on – a few murmured words from a source, a cautious but encouraging response from Pelossi, and silence from Schreiber – but her nose told her she had a story, not a business story but a national political story. It was time to talk to her boss, Christiane Kohl.

Der Spiegel's headquarters is in a large brick building on a quay known as Brandestwiete, facing the Hamburg harbour; the national affairs bureau is on the ninth floor. Here the reporters and editors enjoy a fine view overlooking the old harbour area and the roofs of Hamburg; they can see the city hall from where they sit, and the spires of the city's important churches. The ninth-floor offices at *Der Spiegel* are coveted for both their view and their prestige as the heart of the magazine's best reporting.

Kohl, who was in her mid-thirties, had been a diligent reporter with a reputation as a digger, especially in political matters. Now national editor, she listened carefully when Littmann explained that despite slim leads, she thought it was worth visiting Giorgio Pelossi. Kohl considered it and later walked over to Mathias Blumencron's desk. "I may have something for you," she said. Blumencron, thirty-two and trained as a lawyer, was one of the most talented young reporters at *Der Spiegel*. His cheerful friendliness belied a ferocious resolve. He and Littmann contacted Pelossi and were able to persuade him to see them in Lugano. They flew down immediately.

Pelossi wasn't reluctant to tell the reporters his story, but he did say he expected to be paid for it. It was sensational, he promised them, and well worth the money. Here was a difficulty. Like many informants with a good story, Pelossi expected a five-figure fee for his information. Eventually they reached an agreement. The magazine would pay Pelossi's out-of-pocket expenses, covering the cost of his time away from work. It amounted to three or four thousand Deutschmarks.

"He was very secretive," remembered Blumencron. "He didn't want to have his name mentioned. Ever." And, at the beginning, the reporters were skeptical. Pelossi was quiet and easygoing. He didn't seem the type to be a major player, a holder of secrets that could threaten governments. He sensed their reserve and finally opened his safe and pulled out his papers. They brightened the moment they saw what was there.

That same month, Karlheinz and Barbel Schreiber celebrated their ninth wedding anniversary. He loved his wife and counted himself a lucky man. It should have been a happy time for him, but he couldn't shake the nightmare of Giorgio Pelossi and his threats to ruin him. The message from Littmann at *Der Spiegel* was alarming. Had Pelossi finally gone to the media or, worse, to the authorities? Schreiber had already decided he had better contact someone he hadn't spoken to in years: Renate Rauscher, the woman who had left him ten years earlier, the woman he had cut from his payroll in a fit of pique. He didn't need her animosity on top of Pelossi's.

Later, when authorities interviewed Rauscher, she made it clear their personal relationship had ended long before. "After this time I essentially had no more contact with Mr. Schreiber, that is to say that there was no relationship there, not even one of a friendship nature," she told them. "After this time I was also no longer financially supported by Mr. Schreiber."

Schreiber had hardly seen her since their breakup in 1984. It was a long time ago, but Rauscher no doubt harboured many secrets about Schreiber's friendships and business dealings. On August 26, he wrote, "# Tel. Renate #," in large print in his diary. The next day he wrote out her name in full, Renate Rauscher, just above a bank account number: "Kto No. 18202519 DSK."

On October 10, according to the German prosecutors, Schreiber instructed Lorenzo Wullschleger to draw up a contract between Rauscher and Kensington, IAL's parent company. Schreiber was taking precautions: it was better to have his enemies inside the tent.

Rauscher herself denied knowing anything about a contract when the Augsburg investigators inquired a year later. "When the 10.10.1994 contract . . . is held before me, all I can say to that is that this event is totally unknown to me," she told them. Her interrogators wanted to know why she suddenly renewed a friendship with Schreiber, after all those years.

"There was no specific reason for the re-establishment of the relationship in 1994," she told the prosecutors. "As I recall, I only saw Mr.

Schreiber about twice in 1994 also. An occasion for this was that I had bought him two hunting rifles. This can be proven, as the rifles were re-registered in his name. In order to do this, we met at my office, that is, in front of my office – in the car, in Munich."

Mathias Blumencron and Anette Littmann pored over the documents from Pelossi's safe: bank documents, secret agreements with Thyssen, MBB, and Airbus, faxes from Karlheinz Schreiber, telexes from Stuart Iddles, shell companies in Liechtenstein, payments to secret accounts in Zurich. It was a motherlode.

But there were some weaknesses too. Pelossi had no evidence concerning the whereabouts of the commissions and contingency fees after he sent them to Schreiber's Zurich account 18679. And Pelossi's most sensational revelation – that Schreiber had told him he was going to pay off a Canadian prime minister, Brian Mulroney – was simply a second-hand comment without proof. Pelossi was the first to admit he was only reporting a conversation. Pelossi told Blumencron that Schreiber had said he met Mulroney in Pontresina in 1988 or 1989. Again, there was no proof. Still, the material was powerful, and Pelossi was helpful. He had only two conditions: no one could mention his name for now, and he wanted to be paid, as they'd agreed.

As the senior reporter for national politics, Blumencron took the lead on the story, and the more time he spent going through the Pelossi papers, the more he realized he would need the assistance of a Canadian journalist. Pelossi had described three deals to him – the Airbus sale, the MBB contract, and the proposed Bear Head plant – and all were Canadian. He asked his colleague Hans Leyendecker if he could suggest a Canadian contact. Leyendecker, considered the finest investigative reporter in Germany, was sour on the Pelossi story; the evidence was flimsy and circumstantial, the informant was a disgruntled former employee with a score to settle, and the whole thing was a waste of time. Still, he didn't mind suggesting a Canadian reporter if Blumencron insisted on chasing the story across the Atlantic. He recommended Jock Ferguson, once an investigative reporter for the *Globe and Mail*. Ferguson had specialized in municipal politics, but he possessed the same tough, intuitive tenacity as his German counterparts, and he was famous for his ability to secure and decipher corporate financial documents. When Blumencron called him, Ferguson was working as a freelancer on television projects for Canadian, British, and American producers.

Ferguson had been working with Harvey Cashore, then an associate producer with CBC-TV's investigative documentary show, *the fifth estate*, on another story about kickbacks and bribes in the airline industry. The competition for a Bahamas Air order had been won by de Havilland amidst rumours that the Canadian company, owned by Boeing, had made secret payments to Bahamian politicians. One of the losing bidders told Cashore there was a "far bigger" story out there: he had been told by someone at Airbus Industrie that it had paid substantial secret commissions on the Air Canada sale. "That's the one you ought to be looking at," he said.

Now there were several investigative reporters consumed by the story: the *Der Spiegel* team and Cashore's group at the CBC. They worked out a schedule of assignments and started making calls. One of them was to Stevie Cameron; she shared her files on Schreiber, Airbus, and Bear Head with Ferguson, an old colleague from their days together at the *Globe and Mail*.

That fall Gary Ouellet seemed to run into financial troubles. Despite being one of the most successful lobbyists of the Mulroney era, he declared personal bankruptcy. The magician's money had done a vanishing act: his only asset, he claimed, was a 1990 Jeep Cherokee worth $8,000. He had not a penny to his name and his debts totalled $335,746: $203,490 in unpaid federal and provincial taxes and an outstanding loan of $132,256 at the Toronto-Dominion Bank in Ottawa. News of his bankruptcy was received with little surprise in Ottawa; GCI had left a pile of unpaid tax bills that none of the partners, let alone the new owner, wanted to pay. Fortunately, Ouellet didn't lose his house in Sillery, Quebec – it was in his wife's name.

Now that Schreiber was spending less time in Canada, he saw more of his old German connections. He was in touch with Werner Ströhlein and he made plans to meet Wolfgang Schäuble, deputy chairman of the CDU, in Bonn, and on several occasions met with or spoke to Brigitte Baumeister, treasurer of the CDU, whose name, along with that of Jürgen Massmann, appeared frequently in Schreiber's diaries.

In the middle of September 1994, he transferred C$316,716.81 out of his Canadian-funds subaccount 18679.1 to an unidentified destination. On October 4, he made two further withdrawals: one for C$200,000 and another for C$31,678.99, the latter converted to another currency. His diary for that date notes, "200 CAN, 50 Jürglund, 100 DM" and then another "4088 CAN." For some reason he was taking substantial amounts out of this Canadian-funds subaccount, and by the end of October he'd withdrawn even more.

Records did not indicate to whom Schreiber gave the C$200,000, but the recipient of the DM100,000 was later identified. Schreiber stuffed the money into an envelope and arranged for Baumeister to pick it up at his home in Kaufering; she was to pass it on to Schäuble as a donation to the party. But just like the gift Schreiber had given Kiep in St. Margarethen in 1991, it was never registered in the CDU books as a donation. As Schreiber said years later, the money wasn't given out of admiration for the CDU's goals. "This sum of money had other reasons," Schreiber told a reporter from ARD, Bavarian public television.

Blumencron called Schreiber several times, playing telephone tag until they finally connected. Schreiber would promise to meet him and then put it off. Blumencron went to other names on his list and on November 9, just as Schreiber had feared, he called Renate Rauscher. Rauscher and Schreiber spoke that evening about Blumencron's questions. The journalist had asked her, Schreiber noted in his diary, what she knew about meetings between Schreiber and Brian Mulroney.

At 7 the next morning, Schreiber spoke to his lawyer about Rauscher's call from *Der Spiegel*. He called Fred Doucet at 8 a.m. Ottawa time looking for Mulroney's home and office numbers. The day after, Schreiber learned Blumencron had contacted Helmut Wieczorek as well. Blumencron was becoming a nuisance. The bank accounts would have to be moved.

Schreiber would close his accounts in Zurich and open another set, exactly the same, under Barbel's name. Threatened and spooked by

Der Spiegel's snooping, he moved quickly. On November 14, 1994, he started by withdrawing the remaining C$3.7 million out of his Canadian-funds account 18679.1. He transferred it to another account, in a different currency, where it sat temporarily until he was ready to transfer it into a new Barbara Schreiber account.

On the same day he made several notations in his diary and in tiny handwriting wrote the following lines: "Brian 2+4 / Cretien / Wieczorek." Whatever Schreiber was thinking, he wasn't about to commit all of it to paper.

On Monday, November 21, Schreiber shut down account 18679, including all its code-named subaccounts, in his Swiss Bank Corporation branch in Zurich. He sent the money remaining in these accounts into a mirror copy of 18679 – a new account, 56129, at the same branch, in Barbara Schreiber's name. The process took about two weeks. Britan became subaccount 62684.3; Stewardess, 56129.5; Marc, 56129.4. Pelossi could try anything he liked, but Schreiber convinced himself he would remain one step ahead.

Schreiber made some careful notes in his diary for November 21. He recorded a withdrawal of DM50,000 for himself and C$50,000 from the Britan account. Bank records confirm the latter transaction. It was the first and only time Schreiber wrote the word "Britan" in his 1994 diary. (But he did write "Britan 200.200" under the B's in his 1994 address book, an entry that stumped the prosecutors.) Below his note – "50 Britan CA" – is a reminder to call Greg Alford about a hotel in New York. On the same page are the words "Kathi Pierre NY." It looked as if he planned to stay at the Pierre, one of the finest hotels in the city. On November 23, Schreiber jotted "# Briefe" in the diary, along with several names including Schäuble, Kiep, and Baumeister. He also called Fred Doucet about the meetings in New York.

That same day Schreiber made a note, "Roger Bailly. Fax. On the Take." Bailly was the Airbus lawyer who had overseen the IAL contract. Stevie Cameron had included a section on Schreiber and his connection to the Airbus contract in her book *On the Take*, released three weeks earlier.

Schreiber landed in New York on December 4, 1994. The next day he met Frank Moores at the Pierre. Even thousands of kilometres from home, Schreiber couldn't seem to shake the persistent Mathias Blumencron. Before he left Germany he learned that Blumencron had called Erich Riedl. Once in New York, he heard that he had also called Kurt Pfleiderer of MBB. Schreiber dined the following evening with Elmer MacKay at the Metropolitan Club. On the morning of December 8, he made a note to get Blumencron's telephone number at *Der Spiegel*. After four days in New York, Schreiber was ready to check out of the Pierre and return to Germany, but his diary suggests he had one last commitment: "10:30/Brian."

At the end of January 1995, Schreiber, weary of deflecting Blumencron's calls – and probably curious about what he knew – finally agreed to meet him. Harvey Cashore too had reached Schreiber by telephone and had been charmed by this affable man who knew, by the time their conversation had ended, that Cashore was married and the father of a baby who had just passed his first birthday. Only when the conversation turned to Giorgio Pelossi did Schreiber's anger show, and he balked at doing a formal sitdown interview with the CBC. If the Blumencron session went well, perhaps he could risk Canadian television.

During the *Der Spiegel* interview, Schreiber told Blumencron that IAL was not his company. He knew some of IAL's people, he said, but he refused to tell Blumencron who they were. Sometimes, he added, he used IAL to pay "useful expenditures." He was more than willing to talk about Boeing and the competition for Air Canada's business.

"You see, there was a real mix-up with Boeing at that time. That everything possible was done to get the business going is totally logical. And that I didn't do it for nothing, if I had been involved – that is also logical. There is nothing to hide."

Then why the secrecy about the ownership of IAL? asked Blumencron.

"I will not get into that," Schreiber replied. "That is exclusively a matter between the tax authorities and myself."

What was Schreiber saying? He would not confirm his involvement in the Airbus deal, but he couldn't stop himself from bragging about Airbus's victory over Boeing. He told Blumencron he had no intention of talking to *the fifth estate*. "I have had good experiences with *Der Spiegel*," he confided, "but I can't tell you all I would tell you if a Canadian is on the other side of a table. We do some things which are good for our industry, which are perhaps not that good for Canadians."

Stuart Iddles refused to talk to the CBC as well, though he was very polite on the phone and later sent Cashore a copy of the confidentiality agreement he had signed with Airbus before he left. After their conversation, Cashore thought it through. Iddles said he could not talk about Moores, Schreiber, and IAL because he could not talk about Airbus, but Moores had always maintained publicly he had nothing to do with Airbus. The two statements didn't add up.

He called Iddles back with a single question. "What about meeting people like Frank Moores?" Could Iddles talk about that?

"No, I am sorry," Iddles replied. "I cannot discuss any of the Airbus business."

It was just the response Cashore had been expecting.

"Frank Moores says he didn't do work for Airbus," countered Cashore. "So why couldn't you talk about meeting Frank Moores?"

Iddles was exasperated. "Look, you talk to Frank Moores."

Officially Airbus Industrie denied it had taken part in any agreement with Schreiber. Jean Pierson had by now received a phone call from Schreiber, who wanted to alert him about the annoying media attention. The corporate position was unanimous: deny, deny, deny. David Venz, vice-president of communications for Airbus North America, told Cashore that Airbus didn't need to pay third-party commissions. "I will tell you: our relationship was sound and solid enough with Air Canada, we knew the players very well at Air Canada, that we did not need somebody making introductions for us . . . Airbus has no relationship with Frank Moores or Schreiber. Airbus believes that all this is based upon innuendo and back-alley gossip." No one from Airbus would agree to speak on camera.

Fortunately for *the fifth estate*, there were some people in France who had agreed to talk about the Airbus sale and about Schreiber. Cashore flew to Paris, where on a whim he called Schreiber and left his hotel number. Schreiber called him from a pay phone on the way to

Moscow. This time there was no charm in his voice; the message was grim and blunt.

"I have to caution you," he began, "it is not a game. You can imagine where my position is. I am not going to do anything, you know, to upset them [his clients]. My point is this is not a game with a little Moores or a little Ouellet or a Doucet or whatever," he added.

Ouellet? Doucet? Which Doucet was he talking about, Fred or Gerry? And why was he bringing their names into the conversation?

Proceed with caution, Schreiber advised. "I can only say: do what you want. But be careful. Make sure you have a real and proper case in what you're saying. Otherwise, you are nothing else than a tool . . . And you should play your game, and not be involved in the games of others."

This story was larger than any one person, he said. "And as far as I can see, this company, they don't care about these people."

"What company doesn't care about what people?"

Schreiber became agitated – and almost incoherent. "The companies involved. Jesus Christ, Mr. Cashore, you are touching business interests of companies. You see what I mean? When you look at Moores or Doucet or Ouellet or whoever, where is the power there? Even when you look at me? You know, where is the power there? The power is – and there are interests you have to watch – and the problems you may create when you come out with stories which are not true, you touch directly the companies involved."

Schreiber insisted he wasn't trying to threaten anyone. "I think you are a pretty nice man. And you try to do your job and you have a family and a baby. So I try, I think – I try to be fair."

The conversation wore on, but Schreiber didn't stray from his message track.

"What I still don't understand is why can't you tell me what role you and Moores played on the Air Canada sale for Airbus," Cashore asked.

"I have told you already. Whether you believe it or not. I played no role at all. I played no role at all on the Airbus."

On February 24, 1995, ten days later, Schreiber was at a Vaduz courthouse to provide testimony in a criminal complaint against Giorgio

Pelossi. The court records show that IAL had launched the formal complaint, charging that Pelossi was leaking secret company information. "He misused his authority to look after third-party assets, and has thereby caused great damage to IAL," the charge read. "He has disclosed IAL business secrets for utilization and exploitation abroad. Moreover, Karlheinz Schreiber and Thyssen BHI [Bear Head Industries] have reserved the right to prosecute a claim for damages vis-à-vis IAL in the event of the publication of IAL's internal affairs."

As Schreiber testified in court that day, Pelossi had been his friend for a long time. "He was even manager of one of my firms," Schreiber said. He went on to explain what he knew about IAL, sticking to his story that IAL was owned by "other people" he did not name.

"In general IAL's field of business activities was the arrangement of industrial deals on a commission basis," he said, adding that the company often paid "useful expenditures." Schreiber testified that the "equitable owners of IAL" told him they had not received the expected payments in 1991. Pelossi had stolen the funds.

By mid-March a *fifth estate* crew was in Europe, preparing a documentary on the secret Airbus commissions. Bernard Lathière, the former president of Airbus who had left the company in 1985, agreed to an on-camera interview with the reporter Trish Wood. Lathière was working as a senior executive in the French Ministry of Finance and serving as chairman of the Limoges airport authority. Clearly, life had been kind to him. He and his wife were living in a grand apartment on Avenue de Villières in the Seventeenth Arrondissement. As he sat in an antique wing chair in his large living room, with a tall gilded mirror reflecting the camera lights, Lathière gamely tried to downplay any suggestion of wrongdoing by his former company. It wasn't easy, especially after Wood asked him if Airbus ever paid secret commissions on contracts.

"In some countries," Lathière replied confidently, "they have . . . I still think they have . . . what you can call 'consultants,' who are here to say, 'Okay, this is where you should go to have the right word.' And this is normal; everybody does it. But this is not . . . this has nothing to do with bribing, baksheesh or that kind of thing. These are contracts which are commercial but almost public. If there were any baksheesh, I don't think we would be stupid enough to sign it."

His rambling answer wasn't good enough for Wood. She wanted to know if Airbus had ever paid bribes to get a contract. "I want to ask you directly," she insisted. "Have you ever done it?"

"Never. For what reasons? And any country or any kind of business in which it's done, the boss is protected."

"What do you mean, the boss is protected?" she probed.

The man who had been the boss was nervous now, but his answer was startling. "*I* won't take a dollar and give it to somebody. If we ever did that, somebody *else* will do it."

Which is exactly what Airbus tried to do when it hired IAL. Airbus wouldn't have to know if any laws were broken.

Next, it was Frank Moores's turn to deny the story to the CBC, and he did it with more enthusiasm and vigour than most. He denied ever meeting Stuart Iddles, he denied ever discussing Airbus with Schreiber, he declared he had never had a Swiss bank account.

"You are absolutely full of it," he snapped irritably at Wood. "Whoever told you that is right up to their ears in it. Would I remember if I had an account? Of course. Now, what do you think?"

Schreiber faxed Cashore on March 1, 1995: he would say no more for the moment. But Cashore had to know, once and for all, whether Schreiber was refusing to be interviewed.

"Mr. Schreiber," he wrote, "you will forgive me for wondering if you will ever find a moment to speak with me . . . You have promised me that you will speak to me in detail about my research, but so far that seems like an empty promise."

Schreiber was not amused. He fired back another fax.

Dear Mr. Cashore:

I confirm receipt of your fax dated March 6, 1995. In my opinion this fax shows an obvious lack of culture and intelligence. You seem to have a short memory or do you get carried away with your fantasy?

For a short while I believed in your integrity – unfortunately I failed. It looks to me that you can't stop making a fool out of yourself.

Future developments will prove the reality. I am convinced you will remember my last fax for a long time.

In closing this fax I confirm that I do not want any further contact with you.

Yours truly,

Karlheinz Schreiber

"The Tycoon from Alberta," *Der Spiegel*'s headline blared on March 28, 1995. The magazine said that a Liechtenstein company, International Aircraft Leasing Ltd., received US$11 million in commissions after Air Canada announced its purchase of 34 Airbus passenger aircraft. The money was destined, according to *Der Spiegel*, for Karlheinz Schreiber, a Calgary-based German lobbyist, and for Frank Moores, a former Newfoundland premier and a close friend of Brian Mulroney, prime minister at the time. It pointed to Schreiber's long association with Franz Josef Strauss. Schreiber denied the story and told the magazine that he had no connection to IAL.

The next day, *the fifth estate* aired its documentary. The ratings were better than average, but apart from a piece by Jeff Heinrich in the Montreal *Gazette*, no newspaper in Canada picked up on the story. Canadian Press sent out a shortened version of the *Gazette* article. The stories told by CBC and *Der Spiegel* demonstrated beyond any doubt that Airbus did pay secret commissions to a bank account in Liechtenstein. They also proved that the central characters – Airbus Industrie, Frank Moores, Karlheinz Schreiber – had lied about their involvement.

Maybe the media weren't paying attention, but investigators were taking a close look, on both sides of the Atlantic.

18

On the Run

Ask any acquaintance of Karlheinz Schreiber's about his persona, his sense of national identity, and the immediate response is "Bavarian." But he wasn't Bavarian-born, and perhaps with the acknowledgment of his own mortality, he grew sentimental about his true origins and his home town in the Harz Mountains. He was a great man now, a successful businessman, a friend and confidant of prime ministers, presidents, and premiers – at least in the imagination of most of the citizens of Hohegeiss – and he wanted to do something for the village in which he was born. In April 1995, he decided to give DM160,000 to set up a small museum of local history in Hohegeiss; the local newspaper, the *Goslarsche Zeitung* of Bad Harzburg, sent a reporter to cover the ceremony and Schreiber's speech.

As he spoke, Schreiber boasted about his influence with Brian Mulroney and George Bush on the issue of German reunification. The reporter, Frank Heine, who had interviewed him a day or two earlier, dutifully took down his remarks at the ceremony and wrote a story, which was then typeset and pasted up for printing. But Schreiber had second thoughts about his comments and called the newspaper; the next day, April 22, 1995, Heine's story appeared without the details of Schreiber's advice to Mulroney. Perhaps Schreiber thought it would be better to downplay his claims of influence at this stage, after *Der Spiegel*'s story about the Airbus money. Schreiber also skilfully deflected any negative association with the Strauss Amigos who had fallen into disgrace a year earlier. "Sure, I'm an Amigo!" he told the reporter with bravado. "An amigo of this town!"

Public knowledge of his relationship with Mulroney was new and unsettling to Schreiber. Given the publicity about Airbus, it was prudent to keep a low profile. Besides, his adventures in Canada were at an end. The dream of a tank plant was fading, and by the end of May there was little left but files of useless paper. Thyssen wanted to end the contract with Schreiber; both sides agreed.

On May 24, a formal letter to Winfried Haastert from Bobby Hladun, representing Schreiber's Calgary shell company, Bitucan, confirmed the termination of its business relations with Thyssen. Schreiber wrote to Haastert as well, composing a letter full of invective against the Canadian government, and raising the case of Bombardier winning a German government contract without having to bid, while Thyssen was denied the Bear Head deal.

Beyond any doubt the Canadian government... has violated international standards in a horrible way. And as I have heard in the meantime, this is case number seven in a series of similar kinds of behaviour ...

Confidentially I have received the information that the German defence industry, as they have done in the past, are going to buy Challenger airplanes from Canadair in Montreal, and they are going to do this without a call for bids.

I find this scandalous when German companies in Canada through egregious violations of contracts are kept away from business deals, from being a part of the competition, and at the same time our government spends large amounts of money in Canada.

We should discuss this point in the next few days. As far as I am concerned, you may assume that I have not invested ten years of time and work in order to leave the scene quietly.

I have discussed the content of your letter with Bitucan

Holdings, and received their agreement that the matter that you have mentioned in your letter will be brought to an end.

The letter that you want from Bitucan will be sent to you. A similar conversation has taken place with the representative of the company IAL. I am assuming I will also receive a similar confirmation from them. With that, the contractual agreements that we have entered into, especially your letter of October 31, 1985 [the Bear Head agreement], will be cancelled.

In addition, it should be clear between your company and me that if we should manage to complete this business project in any way, a fair deal would be arrived at for me.

With friendly greetings, your friend ...

KHS.

These disappointments fresh in his mind, Schreiber dashed off another intemperate letter the next day, this one to Paul Heinbecker, Canada's ambassador to Germany. He complained that many large and small German companies such as Thyssen, Daimler-Benz, Siemens, and others felt they were badly dealt with by the Canadian government. Compare their treatment with the approach of the government of Germany, he suggested, "where contracts of considerable volume were awarded to Canadair in Quebec without tendering... I find it hard to imagine how Federal Chancellor Kohl can support such a measure in Germany when German companies which have been located for many years in Canada are being treated by the Canadian Government like Thyssen... I wish to inform you today there will be considerable official intervention."

But there were more serious matters to worry about than the fortunes of Thyssen in Canada. In February, Schreiber had made a pre-emptive attempt to disarm at least one of Pelossi's threats: that he would reveal Schreiber's business arrangements to the tax authorities in Augsburg. Schreiber decided to beat him to it, calling Hans-Jürgen Kolb, a prosecutor and sometime hunting companion, to establish his innocence in advance. Kolb told Schreiber to call Anton Gumpendobler, director of the investigation department at the Augsburg Tax Office. Schreiber offered various records to Gumpendobler and his colleagues.

Instead of being comforted by Schreiber's disclosures, the investigators were sufficiently intrigued to begin an informal investigation.

Schreiber knew he would have to come up with answers to Pelossi's allegations. First and foremost, he would have to explain why he had not paid income tax on some of the money that had flowed through his accounts. For that, Schreiber had at least one explanation, according to an old acquaintance, Sami Jadallah. Although Jadallah said later that he never did any business with Schreiber, he did remember one particular meeting with Schreiber at the Mövenpick Hotel at the Zurich airport. He did not know why Schreiber had requested the meeting, but "I knew at that time he was having some... problems with the tax authority."

According to Jadallah, Schreiber confided that he wanted Jadallah's help: would Jadallah sign a fake loan agreement, one that would make it look as though one of Schreiber's companies owed Jadallah millions of Deutschmarks? Schreiber could then argue that because a significant share of the company's revenues were going to pay off a loan, the company never earned a profit. And with no profit, no taxes would be owed. Jadallah would earn a little on the side for his troubles.

Jadallah recalled he rebuffed the offer at once. He said to Schreiber, "You know I would not do it. This is fraud. This is serious business, when somebody is in a scheme like this." At that point, according to Jadallah, Schreiber dropped the subject and turned to a new topic, a machine that would revolutionize the pasta business. "And that was the last time I talked to him."

Jadallah's relationship with Schreiber remained an intriguing mystery to those investigating Schreiber's affairs. His name appeared frequently in Schreiber's diaries, right next to the names of André Strobel and Winfried Haastert. Among the documents later found by prosecutors was a loan agreement dated October 1, 1988, between Jadallah and Schreiber. It outlined debts of DM14 million owed to Jadallah by Schreiber's Canadian company Bitucan, to be repaid between 1987 and 1993 at 5 percent interest. Investigators could not establish its authenticity; Jadallah later maintained there was no loan.

When the tax authorities read Mathias Blumencron's story in *Der Spiegel* in March 1995, their noses started to twitch. They heard through their own sources that Pelossi – whose role in blowing the whistle on his former employer hadn't been made public – was in a mood to talk. But Pelossi was reluctant to make the first move: as Schreiber's former trustee, he was worried that Swiss law might prevent him from volunteering information about his affairs, even alleged criminal activity. If the authorities came to him, however, he could speak freely.

The tax investigators worked out of a nondescript stone building in the centre of Augsburg, a prosperous city of 250,000, 60 kilometres northwest of Munich. Famous as the place where Martin Luther proclaimed the Lutheran faith in 1530, Augsburg serves as a commuter haven for people who work in Munich but is also home to several Bavarian government offices, among them the local tax investigation department and public prosecutor's headquarters.

Anton Gumpendobler, director of the tax investigation department, was assisted in his inquiries about Schreiber by Winfried Kindler, a tax law specialist. They were members of a dedicated team that handled routine tax investigations throughout the region. If they uncovered a serious case of fraud or other crimes, the matter could be passed to the public prosecutor's office for further investigation.

While the tax officials launched an aggressive search for records, Schreiber met again with Wolfgang Schäuble of the CDU. Though he had formally ended his contract with Thyssen, Schreiber continued to press Schäuble for Kohl's assistance with Bear Head. The appeal may have worked: later that month a letter from Joachim Bitterlich, a senior adviser in Kohl's office, arrived at the Defence Department in Ottawa, asking about the government's intentions regarding a Thyssen plant.

More pressure was applied a few days later in a letter dated July 13 to Jean Chrétien from his former cabinet colleague Marc Lalonde. Representing his client Bear Head, Lalonde questioned the Defence Department vehicle contract that had been awarded to General Motors without a tendering process and said the whole situation was beyond his understanding. All Thyssen wants, he explained, was open competition. Thyssen had incurred millions of dollars in costs while developing a vehicle, based on written assurances – the infamous understanding in principle – from the Canadian government.

Furthermore, Thyssen had a written opinion from its counsel Ian Scott, he said, that the company had the right to compensation because it hadn't been allowed to bid for the vehicle contract. Scott was one of the country's finest courtroom lawyers and most colourful politicians; he had been Ontario's attorney general before returning to private practice. At the very least Jürgen Massmann of Thyssen Henschel deserved a meeting with Defence officials to discuss the whole matter, Lalonde concluded.

Letters went back and forth from one senior government official to another for months. Eventually, on September 1, Chrétien replied to Lalonde, blaming cost factors and operational requirements for the decision to give the contract to General Motors.

By July 24, Giorgio Pelossi was ready to respond to questions from Gumpendobler and Kindler. He gave his first statement on that date, followed by three more sessions, during which Pelossi, whose memory was excellent and who had hundreds of pages of bank statements at his fingertips, revealed the long and tangled tale of his business relationship with Schreiber. Tell us everything, they urged; we have lots of time. And Pelossi did. But once they heard Pelossi's story, they realized his allegations could reach beyond their mandate. They would have to work with a team at the prosecutors' office.

The chief public prosecutor was Jörg Hillinger, a tall, beefy man in his early fifties whose unlikely after-hours pastime was writing entertainment reviews for the local paper. He worked out of a large, cluttered office lined with legal texts. When he needed to talk things over with his colleagues, he pulled a snuff tin out of his vest pocket, took a pinch between his thumb and forefinger, inhaled deeply, and thought hard, his shrewd eyes missing nothing.

Hillinger supervised the case; much of the day-to-day work was done by the prosecutor Klaus-Jochen Weigand. From the start, they were sure of two things: this was a major case, and it was going to be tricky. Franz Josef Strauss was still a hero to many Bavarians, and his son Max was a prominent lawyer in Munich. Hillinger and Weigand thought they could handle the flak, though they intended to tread carefully. After a closer perusal of Schreiber's records, Weigand began drawing up lists of contacts, interviewees, and warrant requests.

On August 2, the investigators were granted a warrant to search the offices of Messerschmitt-Bölkow-Blohm in Ottobrun near Munich and to seize the records of the Canadian Coast Guard helicopter deal. By August 11, Kindler had written an internal memo listing Schreiber's companies, related companies, and his close business associates.

On August 14, a court granted the Augsburg team the right to carry out a search and seizure at Thyssen Industrie. After the raid they decided to interview several senior Thyssen executives, including Ernst Höffken and Winfried Haastert.

While the Germans raced ahead, the RCMP was trying to get an investigation moving in Canada. RCMP officers began by interviewing widely, and word spread that they were examining the Airbus sale. When asked, they said that they were simply looking into the allegations raised by *Der Spiegel* and *the fifth estate* in March. In September, officers questioned Norman Spector, the bureaucrat who had been in charge of the Thyssen file when he worked in the Prime Minister's Office. Spector told the police the project had been killed in 1990 or 1991, after he told the prime minister the tank plant would cost Canadian taxpayers over $100 million. Yet Schreiber had continued to meet with Mulroney to discuss it after that date, and senior Defence officials were forced to see Schreiber again and again.

The Mounties agreed to compare notes with the investigators in Augsburg. On September 11, two officers, Sergeant Fraser Fiegenwald and Inspector Yves Bouchard, both members of the RCMP's Commercial Crime Division in Ottawa, met with Hillinger's people. Three days later, the Augsburg investigators asked for permission to raid the offices of Eurocopter Germany, which had purchased MBB's helicopter business.

By this time, the RCMP was also talking to Giorgio Pelossi, who would later claim he hadn't been interviewed by the Canadians before the end of September. Pelossi was speaking careful legalese; he still wasn't sure whether Swiss law would allow him to reveal anything about Schreiber's activities. Instead of giving the RCMP a full interview, he merely confirmed that he was indeed knowledgeable about the kinds of allegations reported by *Der Spiegel* and *the fifth estate*.

Schreiber kept an eye on coverage in Canadian newspapers

through Greg Alford, who had maintained an office for Bear Head Industries and was clipping the stories. On September 20, Alford faxed Schreiber an item by the *Globe and Mail* business columnist Terence Corcoran that was critical of Stevie Cameron. Headlined "On the Take, or Our Ms. Take," it was promptly sent by Schreiber to the Augsburg investigators. Two days later, Alford faxed Schreiber another story, this one by another *Globe* columnist, Jeffrey Simpson. This too was forwarded to the German investigators.

At the end of September, the Mounties concluded that they had enough information to proceed with a formal investigation. Publicly, however, they continued to tell curious reporters that nothing was official. They were just checking things out, said Fiegenwald.

The true status of their inquiry remained a tightly held secret until a series of events began to unfold on September 29, 1995. On that day, a senior Justice Department lawyer, Kimberly Prost, signed a letter to Swiss justice authorities, in German and English versions, requesting help in gathering evidence about allegations that Brian Mulroney, Frank Moores, and Karlheinz Schreiber had received kickbacks on the Airbus contract. The letter contained allegations that Airbus had paid commissions to IAL, which was controlled by Schreiber, who then shared the money with Moores and Mulroney. Prost's letter went to Switzerland on October 3, hand-delivered by a courier.

Although he wasn't yet aware of the Canadian government's request to Switzerland, Schreiber certainly knew that the Augsburg prosecutors were after him. On October 4, he learned that Pelossi was trying to have criminal charges laid against him in Liechtenstein. Schreiber had made sworn statements that he did not own IAL, but Pelossi said Schreiber was indeed the owner. He claimed in an application to the Liechtenstein court that Schreiber had given false testimony.

The next day, October 5, the Augsburg authorities arrived at Schreiber's Kaufering home with a search warrant. They strode through the house and office, turning out all the drawers and filing cabinets, searching every corner of every room. In a storage area, they found eight files of bank statements from Schreiber's bank in Landsberg and from his Zurich bank. His dressing room yielded his diaries for the years 1991 and 1994, three address books, and a Bank of

Montreal file. His attic contained a box of cards and letters. Even Schreiber's workshop held records from companies for whom he'd worked as a lobbyist, copies of his bankbooks, and microcassettes. In the safe was more paper, including contracts with Thyssen, Pelossi's lawsuit, details of the Saudi tank deal, and records of loans and mortgages.

As the investigators and prosecutors sifted through these papers, they began to understand the extent of his activities and the wider significance of what they had uncovered. Schreiber knew better than anyone what was there, and he took what appeared the safest course of action: he fled the country, leaving Kaufering in the hands of his son, Andreas, and the ever capable Dietlinde Kaupp, who now took instructions by telephone. In the words of the arrest warrant, "The defendant... absconded to Switzerland or Liechtenstein, knowing he would not be extradited from these countries for tax evasion." By this time, the Schreibers had acquired a second condominium in Pontresina, and there they settled in, wondering how long it would be before they could return to Germany.

The Augsburg team had a field day with the Schreiber documents, but the most exciting find was the diary listing the code names of those who were slated to receive payments through his banking transactions. Who did these nicknames represent, they wondered. They called Pelossi, and with his help and the evidence contained in other documents, they believed they had cracked Schreiber's simple codes. As the pace of the investigation quickened, Hillinger's group took statements from several of the executives who had set up deals with Schreiber. Kurt Pfleiderer of MBB, for example, admitted he had negotiated a contract with Schreiber and signed the agreement with IAL. "The letterbox company IAL was brought into this [contract] either by the defendant Schreiber or by Frank Moores," the prosecutors wrote after questioning Pfleiderer.

But the investigation hit a roadblock in October when a judge refused to give permission to search Max Strauss's home. The judge ruled that Strauss's assets were part of an estate, and no one had proven that money had gone to him directly.

In Canada, events were picking up speed. On October 10, Canadian officials heard that the Swiss federal public prosecutor's office had agreed to assist them in their investigation. To win this cooperation, the Mounties had had to meet with Swiss magistrates, review their evidence with them, and persuade them that the Canadian investigation couldn't proceed without access to banking records. If this was a tax case, if Canada was simply attempting to collect taxes on money held in Swiss numbered accounts by its citizens, then there would be no cooperation. The Swiss do not help other countries collect their taxes. Only when a foreign government can produce persuasive evidence of possible criminal activity will they assist. After long deliberation, Swiss authorities finally agreed that the evidence was convincing.

In a sideshow to these delicate manoeuvres, more letters about Bear Head were exchanged during this period between Marc Lalonde and the Privy Council Office. It was an endless litany of blame and counter-blame, with the correspondents oblivious to the fact that authorities in both Canada and Germany were chasing the very man who claimed he and his Thyssen associates had been cheated by the government of Canada.

On October 24, the Swiss federal police sent an order to the Swiss Bank Corporation on behalf of the RCMP, ordering it to freeze any and all accounts belonging to Frank Moores, Brian Mulroney, and Karlheinz Schreiber. Schreiber was not inconvenienced by this order. His accounts remained in place, but the money had already been moved into the mirror accounts under Barbel's name and then transferred again to a bank in Liechtenstein. As for Mulroney, there were no accounts under his name in the Swiss Bank Corporation. Moores's accounts were found and, like Schreiber's, frozen.

Under Swiss law, anyone whose account has been frozen in this way must be notified. When the bank got in touch with Schreiber, it also provided him with a copy of the German letter Prost had sent to the Swiss government. Schreiber read it in shock and rage. He got on the phone to Bobby Hladun in Edmonton, who was well aware of the escalating battle between Pelossi and Schreiber but probably had no idea it would go this far. Hladun immediately hopped on a plane to Switzerland, where he and Schreiber decided to phone Brian Mulroney.

It had been almost a year since Schreiber made a note in his diary to call Fred Doucet for Mulroney's phone numbers after learning *Der Spiegel* had been asking about his relationship with the former prime minister. On November 2, Schreiber called Doucet in Halifax; he tracked down Mulroney in Toronto, where he was attending a board meeting.

Doucet told Mulroney that the call from Schreiber was extremely urgent: Schreiber had said the Canadian government was investigating Mulroney with regard to alleged Airbus commissions. Mulroney tried to reach Schreiber from a phone in Toronto's Royal York Hotel but could not get through. He flew back to Montreal and that evening, before dinner and with his wife, Mila, at his side, he called Schreiber at his home in Pontresina.

Schreiber told Mulroney that the Canadian government had accused him of serious crimes. He did his best to translate the document's key sentences over the phone. The letter accused Mulroney of being involved in an "ongoing conspiracy": the charge was fraud, in the millions, against the Canadian government. It reminded the Swiss of the importance of the investigation, since it concerned "criminal activities on the part of a former prime minister." As he listened to Schreiber's recitation, Mulroney felt sick; he couldn't believe what he was hearing.

As soon as he'd hung up the phone, Mulroney called Yves Fortier, his law partner at Ogilvy Renault and one of his closest friends. Although Fortier was out of town on business, he promised Mulroney he would return to Montreal the next day. At Fortier's suggestion, Mulroney also engaged the services of Roger Tassé, a former deputy minister of justice in Ottawa and one of Mulroney's constitutional advisers, who now practised law in Ottawa.

The next few days were a blur for Mulroney. He was on the phone several times to Schreiber and to Hladun, who was still in Switzerland and who told Mulroney that he had reviewed Schreiber's Swiss bank records, according to William Kaplan's 1998 book, *Presumed Guilty*. Mulroney was not mentioned in these documents, Hladun informed him. Even if Hladun had examined all Schreiber's Zurich bank account records, including the series of coded subaccounts and the account tagged "Britan," there was no reason why he would connect "Britan" to Brian Mulroney.

On November 3, Mulroney spoke to Schreiber again, arranging to obtain an English translation of the Canadian letter of request from Schreiber's Swiss lawyers, Blum & Partner. Meanwhile Tassé rushed to Montreal to meet Mulroney at his home. He advised Mulroney to distance himself from Schreiber's law firm and hire his own Swiss counsel. Yves Fortier arrived at Mulroney's house on the same day. He could not imagine a Canadian government having written such a letter. Nonetheless, he decided to be blunt. "Is there anything to this?" he asked his friend.

"I swear on the head of my mother and my children that I have done nothing wrong," Mulroney replied, according to Kaplan. When he offered to resign from Ogilvy Renault, Fortier rejected the suggestion.

All week long Mulroney worked the phones. He called the chairmen of the company boards on which he sat as a director; there were six international boards, five international advisory boards, and twelve charitable, educational, and public policy organizations. To each, he offered his resignation. "I did not want to subject them to the smear campaign that had been initiated by such a false and odious document that had been transmitted to Switzerland," he said later in court.

"I called them all and said, 'Look, I can't tell you what I've been accused of; they won't give me the documentation. I can't tell you who the accuser is; the accuser is anonymous. I can't tell you what the crime is because the Canadian government won't talk to me... You have read, or will read, that I have been called a criminal by the government of Canada.

"'I feel honour bound to tell you two things: this is a grotesque lie and there is no foundation for it whatsoever, but I feel honour bound to tell you that you have my resignation.'" None of them accepted it.

But as Mulroney himself suggested, the news was spreading. He said later that he believed that board members of the Swiss Bank Corporation would automatically receive a copy of the letter. A few senior public servants knew. It was only a matter of time, he maintained, before everyone knew. During this period he spoke frequently to Schreiber.

"I was almost alone in the world," he explained later. "I had nobody to talk to, nobody would tell me anything in Ottawa, nobody knew anything about it except that the leak was deepening every day. And so obviously I communicated with him to try and find out what he knew." The last thing he wanted, he said, was publicity; he ordered his lawyers to keep the facts strictly confidential.

The specific facts may have been confidential, but to organize his response Mulroney needed to tell dozens of people about the letter, including Paul Desmarais, CEO of Power Corporation, whose son was married to Jean Chrétien's daughter France. He brought in more lawyers, among them Harvey Yarovsky, one of the most prominent criminal lawyers in Quebec. Yarovsky told Mulroney he should consider suing the Canadian government and the RCMP. And Mulroney hired one of the best civil litigators in the province, Gérald Tremblay, a senior partner with McCarthy Tétrault.

As a former deputy minister of justice and a former law partner of Jean Chrétien, Tassé knew how the federal system worked, and he decided to call Canada's minister of justice, Allan Rock. Rock told Tassé he knew nothing about the letter nor anything about Mulroney being investigated. Rock found it astonishing that a lawyer of Tassé's experience would think it appropriate to call a minister of justice about a client – no matter who it was – under criminal investigation. He told Tassé he could not consider any meeting between them.

On Monday, November 6, Mulroney, Fortier, and Yarovsky gathered over breakfast; Tremblay participated by speakerphone. They agreed that they wanted the government to change the wording of the letter, parts of which referred to Mulroney as having been involved in a crime. The RCMP had a right to investigate allegations, but it did not have a right to call Mulroney a criminal.

The government would argue that while certain words in the letter, taken out of context, seemed to brand Mulroney a criminal, they did so only in a context of originating from allegations, still unproven. If the government really knew Mulroney was a criminal, why would it have to send a letter at all? No one could possibly read the entire letter and come away thinking that Mulroney was guilty, the government said, only that he was under investigation.

Tassé continued to meet and speak with officials in Ottawa and succeeded in getting a meeting with Philip Murray, the commissioner of the RCMP. Tassé told Murray it was his responsibility to change the wording in the letter, and he also wanted Murray to know that Mulroney was willing to answer any questions from his investigators. Murray replied that he would mention the offer to his investigators, but when he did, they told Tassé there was no rush. The investigation was just getting under way.

Indeed, it was normal police practice not to interview people at the centre of an investigation until the proper facts could be assembled. Because not all the facts were known, the Mounties believed that at this point they wouldn't even know what to ask Mulroney.

On November 10, 1995, the story broke – but not in Canada. Beat Bieri, a reporter with the program *10 vor 10* (Ten to Ten) on the Swiss television network DRS, broadcast a report that the Swiss government was cooperating with the RCMP in an investigation, and that a senior Canadian politician was involved. Mulroney heard about the Swiss report at once, as did the media in Canada. As he said himself, the television story "clearly indicated that the German version of the document... sent from Canada had fallen into other hands."

The next day Agence France-Presse carried the story, which was published on the front page of the Montreal newspaper *La Presse*. Canadian reporters were aware of it, but no one knew whether the politician who had been named in the letter was Moores, Mulroney, or someone else. Not surprisingly, without a copy of the request to the Swiss, no news organization was willing to publish a story suggesting who the politician might be, but newspapers, magazines, and broadcasters were working frantically to prepare their versions for the inevitable break. No one was more aware of this frenzy than Mulroney.

Although the Canadian government believed the letter would not be seen as proof of anything, but merely a request for assistance in an investigation, Justice officials sent another letter to Switzerland on November 14, re-emphasizing that the letter outlined only allegations. The Canadians also insisted the Swiss keep the original letter confidential. In response, the Swiss assured the RCMP that they fully understood that the Canadians were drawing no conclusions at this point. Fiegenwald told Tassé about the November 14 letter, but Mulroney's team never actually saw it, according to William Kaplan.

On November 15, Fiegenwald offered to withdraw or revise the letter to Switzerland if Mulroney would allow investigators to see his banking records. But Mulroney's camp argued the offer had come far too late: the story was already circulating that a Canadian politician had been named in a letter to Switzerland.

Day by day, the story was building steam. Even the usually conservative *Financial Post* was chomping at the bit, quoting a surprisingly suggestive remark from an unidentified source on November 14. "A one-time senior adviser to prime minister Brian Mulroney claimed yesterday to have knowledge that millions of dollars was laundered through bank accounts in Bermuda, the Cayman Islands, Liechtenstein and Jersey in Britain's Channel Islands. 'There is a paper trail of accounts all over the f——ing world,' said the Tory insider, who asked not to be identified."

That same day Mulroney met with his former press aide Luc Lavoie. The one-time reporter and Parliamentary Press Gallery president had left journalism to work for senior Conservative ministers in Ottawa and for Mulroney himself when he was prime minister. Now he was a public relations specialist; it would be his job to spin the story. He set up a war room in Montreal's Queen Elizabeth Hotel and began working with the lawyers around the clock on a defiant, high-stakes strategy.

The next day Mulroney received a fax full of questions from Mathias Blumencron at *Der Spiegel*. Andrew Phillips, national editor at *Maclean's*, faxed Mulroney a letter very similar to Blumencron's, mentioning the meetings Tassé had held with the Mounties and the Justice Department. Stevie Cameron, working on the story for *Maclean's*, hoped to have his comments for a feature article the following week.

On November 15, Augsburg prosecutor Klaus-Jochen Weigand noticed the press stories out of Canada mentioning Schreiber, the man they were investigating for tax evasion, in a probe of possible Airbus commissions. As his colleagues had just uncovered some slim leads concerning payments to Holger Pfahls, Weigand decided to talk it over with the general prosecutor in Munich. The response was immediate and clear: do not extend this investigation into a corruption case.

The fifth estate was just as interested as Blumencron and *Maclean's* in discovering the identity of the politician named in the request to the Swiss. While no Canadian source would confirm or deny the rumours, a European source told Harvey Cashore that Mulroney had been named in the request, at least in the version he had seen. For his part, Fraser Fiegenwald was doing his best to underplay the story, once again invoking the official line: the RCMP was "simply evaluating what is available as evidence to determine whether we get into it fully or not."

Whether Mulroney was named or not, his appearance in the letter didn't make him guilty. What was important was the actual information, its strengths and its weaknesses. It was time, *the fifth estate* decided, to convince Pelossi to speak publicly about what he knew or didn't know. And *the fifth estate* had one document few others had, the bank card that Pelossi had scribbled on so many years before, when the accounts were set up for Frank Moores in Zurich. "F. Moore + B.M.," he had written above the two account numbers, 34107 and 34117 Devon. (Canadian Press noted in a November 20 story that Devon was the name of the Montreal street where Mulroney lived after his marriage. Moores denied any link to Mulroney, saying in December that the name Devon was associated with the Moores family.) But it was also true that Pelossi did not know if Mulroney had ever received any money, and *the fifth estate* team thought it was time for Pelossi to come forward and say as much.

Although Mulroney had no intention of talking to *Der Spiegel*, *Maclean's*, or *the fifth estate*, he and Lavoie wondered how much Blumencron knew. Was it possible he had a copy of the letter? Lavoie called him but couldn't tell from their conversation.

Lavoie began to prepare for a press conference at which Mulroney's lawyers would announce a massive lawsuit against the government, but it was still too soon to proceed. The Justice Department's letter to the Swiss had not yet surfaced in public. How could Mulroney sue the government for libel without the story being published? Neither *Maclean's* nor *Der Spiegel* had a copy of the letter, nor did any other news organization. That problem was soon solved. A copy of the

Canadian government's letter was leaked to a receptive reporter from the *Financial Post*, Philip Mathias. William Kaplan's theory was that the leaker was Schreiber.

Mathias wasn't the only reporter planning to break the story; Craig Oliver, a reporter with CTV in Ottawa, was getting ready to go with it on the 11 p.m. national news on Friday, November 17, by showing footage of the *Post*'s press run for the next day. When Mulroney heard about this from Conservative senator Marjory LeBreton, he instructed Lavoie to try to stop Oliver. Lavoie reached him at 10:15. "I gave him the strongest possible denial," Lavoie later told the *Globe and Mail*'s Stan Oziewicz. "I said, 'Are you going to air with this at 11?' He says, 'I'll have to talk to the desk but I suppose with such a strong denial I don't think we'll go.'" Oliver recalled later that Lavoie had said there would be a "massive, massive lawsuit," a fact that helped CTV's bosses make their decision. They killed the story.

This left the field to Mathias. On Saturday morning, November 18, 1995, the *Financial Post* published the story many had expected: Mulroney and Moores were under police investigation, and the RCMP had asked the Swiss government for help in obtaining any evidence that the men had received secret commissions. Although the letter was leaked to Mathias on the condition of anonymity, it appears he may have been misled. In one part of his article, Mathias heaped scorn on the RCMP for not doing its homework – but it was Mathias who was confused.

The letter, wrote Mathias, "indicates Mulroney received a secret commission for a Thyssen tank-manufacturing project in Cape Breton Island. That project didn't go ahead." True enough, but what Mathias did not know was that despite the ultimate failure of the project, Thyssen had paid millions in commissions. Mathias hinted he may also have spoken to Robert Hladun, though he did not identify him. "A lawyer for one of the people accused of paying secret commissions to Mulroney goes further. He says the Justice Department letter is a 'fishing expedition' based on a bluff." Finally, Mathias quoted Lavoie: "Mr. Mulroney states unequivocally that he did not in any way influence or try to influence Air Canada's decision to purchase aircraft made by Airbus, a fact which has been repeatedly and publicly confirmed by Air Canada senior officers. Nor was he ever a party to any agreement to influence this decision or to receive any consideration directly or indirectly for so doing. Mr. Mulroney states categorically that he does not now have, nor did he ever have directly or indirectly a bank account in any foreign country. Furthermore no one now has, nor did anyone ever have, such an account on his behalf."

In fairness, Lavoie's denial could not extend to what others might have done without Mulroney's knowledge. All Pelossi ever said was that Schreiber had told him he and Moores were setting up an account through which money could be funnelled to Mulroney.

The *Post*'s story had one more interesting piece of information. "Last week, lawyers for Mulroney and others named in the document met in Toronto to consider their strategies," Mathias wrote, suggesting that Schreiber, Moores, and Mulroney were coordinating their moves. Now that the story had finally been published, Mulroney would sue – not the newspaper that had printed it but the government of Canada.

Lavoie called his news conference to announce the former prime minister would launch a $50-million lawsuit against the RCMP and the federal government for libel. Months later, Lavoie acknowledged the legal action was part of an orchestrated campaign to influence the headlines.

"The strategy was simple," he said in April 1996 to the Ottawa chapter of the Canadian Public Relations Society. "Either the story published by the *Financial Post* would be picked up by the media worldwide and Brian Mulroney would be described as a criminal, or the denial and the lawsuit would be picked up by the media worldwide and the story would be, 'The former prime minister of Canada is suing the government of his country for defaming him.'"

Phil Mathias did not explain publicly how he obtained the RCMP letter, except to say that it did not come from Mulroney or his people. He was not known to be one of the journalists working on the story, and at first glance his scoop seemed odd. A week after Lavoie's speech, Mathias received a National Newspaper Award for the article.

All through the fall of 1995, Gary Ouellet was keeping very quiet. Reporters thought of calling Frank Moores's former partner for his comments on the Airbus affair, but no one could find him. The magician had disappeared.

Two days before the Mulroney press conference, however, Ouellet's traces were discernible in Switzerland. He transferred funds from his Zurich account to another, described in bank records as SBC MMF C$ LUX 595726, a Swiss Bank Corporation money market fund in Canadian dollars in a Luxembourg branch with the account number 595726. The transactions were for more than C$75,000 and eventually brought his balance at the Zurich branch to a mere C$94.90. The account was officially closed on November 22, 1995.

By the weekend of November 18, Harvey Cashore was in Zurich, hoping to convince Pelossi to speak on camera. He had so far refused, but Cashore had another meeting lined up with a different source. On a whim Cashore called Schreiber's Kaufering office too. He wasn't there, of course, but his office staff took the name and number of Cashore's hotel.

On Sunday evening, the day after the *Financial Post* story was published, the phone rang in Cashore's hotel room. It was someone who called himself Emil. His accent was unidentifiable and gruff; it could have been French or German. Emil explained that he was a Swiss banker who had access to Mulroney's Swiss accounts. Would Cashore like to see them? Emil added that he had a large family and would need some money before he could hand over the documents.

Cashore had to laugh. He had flown to Zurich with Trish Wood, who would host *the fifth estate*'s item on the affair, and was soon joined there by a soundman, Alistair Bell, and Colin Allison, the cameraman. Bell was the practical joker of the group, and Cashore figured that the peculiar accent belonged to him. Cashore played along; whoever Emil was, he didn't seem at all credible. Eventually Cashore hung up.

The phone rang again. "Why did you hang up?" asked Emil.

This was getting silly. But Emil insisted he had Mulroney's accounts, maintained that they held dynamite information, and repeated that they were Cashore's for a modest price. Why don't we meet, he asked. It was just possible this was not a practical joke, Cashore thought uneasily. Fine. When? Emil said he would call back the next day.

As Cashore waited for the call the next morning, he opened his copy of the *International Herald Tribune*. There, below the fold, was a front-page headline: "Canada suspects Mulroney got Airbus kickback." Emil did not call back. By this time Pelossi had agreed to an on-camera interview – undisguised by shadow as he had been in the first program – and the CBC crew drove to Lugano to film the session. Emil had their cellphone number but no call came through. No surprise, thought Cashore, since Bell was there in the van beside him.

The team returned to Zurich the next day. Late that night, just before midnight, Emil again called the hotel, waking Cashore. Annoyed at having his sleep disturbed, Cashore decided to turn the tables on Bell or whoever this might be and told Emil he could meet him that night. Emil agreed and gave Cashore the address of a restaurant near the canal where they would rendezvous in half an hour. Cashore had no intention of leaving the hotel and didn't even write down the address. He hung up the phone and went back to sleep.

Cashore learned years later that the mysterious Emil had been Schreiber. The Emil calls were part of an elaborate effort to entrap Cashore. The bait was the promise of Mulroney's bank records. If Cashore was caught handing over money, he would surely lose his job; in Canada, reporters are not allowed to pay for information.

Mulroney would have had no idea that Schreiber was calling a hotel in Zurich, impersonating a Swiss banker; he was busy enough trying to defend himself against scandal. Although many of his acquaintances knew of his connection to Schreiber, there was one trusted confidant who tried to put as much distance as possible between the two men. Sam Wakim was a Toronto Bay Street lawyer and one of Mulroney's most loyal friends. On November 22, Peter Mansbridge of CBC-TV thought Wakim deserved a call. The host of the flagship nightly news program, *The National,* was the network's biggest star. He didn't make the call himself; instead, he assigned the task to Larry Zolf, a CBC veteran who prided himself on his cordial relations with Brian Mulroney and his circle. He once wrote jokes for the prime minister's speeches and would try them out on his colleagues up and down the corridors of the corporation's office. He was one of the few journalists whose requests for an on-camera interview with Mulroney were invariably granted.

According to a memo from Zolf to Mansbridge, Wakim had told him, "Brian is mad as hell and keeping quiet. Keeping quiet for Brian is murder – it's a torture chamber for him. He can't talk to a soul. He can't say anything. It's explosive!

"The people of Canada don't want this Mulroney story to be true. If you gave Mulroney $25 million but the condition was he couldn't talk about it, even if it was a bribe, Mulroney would not take the money, because his number one urge would be to tell the story."

At this point, Zolf underlined Wakim's final comment for emphasis: "Mulroney never met this Schreiber guy, Mulroney doesn't know Schreiber, Moores may have brought Schreiber to a party, but that's all."

Pelossi's *fifth estate* interview was broadcast November 29, 1995, and for the first time Canadians were able to see the face of the man behind the allegations. Pelossi told viewers that it was Schreiber who was lying, not him, and then repeated his claim that Schreiber told him Moores had opened up an account to funnel money to the prime minister of Canada. Pelossi conceded he had no proof. The program also broadcast the image of the bank card on which Pelossi had jotted down "B.M.," referring to the Moores account that he thought was going to be used for the purpose.

Shortly after Pelossi appeared on television, on December 2, the *Toronto Sun* ran a headline on its front page: "Mulroney bribe claim a hoax, dealmaker says former PM 'totally innocent.'" Schreiber told Bob Fife, "As much as I am involved, as much as I know, as much as I have seen, Mr. Mulroney is totally innocent... Since the Hitler diaries, it is the greatest mess of nonsense that I have ever seen," he declared angrily. "What happened to [Mulroney] right now is totally unfair and foolish." Fife quoted Schreiber as saying he would file suit against the CBC, Stevie Cameron, and "lots of others."

"Where is the proof that IAL belongs to Mr. Schreiber?" Schreiber demanded. "Where is the proof that there is a signed agreement between Airbus and IAL? Where is the proof that the bank accounts where the money was transferred belongs to Mr. Schreiber or Mulroney or Mr. Moores? Where is the proof? It's totally nonsense." Schreiber continued theatrically, "I can tell you one thing, sir. You will laugh yourself to death pretty soon. I'm not joking."

In Montreal, Mulroney continued to wage his own campaign just as fiercely. His lawyers asked the chief justice of the Quebec Superior Court to give the former prime minister "special measures" to allow a single judge to hear all the evidence and take the case to its conclusion. It meant fast-tracking the case, and when the court agreed, the judgment was hotly contested by the federal government's lawyer Claude-Armand Sheppard. As a media lawyer who often worked for the Montreal *Gazette*, Sheppard said he had never seen such a special measure granted in a libel action.

By now journalists were paying attention to the business card Pelossi had produced on the *fifth estate* program. Pelossi said he recorded the initials "B.M.," meaning Brian Mulroney. But the scuttlebutt was that Pelossi had lied to *the fifth estate*. Frank Moores's wife agreed. "The 'B.M.' is Beth Moores," she told reporters. "It was never Brian Mulroney."

In fact *the fifth estate* had called Beth Moores long before the issue of initials arose and asked what she might know about any Swiss bank accounts held by her husband. She said she didn't know anything about them. But it was her husband who tried to put an end to the rumours. He spoke to Phil Mathias, admitted for the first time he had a Swiss account, and then tried to remove his wife from the whole story. He may have been capable of lying about his Swiss accounts, but he drew the line at involving his wife.

"Moores said news stories that the account was opened for her... benefit are not correct," Mathias reported in mid-December. "He opened the account, he said, to hold the proceeds of European business deals that were planned, but did not materialize." Moores never said what those European deals were, but it didn't matter; he deserved credit for keeping his wife out of his subterfuge. That the "B.M." account belonged to Beth Moores was repeated as fact in the months and years to follow. Schreiber himself contributed to the smokescreen, telling Jack Major that the CBC and Cameron were all wrong on their stories and that "B.M." represented Mrs. Moores, not Brian Mulroney. People forgot that Moores was the first to say the account was not for his wife.

The initial media focus on alleged wrongdoing by Schreiber, Moores, and Mulroney had turned full circle. Now those who had brought the Airbus story to light were under attack, and Schreiber was emboldened. He launched a new legal action against the government of Canada, claiming his rights under the Canadian Charter of Rights and Freedoms had been violated when the RCMP sent its letter to Switzerland without what he believed to be proper judicial authority. He filed suit against the CBC for $35 million, in part for its reports of Pelossi's comments. The assault didn't stop there. George Wolff, a CTV reporter, helped to undermine Pelossi's credibility. On one program Wolff outlined the details of Pelossi's six-month incarceration and other business problems, but the item did not explore why, if Pelossi was such a questionable character, Schreiber continued to do business with him. CTV could find no evidence that Pelossi had actually misled anyone, but Schreiber would later fax a copy of the CTV transcript to authorities in Augsburg.

Two days after CTV's Pelossi story, Neil Macdonald of CBC-TV quoted Senator Marjory LeBreton as saying Moores and Mulroney had had a falling-out in March 1987, and insisting that the story that Moores collected money for Mulroney had to be false. To the Canadian public, the story was becoming more and more confusing. Some journalists would continue to squabble about how to cover it, others would give up altogether. It was too much work, too complex, and too risky in that litigious atmosphere. Schreiber was scoring points in the public relations war, at least in Canada.

19

They Won't Get Me

While Brian Mulroney and his team of lawyers took on the media, the Mounties, and the federal government in Canada, Schreiber waged his own war in Germany. He was at a disadvantage, fighting his adversaries from Switzerland, and every time the phone rang, it seemed to deliver more bad news. Prosecutors were investigating allegations of tax evasion and fraud arising from four of Schreiber's business deals: MBB, Bear Head, Airbus, and the sale of Fuchs tanks to Saudi Arabia.

Throughout December 1995, the Augsburg authorities moved in on their suspects with search-and-seizure warrants. On December 11, for example, they searched the offices and premises at Thyssen and at two related companies, as they had already done at least once. They obtained permission to search the houses, the offices, and even the cars of Jürgen Massmann, Winfried Haastert, and Holger Pfahls. In the case of Pfahls, they won permission to search his country house at Tegernsee, his city residence, his daughter's house, and any other premises the family used. Pfahls returned to Tegernsee from Brussels for the prosecutors' search. He didn't hide his fear from the men in his house. "This is the end of my career," he told them.

When the prosecutors arrived at Haastert's home on December 14, he too was there and cooperated. He knew they had been told about the private agreement on commissions on the tank deal, so he opened the safe where he had put his copy and voluntarily surrendered it.

Schreiber's strategy now took a new tack. He had kept very little of the money he had received in commissions, his lawyer told the *Frankfurter Allgemeine* on December 19, 1995. As far as Schreiber was concerned, he had done nothing wrong.

> As Stefan von Moers, Schreiber's lawyer, told this newspaper, Schreiber became involved with Strauss at [the time of the Air Canada-IAL contract] because of his good contacts with Canada. At that time, the Bavarian government was involved in Airbus via MBB and Strauss was the chairman of the board of the Airbus Industrie consortium. Moers said that the order, which was vital for Airbus at that time, was brought about through strong competition with the American aircraft manufacturer Boeing. That so-called "useful expenditures" should flow to the customer was a recognized practice and accepted by the Tax Office. The lawyer also confirmed that in one case Schreiber was involved in the transaction of such a payment.

The public comments by von Moers were startlingly different from his client's previous denials, but Schreiber had been forced to shift his position. The authorities already held evidence of his having received commissions; no one would believe his original defence. This latest argument was cleverer, though it forced him to admit to a deeper involvement than he might have wished. He did receive commission money, he conceded, but not all of it was meant for him. He passed on much of it to others in the form of *Schmiergelder*. And as long as he paid the *Schmiergelder* to individuals outside the country, he had broken no German law. Schreiber protested that he had been working for the good of Germany, and the government should not allow him to be harassed in this way nor subjected to such indignities. He wanted the investigation stopped.

Perhaps he was not alone in fending off unwelcome attention from tax officials. On December 28, 1995, he wrote a strange letter to Frank

Moores, one that the Augsburg authorities labelled a fraudulent attempt to disguise taxable revenues. He portrayed some of the money he and Moores had received from Thyssen not as income but as a loan.

"Dear Frank," he wrote. "Re: Loan in the amount of Can.$ 1 million Project Thyssen Bear Head. On March 12, 1992 Thyssen Industrie through myself granted you a loan in the amount of Can.$ 1 million at an interest rate of 4% p.a." The debt was outstanding, the letter reminded Moores, and he should pay it back. That same day Schreiber dissolved Bear Head Industries as a company. Thyssen later denied it had anything to do with a loan to Schreiber or Moores.

On December 29, a judge allowed the prosecutors to search Max Strauss's home. But with plenty of warning, Strauss had had time to destroy his computer's hard drive.

Schreiber continued his attacks on the media. Along with a lawsuit against the CBC, he twice sued Conny Neumann of the *Süddeutsche Zeitung*, though he didn't follow through on either action. When *Der Spiegel* published a story on the Saudi tank deal on January 20, Schreiber and his cronies accused the prosecutors' office of slipping information to *Der Spiegel*. Pfahls complained, Massmann complained, Schreiber complained – and the prosecutors plodded on.

On January 30, 1996, Schreiber repeated the charge in a letter to Rita Süssmuth, the president of the Bundestag, claiming that the Augsburg team had leaked details of their investigation to reporters and that he had been defamed by *Der Spiegel* and by the *Süddeutsche Zeitung*. Two weeks later he was answered by Arno Peters on Süssmuth's behalf, brusquely telling him to take his petition to the Bavarian parliament, where it belonged.

Schreiber had also protested in writing to Anton Gumpendobler in the Augsburg Tax Office. Were individuals selling his confidential tax information to *Der Spiegel* to make extra money? To hurt his public image? To disqualify an annoying competitor on the international export market? Was it, he asked, "for personal reasons, such as jealousy, hatred, revenge, sensationalism, or pure malice?" Or – finally – was it simply politically motivated, aimed at someone who had been a friend of Strauss?

"I would also like to remind you," he scolded, "that in the mid-'80s,

Deutsche Airbus GmbH was on the brink of bankruptcy and the survival of Airbus Industrie would have been impossible without access to the North American market. The 'war' between Boeing and Airbus Industrie in Europe had reached a climate which made it necessary for Franz Josef Strauss to visit the American president Ronald Reagan and make political concessions." Schreiber ended his letter with a passionate appeal to do what was best for Bavarian business interests and end this witch hunt. "The English say: 'Right or wrong – my country'!" he wrote. "I love this country and in particular, the Free State of Bavaria."

Perhaps he hoped for a little friendly support from Renate Schmidt, a Bavarian politician from the opposition Social Democratic Party (known by its German initials as the SPD), whom he met one day in February 1996 when flying from Bonn to Munich. They had such a pleasant chat, reported the magazine *Bunte* in January 2000, that he handed over an envelope of DM5,000 to her during the flight.

In early 1996, Hillinger asked the Swiss police for help in rounding up witnesses; his team also wanted the Swiss to search Schreiber's home in Pontresina. The German authorities put questions to Hans Reiter, the Landsberg bank manager, as well as André Strobel and Paul Schnyder, Schreiber's bankers in Zurich, and his banker in Pontresina. They asked about transactions, code names, payments, and the meanings of certain notations in Schreiber's diaries. By mid-February the Germans believed they had broken most of the codes. For the next several months, it was a matter of interviewing witnesses, deciphering the contracts, and examining in painstaking detail all of the papers they'd acquired.

In the spring of 1996 Luc Lavoie sat in his office one evening, ready to call it a day. It was nearly 6 p.m. and he was exhausted. Since November there hadn't been a day that he hadn't thought of Brian Mulroney and the RCMP and that letter to the Swiss government. The phone rang. The caller was a man who spoke English with a thick accent that Lavoie, whose mother tongue is French, found doubly hard to understand.

"Who is speaking?" Lavoie asked.

"Karlheinz Schreiber here," came the cheerful reply. Schreiber was apparently in a merry mood, laughing and telling Lavoie he had a glass of champagne in his hand. "I read all about you and people send me clippings and you are always quoted in there," Schreiber told him. "I wanted to tell you that you are doing one heck of a job," he said.

Lavoie was a former journalist and his curiosity got the better of him. "Where do you think this is heading, sir?" Lavoie asked.

"This is all a hoax, this is all a joke. In due time people will find out that this was all a hoax and a joke." Lavoie asked him specifically if he had anything to do with the Airbus deal. "No, no," Schreiber said.

Mulroney's lawsuit against the federal government was proceeding quickly and would probably come to trial by the end of the year. If so, the RCMP would not complete their investigation before the trial began; even the most optimistic knew they couldn't secure Schreiber's bank information from Switzerland before then. But there was one advantage in this process for the defendants. Mulroney would be testifying under oath as part of the pretrial preparations, the stage known as examination for discovery. The government had many questions to ask him.

On April 17, 1996, Mulroney walked up the steps of Montreal's Palais de Justice and into the history books; no one could remember a former Canadian prime minister testifying under oath in his own court proceedings. Journalists from every major paper and television station in the country were there, as well as reporters for the *New York Times*, the *Washington Post*, CNN, AFP, and Reuters. The throng followed him into the building, where in a courtroom on the sixteenth floor he sat down to face Claude-Armand Sheppard, the Montreal litigator hired to represent the federal government.

As a university student Mulroney had excelled in debating tournaments, and he did not intend to lose this one. Normally Mulroney would have been counselled by his lawyers to say as little as possible, answering only the questions put to him, never volunteering information. Mulroney took a different approach. He had some things on his mind and he wanted to say them, regardless of what Sheppard asked. First, he wanted to make it clear that his lawsuit had nothing to do with impeding an investigation.

"We never questioned the right of the RCMP to interview whomever they wanted around the world, including former prime ministers or former governors general," he declared. "That's their job. And I respect the responsibility of the RCMP in that regard." What bothered him, he said, was that the Mounties didn't give him a chance to "provide the responses," as he put it, "that might prevail upon the RCMP to say, 'Hey, maybe this information we got is wrong.'"

"This was something straight out of Kafka," Mulroney told the packed courtroom about the moment he received the call from Schreiber, who read out parts of the letter. "I had never been interrogated. Nobody ever spoke to me. This was a document transmitted by stealth, in the middle of the night ... I had no idea what they were talking about."

Above all, he said, he was fighting back for his family.

"This is not an allegation, this is a statement of fact where the Government of Canada is judge, jury, and executioner. When something like this happens, this was a devastating personal experience ... This was the worst thing that's ever happened to me in my life. I have four young children, my mother is eighty-five years of age, my father-in-law is very ill – to have to explain to them what happened and what is going to happen is an extremely painful thing for any father, or any individual to have to go through ... It was a truly overwhelming and devastating human situation."

Even the most cynical journalists were not immune to Mulroney's references to his family; he was getting through to his audience. Sheppard seemed to be sinking in the face of these sentiments, and people later criticized him for his poor performance. Few understood that he thought little about scoring debating points; he was looking for information.

Sheppard began by asking how Mulroney met Schreiber in the first place. He'd known Schreiber since the early 1980s, Mulroney replied. They'd met in "a business context" but he couldn't remember much about it. During the relatively brief period when he was running for the leadership of the Progressive Conservative Party, then serving as leader and then becoming prime minister, there were just too many people for him to be able to recall specifics. What he best remembered was Schreiber's involvement in the Thyssen project in Nova Scotia.

Mulroney was impressed by Schreiber's knowledge of business, and by his thoughts on German reunification, just as Schreiber had informed Frank Heine, the journalist in Hohegeiss, earlier that year. He'd never visited Schreiber at any of his homes in Germany or Switzerland, he said, but he recollected that Schreiber had come to a meeting in his office in Ottawa to talk about Thyssen.

"I knew him, quite frankly, as a well-informed, determined, competent businessman who had immigrated to Canada. And I always believed that this country was enormously strengthened by such immigration."

Mulroney testified that he hadn't known Schreiber was a friend of Franz Josef Strauss's until he read it later in the newspapers. He didn't know the Strauss family, he said. "I did not know Mr. Strauss myself, nor did I know any member of his family," he stated.

Mulroney insisted Schreiber did not talk to him about Airbus, despite admitting he met Schreiber in his Parliament Hill office from time to time. "Never," Mulroney swore, saying he did not even know Schreiber was assigned to sell Airbus planes in Canada. Nor, he said, did he know that Franz Josef Strauss was the chairman of Airbus Industrie; he knew of him only as the premier of Bavaria.

When Mulroney was asked if he kept in touch with Schreiber after leaving office, he replied, "Well, from time to time, not very often. When he was going through Montreal, he would give me a call. We would have a cup of coffee, I think, once or twice."

Mulroney made a number of interesting statements in the course of his deposition. He said, for example, that he had never met Greg Alford and that he had no idea Alford had ever been a vice-president of Frank Moores's lobbying company. He said he had no discussion with anyone – including Schreiber – about the MBB helicopter deal, nor did he know that Schreiber had received a commission on the deal.

When the questioning turned to his relationship with Frank Moores, he was asked if he had nominated Moores to the board of Air Canada in 1985. Mulroney said he had not. He said Moores was nominated by the minister of transport, Don Mazankowski. Technically, this was correct. In reality, the members of the Air Canada board appointed in that year were mostly organizers or fundraisers for Mulroney's leadership campaign, including Moores. Mulroney also testified that he hadn't known anything about possible links between GCI and the Airbus deal until the news stories broke. He said he didn't know who Moores's clients were at GCI.

Sheppard began his questioning on the Airbus purchase with a recitation of facts as he had them. "Mr. Moores resigned from the board of directors on September 12, 1985 ..."

"False," Mulroney jumped in. "The date is wrong." Mulroney was correct. Moores resigned on September 6, 1985.

"... when it became known," Sheppard continued, "that Airbus Industries was one of his clients at GCI ..."

Once again, Mulroney interrupted impatiently. "False. He resigned because, ... as was publicly stated, that Nordair and Wardair were his clients, not Airbus ..."

"... and that he was in a conflict of interest position while Air Canada was negotiating the purchase of a new fleet of aircraft with Airbus ..."

Mulroney challenged Sheppard a third time. "Mr. Moores resigned from the board – he was there for five months – he resigned from the board in September of 1985. Air Canada did not begin to consider and negotiate a new fleet of aircraft until August of 1987, two years after Mr. Moores left the board."

In citing these dates, he may have been referring to the fact that Air Canada set up its formal decision-making teams in August of 1987. But Airbus knew Air Canada intended to make a major fleet purchase well before 1987; consequently, it set up its contract with IAL in March of 1985, only days before Moores was appointed to the Air Canada board.

Mulroney also testified that he and Moores had a falling-out in 1987 after his friend publicly doubted whether Mulroney could win a second federal election. Mulroney said it would be an "understatement" to say that Moores put a damper on their relationship, saying Moores was dropped from his "hit parade."

In one exchange in French, Mulroney asserted that the letters "B.M." that Pelossi had scribbled on the business card referred to Beth Moores and not Brian Mulroney. He said his legal team would establish that Beth Moores was the beneficiary of the account.

Few reporters in the courtroom could examine this testimony in detail or know what evidence the RCMP had gathered as background to Sheppard's questions. What they noticed was that Mulroney won the debate.

Schreiber, too, was fighting hard. He charmed friendly reporters, especially two of the Canadians, Phil Mathias and George Wolff, convincing them he was the victim of a crooked former partner and a few "out of control" journalists. In his view those journalists included Stevie Cameron, who travelled in April to Germany and Switzerland, where she met with Hillinger, Pelossi, and some of the other players. Schreiber later told Bob Fife of the *Toronto Sun* the hotels Cameron stayed in, the cities she visited, and the meetings she attended. When Fife asked Schreiber if he had paid for a detective, Schreiber said it was CTV News. But a CTV News producer denied it. "We wouldn't be allowed to do this," he told Cameron after Fife had relayed Schreiber's gleeful conversation, "and we don't have the money to do it!"

In Germany, the story of the Saudi tank deal died down; Conny Neumann was one of the few reporters who continued to pursue new information. On May 14, 1996, she reported that the Augsburg authorities were looking at evidence that suggested, even then, that money had gone to Max Strauss, Holger Pfahls, and Walther Leisler Kiep as a result of the tank contract. Hillinger had plenty of evidence but, like the Canadians, he needed the details of Schreiber's Swiss accounts to complete his case. He made a formal request to Swiss authorities on June 5 for records from the Swiss Bank Corporation in Zurich and the Schweizerische Kreditanstalt in Pontresina. Schreiber battled him in the courts to keep the banking records out of reach. And Schreiber, as always, remained defiant. Just after Neumann's story appeared, the *Augsburger Allgemeine* published an interview in which he declared, "They had better not even think of taking me into coercive detention."

The same month Canadian tax officials were beginning to work together with their German counterparts. On June 4, two Revenue Canada officers, Bruce Findlay and Guy Bigonesse, met in Augsburg with Gumpendobler, Kindler, and others, to share intelligence. They swapped binders of confidential tax information.

According to Hans Leyendecker, Winfried Maier, one of the prosecutors working with Hillinger and Weigand, received a call on June 24, 1996, from Erich Riedl's wife, Gertrud. She told him that Max Strauss had suddenly appeared in her apartment a day or two before. Apparently he had come in through an unlocked door on her terrace. He didn't waste time on pleasantries. "You have received 500,000 Deutschmarks from Thyssen, and tomorrow morning a house search will take place. My house was searched on Wednesday at 7:30." Gertrud Riedl told Maier that Strauss had warned her to destroy everything that could incriminate her husband, including business cards and telephone numbers. And she should warn her husband immediately – not from the phone in their apartment, but from a pay phone or a friend's house.

Although she had said repeatedly that she and her husband did not have DM500,000 and held no Swiss accounts, Strauss uttered his warning twice before running out through her garden. He had been right about the raid – the Riedls' house was searched.

Towards the end of July, Augsburg authorities received permission to examine Massmann's bank accounts and those of his wife, Ingrid. In late November, Maier and Weigand questioned Max Strauss in Munich. Strauss arrived late, tried to tape-record the session until the prosecutors stopped him, and refused to answer any questions, citing his right to withhold incriminating evidence. Hillinger picked away, relentlessly pursuing new leads and interviewing reluctant witnesses. Slowly but surely, the net was tightening.

In Canada, Mulroney's allies in the press, especially William Thorsell, editor-in-chief of the *Globe and Mail*, argued that what had happened to Mulroney was a travesty. Mulroney's lawyers subpoenaed journalists, including Cameron, Cashore, and several others; in return, the government lawyers initiated their own round of subpoenas, including one to Thorsell and another to Phil Mathias. They wanted to ask when they had received copies of the translation of the Canadian letter of request to Switzerland – and who had sent it to them. They told Thorsell to bring copies of all his correspondence with the former prime minister. The government would argue that there had been no libel to begin with, but if there had, surely it rested with the people who released the document to the media. If it could be shown that Mulroney had caused the document to be given to a journalist, then the suit would collapse. At least that was the theory.

Mulroney's lawyers sought the court's permission to ask dozens of questions of Pascal Gossin, a Swiss police liaison officer who had been working with Canadian government officials. The Mounties had revealed the details of their criminal evidence to Gossin in order to win Swiss support for their case; now the Mulroney team argued that they needed to know these details to mount their lawsuit. Horrified, the RCMP refused. The Justice Department asked that nine of the questions be ruled out, arguing that showing such evidence to Mulroney's lawyers would betray the Mounties' sources and undermine their criminal case. Any line of inquiry like this could reveal strategy, or tip off the guilty. If it came down to it, the government would settle the lawsuit rather than allow its investigation to be jeopardized before it was finished.

By late December, both sides were preparing for what was expected to be a sensational trial. Luc Lavoie asked the judge for a private room in the courthouse; the judge agreed and granted Mulroney a private phone, installed at his own expense, as well. Mulroney's lawyers made it known they expected to call former U.S. president George Bush and former British prime minister Margaret Thatcher as character witnesses. His legal team subpoenaed two of Prime Minister Chrétien's top aides, Eddie Goldenberg and Peter Donolo, asking for all correspondence, memos, and electronic mail they had exchanged with Chrétien concerning Airbus since October 1, 1995. The request made federal lawyers nervous. The word went out that Chrétien wanted this case settled – he didn't want his people dragged into court.

The federal government had nonetheless determined its strategy. As Rod Macdonell reported in the Montreal *Gazette* on January 4, Ottawa took the position that it was not at fault if a leak had sprung somewhere within the Swiss legal or banking apparatus. Furthermore, Mulroney himself was partly to blame for the publicity: his nationally televised press conference announcing a $50-million lawsuit drew

Canadians' attention to the kickback allegations against him.

In the end, the lawsuit did not go forward. On Monday, January 6, 1997, Justice Minister Allan Rock and Solicitor General Herb Gray held a press conference to announce a settlement that would pay Mulroney's expenses. It would also apologize for the wording of several sentences in the letter of request, wording that suggested the Mounties had already concluded Mulroney was a criminal. However, the government had rejected Mulroney's demand for $50 million in damages; "in fact, Mr. Mulroney has now dropped any claim to compensation for damages," said Rock.

As Rock and Gray made clear, the settlement changed nothing in the Mounties' ability to proceed with the investigation. "This agreement does not stop the RCMP's ongoing criminal investigation into Airbus, or give anyone – including Mr. Mulroney – effective immunity from such an investigation. The RCMP will continue its investigation in its entirety, and it is now free to carry it through to whatever conclusion is appropriate."

Mulroney had accepted the fact, said Rock, that "the Airbus investigation was begun by the RCMP on its own, that there was no political interference, and that the Department of Justice and the RCMP, in transmitting the letter of request, acted within their legitimate responsibilities. Mr. Mulroney has also acknowledged that the procedure used in sending the letter of request in this case was the same as that followed in numerous previous requests for assistance under the current government and his own administration."

Gray elaborated on the reasons for settling the case. One was to ensure what he called "the integrity of the ongoing police investigation" – in other words, to protect sources, evidence, and the overall inquiry. If the RCMP had to reveal its criminal evidence under questioning in Switzerland, as the Federal Court of Appeal in Ottawa had ruled three days earlier, it would endanger the RCMP's case.

Furthermore, Gray said, there may have been a leak in this case: an RCMP officer might have disclosed something to an unauthorized third party about who was named in the letter of request. Gray said the Privacy Act prohibited disclosure of the name of either the officer or the third party.

Dear Diary: A page from Schreiber's diary for January 19, 1991, shows his notes on the division of funds from Airbus commissions and reminders concerning Stuart Iddles, "Fred," "Holger," and others.

A career-ending move? At an Ottawa news conference, Justice Minister Allan Rock tries to explain the government's apology to Brian Mulroney and the settlement of his lawsuit. (Fred Chartrand, *Ottawa Citizen*)

Oh, happy day: Brian Mulroney is all smiles as he leaves his house for a walk after settling out of court in his lawsuit against the federal government. (Paul Chiasson, CP)

Sacrificial lamb: RCMP Staff Sergeant Fraser Fiegenwald attends a fundraising barbecue in October 1997 at the Mounties' national headquarters in Ottawa, where his colleagues raised money for his legal fees. (Fred Chartrand, *Ottawa Citizen*)

Breaking news: The chief prosecutor in Augsburg, Jörg Hillinger, who led the investigation into Schreiber's deals, follows the story in Munich's *Süddeutsche Zeitung.* Hillinger was killed in a car crash before charges were laid. (Private collection)

Relentless: Winfried Maier was the prosecutor who wrote the letter to Canada requesting Schreiber's extradition. (dpa)

Code name "Jürglund": Jürgen Massmann, a Thyssen executive, was president of Bear Head Industries and later brought Schreiber into the Saudi tank deal. He was charged with fraud and tax evasion in May 1999. (Frank Darchinger)

Code name "Winter": Winfried Haastert, the second Thyssen executive who worked with Schreiber on the Bear Head and Saudi tank deals, was also arrested in May 1999 and charged with fraud and tax evasion. (dpa)

Spymaster: Holger Pfahls, a former German spy chief and deputy minister of defence, was charged by German prosecutors but disappeared in the Far East in the spring of 1999. (Bonn-Sequenz)

A suitcase in St. Margarethen: Walther Leisler Kiep, treasurer of the Christian Democratic Union, set off the party's slush fund scandal after revelations that he accepted DM1 million in cash from Schreiber at a pizza restaurant in St. Margarethen. (dpa)

Not talking: Former German chancellor Helmut Kohl prepares for an interview on the German ZDF TV network on December 16, 1999, as prosecutors pursue an investigation against him for accepting illegal donations to the CDU.
(Jockel Finck, AP)

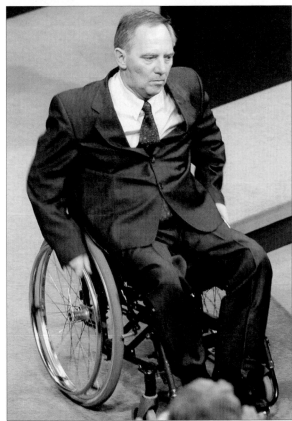

A career in ruins: Wolfgang Schäuble, wheelchair-bound after an assassination attempt in 1992, succeeded Helmut Kohl. In January 2000 he offered an apology in the Bonn parliament for the party's ongoing finance scandal; it didn't end calls for his resignation.
(Roberto Pfeil, AP)

A friend in need: Elmer MacKay, a former Tory cabinet minister, explains to reporters in September 1999 why he put up a bail surety of $100,000 for Schreiber. (Ken Kerr, Sun Media)

Free at last: Schreiber and his wife joyfully leave a Toronto courthouse after winning bail with the support of powerful friends. (Ken Kerr, Sun Media)

The Privacy Act notwithstanding, within hours of the press conference's conclusion, Rock's senior staff and counsel, as well as public relations specialists hired to give him advice on how to handle the affair, were telling reporters openly that the Mountie in question was Staff Sergeant Fraser Fiegenwald and the "third party" was Stevie Cameron. Cameron's response was that she had been working on the story for *Maclean's*; if Fiegenwald had leaked anything of substance to her, if he had confirmed that Mulroney was a subject of investigation, she would have printed it. That was her job. But right up to the magazine's deadline, she had been unable to verify that Mulroney was the politician targeted in the letter to Switzerland.

In the aftermath of the settlement, the Airbus story faded. In the public mind, Mulroney had been exonerated. Everyone should be considered innocent until proven guilty, and on that level the government's apology had a positive effect. Casual observers could be forgiven for thinking that the investigation was for all intents and purposes at an end, or worse, that if it continued, it was only because the RCMP was bent on a senseless vendetta.

A day after the settlement announcement, Frank Moores's lawyer, Edgar Sexton, a respected Bay Street litigator (and later a judge on the Federal Court of Appeal), spoke to the *Globe and Mail* and made an astonishing declaration: his client never received any Airbus money. "[Moores] did not impede the RCMP investigation in Switzerland, and they got the information on his accounts and they've had it for several months," said Sexton. "Obviously the accounts show nothing and substantiate the position of Mr. Moores that he had nothing to do with obtaining the Airbus contract and that he got no money for it." Although Schreiber's banking records would show that Moores did receive Airbus commissions, his lawyer's comments cemented the consensus that the entire investigation was without foundation.[1]

Schreiber and Moores also won apologies from the government. "Some of the language contained in the request for assistance indicates, wrongly, that the RCMP had reached conclusions that you had engaged in criminal activity," said identical letters to the two men. "The government of Canada and the RCMP fully apologize to you." The pair refused to accept the apologies. Sexton responded in a letter to Rock, calling the gesture "inadequate and unsatisfactory" and demanding compensation. Moores might even sue, he added.

Schreiber chimed in. "I would not wish the enormous pain, suffering and embarrassment that you have caused for my family and friends on anyone," he wrote the government. He compared his experience to that of wartime Germany, saying it "reminds me of the nightmare years of my childhood when the Nazi regime set loose the Gestapo on the German public."

Two months after the announcement of the settlement, the Mulroneys purchased a yellow stucco house in the best part of Palm Beach, their favourite vacation retreat. The house is expansive and elegant with six bedrooms, seven bathrooms, and a large swimming pool, all surrounded by palm trees. The price was US$915,000, or about C$1.4 million, and they took possession on March 10, 1997.

The property was owned by a holding company called Golden Memoirs Investment Inc., which was, in turn, owned by Mila Mulroney. Golden Memoirs was incorporated in Montreal but later listed its address as that of the Calgary branch of KPMG, the large accounting and management consulting firm. It appears an American residence was a longstanding dream; in 1990, when Mulroney was still prime minister, Mila, on a visit to South Carolina, took out a U.S. social security number.

To offset Mulroney's expenses from the lawsuit, the federal government made the first payment to him of $450,000 on May 25, 1997; a month later, on June 27, it made a second $450,000 payment. In mid-July Mulroney received a further $300,000. Initially the government had agreed to pay only his legal fees, but a Montreal judge, brought in to arbitrate a dispute over costs, ordered the government to pay Luc Lavoie's bill for public relations services as well. This added another $587,221 to the final costs.

Then on March 13, 1997, in response to an action launched by Schreiber, the Federal Court of Canada ruled that the RCMP letter to the Swiss was unconstitutional. The ruling declared that the Mounties had no right to see Schreiber's bank accounts on demand; instead, the RCMP should have had a judge issue a warrant before it sent the letter. The government announced it would appeal the judgment to the

Supreme Court of Canada, but in the meantime the RCMP would not see Schreiber's bank records.

For the Mounties, these were the darkest days of the Airbus investigation, though the effort continued despite setbacks. Fraser Fiegenwald was pulled off the Airbus file, assigned to "administrative duties," and placed under investigation for allegedly leaking information to Stevie Cameron. Although the internal review cleared him of any wrongdoing, RCMP brass had him charged anyway with disobeying the force's code of conduct. His colleagues held a barbecue on the grounds of RCMP headquarters in Ottawa to help raise money for his legal fees, but a disciplinary hearing on the charges was eventually abandoned. Fellow officers believed he had been thrown to the wolves by those who would protect the politicians' careers above all else. Fiegenwald decided to leave the force for a forensic accounting job in the private sector and received a generous financial package from the government.

The contradiction seemed enormous. An honest cop's RCMP career was destroyed, and the deal-maker who hid those commissions received an apology.

Jörg Hillinger would have read the settlement details with interest, but they made no difference to his work. Broadening his investigation to France, he sent a letter of request to the procurator general at the Court of Appeals of Paris, asking for assistance in executing a search warrant. He explained that he was investigating the Strausses, Schreiber, IAL, and payments for Airbus contracts. Specifically, he needed the files from the Paris bank where the money trail began, and he wanted a search done in Toulouse, the headquarters for Airbus Industrie.

Closer to home, Hillinger seized Schreiber's records at the Sparkasse Landsberg at the end of January. Affidavits were taken from Schreiber's business manager, Albert Birkner, and his secretary, Dietlinde Kaupp. Herbert Leiduck provided his affidavit in February with often hilarious accounts of his dealings with Schreiber in Moscow.

Most of the Augsburg team's activities were invisible to the average German. Occasional stories surfaced in the media: Brigitte Baumeister had used CDU writing paper to lobby for export contracts favourable to Thyssen Henschel, according to *Die Welt* on March 20, 1997. In April, there were reports that bribes may have been paid to the CDU in the Elf-Leuna deal, allegations emphatically denied by Helmut Kohl's associates. But these isolated items were not connected or pursued at the time.

It was on April 22 that Hillinger scored a major victory: the Swiss agreed to a search and seizure of Schreiber's records at the Swiss Bank Corporation in Zurich, and at all its other branches. But even without these records, Hillinger's case was strong. On May 7, he issued an arrest warrant for Schreiber on charges of tax evasion. But Schreiber was sitting tight in his condo in Pontresina. They couldn't touch him there, and he launched an appeal against the Swiss seizure.

Hillinger opened yet another line of attack. On September 18, 1997, he addressed a letter to Kimberly Prost in Canada's Department of Justice. After laying out his case against Schreiber – who, he said, had set up shell companies to hide commissions from Thyssen, MBB, and Airbus, thereby avoiding income tax on those commissions – he asked that the RCMP interview Frank Moores, Fred Doucet, and Erika Lutz. He provided a list of questions for each. He requested that search warrants be served on Schreiber's Ottawa condo, on the Bitucan offices in Calgary, and on several banks: the Royal Bank of Canada at its 10503 Jasper Avenue branch in Edmonton, the Royal Bank at 90 Sparks Street in Ottawa, the main Calgary branch of the Bank of Nova Scotia on 8th Avenue, and the Bank of Montreal on 7th Avenue in Calgary.

Hillinger couldn't send such a request directly to Canadian officials; it had to be forwarded by Germany's Foreign Ministry. Did alarm bells go off in Bonn when senior bureaucrats there saw Schreiber's name on the letter and the details of his deals for Thyssen, MBB, and Airbus? It would be convenient – and far less troublesome – if the correspondence were misplaced. Whatever transpired, Hillinger's September request never reached Canada.

In October Schreiber wrote an appeal of his own, a long, rambling letter to Edmund Stoiber, the premier of Bavaria and a man he had known since the early 1980s, when Stoiber was a cabinet minister in Strauss's government. Schreiber complained to Stoiber about media exposure of his arrest warrant and the details of his case, and he begged Stoiber to put an end to the investigation. "You, as the highest authority of the Free State of Bavaria ... you alone could be in a position, after examining the proceedings, to put a stop to the unbridled craziness of the Augsburg officials. I have reached this conclusion because all of my efforts in this direction through my lawyers, following the usual legal procedures, have failed."

He reminded Stoiber that much of the case had to do with the payment of useful expenditures in the course of his promotion of Bear Head and other ventures. "This activity in some cases brought with it that *nützlichen Abgaben* had to be paid to foreigners in connection with the side which issued the contracts. In order for me to be able to carry out [these payments] in accordance with the wishes of those issuing the contracts, the participation of trustees was necessary."

He reviewed the initiatives one by one. As far as the Saudi tank deal was concerned, everyone knew what was involved. "Aside from industry, taking part in this project were the Federal Chancellor's Office, the Ministry of Foreign Affairs, the Trade Ministry, and the Ministry of Defence. The Federal Security Council played a decisive role in the approval, under the chairperson Chancellor Kohl, Minister of Defence Stoltenberg, Trade Minister [Jürgen] Möllemann, Finance Minister Waigel, and Foreign Minister [Klaus] Kinkel. In addition, the president of the United States, George Bush, the commander of the Gulf forces, Schwarzkopf, and the representatives of the Kingdom of Saudi Arabia."

As for the revelations concerning the Airbus commissions, Schreiber claimed the entire affair was a plot by Boeing and the media: "Existing documents and statements confirm that beyond a doubt. The extent to which the witness Pelossi ... along with the Canadian media representatives, was turned into an advocate for Boeing, is not yet clear, but will be made so in the related court cases that I have started in Canada."

He reminded Stoiber that "the Airbus project in Canada required ten years of work," including his own concerted efforts to persuade Wardair to purchase planes from Airbus. This sale, he said, was the "Trojan horse" into the North American market, a success that had been achieved thanks to the involvement of Franz Josef Strauss, Erich Riedl, numerous Bavarian cabinet ministers, and Stoiber himself. Moving on to Bear Head, he cited another string of names from Germany's political elite – Kohl, Pfahls, Riedl, Kiep, and others – who had been part of the campaign.

Finally, he referred to press reports that Stoiber intended to clean up the "Amigo" culture he had inherited from Strauss and Max Streibl, calling such reports disgraceful and suggesting that attempts were being made to alienate Stoiber from former comrades and supporters. Invoking past and happier memories, he ended with a plea for justice and understanding: "Up to now ... I did not want to give up the hope for reason and due process. This phase is over, which is why I turn to you, even if I regret having to burden you with this matter."

Stoiber never responded personally to Schreiber's letter; instead he forwarded it to the Justice Ministry. The climate in Bavaria had changed and Stoiber would not rise to defend one of the Amigos. From then on, Schreiber regarded Stoiber as an enemy.

In Canada Schreiber was enjoying a friendlier reception. A growing chorus of newspaper editorials in the *Globe and Mail* and *Toronto Sun* demanded that the RCMP withdraw its letter of request to the Swiss. Since all three players named in the letter had by now received public apologies, the demands made little sense. What possible harm could the letter cause at this point?

In November Mulroney told the *Toronto Sun* he had written to the federal government, demanding it withdraw the offending letter of request. "If we don't get that withdrawn, we will take appropriate action in the future," he warned. Months earlier, when the settlement was announced, Mulroney had not asked that the letter be withdrawn and had acknowledged that the RCMP could "investigate until the cows come home." For some reason he appeared to have reconsidered his position and now wanted the letter withdrawn.

In the midst of the clamour to withdraw the letter, one Southam News columnist, Andrew Coyne, appeared to break ranks with prevailing opinion. "It is still hard to see what all the fuss was about," he wrote. "Had Mulroney been convicted on this evidence, had he even been charged, the affair would be full value for all the outrage it has excited. But as things stand, we are left with nothing more than a piece of private correspondence between two countries' legal authorities, such as one imagines is exchanged every day in the course of their duties."

On March 20, 1998, lawyers for Schreiber and for the federal government appeared in the Supreme Court of Canada to argue the constitutionality of the RCMP's 1995 letter of request to Switzerland. Because two lower courts had ruled it was not a legal request, the government had been obliged to ask the Swiss to hold on to Schreiber's banking records. The Supreme Court would decide the matter once and for all. Justice Jack Major excused himself from taking part.

Bobby Hladun, who had helped his client run a grab bag of shell companies, was present to argue Schreiber's case. He maintained that Schreiber's Charter rights had been violated because the RCMP did not obtain a proper search warrant before it sent the letter to Switzerland. The federal government countered that it was up to Switzerland to determine the appropriateness of the letter, since the Swiss set the rules for Switzerland, not the Canadians. The judges soon had Hladun squirming under tough questioning. Why should the constitution of Canada protect Schreiber in his business dealings in Switzerland?

"The problem I'm having is your client chose to put his documents under the laws of Switzerland," Chief Justice Antonio Lamer said to Hladun. "Isn't it that my expectation of privacy will be governed by the laws of where I am?"

While the RCMP officers on the Airbus file waited anxiously for the court's decision, they started to work for the first time with their German counterparts. Though Hillinger's formal request of September 18, 1997, had mysteriously gone astray, the Mounties were aware of his interests. A confidential memo addressed to the German prosecutors and signed by an RCMP liaison officer, Rainer Brettschneider, in Bonn on March 2, 1998, confirms the RCMP had met with the Augsburg staff.

Canada knew about the German arrest warrant, wrote Brettschneider, and the RCMP was aware that Schreiber had renewed his Canadian passport in Bern, Switzerland, in December 1996.

Schreiber was living in Pontresina, he said, although he seemed to spend a lot of time in Liechtenstein, where his mail was being forwarded. Should the Germans apprehend Schreiber, Brettschneider noted, the Canadians wanted to question him too. "Canadian investigators are equally interested in having Schreiber arrested. You will be contacted immediately in the event of any information which would assist you." But he was concerned about the time passing, adding pointedly that the German request had been delayed in Bonn for months.

In April, RCMP officers flew to Europe to meet again with Giorgio Pelossi. Someone had suggested a polygraph test. Pelossi agreed immediately and passed it easily. It was also in April that the RCMP Commercial Crime Unit in Edmonton decided not to pursue charges against Schreiber for the loan he had given to Hugh Horner so many years before. Horner had died in the meantime, and no one thought there was enough evidence to lay charges.

A few weeks later, on May 16, 1998, Jörg Hillinger prepared a second letter of request to Canada, his irritation and suspicion of Bonn's ineptitude barely suppressed. He asked again for the assistance he had sought eight months earlier.

Dear Sirs,
The originals of the letters rogatory with enclosures dated September 18, 1997, which is enclosed as a certified copy, was lost by the Federal Ministry of Justice for reasons unknown to this office. Therefore the transmission is effected again as a certified copy.

By an order dated May 14, 1998, the Augsburg Local Court confirmed by a judge the directives given in the orders issued by Augsburg Local Court on September 04, 1997.
Hillinger

If Hillinger expected speedy action from Canada after the months of delay in Bonn, he was to be disappointed. Despite Brettschneider's helpful attitude, Canadian authorities couldn't proceed. A letter from the Department of Foreign Affairs and International Trade in August 1998 reminded the Germans that there was no treaty between the two countries to cover the request as presented; the Germans had to establish "reasonable grounds that an offence has been committed in the foreign state and that evidence of the offence will be found in Canada." A Canadian police officer would then have to prepare an affidavit with the supporting grounds. After a careful look at the evidence Hillinger had provided, the Canadians decided it wasn't good enough. But a note of encouragement fluttered weakly near the bottom of the response.

"Canadian officials familiar with Canadian legal requirements are prepared to assist the German prosecutor with the preparation of a case and to travel to Germany for this purpose. One of the Canadian officials, fully familiar with the German investigation, could become the affiant for the purpose of applications for court orders in Canada."

It's going to be very expensive, the Canadians warned, and Schreiber's lawyers will "rigorously" oppose any efforts to gather evidence. Be sure of your facts and keep it simple.

Hillinger could read between the lines as well as anyone, but the Canadian letter, delivered to the German Embassy in Ottawa on August 31, 1998, didn't reach him until the middle of October. It took Hillinger until late November to respond. This time he included summaries of the facts, and he accepted the idea of assistance from Canadian officials, specifically Brettschneider. He also reduced the number of search warrants he'd asked the Canadians to execute, removing the premises of the four banks from his list.

Frank Moores kept to himself in these months. Although he had issued a writ against the CBC in the fall of 1995, he had done nothing to pursue the lawsuit. In the spring of 1998 Moores called Keith Miller, whom he had hardly seen since they met to discuss the Airbus deal back in the mid-1980s. The two had not spoken in some time, but out of the blue Moores had suggested a game of golf. Why not, thought Miller.

When they met at Moores's condo in Florida, Moores had two questions for Miller.

"Remember our meetings about Airbus years ago? Did I mention money at the meeting in Ottawa? Did I mention money at the meeting in Toronto?"

"Yes, Frank," Miller replied.

Miller was mildly surprised by Moores's topic of conversation. Moores asked about John Lundrigan, the lobbyist who had worked for Boeing.

"Lundrigan was the one going around saying you got money on Airbus," Miller told Moores.

Moores tried to tell Miller he did not receive any Airbus money and complained that Schreiber had "stiffed" him. Miller asked him why he didn't sue; Moores didn't answer. But after they finished playing an enjoyable round of golf, Moores looked Miller right in the eye.

"Brian Mulroney did not get any of the Airbus money," he said. "At least, not from me."

On May 29, the Supreme Court of Canada ruled that the RCMP had acted properly in sending the letter of request to Switzerland and that no one had violated Schreiber's rights. Then in Switzerland another judgment went against Schreiber. In one of the many legal manoeuvres he had used in an attempt to thwart Hillinger, he had argued that there was not enough evidence for Swiss authorities to link his accounts to commission payments, and therefore the bank records should not be turned over to German investigators. On June 24, 1998, the Appeals Chamber of the Graubünden Canton Court disagreed. It concluded that the code names in Schreiber's bank accounts were not hard to translate.

"Various accounts labelled with the letters IAL and ATG also carry code names, which can with little imagination and through more than coincidence be tied to the fellow accused Haastert, Massmann, Pfahls, Kiep, and Strauss. This phenomenon cannot be explained otherwise."[2] Schreiber had one remaining appeal to make on this file before the Swiss could turn over his bank documents to Augsburg. It held the prosecutors at bay for several more months.

It had been nearly three years since Schreiber had fled from his home in Germany, and now he began to see that he might have to leave Switzerland as well. On September 2, the *Süddeutsche Zeitung* ran an interview with him, conducted at the Zurich airport. "They won't get me," he boasted.

In January 1999, however, came a third defeat in the courts. On

January 13, a three-member panel of the Swiss Federal Court rendered an eighteen-page judgment that granted the release of Karlheinz and Barbara Schreiber's bank records to the German investigators. Gary Ouellet had fought together with the Schreibers against the disclosure of his account information; he lost as well. The Germans could see whatever they wanted.

The Mounties were encouraged by all three court decisions. But Schreiber had begun a separate legal challenge in Switzerland to their request to see his bank records. Unless that appeal was resolved in the RCMP's favour, the Canadian investigators could not share in their German counterparts' wealth.

The January ruling provided a window into Schreiber's defence strategy, a tack hinted at earlier by his lawyer Stefan von Moers. Schreiber continued to claim while in Canada that the entire Airbus affair was a hoax, but in Europe he could no longer deny the facts.

"The central role of Karlheinz Schreiber to the three industrial clients (MBB, Thyssen, Airbus) ... is not being denied by the appellant," the judges stated. Schreiber did, however, deny he kept any of the money. He claimed it was "passed on to foreigners" as payments sanctioned by the tax authorities. The judges may have bought Schreiber's argument, since German law did allow third-party commissions, "useful expenditures," and even bribes. But in order to satisfy the authorities that he had indeed passed on such monies to others, he had to name the recipients. Schreiber might have to inform on his associates in Canada and Saudi Arabia. Friendship and loyalty were too important to him to allow the disclosure of the identities of these men. Not only did he maintain he was not obliged to name names, he said he was simply "not in a position" to do so. Schreiber complained of being exploited and persecuted by this catch-22. He could either betray his friends or end up in jail for tax evasion. Neither option was appealing.

The Swiss judges ruled that while the German authorities' arguments added up to "suspicion" against Schreiber, Schreiber's defence and that of Barbara and Ouellet worked against them. Especially misleading, wrote the judges, was Schreiber's suggestion that he had permission from the German tax authorities to make anonymous *Schmiergelder* payments. The court reminded Schreiber that as far back as December 14, 1992, the tax officials had told him he could deduct *Schmiergelder* only if he named the recipient.

"Karlheinz Schreiber is himself responsible for not following these regulations," scolded the judges.

There was another victory for Augsburg at the end of March 1999 when Airbus Industrie's secretary general, Hanko von Lachner, quietly acknowledged that the company had paid commissions to IAL. He put the total at US$10.867 million. Made well out of the spotlight, the admission was nonetheless an extraordinary about-face for a corporation that had publicly denied its role in the scandal for years.

Investigating Karlheinz Schreiber had been a long and gruelling undertaking for the Augsburg team and in particular for Jörg Hillinger, who developed a brain tumour while on the case. He was just recovering from treatment in the spring of 1999 when, on April 26, he was killed in a head-on collision. He was at the wheel of a new car, travelling a familiar route, and the police could find no simple answer as to the cause of the crash.

His colleagues were stunned by his death, but the investigation continued. By May 19 the prosecutors' office had filed yet another request for assistance to Switzerland, asking for Schreiber's bank records for the years 1994 and 1995. They cited possible charges of tax evasion, bribery, and assisting in breach of trust. Once again Schreiber was allowed to appeal the new request. He had hired the respected German criminal defence lawyer Erich Samson to join Stefan von Moers, and his legal team soon responded with a brief to the Swiss.

The lawyers argued that the bribery charges had been inflated and that the evidence against him was slim. Samson said that according to the law, Holger Pfahls's actions had to be contrary to his line of duty in order to justify the accusation of receiving a bribe. "Even if one wanted to allege that Pfahls received gifts or donations, this is not an offence for which Schreiber can be punished in Switzerland or in Germany."

His lawyers acknowledged Schreiber had refused to share his secrets. "Schreiber claims that all amounts that flowed through the accounts were passed on as *Schmiergelder* to other business partners and middlemen," they stated, "but [he] refuses to name the other recipients." Then the lawyers pointed to the Airbus contract, saying there was no doubt he had paid Airbus money to others, even if he refused to identify them. Schreiber would eventually lose this appeal.

The story began to pick up steam again in Germany for the first time in many months, especially after Conny Neumann reported that the original German letter of request to the Canadians had been "lost" for eight months in Bonn files. Only after the Kohl government had been defeated in September 1998 by the Social Democrats was the request "found" again.

In Canada there was little public excitement over the news that after a four-year struggle, German investigators were finally gaining access to Schreiber's bank accounts. The January 1999 Swiss court ruling was a watershed that would forever change the tempo of the Augsburg investigation, but in Canada the media barely noted it. In late February, however, a series of articles emerged, seemingly out of nowhere, that took a critical view of the RCMP's Airbus investigation.

The first appeared on February 22, 1999; Phil Mathias was now writing for the *National Post*. "The Airbus affair a decade old and going slowly," blared his story's headline. Mathias quoted a former Mulroney cabinet minister, John Crosbie, who complained about RCMP "incompetence." Mathias quoted Schreiber, who seemed amused. "Isn't that funny? Ten years! Jesus Christ!" The allegation was a "crazy hoax," Schreiber added.

On April 1, Mathias published another story that attacked the Mounties' ongoing efforts to investigate Mulroney. He returned to the stale account of what the initials "B.M." stood for, repeating the claim that Frank Moores had said the "account was actually opened for his wife Beth Moores (B.M.)." In fact it was Mathias himself, three and a half years earlier, who had quoted Moores saying the opposite: "Moores said news stories that the account was opened for her [Beth Moores's] benefit are not correct." Mathias rounded off his second story by quoting Schreiber again, this time complaining about the cost of the RCMP investigation.

The following day the *National Post* ran an editorial condemning the RCMP and defending Schreiber. "Mr. Mulroney was not the only victim of the Canadian government's slander," thundered the editorial.

"Karlheinz Schreiber, the financier, was also tarred as a crook in the infamous letter. He has now launched two lawsuits, both winding their way through the Canadian courts. One asks that the letter of request be withdrawn and that the Swiss be informed of its falsehoods. The other seeks $35 million in damages for libel ... Meanwhile, Mr. Schreiber has been prevented from accessing his personal bank accounts, frozen since 1995 by Swiss authorities relying on discredited accusations made by overreaching Canadian bureaucrats." (The *National Post* would not have known that Schreiber had long before moved his funds into Liechtenstein.) Then, on April 3, 1999, Frank Moores rose up in an interview with Bob Fife, again for the *National Post*, to accuse the RCMP of being out to get Brian Mulroney.

What was the catalyst for this flurry of anti-RCMP, pro-Schreiber stories in the *National Post* in the spring of 1999? Doubtless the journalists and editorial writers truly believed in their arguments. Still, the timing could not have been better for Schreiber. The German authorities were now combing through every detail of his bank records; he did not need the RCMP poring over them as well. A little negative publicity against the RCMP would not hurt. Schreiber could not order up the desired newspaper coverage, but he was a convincing salesman, and he had an attentive audience among certain reporters.

In Germany, events were unfolding quickly. On April 22, an Augsburg court had issued an arrest warrant for Winfried Haastert, now the chairman of Thyssen Henschel, relating to irregularities in the Saudi tank deal. In the formalized wording of the warrant, he was accused of not fulfilling his obligations to his employer and of not acting in their financial interests. "Of the DM24.4 million commission, Haastert received three payments of DM1.2 million, DM170,000 and DM120,000," the arrest warrant charged.

"The goal of passing the money through ATG and then through the 'Winter' account was mainly to hide the commission from the financial authorities. Haastert did not declare this taxable income and paid too little income tax. By including ATG (based in Panama) it became possible for Haastert to aid Schreiber in hiding the 24.4 million DM commission and building his convoluted 'house of lies', that the financial authorities could not see through. He therefore supported

Schreiber in hiding receipt of the commission and in tax evasion."

The warrant also accused him of accepting C$500,000 for the Bear Head project and using the money to buy an apartment in Lugano. Jürgen Massmann was arrested on similar charges on the day of Hillinger's funeral.

When Haastert and Massmann were arrested, the alarm went up among the others who had profited from the tank deal. Pfahls was now running the Daimler-Chrysler operations in the Far East out of Singapore. On May 4, he signed a letter at the German Embassy in Singapore, giving his family authority to sell the house in Tegernsee. He knew an arrest warrant had been prepared for him, and he made arrangements to disappear. This was exactly what the Augsburg authorities had feared; a man with his connections would be sure to receive advance warning. According to *Die Zeit*, the prosecutors had tried to keep his warrant secret by not using their computers in his case and by sending the document only to carefully selected police stations. The Munich headquarters was not informed. But word leaked out, and when Hermann Froschauer, the general prosecutor in Munich, learned of the arrest warrant on April 28, he ordered it cancelled. Winfried Maier, who became one of the team leaders after Hillinger's death, was outraged and demanded the directive in writing. Froschauer did not back down and insisted on examining the case.

The warrant was reinstated a few days later, but Pfahls made good use of the delay. On May 6 or 7, he fled from Singapore to Taiwan, which has no extradition treaty with Germany. Although the prosecutors were able to contact him there and he led them to believe he would return to Germany to face arrest, he made other plans. On May 17, 1999, through a company called Fantasy Tours, he booked a ticket for May 19 from Taipei to Munich via Hong Kong. On May 18, the booking was cancelled when his Visa card number was declined. Worried, the people at Fantasy Tours were concerned enough to call him but couldn't get him on the phone. They were told he was ill. He was reportedly seen at the Hong Kong airport, where he bought seven tickets in seven different names to seven different destinations.

On June 2, 1999, a Dr. Shaw in Taiwan confirmed Pfahls's illness in writing, saying Pfahls was unfit to travel. "Right side limbs, numbness and headache," he wrote in a report given to the Augsburg investigators. Pfahls's condition seemed to worsen. "This patient was admitted again with strong symptoms of dizziness and insufficient supply of some parts of brain," Dr. Shaw noted in broken English. "We strongly recommend he needs long term treatment, avoiding all kinds of excitement and traveling for at least three months."

Officials followed one false trail after another, from Taiwan to Zurich to Singapore to Bali, but could not confirm his whereabouts.

Pfahls wasn't the only one who had panicked when Massmann and Haastert were arrested. Schreiber, too, knew that he was in danger and suspected that his own arrest warrant for tax evasion would soon be broadened to include other criminal charges. The Swiss had given the Germans his banking records. He was not a citizen of Switzerland, and Swiss authorities wouldn't hesitate to cooperate with an extradition to Germany. He, too, had to prepare to run. He called Elmer MacKay, a man he knew he could trust and rely upon.

On May 7, MacKay flew to Zurich with two first-class tickets and brought his friend back to Canada the following day. As soon as they could arrange it, they brought Barbel over as well. The story for the world to know, once he surfaced in Canada, was that Karlheinz Schreiber was now in the spaghetti machine business and looking for new investors.

20

Cat on a Cage

In the aftermath of Jörg Hillinger's fatal car accident, no one outside the Augsburg investigative team knew quite what to expect from those who would succeed him. That the investigation had advanced so far was due largely to Hillinger's single-minded determination. Now the eccentric prosecutor was dead, replaced by his deputy, Reinhard Nemetz, who had survived a serious car crash of his own, leaving him with a permanent limp and a glass eye. These disabilities demanded a mental toughness that Nemetz's professional life would test to the limit, but fortunately he was not alone. Winfried Maier, who reported to Nemetz, provided crucial support and showed equal tenacity. Maier had been introduced to the Schreiber file in 1996, and by the summer of 1999 he had an almost encyclopedic knowledge of the case.

On June 22, Schreiber's lawyer Erich Samson approached Nemetz to try to cut a deal for his client. An Augsburg memo dated June 23, 1999, states that Samson knew that if Schreiber were charged and convicted, he could face a prison term of six to eight years. Such a long sentence was completely unacceptable to his client, Samson told Nemetz, but Schreiber did not want to live as a fugitive either. What would Schreiber have to do to avoid prison time? Samson suggested that in exchange for cooperating fully with the investigators, Schreiber would accept a sentence of two years less a day, a sentence that in practical terms meant he would not go to jail. No deal, said Nemetz. Schreiber could not escape a prosecution that could lead to a prison sentence.

The tax investigators on the case signalled their resolve that same month when, over the signature of a senior Finance Ministry official in Bonn, they sent a comprehensive letter of request to Ottawa, this time hoping its revised wording would satisfy the Canadian authorities. In correspondence addressed to Eugene Kucher, a lawyer at Revenue Canada, they asked again for searches to be conducted at Schreiber's condominium in Ottawa, his businesses in Alberta, and his accountant's office in Calgary. They requested that interviews be conducted with Frank Moores, Fred Doucet, and Erika Lutz, raising the same questions that Hillinger had proposed months earlier.

There were routine queries concerning names, ages, professions, and residences, followed by requests for information concerning how long the three had known Schreiber and whether they were related to him in any way. In the case of Fred Doucet, the next questions were about the invoices he had submitted to Schreiber's shell companies: one to Bitucan on November 2, 1988, for $90,000 and another to Merkur Handels for $30,000 on January 29, 1991. For what actual services were these invoices issued, the German investigators wanted to know. Who placed the order with you? Are there written documents? Can we get copies? Who are the people responsible for these companies and do you know them? What else do you know?

For Moores, the list was considerably longer. Again the prosecutors asked about invoices to Bitucan and Merkur Handels. Why did you switch your invoice from Bitucan to Merkur in May 1989? With whom did you agree that the invoice would be paid not by Bitucan but by Merkur instead? Why did Merkur order a payment for you on May 22, 1989, when your invoice didn't arrive until June 8, 1989?

They were interested in the alleged C$1-million loan from Thyssen, via Schreiber, on March 12, 1992: what was the money for, and do you have any paper records of it or any details of repayment? What about the C$746,000 that came into your personal account 34107 from 1986 through 1992? Again, who was the source of this money?

What companies hired you? Were any of the payments from IAL?

Finally the prosecutors asked about two other, seemingly unrelated companies. One was Port Atlantis, a company with which Moores had been associated years earlier. In 1982, Schreiber had purchased land in Newfoundland from Birchpoint Investments; Birchpoint also sold land to Port Atlantis. The second was the German explosives manufacturer Buck Werke GmbH & Co. In which projects was Moores involved, they wanted to know. Who hired you? Who paid you? What did you do? Are there any written documents in this respect?

The Germans' questions for Erika Lutz were related to her bookkeeping procedures for Bitucan. What can you tell us about its contracts? Who made out the invoices? Who gave instructions on the contents of the invoices? Did Bitucan send backdated invoices to Merkur? If so, who gave the orders? Could you explain your notes on these invoices? What did you know about GCI's $250,000 invoice to Bitucan in 1988 and about the $90,000 each billed by Fred and Gerry Doucet, Gary Ouellet, and Frank Moores? Do you have information about Schreiber's sale of Bitucan in 1995? Why did you transmit Bitucan's account balance to Karlheinz Schreiber on March 31, 1995, even after the sale of the company, and why did you ask him for instructions on how to handle the invoices due for payment?

In Canada word began to spread that Schreiber had left Switzerland. The satirical magazine *Frank* reported unconfirmed Schreiber sightings in Montreal and Ottawa. The rumour in Tory circles was that the Schreibers had to get out of Switzerland fast and that Elmer MacKay had come to their aid.

In August, the Tory caucus met in St. John's, Newfoundland, and Elmer's son Peter was among the media favourites. A Tory member of Parliament representing the constituency his father once held, he was the party's House leader. (Joe Clark, who was once again the leader of the Progressive Conservative Party, had so far failed to find a seat in the Commons for himself.) MacKay knew Schreiber well after spending several months working at Thyssen Industrie in Germany, and he may have been aware that Jürgen Massmann and Winfried Haastert had been arrested and briefly jailed that summer while his father offered hospitality to the Schreibers in Nova Scotia.

Interviewed by the *Toronto Star*'s Edison Stewart during the caucus get-together, MacKay took the opportunity to weigh in on the subject of the Airbus investigation. It was scandalous, he declared, that the RCMP was still pursuing Mulroney and the Airbus affair. The Liberal government was behind the investigation in Canada, he claimed, going on to name Prime Minister Jean Chrétien as the architect of the plan.

"I'm told, from people that I think are within the know, that they have not only consistently been investigating but they have actually increased it in the last six months," MacKay told Stewart. "They are combing over documents in the archives. They are trying to interview more people. I think the Prime Minister is battling shadows and it is a narcissist chasing his nemesis. He is very, very concerned that Mr. Mulroney has rehabilitated his reputation almost entirely and is going to continue to do so." Luc Lavoie also spoke to Stewart, telling him it was outrageous that Swiss officials continued to work under the assumption that Mulroney was suspected of corruption. Lavoie said it all proved that the letter, for which Mulroney received an apology, had not been withdrawn. Mulroney was thinking very seriously of suing the government again, Lavoie added.

A few days after the *Star* story appeared, Lavoie gave another interview, this time to Phil Mathias at the *National Post*. Lavoie, speaking on behalf of Mulroney, disclosed that his client had been trying to persuade Schreiber to release his banking records. "This week," reported Mathias, "Mr. Mulroney telephoned his former chief of staff, Fred Doucet, from South Africa, where the former prime minister is vacationing with his family, and asked him to organize another approach to Mr. Schreiber. Mr. Doucet persuaded a former cabinet minister [possibly Elmer MacKay] in Mr. Mulroney's government, a man who knew Mr. Schreiber, to telephone him on Mr. Mulroney's behalf and ask that the documents be released."

"Nothing would make Mr. Mulroney happier than to have these documents opened up so that his innocence would be clear forever," Lavoie told Mathias. Schreiber refused point-blank. "I don't want to release the documents," he told the *National Post*, "because the whole procedure by the Canadian government is illegal, and I want to see them in court to prove this." This exchange was beside the point; the bank records had already been released to the German investigators.

While supporters for Schreiber and Mulroney tried to persuade journalists that the RCMP should end its long investigation or, at the very least, drop Mulroney's name from the letter of request to Switzerland, Schreiber himself suffered a legal setback. On August 30, 1999, in Canada's Federal Court, Justice Andrew MacKay dismissed the latest of Schreiber's appeals against the RCMP's efforts to see his Swiss banking records. MacKay had reviewed the legal wrangles sparked by Kimberly Prost's original letter to Swiss authorities five years earlier, as well as the Supreme Court of Canada's May 1998 decision against Schreiber and the applications MacKay himself had heard in April and July of 1999. The government had every right to send the letter, concluded MacKay. While he agreed that "some language in the Request wrongly indicated that the RCMP had concluded that criminal activities occurred . . . it is not an acknowledgement that the facts alleged in the request are without foundation. Indeed, the apology to the applicant expressly noted that 'the RCMP investigation in this matter continues' and the settlement agreement with the former Prime Minister affirmed that investigation of allegations of illegality would continue, and that the RCMP and the Department of Justice had acted within their responsibilities in sending the request."

During these summer months, the investigators in Germany didn't know Schreiber's whereabouts, only that he was no longer living in Pontresina. It was not until late August that they were able to follow telephone records to a cellphone in Toronto. It was Phil Mathias's good fortune that he was having coffee with Schreiber at the Westin Prince Hotel on August 31, the day after MacKay's judgment came down, when the RCMP moved in to make the arrest. The reporter had a front-row seat for the apprehension of a man who had eluded German authorities for three years.

In a document dated September 3 and later filed in court, Augsburg asked the RCMP for help in tracing Schreiber's cellphone calls. They suspected he had been in touch with Holger Pfahls, who was still on the run in Asia. Pfahls and Schreiber had spoken regularly by phone until Schreiber fled Pontresina in May. The Germans hoped for information concerning any calls between them from mid-May to late August, details that might reveal Pfahls's location. The Mounties, who were tapping Schreiber's phones as his bail conditions required, complied.

At the same time the Germans asked the Canadians to do a "body search of the suspect" to find and secure his computer notebook, a standard notebook, and his cellphone. The RCMP had seized these items at the time of Schreiber's arrest and had returned them during his bail hearing in the first week of September. On October 28, the German Embassy renewed Augsburg's request for the same items, a search that would have to be conducted during one of Schreiber's mandatory appearances before the RCMP during the bail period.

In late September 1999, Erich Samson gave an interview to the CBC's *the fifth estate*. Samson repeated the contention that the commissions Schreiber had collected on the Air Canada and Thyssen deals were just *Schmiergelder*, but even he didn't know who had received the money.

"As has been said all along, Schreiber will not name the recipients and has not named them to me so that I cannot give an answer as to who it is," he told the CBC. Samson added that the Airbus contract with Air Canada was of such magnitude that one had to be naive to think Airbus would not pay commissions. "I am speaking of the sale of Airbus planes to Canada but not only that – also of the entry into the North American market ... No person with half a brain could believe it to be possible without the passing on of a commission."

Why wouldn't Schreiber name the recipients? "Schreiber is asked over and over about who he passed these monies to," Samson said. "He could name names but it does him no good whatsoever, as no receipts are given for such payments and he could never prove who got the money ... He will not name the Canadians that received money."

Samson took the opportunity to draw some fine lines around the term *Schmiergelder*, saying that the expression was being used loosely by his client's legal team. "Um ... the term 'grease money' carries very bad connotations in the German language," he said uncomfortably. "It always refers to something forbidden. That need not be the case. What is being dealt with is the payment for mediation or brokerage accomplishments to other persons who have set up contacts and provided access to important decision-makers and who want to be paid for their efforts. Those are the commissions. 'Grease money' is actually a term that we use for the bribery of officials or public servants."

Samson suggested Schreiber would never identify those he had paid; to do so would end his successful career as a middleman. What the lawyer did confirm in this interview, however, was that his client had indeed paid secret commissions to Canadians on the Air Canada contract.

Schreiber may have been unwilling to say more, but his Zurich bank accounts would offer important clues. In the fall of 1999, *the fifth estate* became the first media organization to obtain access to Schreiber's Zurich account 18679 and to the details of hundreds of banking transactions between the mid-1980s and the mid-1990s, including those of the coded subaccounts for Holgart, Winter, Jürglund, Frankfurt, Marc, Fred, and Britan, plus Gary Ouellet's account. Some transactions involved as little as $5,000; others were for more than a million dollars. Sometimes funds were transferred to unidentified accounts; at other times they were withdrawn in cash. When contacted by *the fifth estate*, Marc Lalonde and Fred Doucet said they had no knowledge of any such accounts in their names. Frank Moores and Gary Ouellet did not return phone calls.

The CBC journalists painstakingly assembled detailed chronologies and covered an office wall with the documents, connecting transactions with string and thumbtacks. Patterns emerged that fit the Liechtenstein banking records Pelossi had revealed in 1994. There were still mysteries but the picture had become clearer. Clearer – yet also more problematic.

The code name Britan was the only one the authorities in Germany had not publicly connected to a particular individual. The Britan subaccount was in Canadian funds – as were those assigned to Fred, Frankfurt, and Marc (the Maxwell account was also in Canadian funds, though no withdrawals appeared for this account) – and Schreiber's coding system was not difficult to interpret.

If there was a chance Britan stood for Brian Mulroney, then the show's producers would have to contact the former prime minister. On October 8, 1999, they faxed Mulroney a letter asking for an interview based on new information. Lavoie replied immediately but wanted to know more before he would set up an interview.

"Can I ask you a couple of things? Does his [Mulroney's] name appear in any document that you have seen, showing that he has received money from anybody? And if so, what kind of money are we talking about?" Lavoie asked Harvey Cashore.

Cashore hesitated.

"His name or a code name?" Lavoie prompted. When Cashore allowed that Lavoie was smart to have asked that question, Lavoie persisted, "So there is a code name that looks like him?... It sounds like his name, it spells like his name?"

"It is very close to," conceded Cashore.

Lavoie couldn't contain his frustration; he told Cashore that they believed Schreiber was not to be trusted. Lavoie suggested that Pelossi may have been telling the truth when he told police officers and journalists that Schreiber said that he was planning to pay off Mulroney. "Why is it that Pelossi was saying what he was saying?" Lavoie said. "I don't know this Pelossi guy. And even if I knew him it wouldn't change my mind, he probably didn't make up the entire thing he said... He might have not made it up."

Lavoie had a possible explanation. "It could be somebody that was trying to convince somebody else that he needed money for a third party, which might have been a head of state or a government. Therefore getting more money for himself. It could be that. We don't know that. And I want to be very careful here. We do not know that. But if ever there is the name of Brian Mulroney anywhere it has to be that. Because there never was any money. And to think otherwise is really to not know Mulroney. He is too smart to do something like that." The coded subaccount might have been part of Schreiber's strategy to persuade Airbus executives and German tax officials that he had paid off Mulroney – when he hadn't.

Lavoie's outburst showed where the Mulroney camp's thinking was headed if indeed Schreiber was linking Mulroney to the accounts. The man Mulroney had praised in his examination for discovery for his energetic entrepreneurship and sound advice about German reunification was now portrayed as someone who might have had another agenda altogether, if he was actually suggesting that an account had been set up for Mulroney.

On Monday, October 18, 1999, two days before *the fifth estate*'s broadcast on the Schreiber affair, Guylaine Saucier, the chairperson of the CBC's board of directors, received a letter from Mulroney's lawyer. It said that Mulroney had no involvement of any kind in the Airbus deal, and it made an unprecedented threat: Mulroney would sue every member of the CBC's board of directors if he thought the documentary was defamatory. The contents of the letter were leaked to Mathias at the *National Post;* it appeared the day the program was scheduled to air. *The fifth estate*'s broadcast went ahead as planned on October 20. Mulroney did not sue, but Schreiber did, bringing a claim of defamation against *the fifth estate* and another, later, against Luc Lavoie.

Since leaving politics in 1992, Walther Leisler Kiep had devoted his energies to boosting German business abroad and to literary pursuits. He had written books about business and economics, and in the fall of 1999 he was promoting the recent publication of his political memoirs, *Was bleibt, ist grosse Zuversicht* (At the End, There Is Optimism). On the evening of November 4, he was driving his Mercedes to a gathering of the Baden-Württemberg Automobile Club in Stuttgart when his wife, Charlotte, called him on his car phone. The police are here, she said nervously, and they want to talk to you.

Kiep had known since 1996 that the Augsburg prosecutors had targeted him in the Schreiber investigation. He'd had more than three years to think about what he would do if they ever knocked on his door. He drove on to his speaking engagement and enjoyed a pleasant time with the members. Returning home later that night, he saw a police car parked in his driveway, two officers waiting inside. Kiep turned around without being seen, then drove to a borrowed apartment in Frankfurt for the night. The next day, Kiep and his lawyer convinced the prosecutors to suspend his arrest warrant in return for a personal bond of DM500,000.

The prosecutors' warrant alleged that Kiep, along with the CDU money manager Horst Weyrauch, met Schreiber on August 26, 1991, in a pizzeria in a shopping centre in the Swiss town of St. Margarethen.

After a brief discussion, the men moved outside to the parking lot, and there Schreiber handed over a small suitcase containing DM1 million in cash. Maier's staff had matched Schreiber's bank records with other documents, including entries in Schreiber's diaries, to establish that Schreiber had made the payment to Kiep. Once they had tracked the trail of the money to its final recipients and had analyzed the travel records of those involved – just as they had done with Massmann, Haastert, and Pfahls – they issued the warrant for Kiep's arrest.

Kiep electrified his fellow Germans with a blunt admission that he had taken the cash from Schreiber. Almost casually, he explained it away as a donation to the CDU, when it was headed by former chancellor Helmut Kohl. But the CDU couldn't find any record of such a donation. Within days Kohl himself was under fire; the law stated clearly that any donation over DM20,000 had to be publicly disclosed. Was the money for some other purpose, the press speculated, perhaps a bribe? Then another sensational fact became public: the sale of Fuchs armoured vehicles to Saudi Arabia during the Gulf War had been worth US$446 million; of that amount, nearly half – $220 million – was distributed as kickbacks and secret commissions. Much of that money, it seems, went to Saudi power-brokers. Did Thyssen also pay millions to German politicians and bureaucrats to win the export permit that made the deal possible?

At age sixty-nine, Kohl was serving as honorary chairman of the CDU, the respected father figure of his party. On November 8, he denied any knowledge of Schreiber's payment to Kiep and stated that other CDU leaders, including his successor, Wolfgang Schäuble, were likewise unaware of the donation. When one reporter pushed for more answers, Kohl lost his temper. "You are trying to make a scandal of this ... I can see it in your face," he snapped. "Get out of my sight."

The controversy could not have come at a worse time. The next day, November 9, was the tenth anniversary of the fall of the Berlin Wall, the event that marked the beginning of the reunification of East and West Germany and the greatest achievement of Kohl's career as chancellor. This historic anniversary was intended to celebrate his status as the hero of a unified Germany; instead, the slush fund crisis poisoned the festivities. Every day brought new revelations that were angrily denied by Kohl. "False and libellous," he retorted as the newspapers printed rumours about the tank deal and allegations that his party had accepted illegal, hidden donations from many sources. On November 21, in an interview with *Die Welt,* he dismissed what he called "insinuations" that the deal was corrupt, explaining that his government had allowed the tank export "exclusively" on foreign policy and security grounds, in consultation with Germany's NATO partners. But just as Kohl was fending off that story, *Der Spiegel* published a report on November 22 claiming that the CDU had also received undeclared donations from the Quelle mail-order company and the Merck chemical company.

By the end of November, a parliamentary inquiry had been called to investigate the allegations. Its members broadened their mandate to look into possible ties between a number of private companies and donations to the CDU. They intended to examine the sale of Airbus aircraft to Canada and Thailand, the sale of helicopters to Canada, the Thyssen Bear Head project, and the takeover of the Leuna oil refinery by the French oil company Elf Aquitaine, as well as the Saudi tank deal. There were news stories that Elf may have artificially inflated the costs of the refinery by FF256 million in order to funnel money to the CDU through companies controlled by Dieter Holzer – and that both Kiep and Pfahls were involved.

Despite outraged denials from Kohl, a picture came into focus of a right-wing government working closely with appreciative business partners over many years. Police raided several addresses in Bavaria, looking for evidence of hidden accounts that had been described to them by Heiner Geissler, general secretary of Kohl's CDU until 1989. Geissler, uncharacteristically loquacious, told reporters he could talk "for hours" about secret slush funds, adding that "former party chairman Helmut Kohl was interested in the origins of donations far less than one million marks." Geissler told reporters that he had frequently argued with Kohl about the secret accounts, and that Kohl knew everything there was to know about them.

In late 1999, German police had proof of a dozen different Swiss bank accounts used by the Christian Democrats to accept illegal payments, many of them opened at the Vontobel Bank in Zurich in the

1980s under the supervision of Kohl's trusted financial counsellor Horst Weyrauch. In one case, it was discovered that CDU officials had disguised the source of illicit donations to the party from bank accounts outside Germany by claiming they were bequests from Jewish emigrants. Mutterings about the infamous "reptile funds" set up by former chancellor Konrad Adenauer filtered through Europe. As the *Independent*'s Berlin correspondent, Imre Karacs, described it, "the latest revelations from Helmut Kohl's laundry suggest his dirty money was but small change from a vast Cold War slush fund set up to bankroll West-oriented parties around the world."

As Karacs reminded his readers, Adenauer, a forceful crusader against Communism and the leader of the CDU in the early 1950s, had established a front organization called the Civic Association to raise money, primarily from business and industry, to support anti-Communist governments in Europe. The funds were kept separate from the party's publicly declared accounts, out of sight in Swiss banks. In 1974, after U.S. secretary of state Henry Kissinger warned the West that the Communists were gaining strength in Portugal and Spain, four German leaders – Willy Brandt, Hans-Dietrich Genscher, Franz Josef Strauss, and Helmut Kohl – reorganized the system under a new name, Operation Octopus. Germany's BND supervised the collection and distribution of the funds. "At least once a month," Karacs wrote, "a BND car would pull up in front of the chancellery in Bonn. The courier was always a BND official, and often its president, Gerhard Wessel. He would hand over a suitcase of cash to a chancellery official."

The money would then go to officials of the CDU and its Bavarian wing, the CSU; they in turn made sure it went to their allies abroad. Some found its way to Central and South America; some, via the Hanns-Seidel-Stiftung, ended up in Costa Rica. In 1983 Kohl transferred the administration of the system from the BND to the Foreign Ministry, but Horst Weyrauch continued as its manager and courier, making almost weekly trips between Bonn and the CDU's bank in Zurich. At the federal party level, it was Kiep who managed the Octopus cash. Kiep's network was formidable. In Canada, for example, he was a member of the board of the Bank of Montreal; in Germany, he was the chairman of Atlantik-Brücke, of which Schreiber and Dieter Holzer were also members.

But Kohl's network was just as large and influential. As a young politician, Kohl had courted powerful businessmen; his principal mentor had been Fritz Ries, a German industrialist and former Nazi who helped Kohl become an adviser to Germany's pharmaceutical and chemical conglomerates. Ries had made his own fortune by taking over expropriated Jewish companies during the war; his chief legal adviser was another notorious Nazi, Eberhard Taubert, who had worked for Joseph Goebbels's Propaganda Ministry. After the war, both men were welcomed into the new business elite of West Germany, and both prospered. "While we may never know the full extent of the current slush-fund scandal," wrote the American journalist Martin Lee, an expert on the post-war activities of German Nazis, "it should serve as a reminder of how closely the Nazi era lies beneath German politics."

On November 28, Kohl's successor as party leader, Wolfgang Schäuble, promised that the CDU would clear up the funding affair quickly and thoroughly. Two days later, following an emergency meeting of the CDU executive, Kohl, humiliated and sullen, capitulated. Yes, he confessed in a terse statement on November 30, he did run secret party bank accounts during his years as chancellor, but he insisted there were no illicit funds involved. He rejected any suggestion that he had enriched himself or sold state favours. While Kohl took responsibility for what had happened, he maintained that "confidential treatment" was necessary for some party finances. "Having separate accounts from the usual accounts under the national party treasury seemed justifiable to me."

Although Schäuble had distanced himself from Kohl and there were reports of longstanding differences between the two men, he dutifully came to Kohl's defence. The CDU's last secret account had been closed a year earlier when the party lost the federal election, he claimed, but he was careful to add that he had known nothing about the funds or their distribution under Kohl. Such comments were discounted by the German public. Opinion polls showed the majority of Germans didn't believe their former chancellor. "A whiff of corruption is wafting across the land," said the weekly *Die Woche*. "The cracks in the Kohl monument are getting bigger day by day."

"We have not had a full explanation," said Volker Neumann, chairman of the parliamentary commission investigating the scandal. "Where did the money come from? How much was there? Was this money used to influence political decisions?"

On December 2, when the Bundestag formally opened its inquiry, Schäuble told his fellow politicians that he had met Schreiber in 1994, but he made no mention of taking donations from him. It was at this point that Schreiber himself joined the fray. Furious to find his old friends backing away from him, he was quick to correct the record. He'd had contacts with many CDU figures over the years, he told a reporter for *Die Welt*, including Schäuble, former defence minister Volker Rühe, and Edmund Stoiber, the premier of Bavaria.

"It simply does not correspond with the facts," he said tersely, "if, on the CDU and CSU side, one pretends today to have had nothing to do with 'that Schreiber,' and that only Mr. Kiep was involved."

By December 5, 1999, Horst Weyrauch, usually reclusive, was giving interviews about his role in Operation Octopus and about the money Kiep had taken from Schreiber in St. Margarethen. "I deposited it into an account at the Hauck Bank," Weyrauch told *Bild*, Germany's largest newspaper, "in three different deposits on the advice of the bank so that the amount of one million Deutschmarks would not appear." Part of the money, he explained, went to pay Kiep's fines for an old tax matter; the rest was divided between himself and Uwe Lüthje as bonuses for their service to the party.

Germans soon learned that the CDU had had seventeen secret bank accounts in the Hauck Bank in Frankfurt alone, along with five regular accounts. In a television interview on December 16, Kohl made an unapologetic admission that he had accepted secret cash donations worth up to DM2 million during the 1990s and that this illegal "black money," as it was called, went to finance CDU branches in the former East Germany. Who gave him the money? He refused to say. On December 18, there came the revelation that important federal government documents concerning the sale of the Leuna oil refinery to Elf Aquitaine had disappeared. The month ended with prosecutors announcing a criminal investigation into Helmut Kohl's activities.

A few supporters rallied; on New Year's Eve, a 200-member civic association raised just over DM25,000 to help Kohl pay his legal costs, but other Germans – including many of his own party colleagues – were less forgiving. The CDU set aside DM8 million to cover the fines the party expected to be charged as a result of Kohl's blatant breach of the law. It was a time of acrimony and finger-pointing; even Max Strauss grew testy when *Bunte* interviewed him about his mentor Schreiber. "He should be put in jail and at best should just shut his mouth," he opined.

If Wolfgang Schäuble expected to escape the scandal's spreading stain by distancing himself from Kohl, he was mistaken. On January 10, 2000, Schäuble admitted he had met Schreiber at a CDU fundraising event in 1994 and later accepted a DM100,000 cash donation from him, which he passed on to the CDU without it being properly declared. When he tried to shift responsibility for his actions onto the shoulders of Brigitte Baumeister, the party's former treasurer, she refused to accept it.

The following day Schäuble rejected calls to resign as leader of the CDU: "I have nothing to hide," he said. But he wasn't prepared for Schreiber's mischief-making back in Canada. On January 12, the *Globe and Mail* published a story by Stan Oziewicz and Alan Freeman in which Schreiber stated firmly that he had lobbied Schäuble in Bonn in September 1994 about the Bear Head project – a day or two after pledging a large donation to him at a fundraising dinner. Schreiber told the reporters he had been pushing the Liberal government in Ottawa to revive the project and had tried hard to get in on the G-7 Summit when Kohl met Jean Chrétien in Halifax in 1995. But Schreiber maintained that the donation and the Bear Head project were not related. "The two things had nothing to do with each other."

That wasn't what German journalists reported. Oziewicz and Freeman discovered an interview with *Die Welt* published a day before their *Globe* story in which Schreiber said the money was indeed tied to Bear Head. In that interview, the *Globe* reported, "he said he was looking for German political support for the Cape Breton contract and that 'implementation of this important project' was behind all his political contacts with both the Christian Democrats and the Social Democrats."

Schreiber's declarations in *Die Welt* that the cash he gave Schäuble was intended to encourage government support for a Thyssen military plant in Canada created another sensation in Europe; Schäuble denied the story vehemently. On January 13, the *Daily Mail* summed up the situation succinctly: "The crisis engulfing Germany's Christian Democrat party worsened yesterday when a fugitive arms dealer said party leader Wolfgang Schäuble knowingly accepted a [DM100,000] bribe. Karlheinz Schreiber was head of the Bear Head arm of the German industrial giant Thyssen when he made the payment to the party. He said the cash was clearly to obtain the influence of the government, then headed by Helmut Kohl, in securing a contract to set up a tank parts plant in Canada."

The following day, former interior minister Manfred Kanther, who had served in Kohl's government from 1993 to 1998, admitted that during his term as CDU chief in Hesse state in the 1980s, the party had stashed over DM7 million abroad. Some DM13 million was later transferred back to Germany as anonymous bequests without being declared in the party's accounts. Kohl, Schäuble, and other key witnesses were summoned to appear before the parliamentary inquiry. *Bild*'s headline was typical of public reaction: "CDU – money laundering like the Mafia."

Schäuble was booed and heckled at a CDU campaign rally, but Kohl was finished. By January 18, the pressure to resign as honorary chairman of the CDU was enormous and, in the end, he was given no choice; his party told him he had to step down unless he named the party's anonymous donors. Kohl resigned, angrily defending his silence to the end. "In my whole life, I have never given up my honour and I will not do this today either," he said. "I am fighting for my honour and part of this battle is that I will stick to the word I have given."

Accusations, revelations, and unexpected twists were becoming daily occurrences, but the most dramatic episode of the affair came the day after Kohl made these defiant remarks. Wolfgang Hüllen, the budget director of the CDU parliamentary group, lived in a small one-room apartment in Berlin during the work week. On January 20, he called his wife at their suburban Bonn home at 7 a.m. Hüllen told her he'd call again at 8; when he didn't phone, she tried to reach him. At 9 she checked his office to see if he had called in sick; by 11 she was frantic and contacted the police. Forty minutes later the police broke into Hüllen's apartment to find his body hanging in the bathroom and two suicide notes nearby.

When news of his death reached the halls of government, all proceedings in the Reichstag came to a halt. By the end of the day, some reporters were saying Hüllen had been under investigation by the parliamentary commission of inquiry, but a senior CDU official said Hüllen's suicide notes gave personal reasons. Roger Boyes of the London *Times* reported, "The sudden, solitary death of Wolfgang Hüllen [has] sent German politicians into a frenzy, deeply uncertain as to how the corruption scandal, known as Kohlgate, will end. The German flag flew at half mast over the Reichstag yesterday, and in the parliament building grim-faced deputies who have been snapping at one another for a fortnight were shaking hands and exchanging tense greetings: the political class regards Kohlgate as a crisis of the State rather than merely a body blow to the CDU."

Although homicide police were called in, the suicide letters – one to his wife and one to the CDU leadership – convinced most people that Hüllen, fearful that he would be made the scapegoat for the affair, had taken his own life.

Most politicians believe that they can ride out even the worst scandals; they know that bad press lingers in print for little more than two weeks, while television has an attention span of roughly three days for even the most salacious stories. "Kohlgate" was different, dominating news reports and public life in Germany for months. After Hüllen's suicide came the information that the government of the late French president François Mitterrand had helped encourage Germany's acceptance of the European single currency by contributing up to FF85 million to Kohl's 1994 election campaign. That was followed by a story out of London that the Augsburg prosecutors had named the former Airbus executive Stuart Iddles as the recipient of at least US$2.8 million in kickbacks from Schreiber on the Canadian Airbus sale. Then, when Schreiber's dealings with Werner Ströhlein in Costa

Rica and Dieter Holzer's role in the Elf Aquitaine matter surfaced publicly – along with the fact that both men had been working for the BND – the connections between Germany's intelligence community and the CDU's finance system were exposed.

The CDU's popularity had evaporated, and in a by-election held on January 30, it lost a seat in the former East Germany that it had held since reunification. Horst Weyrauch, fed up with being targeted as one of the architects of the scandal, resigned as financial adviser to the CDU.

Losing Weyrauch proved to be more catastrophic than losing the election. Party officials had grilled the unhappy money manager for more than six hours at the end of January, and what he had to say quickly became public. The "black accounts" went back to 1971, he'd admitted; the party's branch in Hesse state held about DM20 million, which was now in a Swiss bank – at least DM2 million more than party leaders had so far acknowledged – and there were other accounts in Switzerland and Liechtenstein. Scores of party donations between DM20,000 and DM40,000 had never been entered into CDU books.

It was at this time as well that Germans began to understand just how much money had gone to Schreiber and Dieter Holzer for their work on the Saudi tank and Elf Leuna projects. At least DM140 million in total, according to the prosecutors – maybe more. But getting to the bottom of it all was impossible. Three-quarters of the government's files dealing with the tank sale, the Elf takeover, and the Bear Head project were missing from the chancellery offices. Vast numbers of other sensitive files on privatization deals and arms exports during the Kohl years were not to be found either.

"This is a catastrophe – never before have such important documents vanished without a trace," said Frank Hofmann, the head of the SPD section of the parliamentary commission. Perhaps as a result of this disclosure, the inquiry expanded its frame of reference in an attempt to find out who had donated money to Kohl's secret slush funds. Prosecutors moved quickly to seize what records they could at his offices and those of the CDU.

As far as the CDU was concerned, it could do no more. At a press conference in early February, the CDU's general secretary, Angela Merkel, said she and her colleagues had not been able to identify many of the donors despite the fact, as she put it, that the "cartel of silence" of Kohl's colleagues had been broken. The party intended to launch a lawsuit against its former leader to help meet the fines being levied against it.

Schäuble's reputation was almost as tattered as Kohl's. He was forced to admit that he had met a second time with Schreiber, who had been taking great delight in contradicting the CDU leader from Toronto. Schreiber predicted to the reporter Christian Nitsche that Schäuble would have to resign within the week. In fact it was two weeks. Schäuble took his leave on February 15, a bombshell that almost obscured the latest story: Augsburg prosecutors were now investigating Max Strauss's role in the diversion and laundering of DM400,000 connected to the Elf deal.

As spring approached, Kohl's troubles only multiplied. A story broke that since the late 1970s the Stasi, the notorious East German intelligence agency, had taped hundreds of hours of conversations between Kohl's aides and Kiep, Lüthje, or Weyrauch about illicit donations. Kohl continued to raise money in an attempt to cover the party's fines, but by June the party's debts had ballooned to DM100 million. And although Angela Merkel had won the CDU leadership in March and was bringing disenchanted supporters back into the CDU fold, Kohl himself remained isolated and shunned. When former colleagues trooped through the parliament buildings in Bonn to give their testimony at the inquiry, they took care to avoid their old boss. Even Uwe Lüthje decided it was time to save his own skin. Lüthje testified that he'd told Kohl in 1992 that a Swiss party account holding DM1.5 million was being closed, and that he and Weyrauch had received some of the money as bonuses from Kiep. When Kiep and Kohl denied the story, Lüthje countered with the claim that Kohl had called him months earlier, telling him what to say before the inquiry.

Soon it was Kohl's turn to face the parliamentary inquiry. Well rehearsed and icily contemptuous of his accusers, Kohl mounted a strong counteroffensive, demanding acknowledgment of his "sixteen good, successful years working for Germany." No, he growled, he wouldn't name the secret donors. When asked about a massive shredding of files three weeks before the CDU lost the 1998 election, Kohl shouted, "That's not true!" For the rest, he was forgetful and evasive, especially on the subject of Schreiber. He didn't know him, he said.

Investigators later found Schreiber's business card among those of Kohl's files still remaining. On the back of the card, Kohl had scrawled, "Who is he?" Kohl pointed to the notation as evidence that he was not acquainted with the Bavarian middleman; Schreiber could scarcely have influenced him on the matter of the export permit for Thyssen's tanks. What was more interesting, however, was the fact that the card was found in a collection of 1995 documents about Bear Head. When questioned more carefully, Kohl's answers were convoluted. "If you mean by 'knowing' that the two of us knew each other, then I say yes," Kohl told the befuddled panel of parliamentarians. "I've never consciously seen Herr Schreiber," he added. Nor did he know about Bear Head – a surprising statement given that he was briefed on the project in 1995, just before a visit to Canada for talks with Jean Chrétien and just after Schreiber gave Wolfgang Schäuble DM100,000 in cash as a donation to the party. The contribution was followed up with a letter asking Schäuble to lobby for Schreiber's perennial hobbyhorse.

Aside from Schreiber, the missing player in the party finance drama was Holger Pfahls. That summer, attention shifted from the Saudi tank deal to Elf-Leuna and to news that Pfahls had received DM17 million for "services rendered" on the deal. Swiss officials had turned over records to the German prosecutors with details of the transactions; these showed that the money had been deposited in several large instalments in accounts controlled by Pfahls. How much he kept for himself was not known, but the prosecutors believed most of it was destined for CDU coffers. In September 2000 the *Times* reported that Germany had asked Great Britain's Home Office for assistance in locating Pfahls; it turned out that the former spymaster had been in England in July 1999 with his twenty-seven-year-old British mistress. The Germans had found him the same way they had tracked Schreiber in Canada – through a cellphone. While he was in

London, Pfahls, who should have known better, called his wife, Birgit, in Stuttgart. Her phone was being tapped.

After his arrest at Toronto's Westin Prince Hotel, Schreiber became a minor celebrity in the city, recognized on the street and in expensive boutiques. At breakfast he might be found at the Mövenpick restaurant on Yorkville Avenue in Toronto's most exclusive shopping district. Lunch would be at fashionable restaurants like Biagio's on King Street East; drinks and dinner, at Morton's Steakhouse in the new Hyatt Regency Hotel. (That's where he met Bob Fife to ask if the journalist would like to write his life story. No thanks, said Fife.) When the pianist at the Four Seasons Hotel saw Schreiber enter the bar, he would play the Nat King Cole numbers Schreiber loves. The waiter knew to suggest a bottle of his favourite Orpale champagne. He and Barbara wandered in and out of the designer shops along Bloor Street; Louis Vuitton is next door to their apartment hotel, Chanel and Cartier just steps away. Sometimes, when he got bored, they drove to Ottawa for a day or two at their Rockcliffe Park condominium.

Schreiber made new friends, and none closer than his lawyer Eddie Greenspan. When Greenspan threw a lavish New Year's Eve party to welcome the new millennium, Schreiber, with Barbara at his side, was the guest of honour, a star amidst the horde of judges, journalists, politicians, and executives. Greenspan was thrilled by his guest's notoriety. "Karlheinz, you were the sensation of my party!" the lawyer exclaimed the next day when he called Schreiber to thank him for coming.

Living under bail conditions, with his phones tapped and his passports taken, was restrictive but not crippling. He was able to cultivate his contacts and pursue new opportunities. One favourite haunt was the private lounge of an exclusive bed-and-breakfast in Toronto's Annex neighbourhood, where he often met with others who shared his business interests. Presumably, he and Mövenpick's Hans Reichert continued to tinker with the spaghetti machine to see if they could make it pay. Elmer MacKay dropped in from time to time. Occasionally Schreiber yanked the chains of his Mountie watchers; he was nearly thrown back into custody after police found out he was using a fax machine in violation of his bail conditions. All his phones were supposed to be tapped – including, the police insisted, fax machines.

Fighting on every front, Schreiber instructed Greenspan to sue the Canadian and German governments for wrongful arrest, arguing that he had been wanted only on suspicion of tax evasion when he was picked up and that tax evasion is not an extraditable offence in Canada. He claimed $1 million in compensation for mental distress, loss of liberty, and damage to his reputation, but in February 2001, Ontario's top court ruled he could not sue Germany since it was a "sovereign nation." Greenspan announced he would appeal. At the same time Schreiber continued to wage his $35-million lawsuit against the federal government in an Alberta court over the 1995 letter of request to Switzerland. As for his extradition hearing, it was delayed by a desultory series of legal motions and had yet to formally begin by early March. No substantive evidence had yet been heard.

While Schreiber looked for appeals, delays, and chinks in his enemies' armour, the RCMP kept busy, working quietly behind the scenes. To those who wondered what the RCMP had been doing for nearly five years, the Mounties' explanation was that until they received the records of Schreiber's Swiss bank accounts, they would never be able to complete their investigation. In the fall of 1999, there were at least half a dozen full-time RCMP officers assigned to the file; while awaiting the verdict of the Swiss courts, they were interviewing people all over the globe, from Airbus officials in the United States to Stuart Iddles in Puerto Vallarta to airline executives in Canada. They had been cheered by their victories in court to that point, but they had nothing that could be made public.

On December 8, 1999, Inspector Al Matthews signed an application for a search warrant, seeking permission from the courts to enter two places of business, one in Ontario and another in Alberta. Normally search warrants are public documents, but Matthews and his colleagues asked that the contents of these be sealed. The judge agreed. The Mounties intended to search the premises of Eurocopter Canada, new owners of MBB Helicopter Canada Ltd. in Fort Erie, and of Buchanan Barry, the Calgary accounting firm that audited

Schreiber's books for Bitucan in Alberta.

The RCMP believed that MBB had defrauded the Canadian government by paying secret commissions to Schreiber and to Frank Moores. The contract its Canadian subsidiary, MCL, had signed for the Coast Guard helicopters specifically forbade them. Under a clause titled "No Bribes," the contract specifically disallowed any inducement to decision-makers or any payment of third-party commissions.

The Mounties received permission to retrieve any documents pertaining to the sale of the helicopters, or any documents referring to a long list of individuals, including Frank Moores, Gary Ouellet, Giorgio Pelossi, Ramsey Withers, Karlheinz Schreiber, Helge Wittholz, James Grant, Kurt Pfleiderer, and Heinz Pluckthun, or any documents mentioning Bitucan Holdings, Government Consultants International, IAL, Merkur Handels, or Kensington. There was no suggestion that any person on this list was guilty of a crime, and of course, a search warrant on its own is not proof of criminal activity. No charges had resulted from these searches as of February 2001, but the warrant demonstrated that the RCMP was serious in its intent.

There were two counts. The first said that MBB, Pluckthun, Pfleiderer, and "persons unknown" conspired together to "commit the indictable offences of fraud under section 465 (1) (c) of the Criminal Code by placing the economic interests of Canada at risk." The second count said that the same business and people, "by deceit, falsehood or other fraudulent means," defrauded the government of Canada again by placing the economic interests of the country at risk under section 380 (1) (a) of the Criminal Code.

On February 17, 2000, the Supreme Court of Switzerland finally reached a decision to allow Schreiber's Swiss bank records to go to the RCMP. It was the culmination of five years' effort. The Mounties did not reveal what they found in the documents. Schreiber and his lawyers were not permitted to see the pile of evidence the Mounties had gathered over the years, although he made attempts. In May 2000, he sought a court order to instruct the police to turn it over to him. He wanted to see not only Germany's September 1999 warrant but also the thousands of pages of evidence sent to Canada to support Germany's request for his extradition. On July 7, 2000, Justice David

Watt ruled that he had no power to order disclosure of the RCMP's confidential files. Greenspan said he would find another way to obtain the material. "I never look at a clock when I'm involved in a criminal case," he told the *Toronto Star*'s Tracey Tyler. "I just look at the due process of the law."

What Schreiber could not ignore was the steady drumbeat of the investigating army in Augsburg. In March 2000, after a lengthy in-house investigation, Thyssen Krupp AG, as the company had been renamed, issued a six-page statement listing its payments to Schreiber and the companies associated with him over a fifteen-year period. For his Bear Head work, he had earned DM9,986,200. There was DM3,760,000 for the Saudi tank deal, DM6,000,000 to open markets for icebreakers in Canada's north, DM24,500,000 paid to his Panama-based company ATG, and another DM4,780,000 for marketing services related to the "acquisition of orders for defence equipment in Kuwait." It added up to almost DM50 million (in 2001, about C$35.5 million). Unless the Germans or the Canadians were able to freeze the accounts holding his funds, Greenspan's hefty hourly rate should have presented no difficulties.

Thyssen's admission wasn't enough to forestall still more raids on its premises. Prosecutors in Düsseldorf said they had searched the offices of the Thyssen Krupp industrial group and six private residences on June 19, 2000. *Die Welt* reported that they had raided the homes of Jürgen Massmann and former Thyssen CEO Eckhard Rohkamm as well. This would have been the second time, at least, that Massmann's home had been searched.

In May, Bavaria's Green Party had demanded charges against Hermann Froschauer, the general prosecutor who had created a delay in serving Holger Pfahls's arrest warrant, throwing the arrest and prosecution in jeopardy. It wasn't the only obstacle Froschauer had thrown in the prosecutors' path. Not only did he refuse Nemetz's request to interview Helmut Kohl about the million marks Schreiber gave to Kiep, but he brought the Augsburg team to Munich to deliver a reprimand for restricting information about Pfahls's warrant.

The long investigation had exacted a price and, not surprisingly, the hardest hit was Winfried Maier. Since Schreiber's arrest in August

1999, the pressure on Maier had been extraordinary. When he asked for assistance, Froschauer's office called him to a meeting with Nemetz on May 27, 2000, and ordered the investigation divided into four regions – Munich, Frankfurt, Essen, and Kassel. Local prosecutors would take the cases that fell into their territories, though none had any experience in the case. Maier was directed to draft a report in which he would make this recommendation himself. When Manfred Weiss, justice minister of Bavaria, was asked about this twist in the investigation, he said it was the wish of the legal staff in Augsburg.

One senior legal officer who was closely involved attributed these developments to a fear, at the highest political levels, that Pfahls had used some of the money set aside for him in the tank deal – DM3.8 million – to buy the favour of those who ultimately made the decision on the export permit.

By June 2000, an inexperienced prosecutor still on probation was handling the file. Maier left the prosecutors' office, his career there finished, his solace a decent position as a judge, far away from this case.

Nonetheless, on August 1, 2000, an Augsburg judge, Maximilian Hofmeister, ordered Schreiber to stand trial in Germany in connection with allegations of bribery and tax evasion related to the 1991 sale of Thyssen tanks to Saudi Arabia. Jürgen Massmann and Winfried Haastert were ordered to stand trial for the same offences.

Greenspan admitted that he would probably not be able to continue fighting extradition on the grounds that Schreiber was wanted on what he called a mere "investigative proceeding." Nonetheless, it was unconscionable, he fulminated, that his client might be extradited for nothing more than an investigator's suspicions. Once again, the extradition case was adjourned while all the players studied the German decision. A few weeks later, Schreiber returned to court, this time to ask if he could retrieve $200,000 of his bail money so that he and his wife could pursue a business opportunity in the restaurant industry.

If Schreiber hasn't been extradited by the time the trial begins in late 2001, he could be tried in absentia, though German authorities would prefer to wait for his extradition. Germany's statute of limitations allows him to be tried up to fifteen years after an alleged crime, a time frame that may save him from prosecution on charges relating to the Messerschmitt-Bölkow-Blohm case in Canada but will not prevent a criminal trial in Germany over the Saudi tank deal.

Germany continues to press Canadian authorities for Schreiber's extradition, but Greenspan has been frank with reporters in saying he is not in any hurry and will challenge on every legal issue he can think of. He is buying time for his client; Schreiber has promised to take him on a trip down the Rhine, he jokes – in twenty years. His defence arguments were laid out during brief court appearances in May and June 2000, when he argued that his client does not own IAL or Kensington Anstalt, that the Augsburg case is entirely based on the word of one disgruntled employee, Giorgio Pelossi, and that Schreiber is the victim of bungling cops, venal politicians, and malicious journalists.

In December 2000, a Munich tax court ruled that IAL did indeed belong to Schreiber. Seizing on another part of the judgment, Greenspan drew attention to the court's ruling that Schreiber did not have to name the recipients of the *Schmiergelder* he had paid in order to claim such payments as tax deductions. It was a controversial finding, however, and German tax officials intend to appeal the decision. Journalists from Germany and some in Canada call Schreiber frequently. He retains his ability to befriend and charm certain members of the press, to confide tantalizing tidbits, to seduce them with the promise of the big story: the truth behind Kohl's secret donations or the insider's account of the tank sale to Saudi Arabia.

He blusters and swaggers, but sometimes there is real menace in his remarks. "If somebody lies, I will make him face up to his lie," he told a reporter from *Die Welt*. "If somebody tries to knife me in the back, I will do something about it. And this concerns politicians in all parties."

During his Ottawa interviews with Bruno Schirra for an article in *Die Zeit*, Schreiber expressed his anger at Giorgio Pelossi's betrayal, dismissing him as a "Mafia pig." He mused that it was cheaper to hire a contract killer in Montreal than in Ottawa – a comment he later explained as a misinterpreted joke. In April 2000, he told Mathias

Blumencron that Luc Lavoie would be made to pay for his intemperate remarks to *the fifth estate*. On another occasion, one cited in the German arrest warrant, he assured reporters, "One day, someone will pay for all this."

He is watching and waiting, Schreiber told Blumencron. "I could create the most horrible Watergate here in Canada when I want to . . . but I'm keeping my bullets for the opportune time."

Epilogue

Following months of negotiations, Karl-Heinz Dahlheimer, chief prosecutor for Berlin, travelled to Canada in mid-January 2001 to interview Schreiber. They met at the German consulate in midtown Toronto where, over the course of several days, Dahlheimer took Schreiber's testimony in the matter of the DM100,000 payment to Wolfgang Schäuble: did Schreiber hand the money directly to Schäuble or did he give it to Brigitte Baumeister to pass on to Schäuble? The pair had offered conflicting stories to the parliamentary inquiry.

"When the treasurer [Baumeister] came to my house to pick up the donation, I was not around," Schreiber told the *Toronto Star*'s Tracey Tyler, confirming Baumeister's version of events. "I was in court and I didn't come back early enough to hand it over, so my wife gave it to her in an envelope. Big deal." It was a big deal for Schäuble, who had said he picked it up personally from Schreiber. Now it was clear he had lied about how he received it.

While the work of the German investigators has been documented and widely reported from the beginning, in Canada the RCMP says nothing. The Mounties have spent as much time as their Augsburg counterparts and devoted comparable resources but have issued no statements on their progress. Having been badly scalded by the

Mulroney lawsuit, they are proceeding with great caution.

In the meantime, Schreiber remains in his Bloor Street apartment with Barbel, waiting to hear when the RCMP will lift the phone taps and return his passports, hoping that they will drop the investigation altogether and declare the case closed.

Frank Moores has not been heard from for many months and appears unconcerned about the whole affair. Not long after the Swiss government agreed to turn over bank records to the RCMP, Moores decided not to contest the ruling as Schreiber had done. He made a voluntary declaration to Canadian tax authorities and paid any tax owing, and he has lived quietly in Florida and at his Chaffeys Locks cottage ever since. One rare public appearance was a charity roast in his honour in St. John's in 2000, a predictably noisy and unruly evening. John Crosbie was one of the speakers and hurled good-natured abuse at his former colleague. According to a report by Bernie Bennett in the St. John's *Telegram*, Crosbie began by calling him devious, then went on to declare, "Everyone was thinking he was just a bay boy from Harbour Grace who didn't know what he was doing. But I don't care what anyone says about you, you were one diabolical, clever son of a bitch." In front of hundreds of people, Moores laughed louder than anyone, and the story reverberated around St. John's for weeks afterwards.

Moores's former lobbying partners and friends have almost disappeared from view. Gary Ouellet left David Copperfield's show years ago and now, based in California, produces magic shows in Europe. Fred Doucet lives quietly in Ottawa. His brother Gerry continues to practise law in Halifax.

In Alberta, many of Schreiber's associates are still around, although Hugh Horner and Christian Graef have died. Horst Schmid has withdrawn from public life and is a consultant in Edmonton; Bobby Hladun is still practising law in Calgary. The RCMP would like to interview Erika Lutz, but she has left Canada; she now runs a bed-and-breakfast on the Caribbean island of St. Lucia and charmingly rebuffs all phone inquiries about her work as the Bitucan paymaster.

The crowd in Quebec don't see as much of one another as they used to. Michel Cogger has distanced himself from many old friends;

in 1998, after many appeals, he was convicted of influence-peddling back in 1988, two years after Mulroney appointed him to the Senate. Although he avoided prison, he was fined $3,000, put on twelve months' probation, and ordered to do 120 hours of community service. In September 2000, he resigned from his Senate seat and returned to private life in Quebec.

Pierre Jeanniot left Air Canada after its privatization, and the airline has been run since by a series of American businessmen. Former chairman Claude Taylor is retired and lives in Montreal. Marc Lalonde is practising law in Montreal. In December 2000, Luc Lavoie left his position as a vice-president of National Public Relations to become a senior executive at the Montreal media conglomerate Quebecor. The same company had earlier appointed Brian Mulroney publisher of the *Toronto Sun*.

Airbus Industrie, the company that was desperate to break Boeing's stranglehold on the world's passenger airline fleets in the 1980s, prospered in the decade following. By 1987, it had chipped away at Boeing's control of the market to win 30 percent of passenger aircraft orders, a share that grows greater every year. Airbus and Boeing enjoyed a brief flirtation when the companies thought they might build a jumbo carrier together, but today they have reverted to their more familiar competitive stance. Both are engaged in developing larger and longer-range megaliners for launch within the next five years.

However, controversy and scandal seem to dog Airbus Industrie. In January 2001, four Syrian politicians were facing charges for taking kickbacks in the purchase of six Airbus jets. Syria's prime minister was under investigation in the same case; he committed suicide in May 2000 before charges were laid.

There has been a great change in Ottawa since the heady days when Schreiber had the run of Parliament Hill. Paul Tellier was appointed the president of Canadian National Railways in Montreal. Robert Fowler moved to New York as Canada's ambassador to the United Nations; more recently, he was posted to Rome as Canada's ambassador to Italy. Pat MacAdam was convicted of tax evasion and now works as an occasional columnist for the *Ottawa Citizen*.

In January 2001, Tom Beveridge, the federal government lawyer who had acted for the German government in the extradition case against Schreiber, was promoted to head of the International Assistance Group in the federal Department of Justice, Kimberly Prost's old job. Because Schreiber is suing this group for more than C$35 million in two lawsuits, a judge of the Ontario Superior Court removed him from the case. Beveridge's personal conduct has been exemplary, Justice David Watt told the court, but the lawyer couldn't continue in the job because, as the judge put it, "the optics aren't quite right."

Elmer MacKay is essentially retired, and he turned up in Toronto to hear the arguments about whether Beveridge should continue to act for Germany in Schreiber's extradition case. He sat with Barbel in the front row of the courtroom – at Schreiber's request, he told the *Star*'s Tracey Tyler. He also told Tyler that he had accompanied Schreiber to the German consulate when his friend met with the visiting prosecutors. "I know a bit of German," MacKay explained to Tyler, and he wanted to make sure the questions were sufficiently "narrow."

In Germany, the parliamentary inquiry in Berlin continues to hear evidence, while the prosecutors in Augsburg prepare for trials later in 2001. Charged with tax evasion, embezzlement, and fraud, Winfried Haastert resigned from the governing board of Thyssen's automobile division in March 2000. Jürgen Massmann, who also left Thyssen, will face the same charges later this year. He has endured the added embarrassment of public exposure of his long affair with Brigitte Baumeister in the 1990s, a story that was splashed across the pages of Germany's major newspapers. "Sex was the one thing missing from the scandal sweeping Germany's Christian Democrats – but no longer," chortled Leon Mangasarian, a reporter with the press service Deutsche Presse Agentur. "On Monday it was added to the piquant stew of murky millions, secret Swiss bank accounts and a fugitive arms dealer."

By contrast, some of the players in this story have been quite lucky. Max Strauss has been named in almost every document pertaining to these cases, but so far, no prosecutor has laid a charge against him. Walther Leisler Kiep also leads a charmed life – the investigation against him in the slush fund scandal was dropped completely. In February 2001, he was found guilty for the second time of income-tax evasion and paid a relatively modest fine of DM45,000.

Holger Pfahls, "Germany's most wanted man," as the *Times* of London describes him, has disappeared completely despite the best efforts of police around the world. The former spymaster, who has taken the precaution of training his wife to phone him in twenty-second bursts – calls too short to be traced – could be living almost anywhere.

Those other slush fund alumni not inclined to running and hiding seem to be taking a different tack – they're telling all. Uwe Lüthje, the CDU's former financial guru, who challenged Kohl's version of events at the Berlin inquiry, is said to be contemplating writing his own memoirs; now in his late eighties, he has little to fear from reprisals and wants to set the record straight. Not long after Kohl published the first volume of his autobiography, Wolfgang Schäuble released a bitter political memoir, in October 2000, called *Mitten im Leben* (In the Thick of Life), attacking Kohl in what one reviewer described as a "score-settling book that portrays him [Kohl] as a scheming, destructive ogre who blames others for the political damage caused by his party's financing scandal." According to Schäuble, Kohl refused his request to name the secret donors to the CDU and accused Schäuble of being the worst culprit in the affair because he accepted the DM100,000 from Schreiber.

"At that point, I ended the conversation by saying that I had already spent far too much of my short life with him," wrote Schäuble.

By the middle of February 2001, Kohl's lawyers had worked out a deal with the prosecutors in Bonn who were handling the investigation against him. They agreed to drop the case in return for his payment of a DM300,000 fine, but the damage to the reputation of the former statesman is irreparable.

There is one man who remains serene, his daily life little troubled by the tremendous upheavals his disclosures created. This is Giorgio Pelossi. He and his wife, Christa, enjoy their lives by the shores of Lake Lugano, one of Europe's most idyllic locales. They spend their time with their children and with close friends, and Pelossi still manages the financial affairs of a few valued clients. He looks forward to the day when he can step up to the witness stand in a courtroom and give his testimony.

Notes

Chapter 6

1. Noghaven's true occupation is still a mystery, but some facts are known. In 1988 he and his wife were divorced after sixteen years of marriage because of his adultery, and court files also show that he used his Diners Club card to rack up thousands of dollars' worth of bills at Robert Buckland Rare Carpets in Montreal, followed immediately by first-class flights to the Virgin Islands and sea cruises. He bought Louis XVI chairs and other fine furniture from Montreal antiques dealers in the early 1980s, charged up more thousands of dollars while shopping at Hermès, Gucci, and other luxury stores in France, ate in the best restaurants, and stayed in the swankiest hotels. What he was doing, no one knows. But he wasn't paying his Diners Club card, and people began to sue him. When one antiques dealer loaned him about $30,000 and couldn't get it back, he finally went to court in 1992. The judge ordered the seizure and sale of a gelded seven-year-old South American race-horse owned by Noghaven to pay the debt. The Diners Club of France also took Noghaven to court in 1992 over hundreds of thousands of francs in unpaid bills. The transactions added up to

well over FF1 million, much of it charged to Robert Buckland Rare Carpets in Montreal. This case was settled out of court.

Chapter 9

1. Pelossi has held consistently to his recollection that Schreiber told him commission money was to go to Mulroney. He has repeated his version several times in sworn statements to German and Canadian investigators. There is no evidence that Mulroney received commission money.

2. German investigators studying Schreiber's papers in 1995 found a reference in one of his address books to "Frankfurt 34104." They assumed this was an account at the Swiss Bank Corporation because of the two similarly numbered accounts Moores had opened there. The bank issued its account numbers in strict numerical order, so this account would have to have been opened just hours or even minutes before 34107 and 34117; it could have been opened at the same meeting of Schreiber, Moores, and Pelossi with Schnyder in Zurich. But Pelossi knows nothing about this account.

   It is likely that Schreiber's notation actually refers to account 34107; he may have written it down incorrectly because the European style of writing a 7 makes it easy to confuse with a 4. Account 34107 was given no name by Moores, but Schreiber often used simple codes in his own notes; German investigators believe Frankfurt could mean Frank Moores. However, this interpretation of the name Frankfurt in connection with this account has not been conclusively established. Schreiber would attach the Frankfurt moniker to another account, one of his coded subaccounts.

Chapter 10

1. Under pressure from American businesses that claimed their Asian and European competitors held an unfair advantage because they could pay bribes to win contracts, Congress amended the act in 1988, softening the laws to allow, among other things, American companies to pay bribes if the payments are legal in the foreign countries in question and if the payments are

reasonable expenditures, directly related to winning a contract. At the same time, it doubled the fines for conviction under the FCPA to $2 million and kept the further penalty of a prison sentence of up to five years.

In August 2000 the *Journal of Business Ethics* looked at the twenty-year history of the Foreign Corrupt Practices Act, pointing out that "some analysts suggest that bribery is so widespread in international business dealings that efforts to stamp it out will prove fruitless." The International Monetary Fund, reported the *Journal*, "estimates that half of the $300 billion external debt of the world's 15 most heavily indebted countries is being held in private accounts transferred to tax havens." And a World Bank survey of 3,600 companies in sixty-nine countries, the *Journal* stated, showed that 40 percent of firms paid bribes.

Chapter 13

1. A memo to file signed by Winfried Kindler of the Augsburg Tax Office on April 20, 1999, identified Maxwell as Max Strauss, Stewardess as Stuart Iddles, Jürglund as Jürgen Massmann, Pitak as Pitak Intrawityanunt, Holgart as Holger Pfahls, Fred as Fred Doucet, Frankfurt as Frank Moores, Winter as Winfried Haastert, Marc as Marc Lalonde, and Waldherr as Walther Leisler Kiep. An earlier memo to file from Kindler making the same identifications (except for Pitak, whose last name was not yet confirmed) was prepared on December 7, 1995, in a period when the investigators were filing information with the courts in support of requests for search-and-seizure warrants.

   The Appeals Chamber of the Graubünden Canton Court ruled on June 24, 1998, that the five German code names "can with little imagination and through more than coincidence be tied to... Haastert, Massmann, Pfahls, Kiep, and Strauss." This portion of the Swiss court decision is quoted in the arrest warrant for Haastert, issued April 22, 1999.

2. The irony inherent in Saudi Arabia's urgent need for Thyssen's celebrated sniffer tanks was that it was Thyssen itself that had built one of Iraq's biological weapons plants. The facility at Salman Pak

stored thousands of canisters full of anthrax, botulism, gas gangrene, and rabbit fever bacteria, according to *Critical Mass: The Dangerous Race for Superweapons in a Fragmenting World* (1994), by William Burroughs and Robert Windrem.

Chapter 14

1. See Chapter 13, note 1.

Chapter 15

1. See "Record of Case for the Extradition of the Defendant Schreiber from Canada for the Purpose of Criminal Prosecution," prepared October 11, 1999, by the Augsburg Public Prosecutors' Office and filed in the Ontario Superior Court of Justice.
2. A reference to the Westray coal mine explosion of May 9, 1992, in which twenty-six miners lost their lives. In the inquiry that followed the disaster, the mine's owner, Curragh Resources, and its manager, Clifford Frame, were alleged to have failed to implement proper safety prevention measures.
3. A section was deleted here in the copy provided to the authors in response to their request under the Access to Information Act. Also, a hand-written question mark appears in the margin next to the paragraph discussing Corbeil's support.
4. Leiduck provided much of this account in an affidavit to German authorities dated February 20, 1998. In the affidavit, Leiduck admitted he had had serious brushes with the law and had been jailed in Monaco in 1997, though he was released on US$5 million bail. He also lost two multi-million-dollar lawsuits to the Liebherr company, which had sued him to recover lost funds. Leiduck and Schreiber later became involved in a dispute over DM8.5 million.

Chapter 16

1. See Chapter 13, note 1.

Chapter 19

1. Today, Sexton refuses to discuss his remarks, except to make the general observation that any comments he made were "on my

clients' instructions and based upon my review of the information they provided to me and any other information at my disposal. I did not at any time make a statement to the press that I had reason to believe was untrue."

2. This portion of the Swiss court's ruling is quoted in the arrest warrant for Winfried Haastert, issued April 22, 1999.

Index

The text of this book was set in Minion, designed by
Robert Slimbach for Adobe Systems in 1989.
Minion exhibits the graceful letter forms of classical
Renaissance type and sets clearly even at small sizes.

Book design by Ingrid Paulson
Typeset by Marie Jircik